A Fireside Book

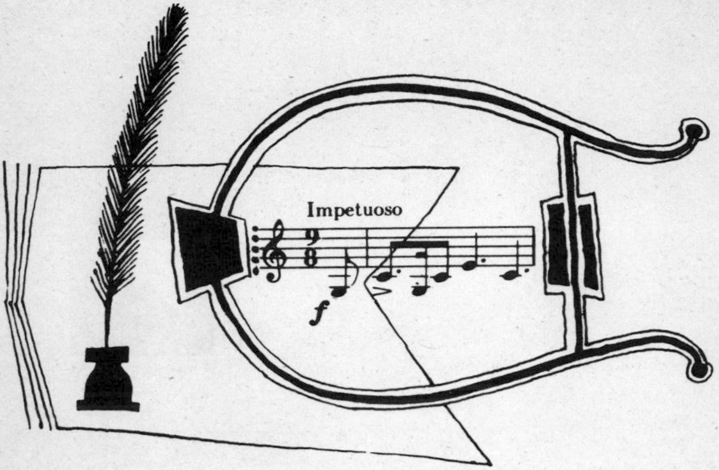
Impetuoso

OPERA THEMES AND PLOTS

by Rudolph Fellner

PREFACE BY ERICH LEINSDORF

A Fireside Book published by
SIMON AND SCHUSTER • NEW YORK

A FIRESIDE BOOK
PUBLISHED BY SIMON AND SCHUSTER
A DIVISION OF GULF & WESTERN CORPORATION
SIMON & SCHUSTER BUILDING
ROCKEFELLER CENTER
1230 AVENUE OF THE AMERICAS
NEW YORK, N.Y. 10020

ISBN 0-671-21215-X FIRESIDE PAPERBACK EDITION
LIBRARY OF CONGRESS CATALOG CARD NUMBER 57-12409
MANUFACTURED IN THE UNITED STATES OF AMERICA
PRINTED BY THE MURRAY PRINTING CO., FORGE VILLAGE, MASS.

10 11 12 13 14 15 16 17 18 19 20

To

Kirk Browning

CONTENTS

PREFACE

by Erich Leinsdorf

WHEN I WAS *a student in Vienna, one of my favorite sports was hunting—hunting not for the fox or the deer, but for inexpensive second-hand scores of symphonies and operas. While browsing through the stacks in the larger music houses, I used to come across pamphlets and small, bound volumes containing thematic analyses of symphonies or identification of leitmotifs from the Wagnerian operas, or the voice parts of the best-known Italian operas. These various guides to the better understanding of symphony, music drama, and opera defied easy classification as they were neither entirely books nor wholly musical scores. They fascinated me, and from them I gained, during my years of study, a better understanding of the intricate organism which a finished work in the operatic and symphonic field represents.*

It is a sign of growing interest and more penetrating curiosity that our music-loving public in the United States is demanding more information than a mere introduction to the great musical masterpieces. Now that the map of the United States has been rapidly filling up with colored pins indicating the location of various musical organizations, the main stream of musical activity seems to carry more operatic enterprise than ever before. The broadcasts of the Metropolitan Opera on Saturday afternoons, the telecasts of operas old and new by the NBC Opera Theater, and the continuing issues of full-length operas on records have immensely broadened the audiences. More than 250 different operatic works have been recorded in their entirety, and there are frequent broadcasts, in many parts of the country, of these works.

The uninstructed listener may first find only a naïve pleasure in the beautiful sounds and obvious passion expressed in the great climactic arias and duets. Then comes the curiosity which prompts the desire to know more about it; and here we are at the point where the demand for more specific guidebooks must be met. As I recall with gratitude the thematic analysis booklets of my student days, so have I retained a great affection and fondness for all good guides, be they to a strange city for a new traveler, or to a masterpiece of opera to be discovered by a listener. A book such as Mr. Fellner's Opera Themes and Plots *offers something beyond the introductory and explanatory words or a summary of the story: it gives many musical examples which can easily satisfy the desire of the reader to try his own voice or his own fingers on a piano to reproduce for himself those themes, motifs and melodies which he likes best in professional performance. These musical samples should be and can be like the snapshots which recall, on winter evenings, last summer's trip. They show the main stops en route and the most noteworthy incidents.*

With musical examples such as we have in this volume, more than just looking at them is needed. They should be played and sung. Be it with two fingers on the piano or be it with an untrained, croaking voice (which is best reverberated by the tiles in the bathroom), the pleasure of reproducing these motifs and melodies will far surpass any of the purely passive ways of appreciation.

The musical samples are far more numerous than any program book can ever supply. They are in their original keys, which may sometimes prove taxing for the amateur voice when trying to sing such music as Otello's entrance; yet the public today is interested in getting acquainted with the original, and part of the original is accurate keys. Transposition means a change of color, and just as we like our reproductions of great paintings in art books to be as close to the original coloring as possible, so do we prefer our music in the original keys.

Here, then, is a new kind of volume for the lover of opera and, like most new things, a return to something known before, though on a somewhat different basis. The great operas musically and dramatically described are truly like the great old cities of the world. You can learn to know them more and more intimately and your enjoyment will increase in proportion to your acquaintance with them. Mr. Fellner's book should prove an enormous help.

INTRODUCTION

THE PURPOSE of this book is to present to the reader the essential materials of thirty-two operas from the standard repertory in as straightforward and simple a way as possible—the musical materials in general on the left-hand page, the corresponding dramatic materials on the right. Occasionally, however, it has been found advisable, for the sake of keeping details of the story and the music on the same spread wherever possible, to print some of the music on the text page, or vice versa.

Opera Themes and Plots can be used to advantage by the man who is hearing any given work for the first time over the radio or on the phonograph, as well as by the advanced student or critic who wishes to survey the essential materials of the score for the purpose of refreshing his memory or for more detailed analysis. In fact, the book may be used in many different ways for different purposes. For example, a man unfamiliar with a given opera may first wish simply to read the story as it appears on the right-hand pages. Next, he may wish to get some advance idea of the musical materials by picking out on the piano (or whatever other instrument he has at his disposal) the themes as they appear on the left-hand pages. And then, while listening to the work on the radio or phonograph, he may follow the action by reading the right-hand page and listening for the quotations on the opposite side as each numbered theme is referred to in the narration.

Again, one who is already acquainted with a certain aria or other number from an opera may wish to ascertain the content of such an item and to establish at what point of the story it occurs by finding first the music on the left-hand page and then referring to the corresponding number on the opposite page. And one who remembers only the name or the first words of an aria or other set number, even without knowing from what opera it is, may look it up in the index and proceed from there.

Finally, even one quite familiar with a work may still gain new insights—especially in the operas using a good deal of thematic material, such as the works of Wagner and Strauss (but also others)—by noticing the thousands of subtle ways in which the same basic musical materials are used over and over again, and, at times, their amazing meanings. To be sure, nobody will be surprised, when he reads in the story of *Pagliacci,* that Canio "demands from Nedda the name of her lover [3]" and, looking up the music quotation, finds it entitled "Canio's Jealousy." However, the case is much more interesting when Salome is said to be "ready to dance for Herod (motive [35b])," and [35b] will be a quotation showing that Salome at a later point sings to that same music the words "Give me the head of Jokanaan." For it is thus that Richard Strauss has intended Salome to reveal to the listener—through the music—her motivation for dancing, a motivation she has been most careful to conceal from Herod.

One more word about the names of the motives may be in order. The names do not originate with the composers, but they are a handy device for criticism and analysis, even though there is not always agreement on the names themselves. When a motive is associated throughout with a given character or situation, there is no great problem. Yet characters are sometimes described in different ways at different times, depending on what aspect of their characters are relevant at the moment. Thus, in the opera *Aïda*, Amneris is characterized by two different motives, which describe her in her relationship to the hero Radames ([4] "Amneris' Love") and in her reaction to her rival, Aïda ([5] "Amneris' Jealousy"). Aïda, on the other hand, is characterized by only one theme, which could have been called "Aïda's Love"; but since this love is her basic and paramount characteristic, the theme has been called merely [1] "Aïda." At times the theme depends on who or how one is looking at a character. Thus Fafner, in *The Ring of the Nibelung*, may be at one time musically described as [66] "Fafner, the Dragon," a derivation of motive [25] "Dragon," when he is thought of in his assumed shape, or he may be considered as the former ruler of the giants, [81] "Fafner, the Giant," a derivation of motive [14] "Giants."

The problem gets even more involved where a theme is associated with a certain emotion or with an abstract idea. Here the naming is difficult not because one cannot ascertain the musical content of the motive but because feelings are not easily expressed in words, and ideas stated in music are not easily translated into a less flexible language. However, with the exception of quotations with text, where the significance follows from the words, thematic material has been given names wherever possible. For names help the memory and facilitate analysis. Yet in the end, the reader must be left to his own resources to establish in his own mind and to his own satisfaction what exactly constitutes the connection between, e.g., the musically related [77] "Triumph" and [17d] "Loge" ("Fire") in *The Ring of the Nibelung*, or what it means when, in the same cycle, Brünnhilde "vehemently [25] . . . embraces Siegfried"—[25] which is, again, the "Dragon" motive. This is as it should be, for it will serve as a reminder that a real "literal," translation of musical expression into abstract words is neither intended here nor, as a matter of fact, at all possible.

Some of the special devices used in this book should be explained. The reader will find a system of sublettering for motives ([9ab] is an example) for those quotations where, on occasion, only a portion of the theme is used; again, where themes underwent too much variation for quotation by a single example; and finally for those cases—especially in the Wagnerian operas—where different themes are used for different aspects of the same idea.

Where there are several quotations belonging to one set number—several parts of a single aria, duet, etc.—this fact is indicated by a bracket in the margin of the music.

The word "scene" has been used in the modern sense—that is, to indicate a change of scenery within an act. The one exception is the one-act opera *Cavalleria Rusticana*, where the two scenes are separated by the playing of the "Intermezzo" while the curtain remains open on an empty stage.

R. F.

OPERA THEMES AND PLOTS

THEMES

[1] AIDA

Andante mosso

pp

[2] THE PRIESTS

Andante mosso

ppp

[3] ARIA *CELESTE AIDA* (Radames)

Andantino

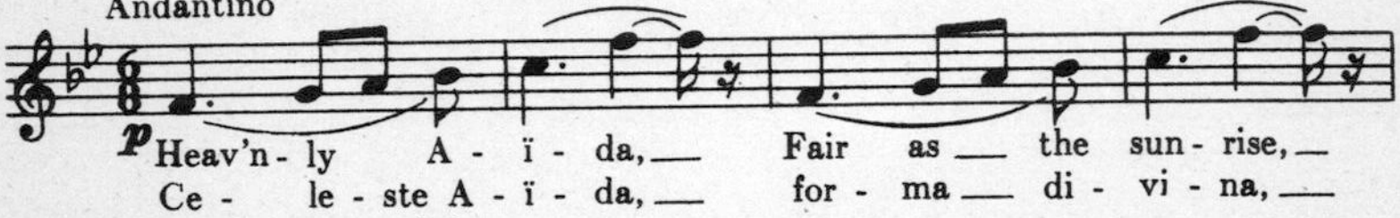
p
Heav'n-ly A - ï - da, Fair as the sun-rise,
Ce - le - ste A - ï - da, for - ma di - vi - na,

[4] AMNERIS' LOVE

Allegro assai moderato

p

[5] AMNERIS' JEALOUSY

Allegro agitato e presto

pp

[6] CALL TO ARMS

Allegro maestoso

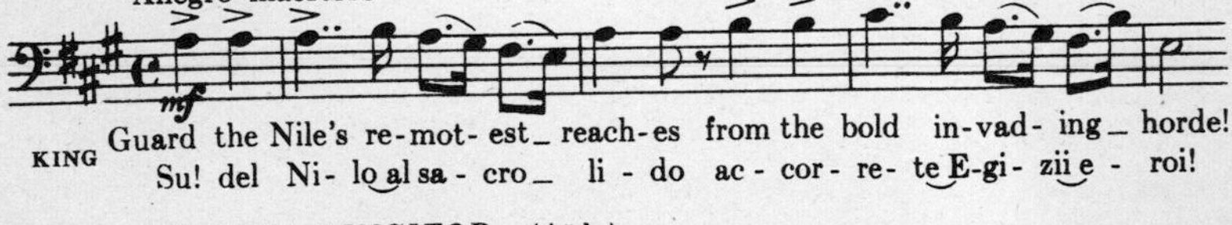
mf
KING
Guard the Nile's re-mot- est reach-es from the bold in-vad- ing horde!
Su! del Ni- lo al sa - cro li - do ac - cor- re- te E-gi- zii e - roi!

[7] ARIA *RITORNA VINCITOR* (Aïda)

Allegro agitato

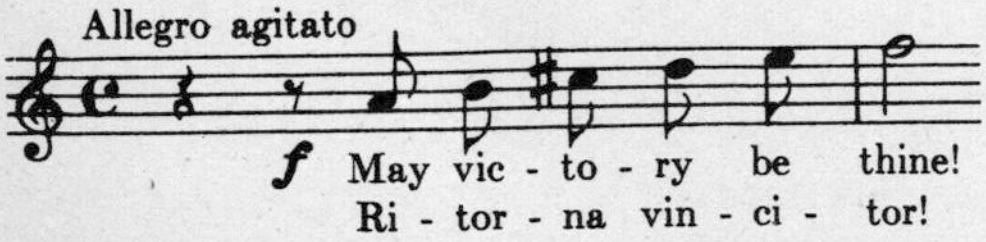
f
May vic - to - ry be thine!
Ri - tor - na vin - ci - tor!

Aïda

Opera in four acts by Giuseppe Verdi. Libretto by Antonio Ghislanzoni. First performance: Cairo, December 24, 1871.

Characters: THE KING (bass); AMNERIS, his daughter (contralto); RADAMES, a young Egyptian captain (tenor); RAMFIS, High Priest (bass); AMONASRO, King of the Ethiopians (baritone); AÏDA, his daughter, favorite slave of Amneris (soprano); A MESSENGER (tenor); VOICE OF THE HIGH PRIESTESS (soprano).
Memphis and Thebes, in the days of the Pharaohs.

Prelude: The music uses the melody characteristic of Aïda [1] and that of the priests' chant [2], thus introducing the basic conflict underlying the tragedy.

Act I, Scene 1: Passing through a large hall in the King's palace in Memphis, Ramfis meets Radames and tells him that Isis has already designated the leader for the armies against the invading Ethiopians. Radames hopes that the goddess has chosen him (Recitative *Se quel guerrier io fossi:* "Ah, would that I were chosen"), so that he can, as the victor, ask the King a favor: that the Ethiopian slave girl Aïda, Radames' beautiful beloved, be allowed to return to her homeland (Aria *Celeste Aïda:* "Heav'nly Aïda") [3].

Amneris [4] enters and subtly tries to discover whether her love for Radames meets with any response. Radames realizes what lurks behind Amneris' questioning [5], and his embarrassment only sharpens her jealousy [5]. When Aïda enters [1], Pharaoh's daughter suspects that this slave girl is her rival [5]. Although she speaks to Aïda in carefully chosen accents, a tense atmosphere prevails [Trio 5] as each follows his own disquieting thoughts.

Presently the King, the High Priest, and their retinues arrive. A Messenger reports that the Ethiopians, led by Amonasro, are already advancing toward Thebes. Radames is named commander-in-chief by the King, whose call to arms [6] is repeated by the crowd. Everybody joins Amneris in wishing Radames a victorious return [7 major], and all leave for the temple of Vulcan. Only Aïda remains to repeat with horror the traitorous words she has just uttered. (Scena *Ritorna vincitor:* "May victory be thine!") [7] Bewildered, she contemplates a fate that will bring disaster either to her family and country, or to Radames her beloved [1, 8]. Heartbroken, she implores the mercy of the gods [9].

Act I, Scene 2: At the temple of Vulcan, the new commander, to the

[8] ARIA *RITORNA VINCITOR!* (Aïda) *continued*

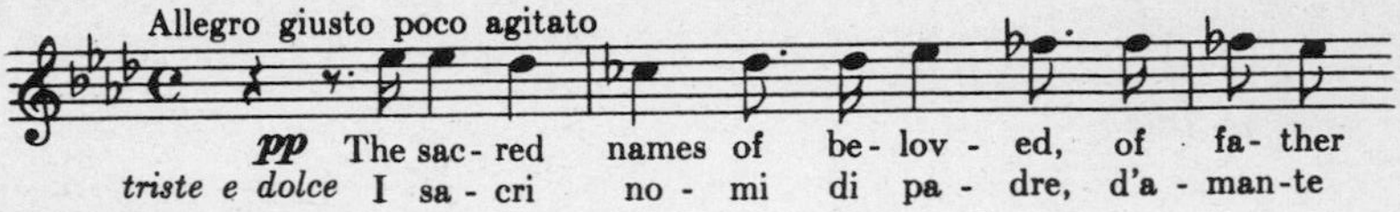

[9]

[10] CHANT OF THE HIGH-PRIESTESS

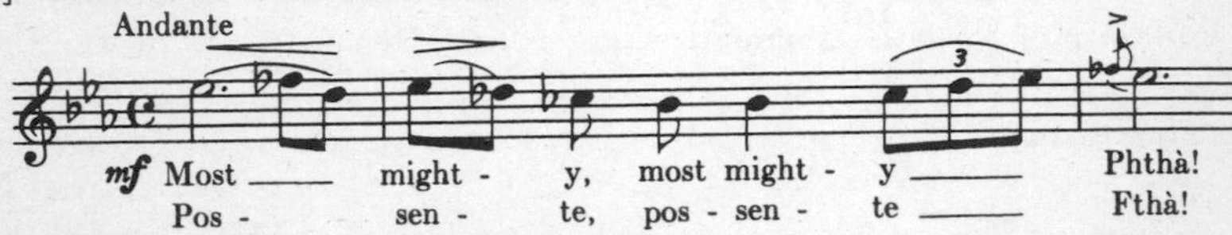

[11] DANCE OF THE PRIESTESSES

[12] INVOCATION

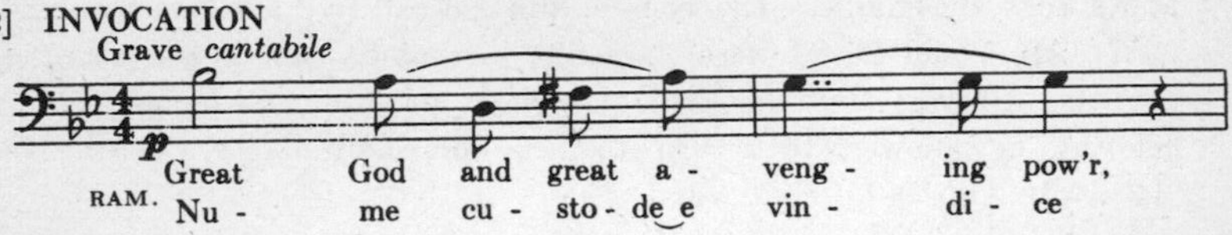

[13]

[14]

[15] DANCE OF THE LITTLE BLACK SLAVES

chanting [10] and dancing [11] of the priestesses, is presented with the sacred sword, and all join in a prayer to the gods [12].

Act II, Scene 1: In the apartments of Amneris, slave girls prepare their mistress for the triumphal reception of the victorious Egyptian army. The girls sing of the proud commander [13], and Amneris answers: "Come, my beloved" [14]. A group of black slave boys entertains with a dance [15]. When Aïda approaches [1], Amneris stops the singing and sends the slaves away out of respect for Aïda's feelings at the loss of her people's cause; but doubt reawakens in her breast and drives her to uncover Aïda's feelings toward Radames. Feigning compassion, she subtly brings up the healing power of love. When Aïda is lost in thoughts of the joys and torments of this emotion [1], Amneris sweetly suggests [16] that she confide in her. Has she perhaps fallen in love with one of the Egyptian soldiers? She should take comfort; fate was gentle to many of them even though the leader was killed [16]. When Aïda cannot hide her despair, Amneris declares that she has deceived her and that Radames is alive. Aïda sinks upon her knees to thank the gods, and Amneris, now sure that Aïda loves Radames, threateningly informs the slave girl that she has a daughter of the Pharaohs for a rival. For one moment the two princesses face each other haughtily, but Aïda suddenly remembers her position and, falling on her knees before Amneris, begs for mercy [17]. She is informed that she can expect only pitiless vengeance [18].

Strains of martial music are heard from outside [6]. Amneris, ignoring the pitiful plea of her rival, already relishes the thought of the impending ceremony, when the slave will kneel at her feet while she, Amneris, will crown Radames with the victor's wreath. Triumphantly she departs, and Aïda, her hopes shattered and her spirit broken, wretchedly repeats her supplication to the gods [9].

Act II, Scene 2: In a big square at the entrance of Thebes, the court, the priests, and the people have gathered to greet the returning army. The people sing a *"Gloria"* [19]; and the priests exhort them to give thanks to the gods [2]. Presently the joyous sound of Egyptian trumpets heralds the entry of the army [20]. After a ballet [21, 22] the people greet the hero as he enters [19]. Radames receives the laurel from the hand of Amneris [4], and the King asks him what reward he desires, swearing to give him anything he asks for. Before answering, Radames has the prisoners brought in, and Aïda quickly discovers her father among them. Called before the King, Amonasro claims to be only an officer; and, pretending that he saw his king die, he launches into a plea for mercy [23] in which he is joined by the other Ethiopians, prisoners and slaves. Although the priests object [24], Radames asks that all the Ethiopians be freed. Again Ramfis objects, and the King decides that all may leave except Aïda and her father, who will be held as hostages. In addition, the King promises Radames the hand of Amneris. The people renew their jubilation [19, 2, 20]. Above their shouts

[16] Andante espressivo

[17] Adagio cantabile

Let this my sor - row thy warm heart move;
AIDA
Pie - tà ti pren - da del mio do - lor - - -

[18] Adagio

Trem - ble vile min - - ion, be — ye heart - bro - ken
AMN.
Tre - ma, vil schia - - va! spez - za il tuo co - re

[19] TRIUMPHAL CHORUS

Maestoso

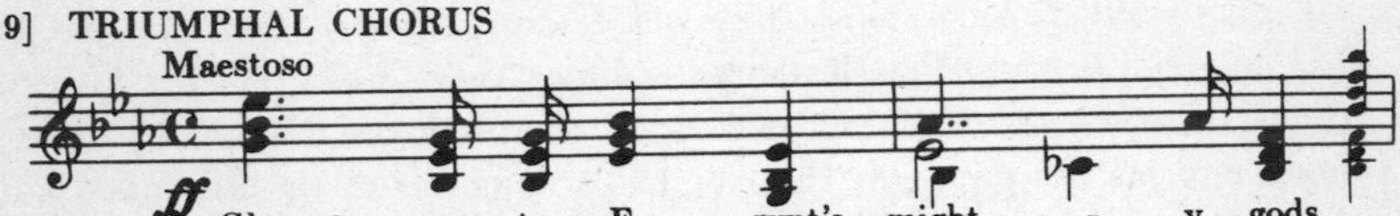
Glo - ry to E - gypt's might - - y gods,
CHO.
Glo - ria al E - git - to ad I - - si - de

[20] TRIUMPHAL MARCH AND DANCES

Maestoso

[21] Mosso

staccato

[22] Mosso

[23] Andante

Ah, great King, at the height of your splen - dor,
AMON.
Ma tu, Re, tu si - gno - re pos - sen - te,

[24] Andante mosso

Death, o King —— be their just des - ti - na - tion,
PRIESTS
Strug - gi, o Re, —— que - ste ciur - me fe - ro - ci,

of "*Gloria*" and Amneris' triumphant exclamations soar the sad voices of Radames and Aïda.

Act III: The chants of the High Priestess and the priests from the temple of Isis permeate the stillness of the night as, passing a clearing by the Nile, Ramfis conducts Amneris to the temple to pray to the goddess on the eve of her marriage to Radames. Immediately afterward Aïda enters [1]. She is expecting the Egyptian hero (Romanza *Qui Radames verrà:* "Here I'll meet Radames"—generally known as *O patria mia:* "Land of my fathers"). Will this be their last farewell? If so, the Nile will be her grave and she will never again see her homeland with its verdant hills, nor breathe its sweet-scented air [25].

Unexpectedly, Amonasro appears. He knows why Aïda has come here, and he promises her the restoration of home, throne, and love [26]. Their people are already preparing a new attack and they are sure to overcome the hated Egyptians. All they need to know is what route the enemy will take. And since the leader of the enemy loves Aïda . . . Horrified, Aïda exclaims, "No, never!" whereupon her father, in a fury, summons up a picture of Ethiopian cities destroyed by the Egyptians' wrath [27]. From their ruins will rise the ghost of Aïda's mother to curse her as the author of their destruction. As Aïda begs for mercy, Amonasro violently pushes her to the ground. She does not behave like his daughter, and he has no mercy for a slave of the Pharaohs. Aïda, cowering at her father's feet, now promises co-operation, and Amonasro, once more impressing on her the tragic situation of her people [28], hides nearby.

Radames arrives glowing with love [29], and Aïda tries to convince him that, if he really loves her, their only salvation is flight—flight to her country, where in love's bliss they will be able to forget the cares of the world [30]. Radames still hesitates, but a final challenge to decide between her and Amneris moves him to agree to flight [31]. As they are about to leave [29], Aïda asks what road they will have to take to avoid the Egyptian army. Radames mentions the route of his troops, and at once Amonasro comes forward. To his horror, Radames learns that this is the King of the Ethiopians. He feels that he has betrayed his country, but is persuaded to follow Aïda and her father. At this moment they are discovered by Amneris, returning from the temple. Amonasro's attempt to stab her is frustrated by Radames. Just then Ramfis appears with guards and sends them after the fleeing slaves. Radames hands over his sword: "I am at your disposal, priest."

Act IV, Scene 1: In a hall at the King's palace Amneris paces restlessly, torn between her jealousy [5] of Aïda, who has eluded the pursuers, and her love for Radames [4]. She has him brought from his prison and begs him to defend himself before the priests, while she will ask the King's pardon [32]. Radames declines; it will be useless [32], since he does not want to live without Aïda. A passionate declaration of love by Amneris [33] only brings

[25] FROM ROMANZA *O PATRIA MIA* (Aïda)

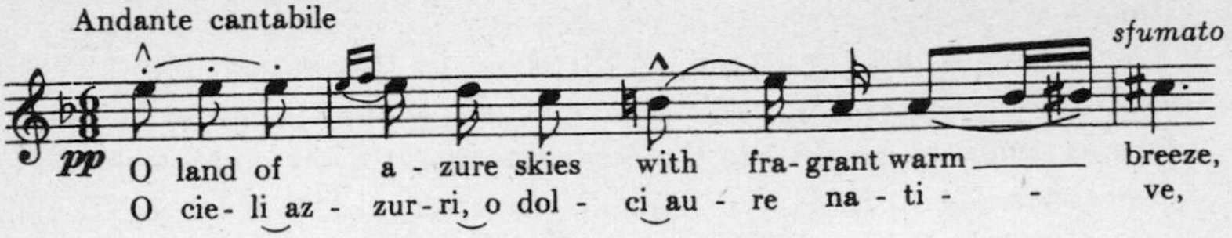
Andante cantabile
sfumato
pp
O land of a - zure skies with fra-grant warm ___ breeze,
O cie- li az - zur-ri, o dol - ci au - re na - ti - - ve,

[26] FROM DUET *A TE GRAVE CAGION* (Amonasro, Aïda)

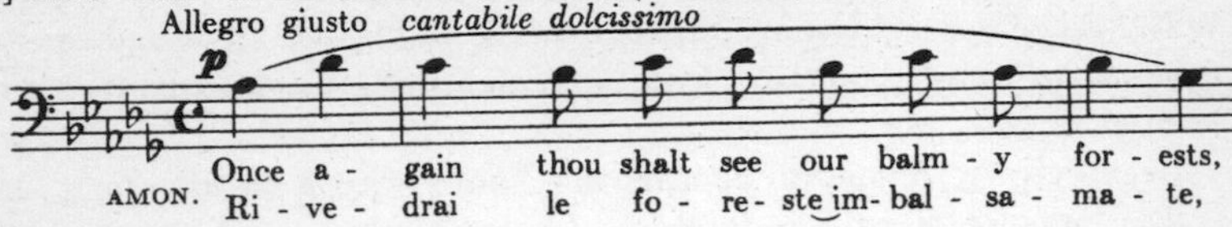
Allegro giusto *cantabile dolcissimo*
p
Once a - gain thou shalt see our balm - y for - ests,
AMON. Ri - ve - drai le fo - re- ste im- bal - sa - ma - te,

[27]

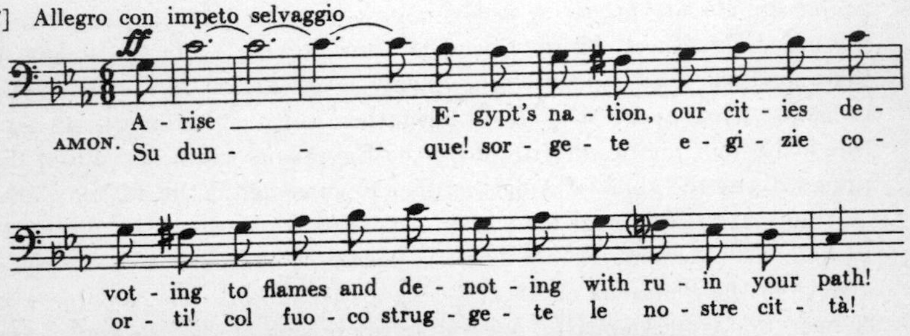
Allegro con impeto selvaggio
ff
A - rise ___ E- gypt's na - tion, our cit - ies de -
AMON. Su dun - - - que! sor - ge - te e - gi - zie co -
vot - ing to flames and de - not - ing with ru - in your path!
or - ti! col fuo - co strug - ge - te le no - stre cit - tà!

[28]

Andante sostenuto
p
Think ___ how thy race, ___ down-trod-den by the con-qu'ror,
AMON. Pen - sa che un po - - po - lo vin- to stra-zia - to,

[29] DUET *PUR TI RIVEGGO* (Radames, Aïda)

Allegro giusto *con trasporto*
f
A- gain I find ___ thee, sweet-est A - ï - - da
RAD. Pur ti ri - veg - - go, mia dol-ce A - ï - - da

[30]

Andantino *dolcissimo*
There, where ___ the age - old for - est sleeps
AIDA Là, tra ___ fo - re - ste ver - gi - ni,

[31]

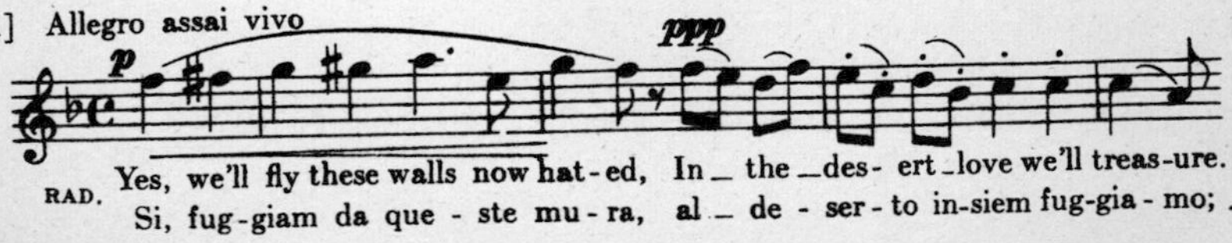
Allegro assai vivo
p
ppp
Yes, we'll fly these walls now hat-ed, In _ the _des- ert _love we'll treas-ure.
RAD. Si, fug-giam da que - ste mu-ra, al _ de - ser-to in-siem fug-gia - mo;

forth another avowal by Radames of his love for Aïda [33]. He is ready to die, and Amneris' ragings only revolt him. He leaves.

Now the priests pass [2] to descend into the subterranean vault as Amneris curses her own jealousy which has delivered Radames into their hands. From below, the inexorable voices are heard condemning Radames to death for treason as, in stubborn silence, he refuses to defend himself.

Amneris, who has been listening in helpless misery, now tries to argue with the priests as they pass by again [2], but they only keep repeating: "He is a traitor; he must die." After they have disappeared, Amneris calls the curse of the heavens upon them and rushes off in desperation.

Act IV, Scene 2: Under Vulcan's temple, in a dark vault sealed by a heavy rock, Radames is awaiting death. Suddenly he discovers Aïda at his side. Divining his fate, she relates, she had entered the tomb to die with him. He is overcome by despair that such youth and beauty should have to perish for his sake [34]. Already she sees the angel of death approaching to guide her to heaven and to eternal love [35]. To the chant of the priests and priestesses [10], Aïda and Radames join in a tender farewell to the world of tears [36], while Amneris, in deep mourning, offers a prayer in the temple above the tomb. Aïda dies peacefully in Radames' arms.

[32] DUET *GIA I SACERDOTI* (Radames, Amneris)

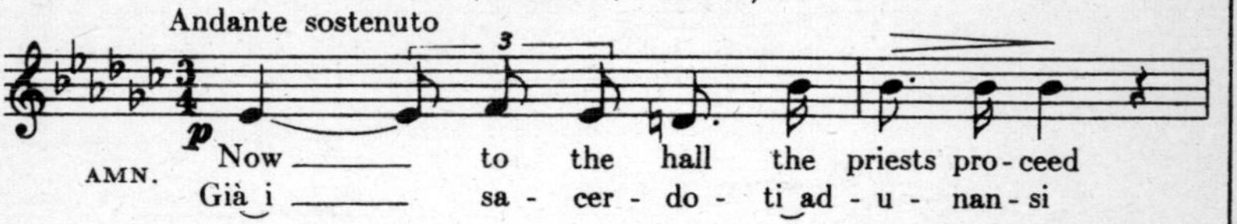
Andante sostenuto
AMN.
Now to the hall the priests pro-ceed
Già i sa-cer-do-ti ad-u-nan-si

[33]

Andante cantabile
AMN.
Ah do con-sent to live! Live of my fond love as-sured.
Ah tu dei vi-ve-re! Sì, al-l'a-mor mio vi-vra-i;

[34] Larghetto

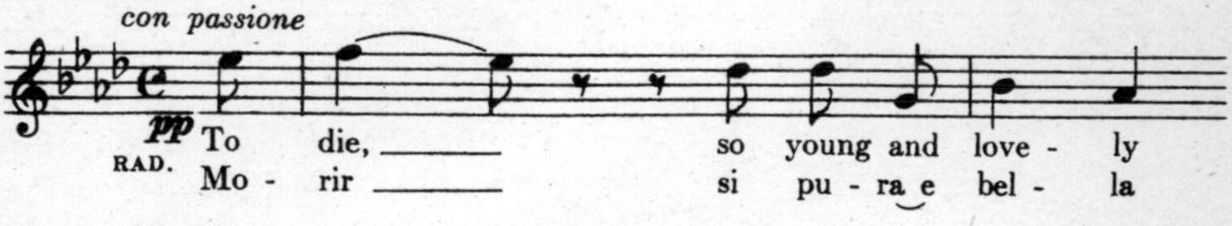
con passione
RAD.
To die, so young and love-ly
Mo-rir si pu-ra e bel-la

[35]

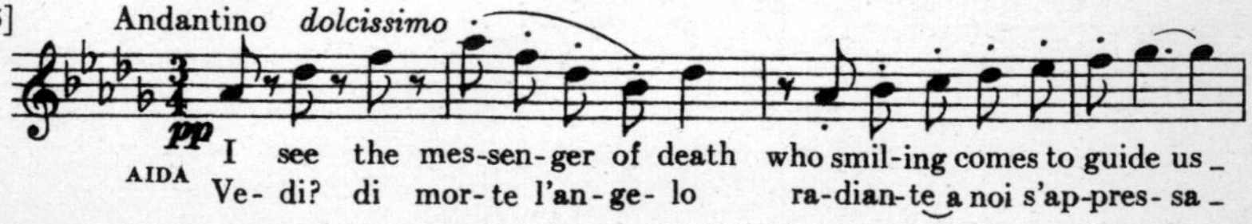
Andantino dolcissimo
AIDA
I see the mes-sen-ger of death who smil-ing comes to guide us
Ve-di? di mor-te l'an-ge-lo ra-dian-te a noi s'ap-pres-sa

[36] DUET *O TERRA, ADDIO* (Aïda, Radames)

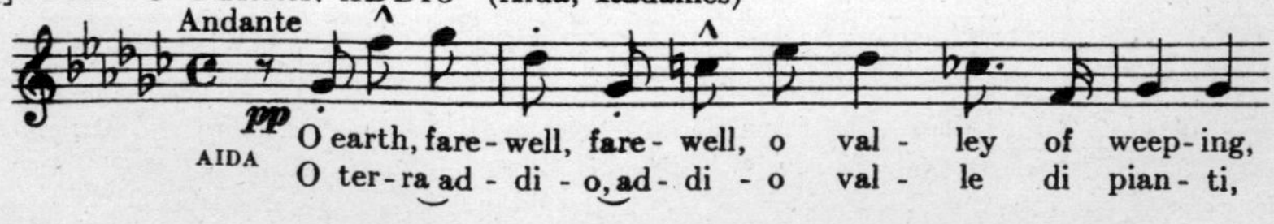
Andante
AIDA
O earth, fare-well, fare-well, o val-ley of weep-ing,
O ter-ra ad-di-o, ad-di-o val-le di pian-ti,

THEMES

[1] Allegro assai moderato

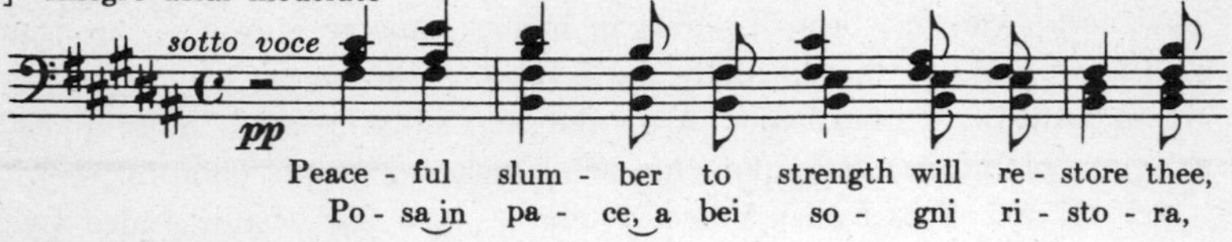
sotto voce
pp
Peace - ful slum - ber to strength will re - store thee,
Po - sa in pa - ce, a bei so - gni ri - sto - ra,

[2] THE CONSPIRATORS

Allegro assai moderato
sotto voce
pp
Watch - ful ha - tred thy doom is pre - par - ing,
E sta l'o - dio, che pre - pa - ra il fi - o,

[3] RICCARDO'S LOVE

Allegro assai moderato cantabile
p
I shall be - hold A - me - li - a with
La ri - ve - drà nell' e - sta - si, rag -
ra - diant beau - ty beam - - ing,
gian - te di pal - lo - - re,

[4] ARIA *ALLA VITA* (Renato)

Andante
mf
On the life thou now dost cher - ish, fraught with
Al - la vi - ta che t'ar - ri - de di spe-
pleas - ure, with hope re - splen - dent,
ran - za e gau - dio pie - na,

[5] BALLATA *VOLTA LA TERREA FRONTE* (Oscar)

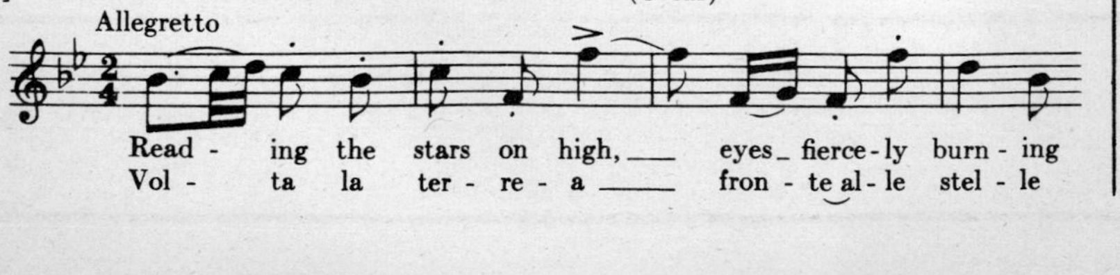
Allegretto
Read - ing the stars on high, eyes fierce - ly burn - ing
Vol - ta la ter - re - a fron - te al - le stel - le

Un Ballo in Maschera

A MASKED BALL

Opera in three acts by Giuseppe Verdi. Libretto by Francesco Piave. First performance: Rome, February 17, 1859.

Characters: RICCARDO, Earl of Warwick, Governor of Boston (tenor); RENATO, his Creole secretary (baritone); AMELIA, Renato's wife (soprano); ULRICA, Negro fortuneteller (contralto); OSCAR, a page (soprano); SAM, (bass) and TOM (bass), conspirators; SILVANO, a sailor (bass).
*In and near Boston (in other versions Naples or Stockholm *) during the second half of the eighteenth century.*

Prelude: After a few opening measures the orchestra introduces the chorus of the Earl's adherents [1], the motive of the conspirators [2], and Riccardo's love theme [3]. The last, after an interruption by [2], concludes the Prelude.

Act I, Scene 1: At the Governor's mansion soldiers, petitioners, and courtiers await the Earl's appearance for the morning audience. His loyal followers hope that he has had a pleasant rest [1], but the conspirators are planning his death [2]. Riccardo arrives, promises to do what he can for the petitioners, and receives from Oscar a list of guests invited to attend a masked ball the following evening. When the Earl reads the name of Amelia, he exults in anticipation of the joy of seeing her [3]. All are asked to await the Earl's decisions in the antechamber. As he breathes a sigh, thinking of the futility of his love for Amelia, her husband, Renato, enters. Mistaking Riccardo's sad mien for anxiety concerning the conspiracy, Renato offers to reveal the names of the traitors. However, Riccardo does not want to hear them. His worried secretary strongly urges caution, since the happiness of the people depends on the life of a good governor (Aria *Alla vita che t'arride:* "On the life thou now dost cherish") [4].

Announced by Oscar, the page, the chief judge enters and submits some legal decisions for signature. When the Earl inquires about the banishment of a woman, the fortune-teller Ulrica, the page describes the wonderful magical activities and prophecies of the witch (Ballata *Volta la terrea fronte alle stelle:* "Reading the stars on high, eyes fiercely burning") [5] and gaily asserts that Ulrica is doubtless in league with Lucifer himself [6]. Thereupon the Earl has everybody called in and, despite Renato's objections, invites them to forget all their cares for the afternoon [7] and to join him, disguised as common people, at Ulrica's hut [8].

* Stockholm is the historical locale of the events that Scribe fashioned into the play "*Gustave III ou le bal masqué*" which, in turn, served as the basis for Piave's libretto. The Stockholm version uses the names of the historical characters: King Gustave III (Riccardo); Count Anckarstroem (Renato); Count De Horn and Count Ribbing (Sam and Tom); Arvidson (Ulrica).

[6] BALLATA *VOLTA LA TERREA FRONTE* (Oscar) *continued*

Brillante

f
Ah!___ she's with Sir Lu - ci - fer sworn friends __ I de - clare!
Ah!___ è con Lu - ci - fe - ro d'ac - cor - - do o - gnor!

[7] Allegro brillante e presto

leggierissimo
RIC. Think of naught now, my friends, save your pleas - ure
O - gni cu - ra si do - ni al di - let - to,

[8] Allegro brillante e presto

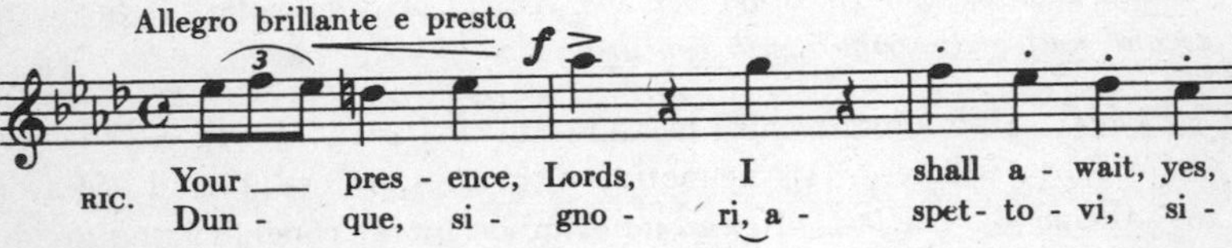
f
RIC. Your __ pres - ence, Lords, I shall a - wait, yes,
Dun - que, si - gno - ri, a - spet - to - vi, si -

Lords, I shall a - wait
gno - ri, a - spet - to - vi

[9] INVOCATION *RE DELL' ABISSO* (Ulrica)

Andante sostenuto

p
King ___ of the shades, I sum - mon thee,
Re ___ dell' a - bis - so af - fret - ta - ti;

[10] Allegro agitato e prestissimo

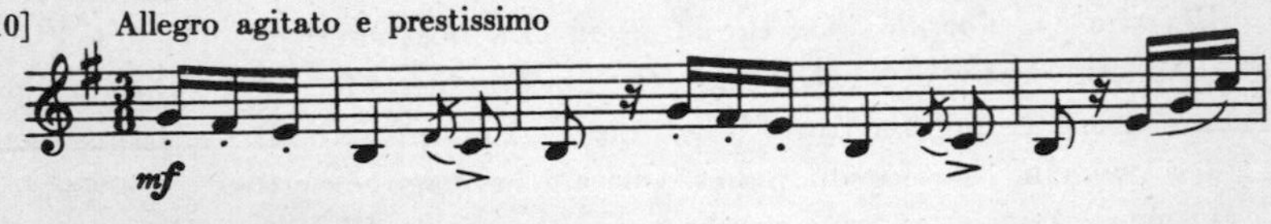
mf

[11] Cantabile

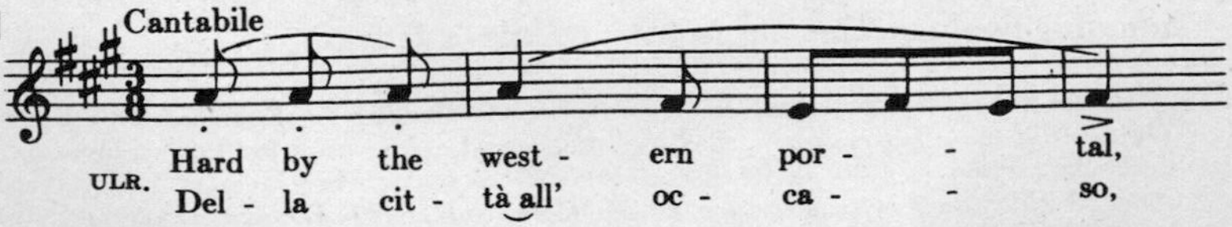
ULR. Hard by the west - ern por - - tal,
Del - la cit - tà all' oc - ca - - so,

Act I, Scene 2: Before an awed crowd of women and children, Ulrica, bent over a caldron in her hut, calls on Satan for assistance (Invocation *Re dell' abisso affrettati:* "King of the Shades, I summon thee") [9], interrupted only for a moment by the entrance of the Earl, who is dressed in sailor's clothes. All secrets of the future, Ulrica declares, now lie revealed before her eyes.

Silvano, a sailor, boisterously pushes his way to Ulrica, and she prophesies that he will receive both gold and rank. Hearing this, the Earl quickly writes a note of promotion and puts it, with a roll of gold, into the sailor's pocket. Silvano, about to pay the sorceress, discovers the strange objects in his pocket and reads aloud the note signed by Riccardo. All pay tribute to Ulrica's wisdom.

There is a knock at the secret door, and a servant of Amelia's asks for a private consultation for his mistress. Ulrica concocts a pretext to bid all wait outside, but the Earl, who has recognized the servant, hides and remains.

Amelia excitedly enters [10], and Riccardo hears her asking for a cure for her love for him. The seeress orders her to pluck a certain herb at midnight near the gallows at the edge of the town [11]. The Earl decides that he will be there to protect her and to be near her (Trio), and Ulrica promises relief, while Amelia asks the Lord for strength [12].

As Amelia flees by the secret door, the crowd, augmented by the page and courtiers, re-enters. The Earl boldly asks for a prophecy (Canzone *Dì tu se fedele:* "Oh, tell if the ocean") [13]. When Ulrica has scrutinized his hand, she refuses to tell his future; but the Earl insists, and she horrifies all by predicting that he will be assassinated by a friend. While Riccardo attempts to make light of the prophecy [14], Ulrica (Ensemble), passing among the conspirators, asks them pointedly why they take her words so seriously; Sam and Tom are afraid of being discovered [15]; and Oscar's heart goes out in sympathy for his master [16]. Riccardo asks Ulrica to name the supposed murderer, and she answers that it will be the next man to shake his hand. In an attempt to disprove her, Riccardo asks those

[12]

[13] CANZONE *DI TU* (Riccardo)

Allegro giusto

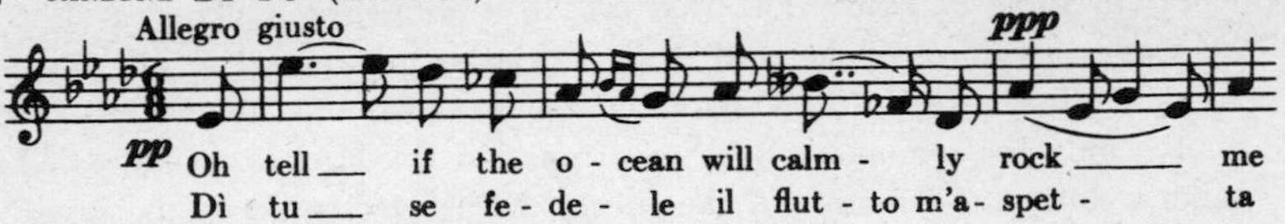
ppp
pp
Oh tell — if the o - cean will calm - ly rock — me
Dì tu — se fe - de - le il flut - to m'a - spet - ta

[14] Andante mosso quasi allegretto *con eleganza*

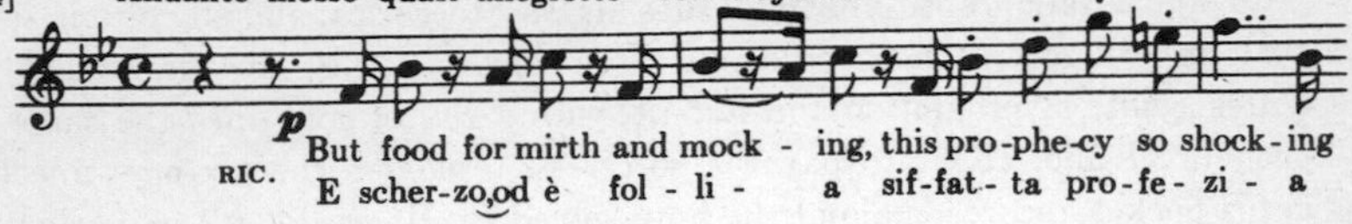
p
RIC.
But food for mirth and mock - ing, this pro-phe-cy so shock - ing
E scher-zo od è fol - li - a sif-fat - ta pro-fe - zi - a

[15] Andante mosso quasi allegretto

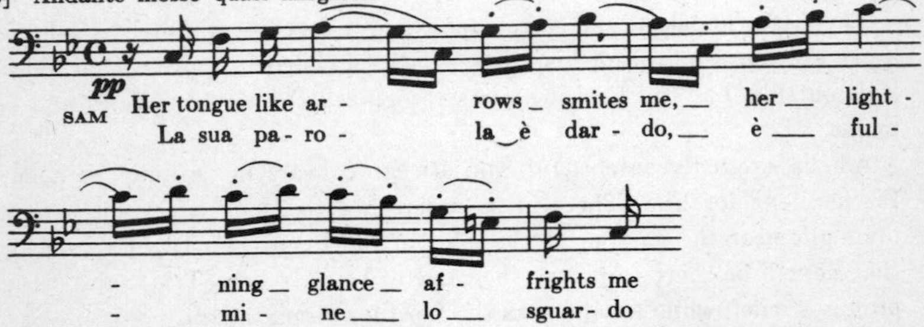
pp
SAM
Her tongue like ar - rows — smites me, — her — light -
La sua pa - ro - la è dar - do, — è — ful -
- ning — glance — af - frights me
- mi - ne — lo — sguar - do

[16] Andante mosso quasi allegretto

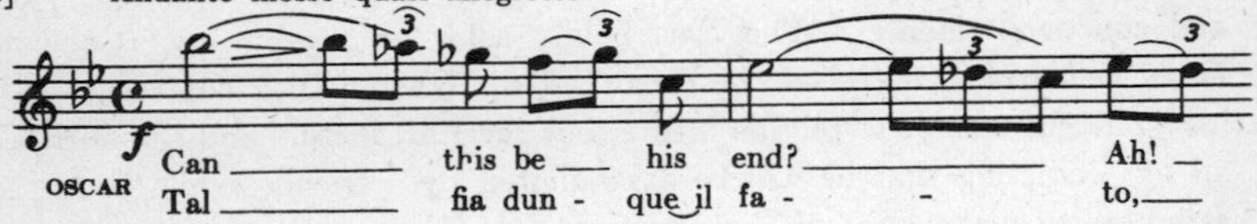
f
OSCAR
Can — this be — his end? — Ah! —
Tal — fia dun - que il fa - - to, —

[17] ANTHEM *O FIGLIO D'INGHILTERRA*

Allegro assai sostenuto

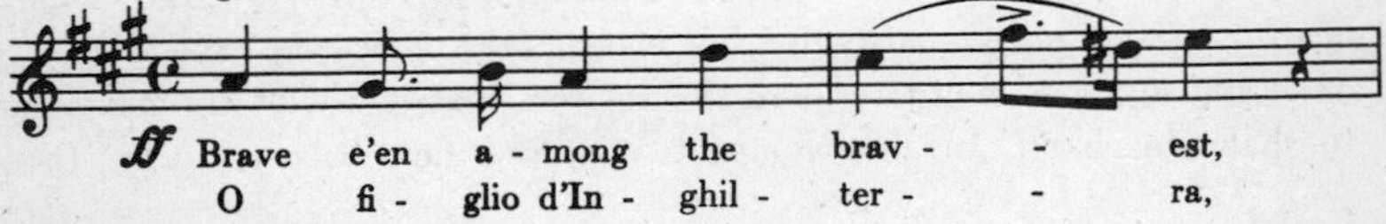
ff
Brave e'en a - mong the brav - - est,
O fi - glio d'In - ghil - ter - - ra,

[18] ARIA *MA DALL'ARIDO STELO* (Amelia)

Andante *con espressione*

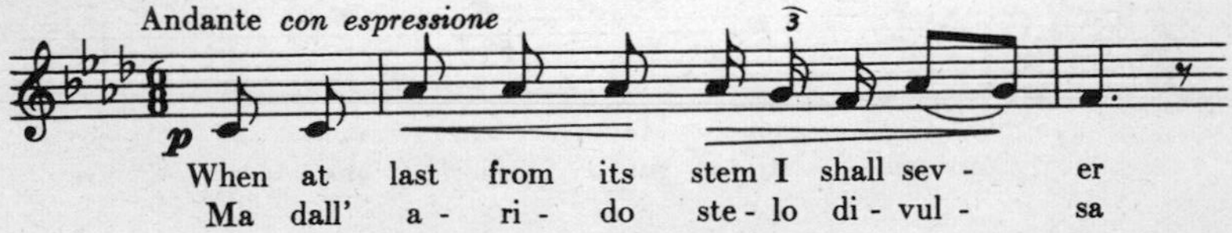
p
When at last from its stem I shall sev - er
Ma dall' a - ri - do ste - lo di - vul - sa

[19] Andante *con passione*

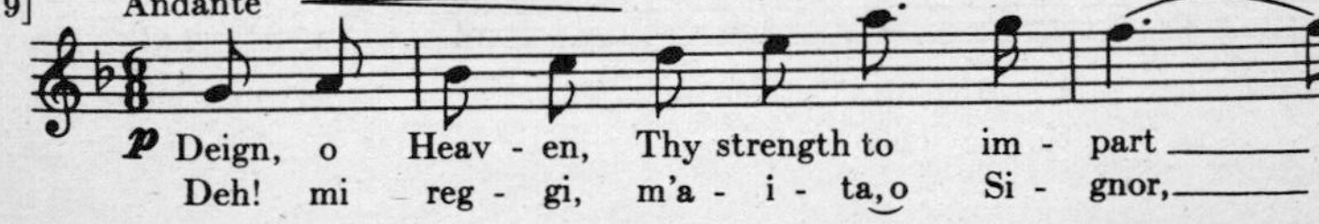
p
Deign, o Heav - en, Thy strength to im - part —
Deh! mi reg - gi, m'a - i - ta, o Si - gnor, —

present to shake hands with him, but all refuse. Just then Renato enters and gladly grasps the Earl's hand. Knowing that Renato is his closest friend, all are convinced that the seeress must be mistaken. Shouts of "*Viva Riccardo*" are heard, and Silvano returns with sailors to pay homage to the Governor [17].

Act II: After a short, agitated orchestral introduction, Amelia approaches and slowly descends [motive 12] toward the clearing where the gallows is outlined against the moon. After a silent prayer, she prepares to pluck the magic herb (Recitative *Ecco l'orrido campo:* "Here's the horrible place"; Aria *Ma dall' arido stelo divulsa:* "When at last from its stem I shall sever") [18]. At the stroke of midnight, terrifying visions assail her, and she again prays to God for strength [19]. Riccardo approaches to protect her (Duet *Teco io sto:* "I'm with you") but Amelia frantically begs him to leave. However, under the pressure of his passionate avowal of love [20], she eventually confesses her own infatuation, and for one fleeting moment they rejoice in the knowledge of their mutual love [21].

Suddenly they hear the sound of approaching steps, and as Amelia quickly veils herself, Renato hurries toward Riccardo (Trio *Tu qui:* "You here?"), informing him that the conspirators are near. He exchanges his cape for Riccardo's and urges him to flee. Riccardo's reluctance to leave Amelia thus with her husband is overcome only when Amelia threatens to unveil. Thereupon Riccardo asks Renato to bring the veiled lady, without talking to her, to the city gates and there to leave her. In whispers, Amelia and Renato urge the Earl to flee [22], and reluctantly he rushes off.

As Renato prepares to take the lady back to the city, the conspirators appear [2]. Renato takes off the cape, and the murderers, disappointed at finding Renato instead of the Earl, insist that at least they must see the face of

[20] FROM DUET *TECO IO STO* (Riccardo, Amelia)

Allegretto un poco sostenuto *a mezza voce*
RIC.
Know'st thou not, though the spir - it with - in me, con-science-
Non sai tu che se l'a - ni - ma mi - a il ri -
strick-en, is wound - ed and bleed - ing,
mor - so di - la - ce - ra e ro - de,

[21] Allegro vivo *a mezza voce dolcissimo*

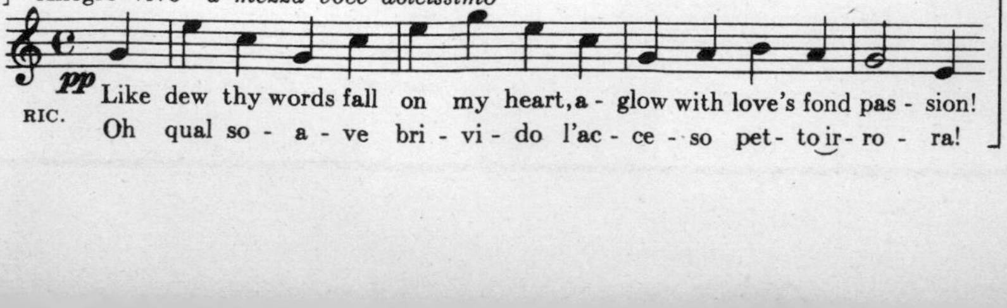
pp
RIC.
Like dew thy words fall on my heart, a - glow with love's fond pas - sion!
Oh qual so - a - ve bri - vi - do l'ac - ce - so pet - to ir - ro - ra!

[22] FROM TRIO TU QUI (Renato, Riccardo, Amelia)

Presto assai *sotto voce*

Do you hear, o Ric - car - do, the dread - ful sounds of

AM. O - di tu co - me fre - mo - no cu - pi per quest'

death and of mur - der ap - proach - ing?

au - ra gli ac - cen - ti di mor - te?

[23] Andante mosso quasi allegretto *con eleganza*

Look at the spous - es court - ing by moon - light

SAM Ve', se di not - te, quì col - la spo - sa

[24] Andante mosso quasi allegretto *leggermente*

How tongues will clat - ter o'er such a mat - ter, gos - sip

SAM & TOM E che bac - ca - no sul ca - so stra - no, e che com -

strange in the town will pass!

men - ti per la cit - tà!

[25] ARIA *MORRO* (Amelia)

Andante *con dolore*

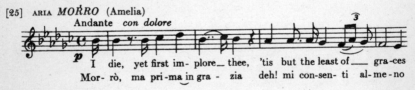

I die, yet first im - plore — thee, 'tis but the least of — gra - ces

Mor - rò, ma pri - ma in gra - zia deh! mi con - sen - ti al - me - no

[26] ARIA *ERI TU* (Renato)

Andante sostenuto

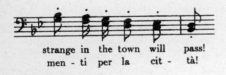

Ah, it's you who has
E - ri tu che mac-

the veiled lady. Renato draws his sword. Rushing between the men, Amelia drops her veil and is recognized by her astonished husband and by the amused conspirators [23], who feel that the situation will provide interesting gossip in town [24]. Sam and Tom accept Renato's invitation to see him at his house the next morning. As the conspirators leave, laughing ironically [24], Renato furiously declares that he will fulfill his oath and bring Amelia to the gates of the city.

Act III, Scene 1: Renato enters his house with Amelia, declaring that she must die. When all Amelia's efforts at explanation are in vain, she kneels and asks as a last favor that she be allowed once more to see her only son (Aria *Morrò:* "I'll die") [25]. Renato grants her wish (Recitative *Alzati!:* "Arise!"). When she has left, he muses that he should take revenge on the Earl (Aria *Eri tu:* "Ah, it's you") [26] rather than on her, for it is the Earl who has deprived him of his honor and robbed him of all the delights life had held for him [27].

Sam and Tom [2] come to keep their appointment. They are surprised to learn that Renato wants to join their plot, but he convinces them of his sincerity, and together they swear vengeance (Vengeance Trio *Dunque l'onta:* "One for all") [28]. As they prepare to draw lots for the privilege of striking the fatal blow, Amelia enters, announcing that Oscar is here with an invitation from the Governor. Renato forces her to draw a name from the urn. Frightened, she complies and Sam reads "Renato." As the men renew

[26] *continued*

[27] Andante sostenuto

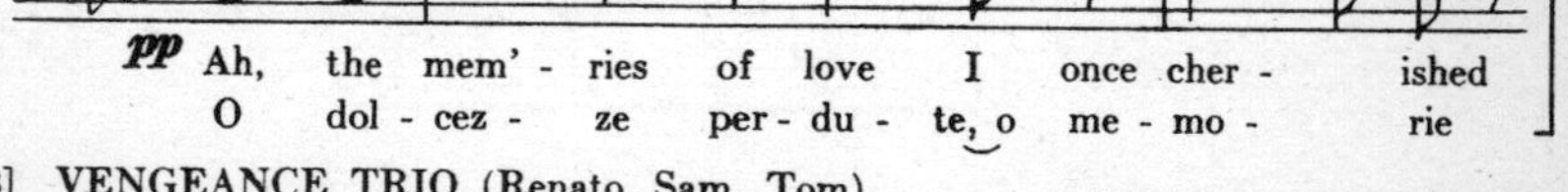

[28] VENGEANCE TRIO (Renato, Sam, Tom)

Andante mosso

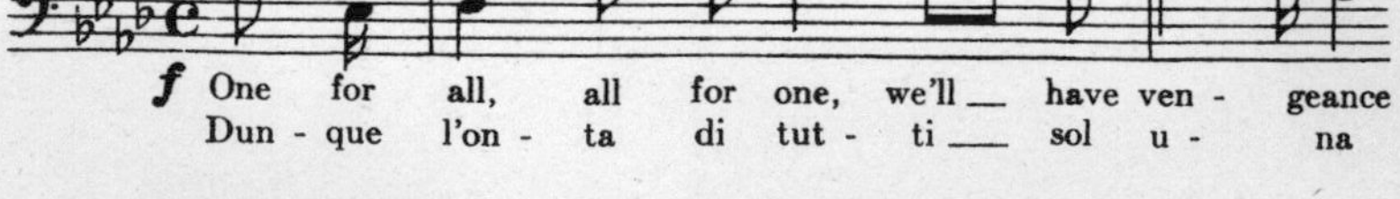

[29] BALLATA *DI CHE FULGOR* (Oscar)

Allegro brillante

What dazzling light, what music bright in yon halls will be reign - ing!
Di che ful - gor, che mu - si - che e - sul - te - ran le so - glie,

[30] ARIA *MA SE M'E FORZA* (Riccardo)

Andante

But though for aye from thee I'm torn, bright star who was my bea - con
Ma se m'è for - za per - der - ti per sem - pre, o lu - ce mi - a

[31] Allegro vivissimo

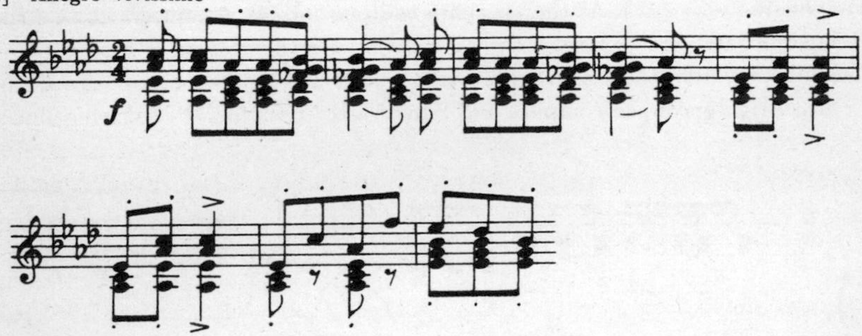

[32] CANZONE *SAPER VORRESTE* (Oscar)

Allegro *scherzando*

You ask me sly - ly but I am wil - y,
Sa - per vor - re - ste di che si ve - ste,

[33] Assai moderato

[34] Prestissimo *con furore*

CHO.
Ah, per - ish the trai - tor, ah, per - ish the trai - tor vile,
Ah, mor - te, in - fa - mia, in - fa - mia sul tra - di - tor,

their vow of revenge [28], Amelia realizes with terror that she has been a tool in the planning of Riccardo's murder.

Renato now asks Oscar to enter and receives from him an invitation to the masked ball. The conspirators see a chance to accomplish their business, and Renato accepts for himself and Amelia. The page paints a glowing picture of the planned festivities (Ballata and Quintet *Di che fulgor:* "What dazzling light") [29], while the conspirators plan for action, and Amelia sorrowfully [29 minor] ponders means to warn the Earl without betraying her husband.

Act III, Scene 2: In his study, curtained off from the grand ballroom, Riccardo wonders whether Amelia has reached home safely [3]. Conquering his own deepest wishes, he signs an order that will take Renato and his wife to England. Oceans will separate them, but his thoughts will always be with her (Romanza *Ma se m'è forza perderti:* "But though for aye from thee I'm torn") [30]. The band is heard playing in the ballroom [31]. Amelia must have arrived, but Riccardo does not intend to talk to her again.

Oscar comes in to deliver a note from an unknown lady. Riccardo learns from it that an attempt on his life will be made at the ball, but he decides to ignore the warning. As the page leaves, Riccardo once more looks forward to enjoying Amelia's presence for the last time [3]. He goes to his rooms, and the curtains are drawn apart, revealing the ballroom.

Act III, Scene 3: A festive, masked crowd is dancing and enjoying itself [31]. Sam, Tom, and Renato meet, the last expressing his doubts as to Riccardo's presence. Renato is recognized by the page, who tells him that the Governor is actually at the ball. However, when Renato asks how the Earl is dressed, the page laughingly refuses the information (Canzone *Saper vorreste:* "You ask me slyly") [32]. Renato now claims that he has to talk to the Earl on urgent affairs of state, thus forcing the page to describe his master's costume.

As a string orchestra starts the minuet [33], a masked lady approaches the Earl and desperately implores him to leave the ball. Almost at once he recognizes Amelia, and when she begs him to flee for her love's sake, he answers that, being loved, he has no fear of death. He tells her that by the next morning she will be sailing to England with her husband, and they bid each other a fond last goodbye. At this moment Renato stabs Riccardo. Renato is seized and unmasked by the guards while the shocked crowd calls for his death [34]. The Governor, fatally wounded, commands that Renato be freed. He admits loving Amelia, but swears that she has remained pure, and produces from his pocket the document that orders Renato and Amelia to go to England. He orders a general pardon and dies as the remorseful conspirators join in the general mourning for a noble governor.

THEMES

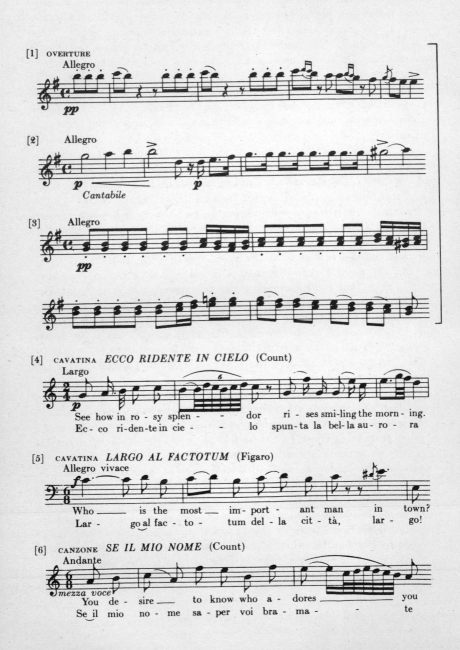

[1] OVERTURE

Allegro

pp

[2] Allegro

p
p
Cantabile

[3] Allegro

pp

[4] CAVATINA *ECCO RIDENTE IN CIELO* (Count)

Largo

p
See how in ro - sy splen - - dor ri - ses smi-ling the morn - ing.
Ec - co ri-den-te in cie - - lo spun-ta la bel-la au - ro - ra

[5] CAVATINA *LARGO AL FACTOTUM* (Figaro)

Allegro vivace

f
Who is the most im - port - ant man in town?
Lar - go al fac - - to - tum del - la cit - tà, lar - go!

[6] CANZONE *SE IL MIO NOME* (Count)

Andante

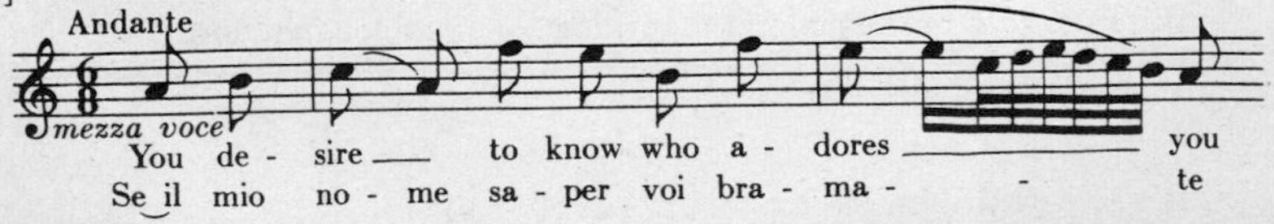
mezza voce
You de - sire to know who a - dores you
Se il mio no - me sa - per voi bra - ma - - te

Il Barbiere di Siviglia

THE BARBER OF SEVILLE

Opera in two acts by Gioacchino Rossini. Libretto by Cesare Sterbini, from the play by Beaumarchais. First performance: Rome, February 20, 1816.

Characters: COUNT ALMAVIVA (tenor); DR. BARTOLO (bass-buffo); ROSINA, his ward (mezzo-soprano *); FIGARO, a barber (baritone); BASILIO, a music master (bass); BERTA, a maid (soprano or mezzo-soprano).
Seville, in the eighteenth century.

Important parts of this opera are cast in the form of recitative accompanied solely by the harpsichord. These "secco recitatives" are indicated in the text by (Recitative).

Overture: After a short introduction, themes [1] and [2] are heard, followed by a sparkling closing theme [3].

Act I, Scene 1: It is shortly before dawn as Fiorello, with a band of musicians, arrives in front of Dr. Bartolo's house to accompany the Count as he sings a morning serenade (Cavatina *Ecco ridente in cielo:* "See how in rosy splendor") [4] to Rosina. When there is no response from her, the Count orders Fiorello to pay off the musicians. The men, excited by the Count's generosity, break into noisy and endless thank-yous. However, the Count manages to drive them off before they have awakened every household on the Piazza. Now the Count dismisses Fiorello (Recitative), but he himself decides to wait in the shadows for Rosina's customary early-morning appearance on the balcony.

Figaro comes by, loudly proclaiming his own fame (Cavatina *Largo al factotum della città:* "Who is the most important man in town?") [5]. The Count recognizes Figaro, whom he knew in Madrid (Recitative), and confides to him his love for Rosina, which has now brought him to Seville. Figaro suggests that he may be able to help, since he is well acquainted with the doctor and his household. As a matter of fact, he holds most of the important positions there.

Rosina (this episode is usually omitted) drops a note for her admirer, and Bartolo, her old guardian, notices that something "fell" from her hand. He rushes outside to retrieve it, but fails to find proof for his suspicions, since by now the note is safely in the hands of the Count, who is hiding around the corner with Figaro. When the doctor has re-entered the house, Figaro reads the missive, which asks that the interesting suitor give his personal data and intentions.

* Often sung, slightly rearranged, by a coloratura soprano.

[7] DUET *ALL' IDEA DI QUEL METALLO*

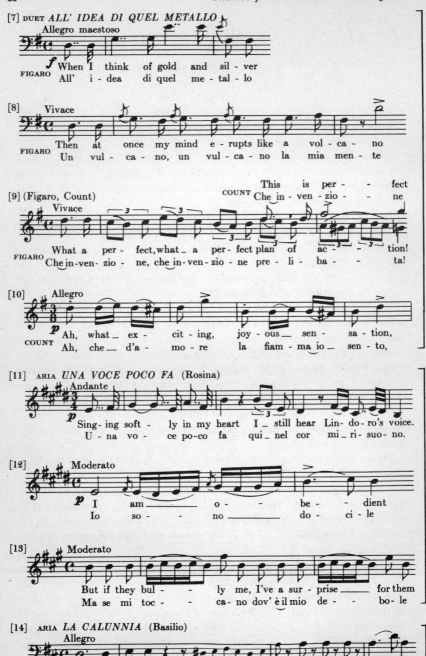

Allegro maestoso
f
FIGARO
When I think of gold and sil - ver
All' i - dea di quel me - tal - lo

[8]

Vivace
FIGARO
Then at once my mind e - rupts like a vol - ca - no
Un vul - ca - no, un vul - ca - no la mia men - te

[9] (Figaro, Count)

Vivace
COUNT
This is per - - fect
Che in - ven - zio - - ne
FIGARO
What a per - fect, what a per - fect plan of ac - tion!
Che in-ven- zio - ne, che in - ven - zio - ne pre - li - ba - - ta!

[10]

Allegro
p
COUNT
Ah, what ex - cit - ing, joy - ous sen - sa - tion,
Ah, che d'a - mo - re la fiam - ma io sen - to,

[11] ARIA *UNA VOCE POCO FA* (Rosina)

Andante
p
Sing- ing soft - ly in my heart I still hear Lin- do- ro's voice.
U - na vo - ce po-co fa qui nel cor mi ri- suo- no.

[12]

Moderato
p
I am o - be - dient
Io so - - no do - ci - le

[13]

Moderato
But if they bul - - ly me, I've a sur - prise for them
Ma se mi toc - - ca- no dov' è il mio de - - bo - le

[14] ARIA *LA CALUNNIA* (Basilio)

Allegro
What is slan- der? It's like a ze - phyr,
La ca - lun - nia è un ven - ti - cel - lo,

The doctor leaves his house, determined that before night he shall be married to his ward.

Figaro suggests that the Count answer Rosina's note with a song. This Almaviva does (Canzone *Se il mio nome saper voi bramate:* "You desire to know who adores you") [6], to the accompaniment of Figaro's guitar; however, he claims to be "Lindoro," poor, but with a heart filled with love. Rosina, standing at the window, encourages her suitor to sing on, and at the end of another verse she starts to reply; but a sudden commotion is heard in her room, and the window is hurriedly closed.

Figaro, promised money for arranging a meeting between the Count and his beloved, declares (Duet *All' idea di quel metallo:* "When I think of gold and silver") [7] that gold inspires his mind to spew forth ideas like a volcano [8]. For example: he would suggest that the Count dress as a soldier and ask to be billeted at the doctor's house . . . or perhaps . . . even better . . . he should come . . . as a drunken soldier, he stammers, at the same time acting out the part. Both find the idea admirable [9]. Asked where he can be found, Figaro explains, in a rapid prattle, where his shop is located, while Almaviva airs his feelings in anticipation of the meeting with Rosina [10].

Act I, Scene 2: Rosina, alone in her room, is thinking about "Lindoro" (Aria *Una voce poco fa:* "Singing softly in my heart"): his voice has deeply affected her [11], and no power on earth, she promises herself, shall prevent her from getting the man she wants. She sits down at her table, quickly writes a little note, and hides it in her bosom. True, she continues, she is an obedient girl [12], but should anyone dare to try to take advantage of her, he had better watch out [13].

Figaro comes to talk to her (Recitative), but hides at the approach of Bartolo. Rosina's guardian is furious with the barber, who has slyly put all the household help out of action by dosing them with his "remedies." Irked by Bartolo's inquisitorial manner in questioning her about Figaro, Rosina declares that she finds him simply adorable and walks out.

Presently Don Basilio arrives and is warmly welcomed by Bartolo. However, he brings the grave news that the secret admirer of Rosina, Count Almaviva, has arrived in Seville. He suggests that the best means of driving him quickly from town is slander (Aria *La calunnia:* "What is slander?"), which may be conceived as a gentle murmur [14] but, once started [15], grows into a deafening roar till its victim, however innocent, is blasted to

[15] ARIA *LA CALUNNIA* (Basilio) *continued*

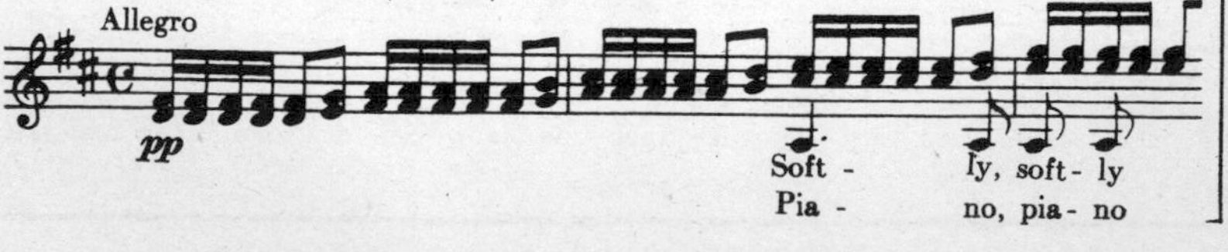

[16] DUET *DUNQUE IO SON* (Rosina, Figaro)

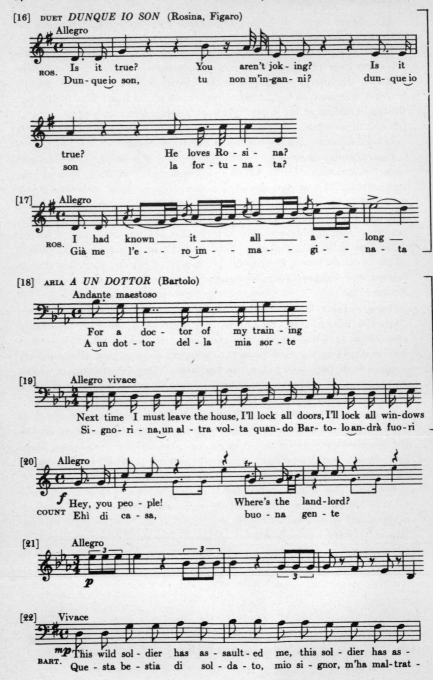

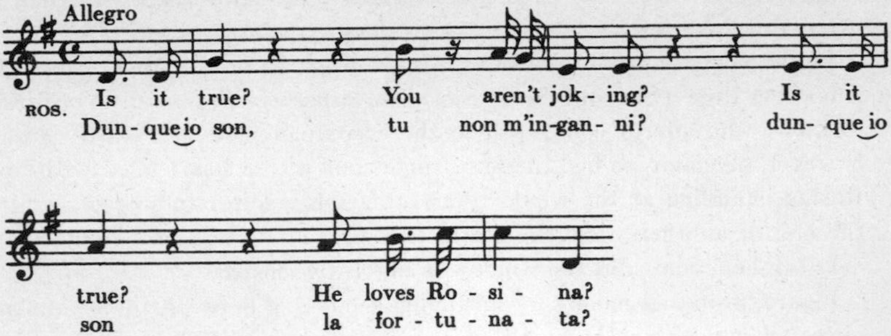
Allegro
ROS.
Is it true? You aren't jok - ing? Is it
Dun - que io son, tu non m'in-gan - ni? dun - que io
true? He loves Ro - si - na?
son la for - tu - na - ta?

[17]

Allegro
ROS.
I had known it all a - long
Già me l'e - ro im - ma - gi - na - ta

[18] ARIA *A UN DOTTOR* (Bartolo)

Andante maestoso
For a doc - tor of my train - ing
A un dot - tor del - la mia sor - te

[19]

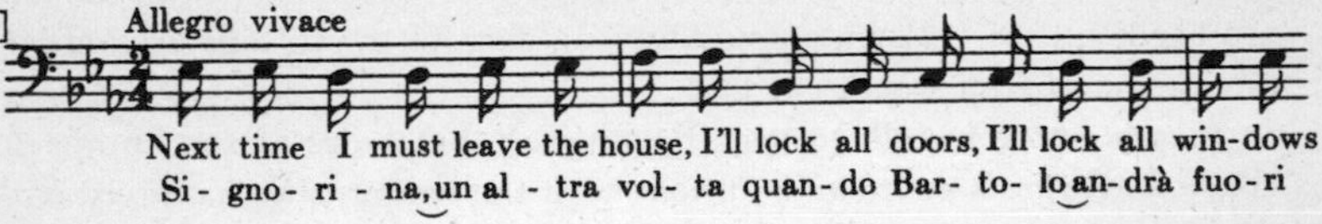
Allegro vivace
Next time I must leave the house, I'll lock all doors, I'll lock all win-dows
Si - gno - ri - na, un al - tra vol - ta quan - do Bar - to - lo an - drà fuo - ri

[20]

Allegro
f
COUNT
Hey, you peo - ple! Where's the land - lord?
Ehi di ca - sa, buo - na gen - te

[21]

Allegro
p

[22]

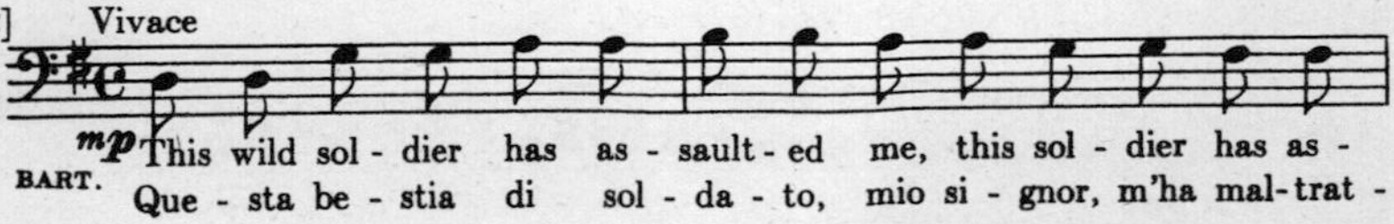
Vivace
mp
BART.
This wild sol - dier has as - sault - ed me, this sol - dier has as -
Que - sta be - stia di sol - da - to, mio si - gnor, m'ha mal - trat -

ignominious doom. That's the way to do it, advises Basilio, but Bartolo prefers quick action. He asks his confidant to come along and help him draw up the marriage contract.

When they have left, Figaro again comes forward, presently followed by Rosina. He informs her that "Lindoro" loves a girl named R-o-s-i-n-a. She coyly feigns surprise (Duet *Dunque io son:* "Is it true?") [16], but admits in an aside that she has known it all along [17]. Asked to write a line to "Lindoro," she shyly protests, but on further urging she produces the note she has just written, all signed and sealed, from its hiding-place. With some caustic remarks about the ways of women [17], Figaro takes the note and departs.

Bartolo comes back and notices with a glance at the desk that his ward must have written a letter (Recitative). Rosina denies it, and summons up an explanation for every suspicious detail, but Bartolo can't be fooled so easily (Aria *A un dottor de la mia sorte:* "For a doctor of my training") [18]. He promises that he will be even more careful to cut all lines of communication the next time he leaves the house [19]. Noticing that Rosina has already left the room, he departs in a rage.

Berta, the maid, enters and goes to answer a knock on the door. It is the Count who staggers in, impersonating a drunken soldier [20] and frightening Berta away. When Bartolo comes, the soldier claims—without ever seeming able to get the doctor's name straight—to have been billeted on this household, all the while trying to discover Rosina. Now she enters and becomes quite excited on hearing the soldier whisper that he is "Lindoro." The doctor, who has been looking for his billeting exemption, eventually finds it, but the soldier won't budge. With saber drawn, and describing a battle, Almaviva effectively keeps the doctor in check while he secretly tries to drop a note for Rosina. Bartolo sees it, but when he finally gets hold of it Rosina has cleverly substituted a laundry list. By now Berta has joined the quarreling group, and Don Basilio has arrived, vocalizing. The confusion and noise continue to increase as the protagonists call one another unflattering names. Even the appearance of Figaro [21] cannot stop the bedlam.

Suddenly an ominous knock is heard, and the police arrive. Their inquiry is met by a deluge of simultaneous explanations of the situation [22]. The Count, about to be arrested by the police sergeant, secretly identifies himself, whereupon the police are ordered to present arms. All stand as if petri-

[22] *continued*

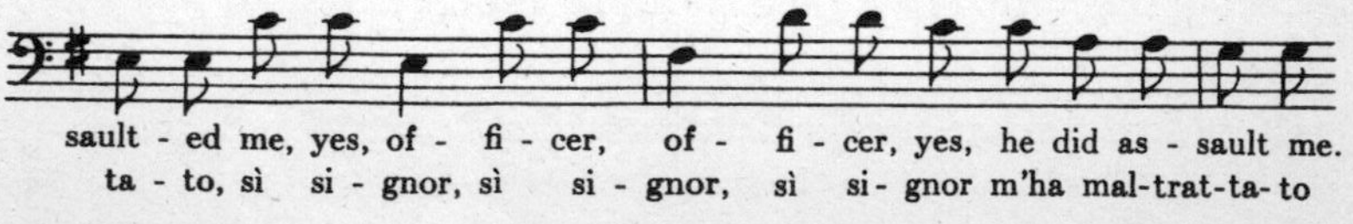
sault - ed me, yes, of - fi - cer, of - fi - cer, yes, he did as - sault me.
ta - to, sì si - gnor, sì si - gnor, sì si - gnor m'ha mal-trat-ta-to

[23]

Andante
p
ROS.
Rig - id and mo - tion - less like a mar - ble mon - u - ment
Fred - do ed im - mo - bi - le co - me u - na sta - tu - a

[24]

Andante
mf
FIGARO
Look at Don Bar - to - lo, how he is pet - ri - fied
Guar - da Don Bar - to - lo, guar - da Don Bar - to - lo

[25]

Vivace sotto voce
pp
In my head a roar - ing thun - der
Mi par d'es - ser col - la te - sta

[26]

Andante moderato
p
COUNT
May God's bles - sing be up - on you
Pa - ce e gio - ia sia con vo - i

[27] FROM THE ARIA OF THE USELESS PRECAUTION (Rosina)

Moderato
p
In my heart sweet thoughts of love I cher - ish
Ca - ra im - ma - gi - ne ri - den - te

[28]

Andantino
p
BART.
Come where the wood will screen us, Thou, sweet-est of Ro - si - - nas
Quan - do mi sei vi - ci - - na, a - ma - bi - le Ro - si - - na

[29]

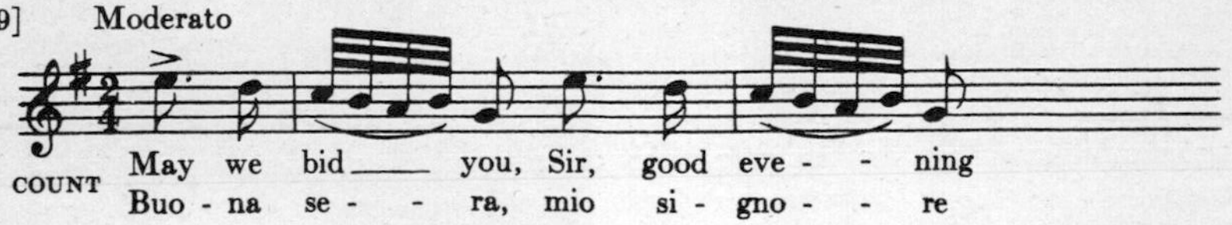
Moderato
COUNT
May we bid you, Sir, good eve - - ning
Buo - na se - - ra, mio si - gno - - re

[30] ARIA *IL VECCHIOTTO CERCA MOGLIE* (Berta)

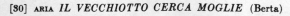

Allegretto
The old doc - tor wants a spouse and the young girl wants a hus - band
Il vec - chiot - to cer - ca mo - glie, vuol ma - ri - to la ra - gaz - za

fied [23], except the highly amused Figaro [24]. When, on regaining their speech, they are rudely told by the police to keep their mouths shut, they begin to wonder if they are not going mad [25].

Act II, Scene 1: The Count, this time masquerading as a music master, enters Bartolo's study with interminable unctuous greetings [26], finally (Recitative) explaining that he, "Don Alonso," has come to replace Don Basilio, who has suddenly fallen ill. To the mistrusting doctor he shows Rosina's letter, which he claims to have purloined from Count Almaviva. By relinquishing it to Bartolo, he worms himself into his confidence. He is permitted to give a voice lesson to Rosina. She enters and, when "Alonso" whispers to her that he really is "Lindoro," sings the "Aria of the Useless Precaution," filled with allusions to tyrannical guardians and young lovers [27]. During the song, teacher and student exchange quick remarks definitely not meant for the ears of Bartolo, who, half asleep, pays no attention. (When Rosina is sung by a soprano, aria [27] and the following duet are replaced with an aria for coloratura soprano or with bravura variations.) Presently, Bartolo wakes up and demonstrates *his* idea of a nice aria [28]. Just then Figaro arrives and with some difficulty persuades the doctor (Recitative) that this is the time for his shave. During the preparations Figaro manages to get possession of the key to the balcony door.

Unexpectedly Don Basilio arrives (Ensemble). After a moment of general embarrassment, Almaviva whispers to Bartolo that Basilio does not know about Rosina's letter. Thereupon Bartolo joins in the effort to make Basilio leave again. With the help of Figaro and a generous purse from the Count, Basilio is persuaded that he is terribly ill and that bed would be the best place for his "fever." He is ceremoniously dismissed [29].

Now, while the guardian finally submits to the razor, the lovers plan a midnight elopement, but the doctor, despite Figaro's various efforts to distract him, manages to overhear "Don Alonso" say something about a disguise. Bartolo threatens to kill everyone (Quartet) as he pursues the fleeing conspirators.

Berta, working her way through the room with her feather duster, soliloquizes about a sickness called love (Aria *Il vecchiotto cerca moglie:* "The old doctor wants a spouse") [30] and complains about the tedium of being an old maid [30].

Act II, Scene 2 (generally no change of scenery, no interruption): Bartolo (this episode is often omitted) sends Basilio for the notary (Recitative) so that the marriage ceremony may be performed at once.

[31]

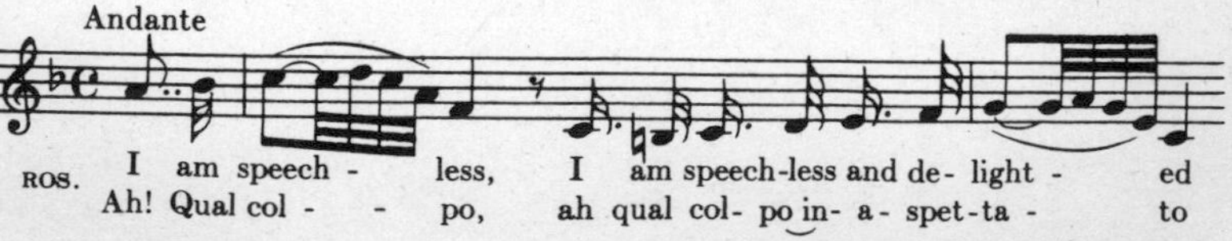
Andante
ROS.
I am speech - less, I am speech-less and de- light - ed
Ah! Qual col - - po, ah qual col- po in- a- spet-ta - to

[32] Allegro

COUNT
Down the lad - der we go quiet - ly and quick- ly from the
Zit- ti, zit - ti, pia - no, pia - no, non fac-cia - mo con - fu -
bal - con - y!
sio - ne

[33] Allegro

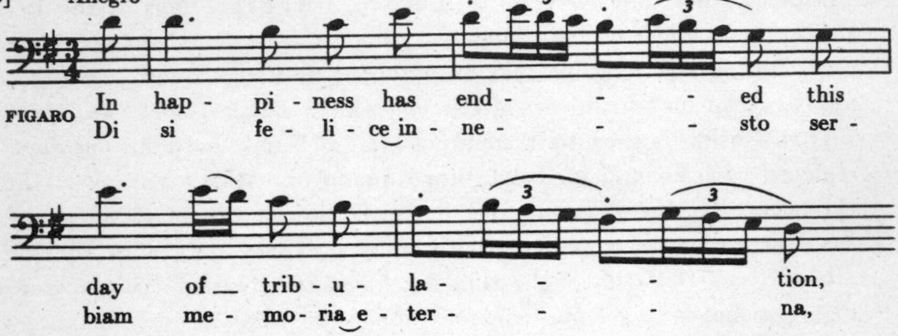
FIGARO
In hap - pi - ness has end - - - ed this
Di si fe - li - ce in - ne - - - sto ser -
day of trib - u - la - - - tion,
biam me - mo - ria e - ter - - - na,

Then he calls Rosina and shows her her own letter to "Lindoro." Claiming that this letter was found with Count Almaviva, Bartolo "proves" to Rosina that "Lindoro" wants to betray her to the Count. Thereupon Rosina, in despair, consents to marry Bartolo immediately, and reveals to him the plan for the elopement. On her guardian's advice, she locks herself in her room while Bartolo goes for the police.

After a thunderstorm (orchestral interlude while the open stage is empty), the Count and Figaro, entering via ladder and balcony door, come for Rosina. At first she accuses "Lindoro" of treachery, but she rejoices on learning that he himself is Count Almaviva [31]. They prepare to escape by the way they had come [32], but discover that the ladder has been taken away. Just then Basilio arrives with the notary (Recitative), who proceeds to marry Rosina to the Count. Basilio, forced to choose between a diamond ring and a bullet through his head, is persuaded to function as a needed witness. Bartolo arrives too late with the police. However, on learning that he may keep Rosina's dowry, he joins in the general jubilation [33].

THEMES

[1] THE BOHEMIANS

Allegro vivace
ff

[2] RODOLFO, THE PENNILESS DREAMER

Allegro vivace
p
ROD.
La - zi - ly ris - ing, see, how the smoke from
Nei cie - li bi - gi guar - do fu - mar dai
thou - sands of chim - neys floats up - ward.
mil - le co - mi - gno - li Pa - ri - gi,

[3] COLLINE

Allegro vivace
ff

[4] SCHAUNARD, THE PROVIDER

Allegro
f

[5] BENOIT, THE ROMEO (See [9])

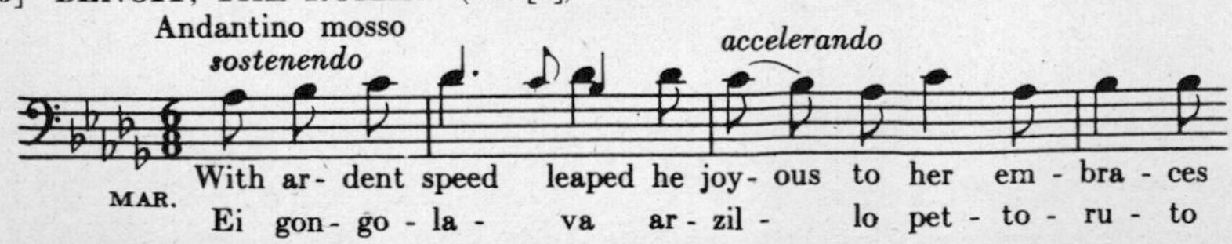
Andantino mosso
sostenendo
accelerando
MAR.
With ar - dent speed leaped he joy - ous to her em - bra - ces
Ei gon - go - la - va ar - zil - lo pet - to - ru - to

Quotations used by permission of G. Ricordi & Co.

La Bohème

Opera in four acts by Giacomo Puccini. Libretto by Giuseppe Giacosa and Luigi Illica. Based on Henry Mürger's *La Vie de Bohème*. First performance: Turin, February 1, 1896.

Characters: RODOLFO, a poet (tenor); MARCELLO, a painter (baritone); SCHAUNARD, a musician (baritone); COLLINE, a philosopher (bass); MIMI, a seamstress (soprano); MUSETTA, a grisette (soprano); BENOIT, a landlord (bass); ALCINDORO, a man about town (bass).
Paris, about 1830.

Act I: In their cold and shabby attic, four friends lead the hard but gay life of poor Bohemians [1]. At present, two of them—Rodolfo, the poet, and Marcello, the painter—hungry and freezing, are trying in vain to concentrate on their work. Rodolfo [2] delivers a tirade against the only idle chimney in Paris—namely, their own. They decide to sacrifice to it Rodolfo's latest drama—all five acts of it. Colline, the philosopher, enters [3], complaining that the pawnshops are closed on Christmas Eve, and tries to warm his hands as Rodolfo's masterpiece is given—to the flames. But the work is too short—to heat the room—and the author is booed.

Triumphant, the musician, Schaunard [4], comes in, astounding and delighting his friends with a good supply of fuel, food, wine, and money. He relates how a crazy Englishman engaged him to play a parrot to death; but his friends are interested only in food. As they prepare to eat, Schaunard reminds them in disgust that on Christmas Eve one may properly drink at home, but one must eat at the Café Momus, where all Paris is celebrating [13 Allegretto mosso—*ppp;* motive 14].

Unexpectedly, Benoit, the landlord, comes for the long-overdue rent. Marcello invites him to have a glass of wine with them [motive 5] and coaxes the old man into admitting that, on occasion, he likes to step out [5] with young and buxom women less troublesome than his haggard and nagging wife. Thereupon the quartet, in a fine show of sudden moral indignation, throw out the dumfounded Benoit without giving him another chance to ask for money.

Now it is time to go to the Momus. Only Rodolfo remains to finish an urgent editorial. When he answers a knock on his door, Mimi, a neighbor, enters [motive 10], apparently exhausted from climbing the stairs. She asks that he relight her candle, then has an attack of coughing [6] and, fainting, drops her key. Revived, and her candle lighted, she prepares to leave. Al-

[6] COUGHING SPELL

Allegro agitato

[7] Andante mosso

MIMI
Oh, how stu - pid, how stu - pid, the key of my poor
Oh! sven-ta - ta, sven-ta - ta! La chia - ve del - la

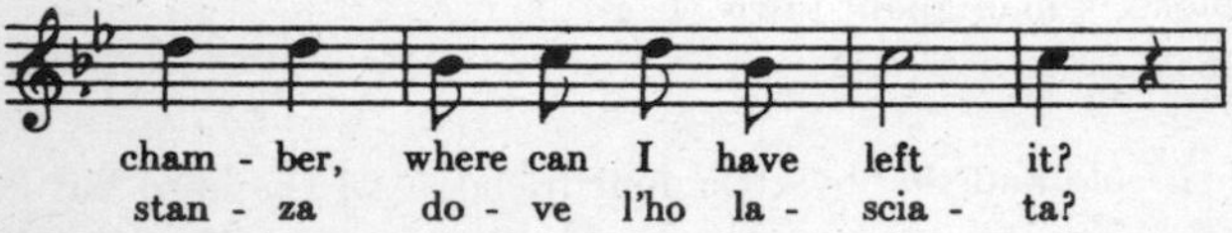
cham - ber, where can I have left it?
stan - za do - ve l'ho la - scia - ta?

[8] ARIA *CHE GELIDA MANINA* (Rodolfo)

a Andante affetuoso

p
Your ti - ny hand is fro- zen! Let me warm it in - to life.
Che ge - li - da ma- ni - na, se la la - sci ri - scal- dar.

b

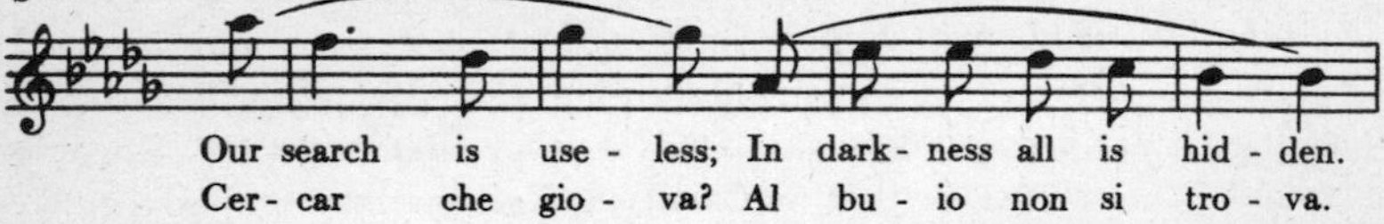
Our search is use - less; In dark- ness all is hid - den.
Cer- car che gio - va? Al bu - io non si tro - va.

[9] Andante lento

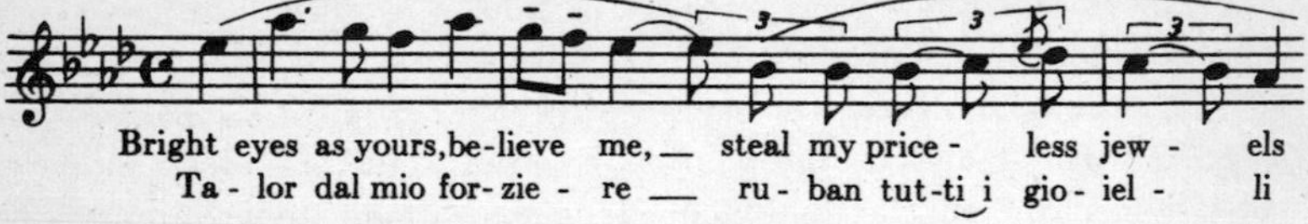
Bright eyes as yours, be-lieve me, __ steal my price - less jew - els
Ta - lor dal mio for- zie - re __ ru - ban tut-ti i gio - iel - li

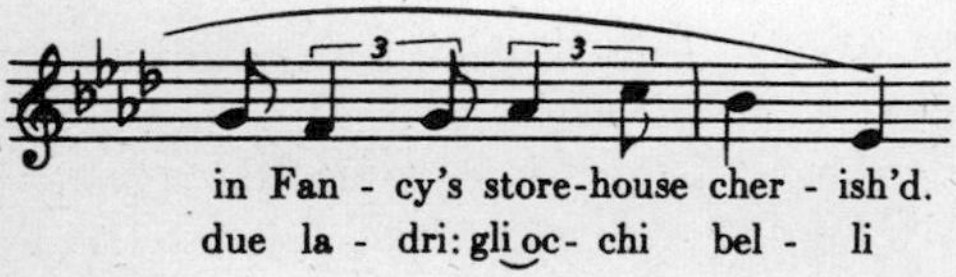
in Fan - cy's store-house cher - ish'd.
due la - dri: gli oc- chi bel - li

ready outside the door, she turns to look for her key [7] and a draft blows out both candles. As, in darkness, Mimi searches for the key and Rodolfo (who has quickly found and pocketed it) pretends to do the same, their hands touch. Rodolfo (Aria *Che gelida manina:* "Your tiny hand is frozen") asks leave to warm her hand in his [8ab] and introduces himself as a poet, poor in worldly possession [2] but rich in fantasy, and prone to be affected by beautiful eyes [9]. Then, at his invitation, Mimi talks about herself (Aria *Mi chiamano Mimì:* "They call me Mimi") [10]. She earns her livelihood by embroidering, and her favorite subject is flowers, which bring a breath of romance [11] to the little room in which she lives [12a]. But when spring sends its sunshine through her window, she likes to have a real rose in a vase [11] and enjoy the sweet perfume that the embroidered facsimile lacks.

His friends call from the street for the tarrying Rodolfo [1]. Let them go ahead! Rodolfo and Mimi (Duet *O soave fanciulla:* "Lovely maid in the moonlight") are glowing with a newly found love [9]. However, for the present he ceremoniously offers her his arm [8ab] in deference to her wish that they go to join his friends.

Act II: Gay crowds are milling about [13] in front of the Café Momus in the Latin Quarter, and hawkers and street venders are loudly offering

[10] ARIA *MI CHIAMANO MIMI* (Mimi)

[11]

ARIA *MI CHIAMANO MIMI* (Mimi) *continued*

[12a] MIMI'S ATTIC-ROOM

Allegretto moderato

p
All by my - self I take my fru - gal sup - per;
So - la mi fo il pran-zo da me stes - sa.
To mass not oft re - pair - ing
Non va - do sem - pre a mes - sa

[12b]* Andantino

[13] CHRISTMAS-EVE ON MONTMARTRE

Allegro focoso

fff

[14] THE HAWKERS

Allegro focoso

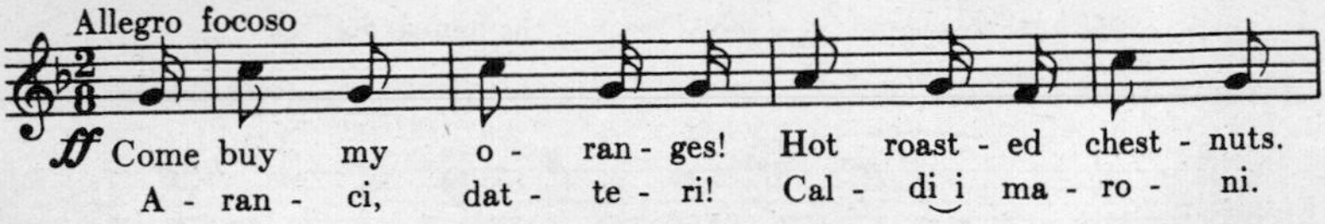
ff Come buy my o - ran - ges! Hot roast - ed chest - nuts.
A - ran - ci, dat - te - ri! Cal - di i ma - ro - ni.

[15] MUSETTA

Allegro moderato

ff

*Variation on accompaniment [12a].

their wares [14]. While Marcello shows interest in the promenading beauties and Rodolfo buys Mimi a pink bonnet, Colline and Schaunard make small purchases with their share of Schaunard's evenly distributed wealth. Eventually all meet at a sidewalk table outside the Café Momus, where Rodolfo extravagantly introduces Mimi, who is cordially received by his friends. They order dinner, but at the first toast Marcello nearly chokes when Musetta appears [15], escorted by old but rich Alcindoro, and sits down at a table nearby. Marcello, whom she loves—if only periodically—describes her fickle character [16] to Mimi. Musetta uses all her wiles to attract Marcello's attention and eventually, angered by his simulated indifference, breaks into a description of her charms, hardly modest but entirely accurate (Musetta's Waltz *Quando me'n vo':* "As through the street") [17]. Caustic remarks from Marcello's table accompany her exhibition, yet he seems ripe for a reconciliation. Musetta suddenly screams that her foot hurts and manages to send Alcindoro to the shoemaker. A moment later she rushes into Marcello's open arms [17]. A military band is heard in the distance [18]. The waiter presents the bill, but Schaunard's money is all spent [4]. While the crowd watches the passing retreat-patrol [18], Musetta takes the friends' bill and leaves it for Alcindoro, while she herself goes off with them. Carrying a new pair of shoes, Alcindoro returns and looks for Musetta. Instead, he finds the waiter waiting for him with the two bills, and sinks overwhelmed into a chair.

[16] MUSETTA

Allegro moderato

[17] MUSETTA'S WALTZ

Tempo di valzer lento

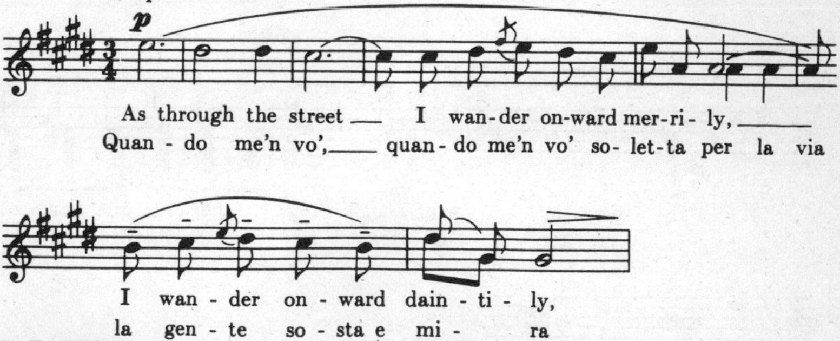
As through the street ___ I wan-der on-ward mer-ri - ly, ______
Quan - do me'n vo',____ quan - do me'n vo' so- let-ta per la via
I wan - der on - ward dain - ti - ly,
la gen - te so - sta e mi - ra

[18] TATTOO

Allegro alla marcia

[19] SNOW

Andantino mosso

pp

[20] Andantino mosso

dolce e con grazia

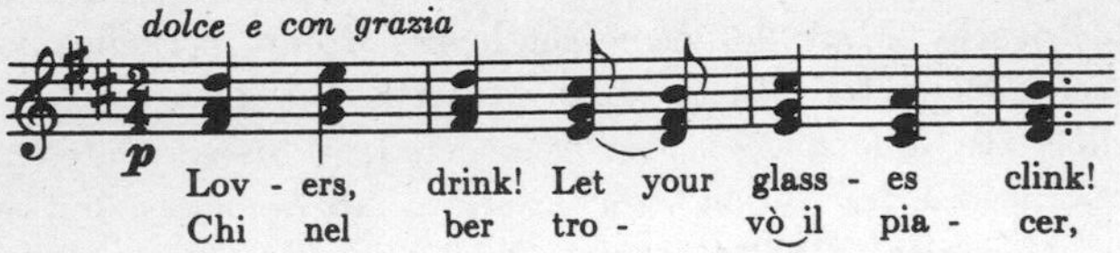
p
Lov - ers, drink! Let your glass - es clink!
Chi nel ber tro - vò il pia - cer,

[21] RODOLFO'S JEALOUSY

Andante

p

[22] ARIA *MIMI E UNA CIVETTA* (Rodolfo)

Allegro moderato

Mi - mi is al - ways flirt - ing; ev - ery man is a tar - get.
Mi - mì è u - na ci - vet - ta che fra - scheg - gia con tut - ti.

[23] Lento triste

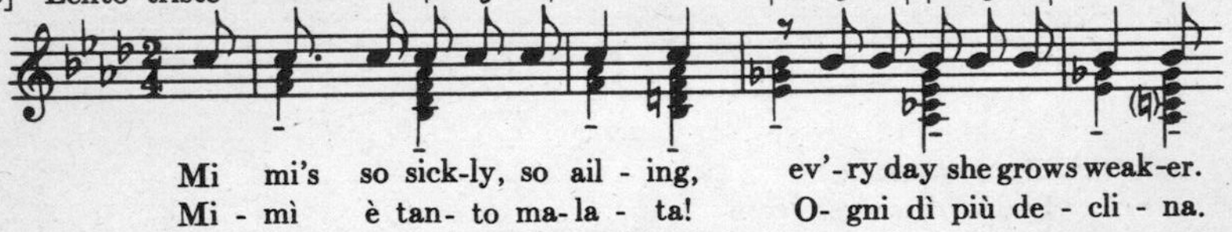
Mi mi's so sick-ly, so ail - ing, ev'-ry day she grows weak-er.
Mi - mì è tan - to ma - la - ta! O- gni dì più de - cli - na.

[24] Sostenuto molto

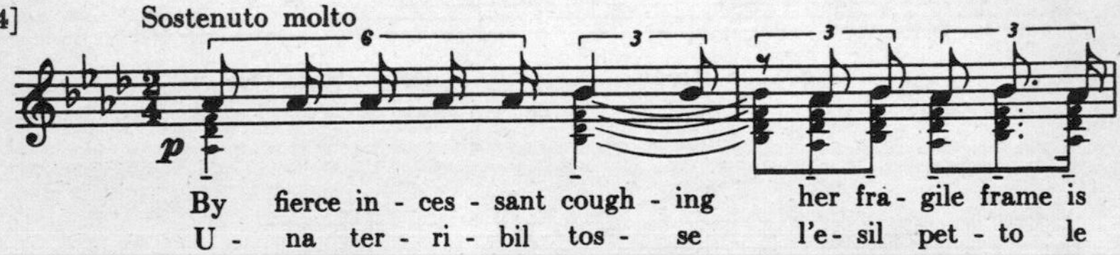
p
By fierce in - ces - sant cough - ing her fra - gile frame is
U - na ter - ri - bil tos - se l'e - sil pet - to le

sha - ken
scuo - te

Act III: Snow is falling [19] as, with the break of day, people from the suburbs arrive at a toll gate at the edge of Paris and rouse the sleepy customs officials. But at the inn close by, where Musetta and Marcello are working for their keep—she teaching singing, he painting murals—the revelers are still awake [20] and Musetta's voice is heard among them [17]. Mimi [10, 6] approaches the inn and has Marcello called out. When he arrives [1], she tells him that Rodolfo, in a fit of jealousy [21], has left her, and Marcello suggests that separation is the only remedy for lovers who make each other suffer [21]. Love should be handled with easy grace and gaiety, he claims, as he and Musetta do. Through a window he now notices that Rodolfo [2], who had come to him for a short rest, is waking, so he quickly sends Mimi home.

Rodolfo comes outside [9 with 2, 1], resolved to leave Mimi, whose flirtatiousness, he claims, he can bear no longer [22]; but, prodded by his friend, he confesses his fervent love for her [22] and also bares the real reason for his behavior: Mimi is terribly ill [23] and her cough will surely bring about her death [24] if she continues living in Rodolfo's cold, damp attic. Marcello is deeply moved, and Mimi, who has returned unnoticed, listens with conflicting emotions to Rodolfo's confession [Trio 23]. Now a dreadful coughing spell seizes her [24], and as she staggers forward, Rodolfo rushes to her side [10, 6].

Musetta's gay laughter is heard from the tavern [16], and in a violent jealous rage Marcello runs to her. Mimi (Aria *Donde lieta uscì:* "To the home that she left"—the *Addio*) decides to return to her attic of bygone days [10, 6, 12b, 11] and says a last farewell to Rodolfo. Musetta and Marcello flounce out of the inn, quarreling [25] and, amid violent name-calling,

[25] QUARREL

Andante con moto

[26]

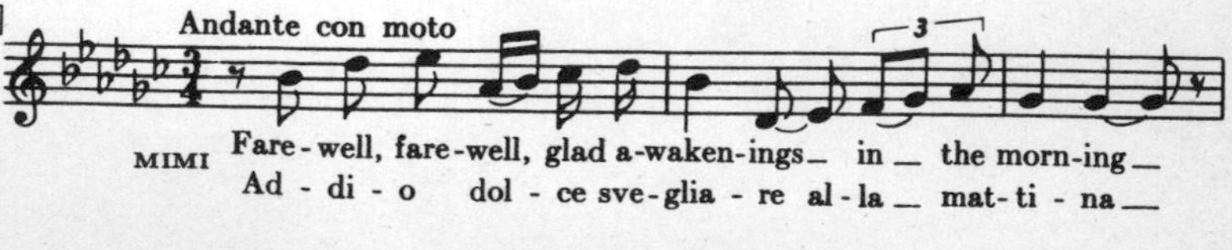
Andante con moto
MIMI
Fare-well, fare-well, glad a-waken-ings in the morn-ing
Ad - di - o dol - ce sve-glia - re al-la mat-ti - na

[27] Andante con moto

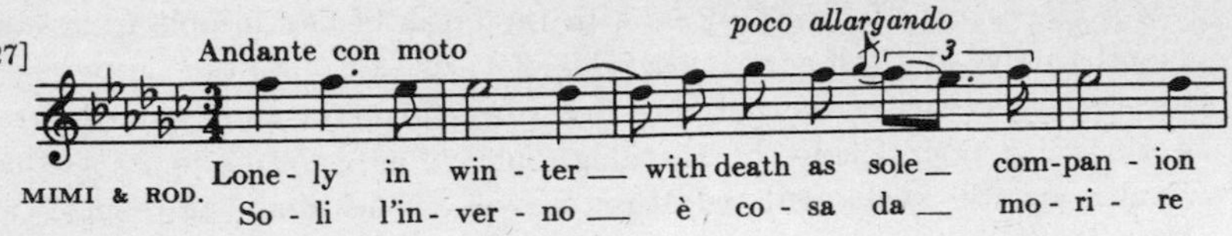
poco allargando
MIMI & ROD.
Lone-ly in win-ter — with death as sole — com-pan-ion
So-li l'in-ver-no — è co-sa da — mo-ri-re

[28] DUET *O MIMI TU PIU NON TORNI* (Rodolfo, Marcello)

Andantino mosso

p
ROD.
Ah, for-ev-er I have lost — you,
O Mi-mì tu più non tor-ni.
ah, beaut-eous days de-part-ed!
O gior-ni — bel-li,

[29] THE QUADRILLE Grazioso

SCHAUN.
Lal-le-ra, lal-le-ra, lal-le-ra, là, lal-le-ra, lal-le-ra, lal-le-ra, là.

[30] ARIA *VECCHIA ZIMARRA* (Colline)

Moderato e triste

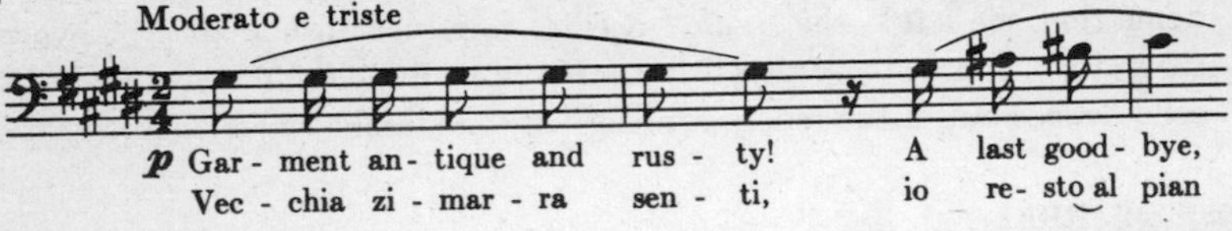
p
Gar-ment an-tique and rus-ty! A last good-bye,
Vec-chia zi-mar-ra sen-ti, io re-sto al pian

[31] Andante calmo

p
MIMI.
Have they left us? I just pre-tend-ed sleep-ing —
So-no an-da-ti? Fin-ge-vo di dor-mi-re —
for I want-ed to be a-lone with you, love —
per-chè vol-li con te so-la re-sta-re —

part company while Rodolfo and Mimi nostalgically recall their days together (Quartet *Addio dolce svegliare:* "Farewell, farewell, glad awakenings") [26, 25]. Musetta angrily runs off, but Rodolfo and Mimi decide that winter is no time for parting [27]. They leave, arm in arm, with the prayer that spring may never come, as Marcello, alone and sad, re-enters the inn.

Act IV: Back in their old quarters [1], Marcello and Rodolfo are in no mood for work. Rodolfo has seen Musetta [15]. She is so luxuriously dressed these days that, she said, she no longer can hear the voice of her heart [16] from below all the satin and silk. Marcello has met Mimi [10]. She, too, looked like a veritable queen. The two friends, each to himself, reminisce nostalgically about their former sweethearts (Duet *O Mimì, tu più non torni:* "Ah, forever I have lost you") [28].

Colline and Schaunard [4] enter with the day's meal: bread and a salted herring. Such meager fare gives rise to all kinds of horseplay. Colline [3] pretends he has to leave quickly for an audience with the King. Yet he remains to join in a quadrille [29] and to fight a poker-and-tongs duel with Schaunard while the other two switch to a rigaudon. Suddenly the fun is harshly interrupted by the entrance of Musetta. She has come to announce the arrival of a very sick Mimi. Rodolfo rushes out to assist her up the stairs [10, 6]. While Mimi is made comfortable on the bed [11], Musetta explains to the others in whispers that Mimi, feeling her end approaching, had left her viscount and expressed the desire to die near Rodolfo. Now Mimi is back and happy. If only she had a muff to warm her hands! Musetta [16] goes with Marcello to fulfill what will probably be Mimi's last wish and to get some medicine and a doctor. Colline leaves to pawn his coat (Aria *Vecchia zimarra:* "Garment antique") [30], and Schaunard [4] pretends to go for water. Alone now [9], Rodolfo and Mimi, who reiterates her undying love for him [31], recall their first meeting—how she told him her name [10, 12], how they looked for the key [7], and how he warmed her hand [8ab].

A violent coughing attack [6] brings back Schaunard, and soon Marcello and Musetta return. Mimi accepts the muff with childlike delight. Never again will she have cold hands [8b]. Gently she leans back and falls asleep. Musetta, while preparing the medicine, prays to the Madonna for Mimi's recovery. When Colline returns, Schaunard has already discovered Mimi's passing, but Rodolfo tells Colline that he is still hopeful. Suddenly he notices the agitation of the others, and with an anguished outcry he rushes to the bed and falls sobbing over Mimi's body [31].

THEMES

[1] INTRODUCTION

Andante
p

[2] POLICE

Allegro moderato
f
a

[3]

Allegro molto moderato
f
Why for - sake us all, leave_ us_ help - less, kind_fa - ther?

[4]

Moderato
pp
Glo - ry to Thee, O Lord, cre - a - tor of heav - en

[5] THE BELLS OF THE KREMLIN

Moderato
a

[6] HYMN OF GLORY

Allegretto moderato
Like the sun in the skies_ su-preme in his glo - ry Tsar Bo - ris

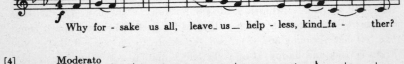

Boris Godunoff

Opera in four acts and a prologue by Modest Mussorgsky. Libretto by the composer after the play by Alexander Pushkin. First performance: St. Petersburg, January 24, 1874.*

Characters: BORIS GODUNOFF, Tsar of Russia (bass-baritone); FYODOR, his son (mezzo-soprano); XENIA, his daughter (soprano); Xenia's NURSE (contralto); PRINCE VASSILI IVANOVICH SHUISKI (tenor); ANDREI SHCHELKALOFF, Secretary of the Duma (baritone); PIMEN, a monk and chronicler (bass); GRIGORI OTREPIEFF (the false DIMITRI) (tenor); MARINA MNISHEK, daughter of the Lord of Sandomir (mezzo-soprano); RANGONI, a Jesuit (baritone); THE INNKEEPER (mezzo-soprano); VARLAAM (bass) and MISSAIL (tenor), vagrant monks; THE SIMPLETON (tenor); THE BOYAR IN ATTENDANCE (tenor); LAVITSKI (bass) and CHERNIKOFFSKI (bass), Jesuits; KHRUSHCHOFF, a boyar (tenor).
Russia and Poland, 1598–1605.

Prologue, Scene 1: As the people are moving about aimlessly [1] in the courtyard of the Novodievichy Monastery at Moscow, a police officer [2] appears and with threats forces them to kneel and resume their prayer [3]. Scarcely has the officer left when the people start chatting, but he returns and with raised cudgel makes them pray again [3]. Shchelkaloff comes from the monastery to announce that Boris is still reluctant to ascend the throne, and asks all to pray God that He may change Boris' mind. Slowly a procession of pilgrims approaches [4], denouncing the lawlessness and corruption in the land and exhorting the people to be true to the Orthodox Church. Distributing amulets to the kneeling population, they move into the monastery.

Prologue, Scene 2: All the bells of the Kremlin are ringing [5] as the procession of boyars moves from the palace to the Cathedral of the Assumption, carrying the royal insignia for the coronation of Boris. While the people who fill the entire square sing the new Tsar's praises (Hymn of Glory: "Like the sun in the skies") [6], the procession leaves the Church of the Assumption and moves across the square toward the Church of the Archangels. Last of all, Boris appears with crown and scepter, accompanied by his children and Shuiski. Boris is haunted by gloomy forebodings (Coronation Monologue: "My soul is sad") [7], but after a short prayer he invites

* The version here described is that by Nicolai Rimski-Korsakoff, the one most generally in use. It differs from the 1874 edition mainly in the reversal of the last two scenes—aside, of course, from Rimski-Korsakoff's completely new orchestration.

[7] FOREBODINGS–CORONATION MONOLOGUE (Boris)

Andante
dim.
p
f
My soul is sad

[8] PIMEN

Mosso

[9] DIMITRI

Moderato assai

[10] THE INNKEEPER'S SONG

Andantino
I have_caught_a duck,_ what a_ stroke_of luck,_

[11] THE VAGRANT MONKS

Moderato assai
Kind Christ- ian peo - ple, du - ti - ful and faith - ful

[12] BALLAD OF KAZAN (Varlaam)

Allegro
f By the walls of Ka - zan, the might-y strong - hold

[13]

Allegretto
VARL. Lurch- ing a - long_ walks_ all day long_

[14]

Andante
mf
3
XENIA Where are you, sweet - heart, where are you, be - lov - ed?

all to celebrate this day with him. Passing the boyars, who now are lining the way, he precedes them into the Cathedral of the Archangels to pay homage at the tombs of Russia's rulers. While the people continue to hail the new Tsar [6], Boris reappears from the cathedral and returns to the palace.

Act I, Scene 1: In a cell of the Chudoff Monastery the young monk Grigori lies asleep while the ancient Pimen, by the light of a dim lamp, writes the last chapter of his chronicle and recalls his younger days [8]. As the night passes and the chanting of praying monks penetrates to the cell, Grigori awakes from a nightmare, which he relates to Pimen: he was climbing a steep stairway up to a tower while all the people of Moscow watched from below with mocking laughter, until in shame and terror he fell—and awoke. Pimen admits that he, too, when he falls asleep without saying his prayers, has wild dreams filled with memories of his wayward youth [8]: Grigori, who has been in monasteries ever since he can remember, laments passionately that he, unlike his older companion, has never seen anything of the world and has never been at the Tsar's court. His discontent is not assuaged by Pimen's tales of Tsars who came to the monastery to find peace, of Tsars different in nature from the murderer Boris. Grigori now asks at what age the Tsarevich Dimitri had been killed and learns that Dimitri, were he alive, would be about Grigori's age. The bell calls to matins, and Grigori guides Pimen over the threshold. Then, turning and looking toward the chronicle, he promises the still all-powerful murderer of Dimitri [9 minor] a dire reckoning before God and the world.

Introduction to Act I, Scene 2: Preparing the mood for the following scene, motives [12], [11], and [9] are presented.

Act I, Scene 2: At an inn near the Lithuanian border, the innkeeper sings a song expressing her longing for male companionship (Song: "I have caught a duck") [10]. She hears steps outside, but her hopes for interesting guests are quickly dashed when the chant of the approaching men [11] reveals them to be mendicant friars. Missail and Varlaam enter and ask for food and wine, and the pious innkeeper quickly goes to bring it [10]. Meanwhile a third man, who has traveled with the monks—Grigori, now dressed in peasant clothes [9 minor]—has entered. His anxiety to get across the border to Lithuania puzzles Varlaam, whose only problem in life is to obtain wine. When the hostess [10] brings that, he breaks into a ballad about the storming of the city of Kazan (Ballad: "By the walls of Kazan") [12]. Now Varlaam expresses his disgust with Grigori, who does not drink, but soon he is himself too drunk to care. While Varlaam goes on singing [13] and gradually falls asleep as Missail has before him, Grigori finds out from the innkeeper how he can bypass the guards and reach the Lithuanian border.

A patrol [2a] enters, and, in answer to the shouted command that suddenly has wakened them, Varlaam and Missail identify themselves as mendicant friars [11], while Grigori [9] claims to have accompanied the

[15] SONG OF THE GNAT (Nurse)

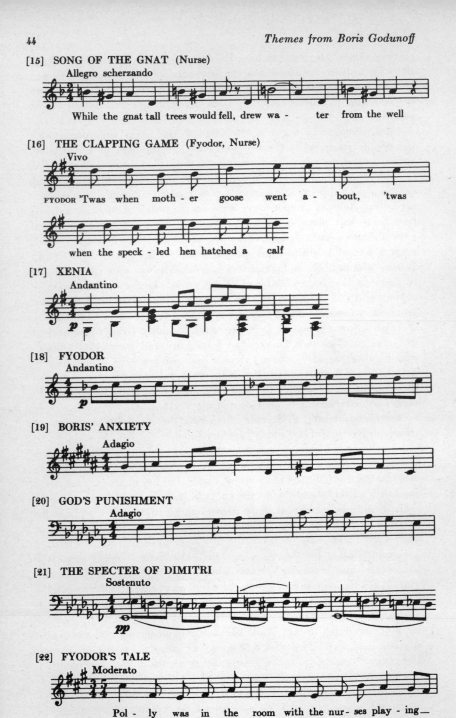

Allegro scherzando
While the gnat tall trees would fell, drew wa - ter from the well

[16] THE CLAPPING GAME (Fyodor, Nurse)

Vivo
FYODOR 'Twas when moth - er goose went a - bout, 'twas

when the speck - led hen hatched a calf

[17] XENIA

Andantino
p

[18] FYODOR

Andantino
p

[19] BORIS' ANXIETY

Adagio

[20] GOD'S PUNISHMENT

Adagio

[21] THE SPECTER OF DIMITRI

Sostenuto
pp

[22] FYODOR'S TALE

Moderato
Pol - ly was in the room with the nur- ses play - ing—

monks from the next village, to which he is about to return. The officer wonders which one of the three would make a shake-down worth while, then decides [2a] to accuse Varlaam of being the renegade monk who has flown from Moscow and whom the patrol is trying to find. He produces a warrant, but Grigori turns out to be the only one who can read. As he reads aloud [9] what is written in the warrant, he changes the description of the fugitive to fit Varlaam. Thereupon the old vagrant, outraged, decides that he might, after all, not have forgotten his reading entirely. Slowly, spelling out each word, he reads the warrant as written. When Grigori is recognized, he quickly escapes through the window.

Act II: In one of the rooms of the palace, Fyodor sits at a large table studying a map, while the old nurse is occupied with sewing and Xenia sighs over the picture of her dead fiancé [14]. The nurse tells her that many girls who have lost one sweetheart find consolation with another, and tries to cheer her up with the story of a gnat and a flea, both of which die grievously through most trivial accidents (Song of the Gnat: "While the gnat tall trees would fell") [15]. However, the Tsarevich does not think this cheerful enough, and he starts to sing a children's song to which a clapping game is played (Clapping Game: " 'Twas when mother goose went about") [16]. The nurse is drawn into the game as a clapping partner, and just as Fyodor gives her a smart smack on the shoulder, Boris enters. The Tsar tries to console Xenia and then sends her [17] to find comfort among her companions. Fyodor [18] shows his father the map of Russia, and Boris encourages him to keep on studying, for someday, perhaps soon [motive 41], he will need this knowledge. In a somber mood [7] the Tsar weighs the outward success of his six years' rule (Aria: "I stand supreme in power") against his sadness [19], unrelieved despite the favorable predictions of his seers; against his private sorrows—Xenia's shattered happiness [17]; and against his foreboding of doom as God's punishment [20] for his sins. He is in constant anxiety [19]. The restive population of his land lives in misery and blames him for God's wrath against Russia [20]. At night the vision of a blood-spattered child [21] prevents him from sleeping. May God have mercy on him!

When loud shouts are heard from the inner rooms, Boris sends Fyodor to investigate. The boyar in attendance enters to announce Prince Shuiski, and informs the Tsar that during the preceding night the Prince had taken part in a secret meeting of boyars with a messenger from Poland. As the boyar leaves, Fyodor returns [18] and with childish delight informs the Tsar of the reason for the commotion (Fyodor's Tale: "Polly was in the room") [22]: the parrot, in an attack of bad temper, had dealt each one of the nurses a violent blow with his beak.

Now Shuiski enters, and Boris receives him with a violent outburst, calling him a cunning schemer and traitor; but the Prince, smoothly ignoring the tirade, reports to his sovereign the appearance in Poland of a pretender

[23] SOUL'S TORMENT

Adagio

[24] Allegretto con grazia

[25] FROM MARINA'S ARIA

Alla mazurka

[26] Andante non troppo

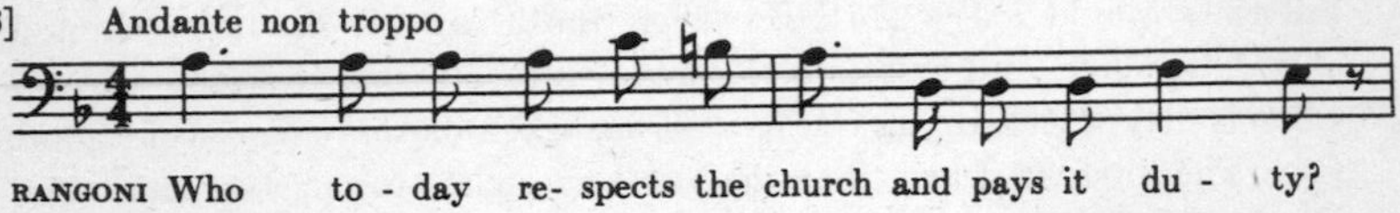

[27] THE JESUIT

[28] Andante non troppo

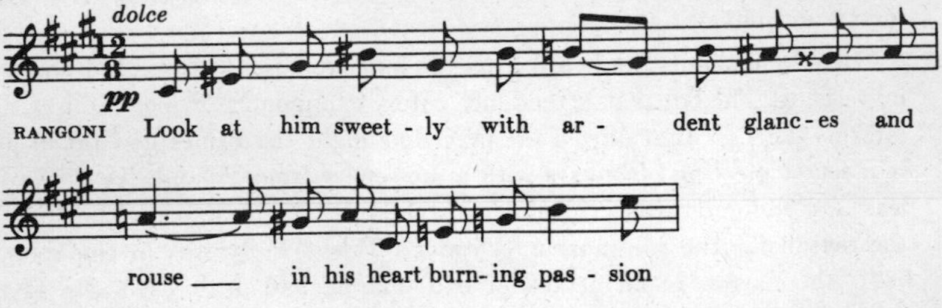

[29] POLACCA

Tempo di polacca

to the Russian throne who has the support of the Polish King and the Pope. Though, naturally, the Tsar is well loved by his people, Shuiski continues, it is not impossible that the pretender may win many followers through the power of the name he has assumed: Dimitri [9]. Hearing this, Boris commands the reluctant Fyodor [18] to leave, and then asks the Prince whether he ever has heard of anything so ridiculous as the possibility that a dead child could return from his grave to torment a lawful Tsar [23]. He adjures Shuiski to tell him [19] whether the child found murdered in Uglich was really Dimitri. The Prince describes so vividly the scene of the decomposing corpses of murdered children with the dead Tsarevich [9] in their midst still looking like a child merely asleep, that Boris with a tormented outcry sends Shuiski away. Trembling, he sinks into a chair [23]. He feels (Clock Scene: "Phew! I am spent!") that he cannot escape his sins. Relentlessly (like the ticking of the clock in the corner, which suddenly becomes unbearable) his conscience haunts him. The mechanism of the clock starts whirring and then the clock strikes eight. A ray of moonlight suddenly illuminates its face, and Boris has a vision of the murdered Tsarevich advancing threateningly toward him [21, 23]. Presently he comes to his senses and sinks to his knees to pray to God for forgiveness.

Act III, Scene 1: In her room in Sandomir Castle, Marina is having her hair arranged while a group of young women sings a song extolling her beauty [24]. However, Marina has no interest in such idle prattle; the only songs she likes are those that treat of Poland's glory. She dismisses the maidens and confesses (Aria: "Oh, life is tedious") that she is bored [25] by the swarm of suitors surrounding her. Her only interest is in the pretender, Dimitri, and on him, she decides, she will use all her arts, because what she longs for is the power and the glory of the Russian throne!

She starts when she notices Rangoni's presence, but she receives him in humbleness and listens to his sorrowful description of the sad state of the Holy Church [26]. He promises her the title of a saint if she will convert the Russians, but Marina, though greatly flattered for a moment, declares herself unwilling—she is incapable of such a mission (Alla mazurka). Thereupon Rangoni [27] advises her [28] to use her charms on Dimitri, putting her soul and body completely in the service of the Church. Marina, in a rage, curses the priest, but when Rangoni threatens her with hell and damnation, she collapses at his feet in complete submission [27].

Act III, Scene 2: In the moonlit garden of Sandomir Castle, Dimitri [9] is waiting for Marina, hoping that she has not forgotten him. Rangoni [27] approaches (this episode is usually omitted) and assures him that Marina, though she has to suffer derision on account of her affection for Dimitri, will come to meet him. In great excitement, Dimitri promises to raise her to the throne of Russia and to take Rangoni along as adviser.

Both retire as a crowd of nobles led by Marina comes from the castle (Polacca) [29]. In gay spirits, they pass through the garden, confident that

[29] *continued*

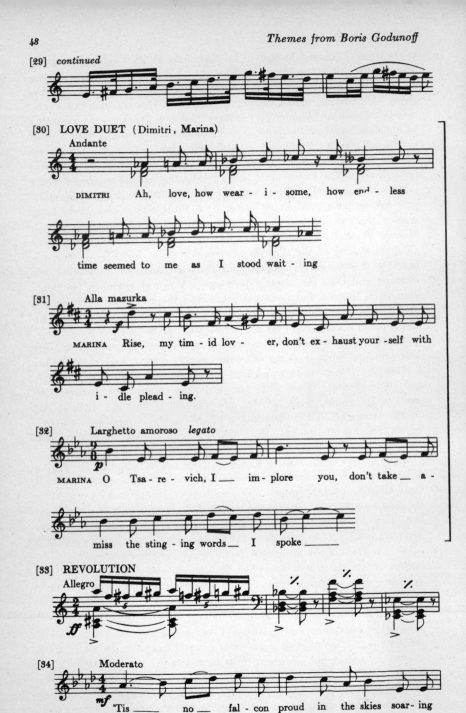

[30] LOVE DUET (Dimitri, Marina)

Andante

DIMITRI Ah, love, how wear - i - some, how end - less

time seemed to me as I stood wait - ing

[31] Alla mazurka

MARINA Rise, my tim - id lov - er, don't ex - haust your - self with

i - dle plead - ing.

[32] Larghetto amoroso *legato*

MARINA O Tsa - re - vich, I ___ im - plore you, don't take ___ a -

miss the sting - ing words ___ I spoke ______

[33] REVOLUTION

Allegro

[34] Moderato

'Tis ___ no ___ fal - con proud in the skies soar - ing

soon they will conquer Moscow; then they return again to drink a toast to their hostess, Marina.

Dimitri emerges from hiding, angrily reflecting on the way the Jesuit has succeeded in imposing his will on him. Disgusted also with the smile that Marina has bestowed on the old count escorting her, he is burning only to do battle for his throne. (This episode is usually omitted.)

Marina comes to meet him, but when he talks of his longing [30] she makes sport of him. She cares nothing for pining and sighing: when will he be Tsar? Dimitri is shaken. What about love? he demands; and Marina remarks with caustic irony (Alla mazurka) that in Moscow he will find many girls willing to slake his thirst for love. Dimitri's confession that his love is only for her is answered by a cold statement that only the crown of Russia can tempt her. When he once more pleads for her love, she cruelly derides his servile fawning [31] and haughtily repulses him. Thereupon Dimitri proudly prophesies that he will win the throne [9] and then, from his lofty height, will laugh at the stupid Polish maiden in the dust before him! Now (Duet: "O Tsarevich, I implore you") [32] Marina tenderly declares that her words were meant only to spur him on to heroic deeds, and, although Dimitri at first does not believe her, he is soon won over. When they embrace, Rangoni [27] appears and watches them with satisfaction from afar. Gay shouts of *Vivat!* are heard from the castle.

Act IV, Scene 1: A wild mob [33] drags the bound boyar Khrushchoff into a clearing of the forest near Kromy. They gag him, set him down on a stump, put the oldest woman next to him as a fitting sweetheart, and sing a mocking song of praise in his honor [34, 35]. The Simpleton appears, chased by a horde of boys, and sings a melancholy song [36]. When the boys take away his penny, he breaks into a heart-rending lament, which is interrupted by the approach of Varlaam and Missail [37], who vehemently denounce Boris. The crowd breaks out in a call to revolution [38], and the two monks agitate for Dimitri. When two Jesuits approach proclaiming the new Tsar, Varlaam and Missail decide they do not like such competition, and they incite the crowd to hang them. As the Jesuits are being dragged away, the sound of trumpets is heard and the pretender Dimitri arrives with his army, hailed by the monks and the crowd. The Tsarevich [9] promises protection to all those oppressed by Boris. Khrushchoff, who has been forgotten by the excited crowd, rushes to Dimitri's feet to make his obeisance, and is invited, together with all others, to follow the Tsarevich into battle and to the Kremlin [9]. The two Jesuits also join the procession. Now, as the tocsin is heard in the distance, the Simpleton, who has remained alone, rouses himself from his apathy and, looking toward a conflagration in the distance, weeps for the Russian people [36].

Act IV, Scene 2: A session of the Duma [39] is in progress in the great reception hall of the Kremlin. The boyars decide that the false pretender must be captured, tortured, hanged, and left hanging for the ravens to feed

[35]

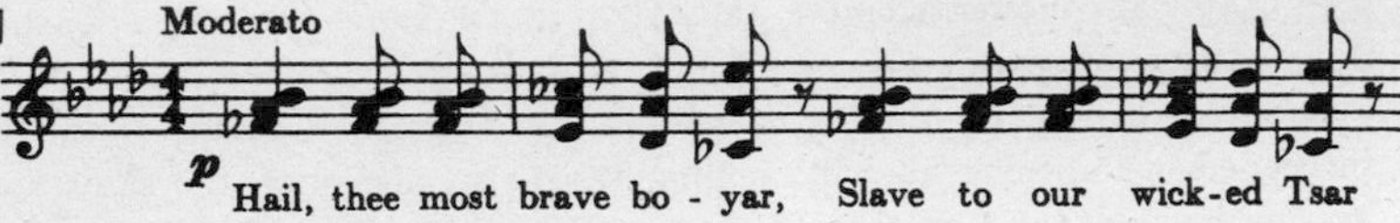
Moderato
p
Hail, thee most brave bo - yar, Slave to our wick-ed Tsar

[36] THE SIMPLETON'S LAMENT

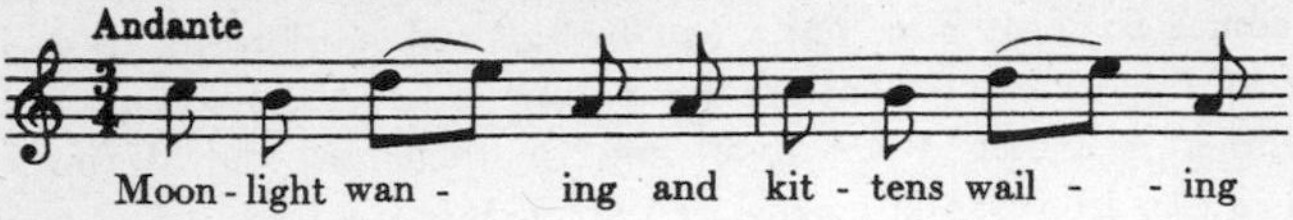
Andante
Moon-light wan - ing and kit - tens wail - - ing

[37]

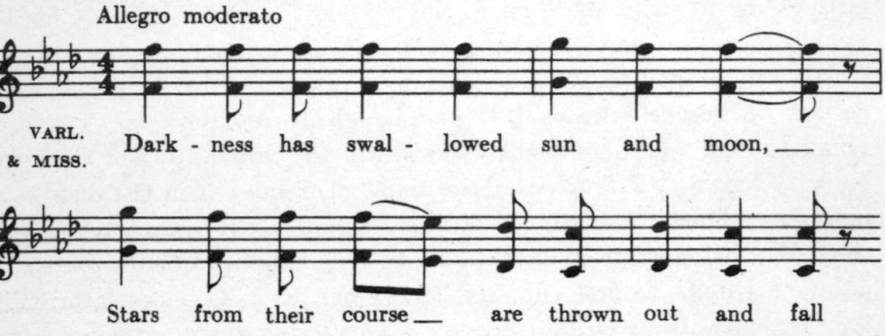
Allegro moderato
VARL. & MISS.
Dark - ness has swal - lowed sun and moon,
Stars from their course are thrown out and fall

[38]

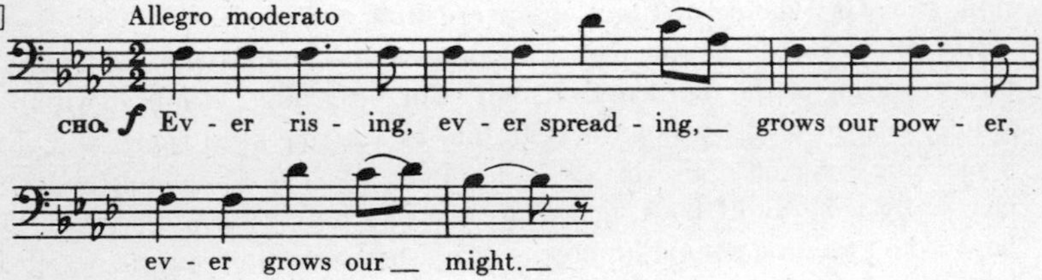
Allegro moderato
CHO. f
Ev - er ris - ing, ev - er spread - ing, grows our pow - er,
ev - er grows our might.

[39] THE DUMA

Moderato
p

[40] PIMEN'S TALE

Andante non troppo
p
One eve-ning, I was a - lone, a shep-herd came to me

[41] THE DEATH OF BORIS

Andante
p
3
Fare-well, my son, I am dy - ing.

on. Then his body shall be publicly burned, and his ashes shall be cursed and scattered [39]. Throughout the country it shall be proclaimed that whosoever joins him will share his fate, and prayers for peace shall be offered in all churches.

Shuiski enters and tells the boyars how on the previous day he had noticed that the Tsar was behaving rather strangely. After leaving the Tsar's presence, he had observed him through a chink in the door and had seen him sitting in his chair, pale and perspiring, trembling and stammering, staring into a corner and asking the ghost of the Tsarevich to leave him: "Go, go! Leave me, child!" [21]. The boyars are little inclined to believe the crafty Prince, but just then the Tsar enters the hall, apparently trying to fend off an invisible pursuer and repeating the exact words just quoted by Shuiski. Unaware of his surroundings, the distraught Boris protests that he is no murderer, and that Dimitri is alive, and he swears that Shuiski will suffer a dreadful fate for spreading the lie that the Tsarevich has been killed.

When Shuiski solemnly addresses the Tsar, Boris regains his senses, walks to his throne [motive 41], and greets the boyars. Shuiski asks leave to bring before him an old and righteous hermit who has an important message for the Tsar. Pimen is brought in [8] and tells (Pimen's Narrative: "One evening, I was alone") [40] of an old shepherd who had been blind since childhood and who even dreamed only in sounds. One night the shepherd had heard a child's voice asking him to go and pray at his, the Tsarevich Dimitri's [9], grave in the Cathedral at Uglich, for he was now one of the Lord's wonder-working angels. The old shepherd had done as bidden, and scarcely had he kneeled at the grave when his eyesight was restored.

The Tsar, who has been listening to this report with growing anxiety, suddenly gasps for air. He loses consciousness for a moment [21], then, sensing death approaching, calls for the Tsarevich and asks that his death shroud be brought. When Fyodor enters [18], Boris orders the boyars to leave and bids farewell to his son (Boris' Farewell: "Farewell, my son") [41]. How Boris had ascended the throne is a question that his son [18], his lawful successor, should never ask. Never must he trust the treacherous boyars, but he must rule firmly and mercilessly. He must protect the Holy Church and watch over his sister [17]. As Boris asks the heavens to guard his children, the death knell sounds [5a] and a procession approaches chanting a dirge. While Boris desperately begs for the Lord's forgiveness, they enter, their chant recounting the tale of a child mercilessly murdered. Suddenly Boris rises majestically and halts them. He is still Tsar! But his strength is ebbing and he sinks back into his chair. With a last effort, he points to his son as the new Tsar, and dies [19].

THEMES

[1] OVERTURE

Allegro giocoso

[2] Allegro giocoso

[3a] CARMEN'S FATE

Andante moderato

[3b] Allegro moderato

[4] Allegretto

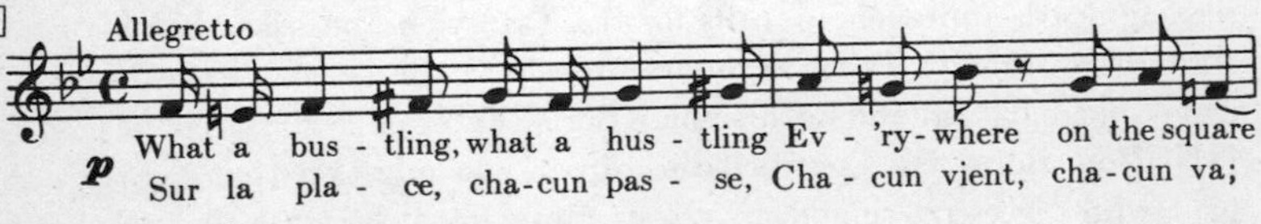
What a bus - tling, what a hus - tling Ev - 'ry- where on the square
Sur la pla - ce, cha-cun pas - se, Cha - cun vient, cha-cun va;

[5] Allegretto mosso

MORALES
For you must know, his guard will soon re - lieve _ us
Il y se - ra Quand la gar- de mon- tan - te

[6] THE CHANGING OF THE GUARDS

Tempo di marcia

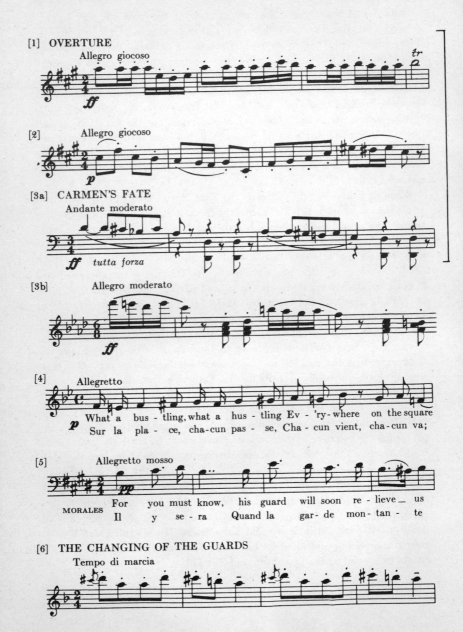

Carmen

Opera in four acts by Georges Bizet. Libretto by Henri Meilhac and Ludovic Halévy after a novel by Prosper Merimée. First performance: Paris, March 3, 1875.

Characters: DON JOSÉ, a corporal of the guard (tenor); ZUNIGA, his captain (bass); MORALÈS, an officer (baritone); ESCAMILLO, toreador (baritone); CARMEN, a gypsy (mezzo-soprano); MICAËLA, José's childhood sweetheart (soprano); FRASQUITA (soprano) and MERCÉDÈS (soprano or mezzo-soprano), gypsies; LE DANCAÏRE (tenor) and LE REMENDADO (tenor or baritone), smugglers.
In and near Seville, about 1820.

Prelude: Between strains characterizing the gaiety and excitement attending the bullfight [1, 2], the Toreador Song [motive 17] is heard. The fate motive [3a] is introduced and developed to a climactic silence—after which the curtain rises.

Act I: Soldiers in front of their post on a square in Seville are watching the passers-by [4] when Micaëla comes looking for a corporal called Don José. Informed by Moralès, the officer in charge, that José belongs to the next relief [5], she gracefully refuses the soldiers' invitation to wait for him inside and runs off. The soldiers resume their gazing at the crowds [4].

Now, "assisted" by a group of street urchins, the guard changes [6]. Presently the bell of the cigarette factory facing the guard post rings, and men gather in the square to get a look at the cigarette girls who are coming out for a break. Unconcerned with their audience, the girls leisurely enjoy their cigarettes [7].

Last of all comes Carmen [3b], and all the men crowd around her. But as

[6] *continued*

[7]

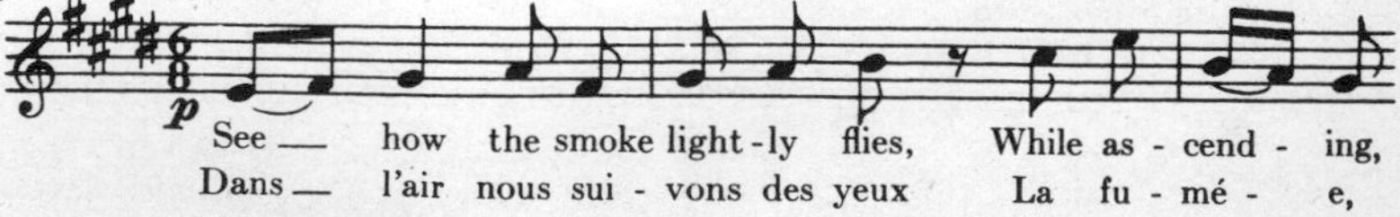
Andantino
See — how the smoke light-ly flies, While as - cend - ing,
Dans — l'air nous sui - vons des yeux La fu - mé - e,

[8] **HABANERA** (Carmen)

Allegretto, quasi andantino

Gyp - sy love is a rov - ing rap - ture, A wan - ton
L'a - mour est un oi - seau re - bel - le Que nul ne
bird that none can tame.
peut ap - pri - voi - ser.

[9] Allegretto, quasi andantino

Oh, love is just a gyp - sy lad, He nev - er
L'a - mour est en - fant de Bo - hême, Il n'a ja -
could and nev - er would play fair,
mais, ja - mais con- nu de loi,

[10] FROM DUET *PARLE-MOI DE MA MERE* (José, Micaëla)

Andantino non troppo

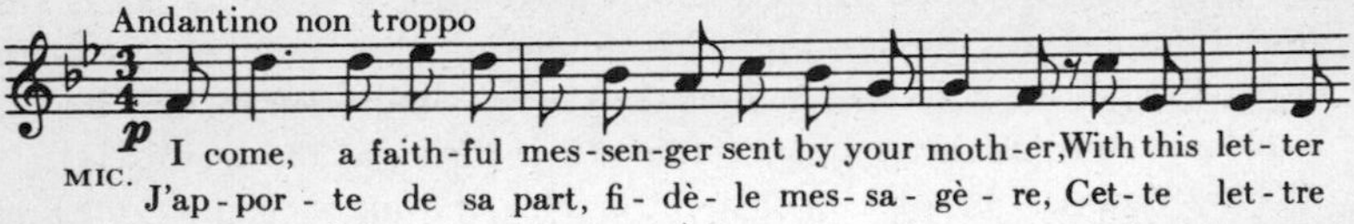
MIC.
I come, a faith-ful mes-sen-ger sent by your moth-er,With this let- ter
J'ap - por - te de sa part, fi - dè - le mes - sa - gè - re, Cet - te let - tre

[11] Allegro moderato *espressivo*

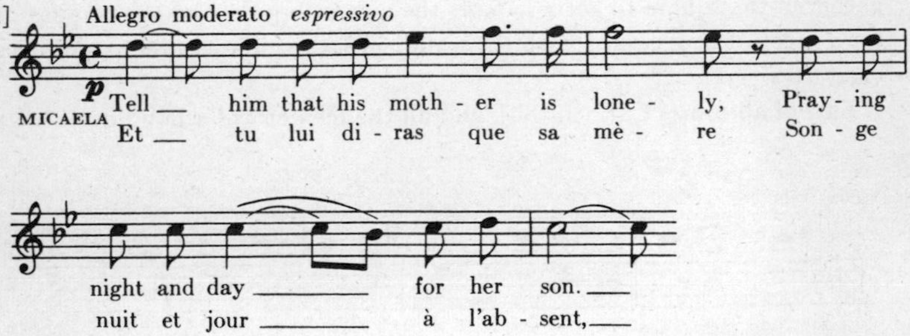
MICAELA
Tell him that his moth - er is lone - ly, Pray - ing
Et tu lui di - ras que sa mè - re Son - ge
night and day for her son.
nuit et jour à l'ab - sent,

[12] Allegro moderato

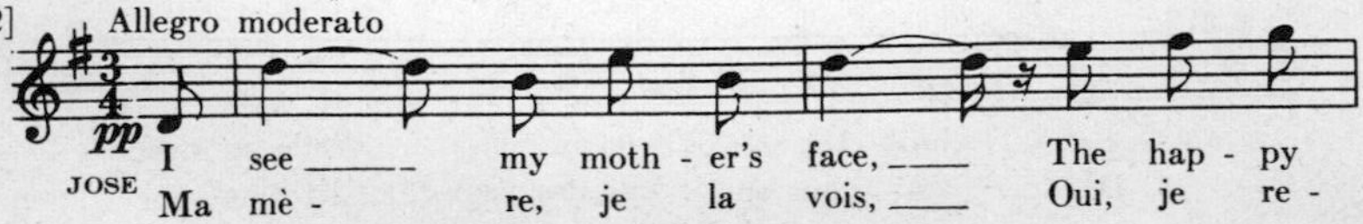
JOSE
I see my moth - er's face, The hap - py
Ma mè - re, je la vois, Oui, je re -

her eyes come to rest on Don José [3b], who pays her no attention whatsoever, she airily dismisses them, explaining (Habanera *L'amour est un oiseau rebelle:* "Gypsy love is a roving rapture") [8] that love is like a capricious bird that alights only near those who ignore it [9]. Suddenly she throws a flower at José and, with the other girls, re-enters the factory.

José has hardly recovered from his surprise and hidden the flower in his coat [3b] when Micaëla returns. She brings him (Duet *Parle-moi de ma mère:* "Tell me, how is my mother") a letter from his mother [10], his mother's love [11], and a kiss; and memories of his native village come alive in José's mind (Duet *Ma mère, je la vois:* "I see my mother's face") [12]. He sends back his love [11] and a kiss, but Micaëla prefers not to be present while he reads his mother's letter. When he opens it [11], he finds in it the welcome suggestion that he marry Micaëla.

Suddenly girls come rushing from the factory, excitedly calling for help and giving their conflicting versions of a fight in which Carmen has cut another girl with a knife. Brought before Captain Zuniga by José, Carmen replies to all questions with an insolent little ditty [13]. "What a pity," says the Captain, "we will have to send her to jail." While the square is cleared and the girls return to the factory, Zuniga goes inside to write out the warrant. As José ties Carmen's hands [3b], she insists that a charm in the flower which he still is hiding in his coat has made him love her and do her bidding. She invites him to come to Lillas Pastia's tavern, where she will be waiting for him (Seguidilla *Près des remparts de Séville:* "There's a café in Sevilla") [14]. Completely under the spell of Carmen's charms and promises, José loosens the rope around her wrists. When the Captain returns with the warrant, Carmen, after whispering to José, impudently repeats her

[12] *continued*

home ___ I love so well! ___
vois ___ mon vil - la - ge!

[13]

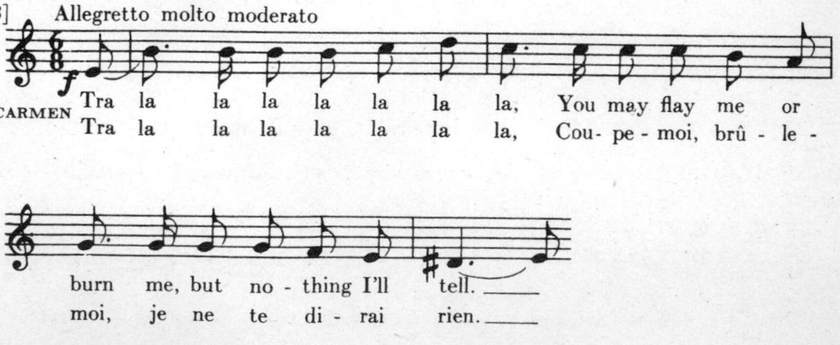
Allegretto molto moderato
CARMEN
Tra la la la la la la la, You may flay me or
Tra la la la la la la la, Cou- pe - moi, brû - le -
burn me, but no - thing I'll tell. ___
moi, je ne te di - rai rien. ___

[14] SEGUIDILLA (Carmen)

[15] GYPSY SONG (Carmen, Frasquita, Mercédès)

[16] TOREADOR SONG (Escamillo)

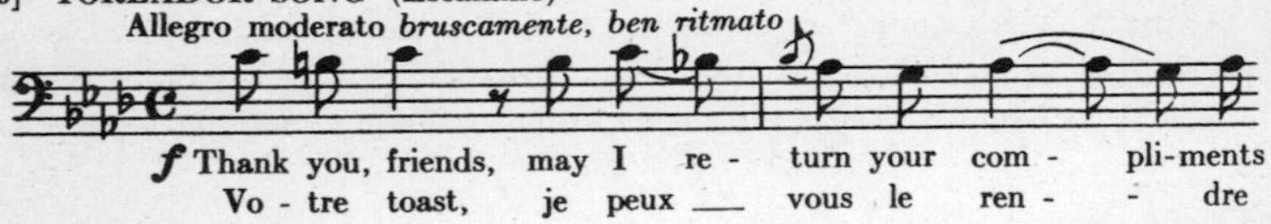

[17] Allegro moderato

[18] SMUGGLER QUINTET (Dancaïre, Remendado, Carmen, Frasquita, Mercédès)

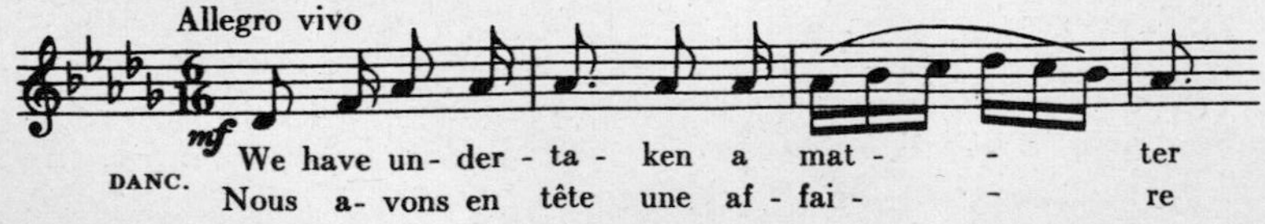

little refrain about love [9]. José leads her away, but after a few steps she pushes him to the ground and escapes. Amid the laughter of the onlookers, José is arrested.

Entr'acte music: Motive [21].

Act II: At Lillas Pastia's, Carmen, Frasquita, and Mercédès are singing and dancing for the soldiers [Gypsy Song 15]. Zuniga has just informed Carmen that José has been released from prison when a *vivat* is heard and a crowd acclaiming Escamillo approaches. Invited in for a glass of wine, the toreador proudly discourses on his profession and its rewards (Toreador Song *Votre toast:* "Thank you, friends!" [16] and *Toréador en garde:* "Toreador, be on your guard") [17]. However, his declaration of love to Carmen meets with no apparent response. He leaves [17] and all the guests leave with him. The inn is closed.

Le Remendado and Le Dancaïre, the chiefs of the smugglers, come from the back room and explain to the three gypsy girls their plans for the impending smuggling expedition (Quintet *Nous avons en tête une affaire:* "We have undertaken a matter") [18] in which they will need the girls' help [19]. However, tonight Carmen will not join them. She is in love, she declares. This statement causes incredulous amusement among her companions [20], but already the object of her affections can be heard approaching in the distance [21].

When José enters, Carmen receives him alone. She dances for him [22], and when he calls her attention to the sounding of the retreat, she gaily continues her dance to the accompaniment of the bugles. However, when he explains that he must return to his company, she becomes furious and screams: "Run along then, my boy, run home to your barracks." But José

[19] SMUGGLER QUINTET
(Dancaïre, Remendado, Carmen, Frasquita, Mercédès) *continued*

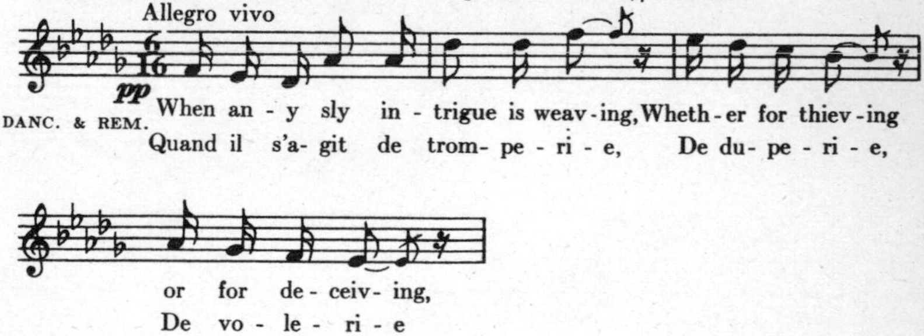
Allegro vivo
pp
DANC. & REM.
When an - y sly in - trigue is weav - ing, Wheth - er for thiev - ing
Quand il s'a- git de trom- pe - ri - e, De du- pe - ri - e,
or for de - ceiv - ing,
De vo - le - ri - e

[20] Un poco ritenuto

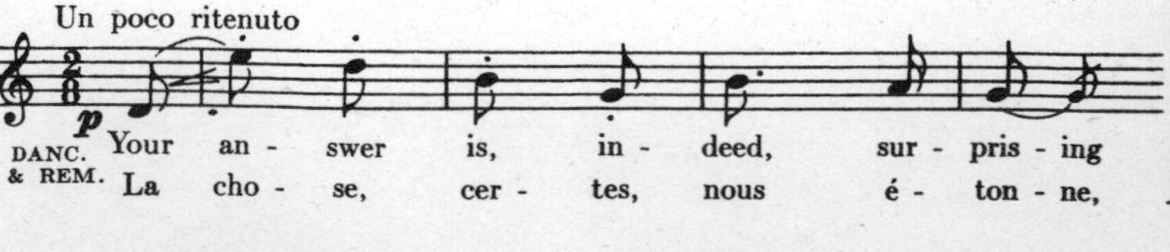
p
DANC. & REM.
Your an - swer is, in - deed, sur - pris - ing
La cho - se, cer - tes, nous é - ton - ne,

[21] Allegro moderato

f
JOSE
Friend or foe? We must know, Son of Al - ca - la! ___
Hal - te là! Qui va là? Dra - gon d'Al - ca - la! ___

[22] CARMEN'S DANCE

Allegretto

p
La ___ la _ la ___ la _ la ___ la _ la ___ la _

[23] FLOWER SONG (José)

Andantino *con amore*

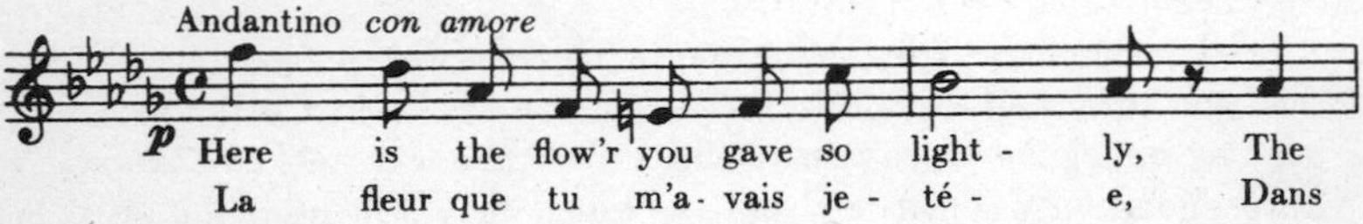
p
Here is the flow'r you gave so light - ly, The
La fleur que tu m'a- vais je - té - e, Dans

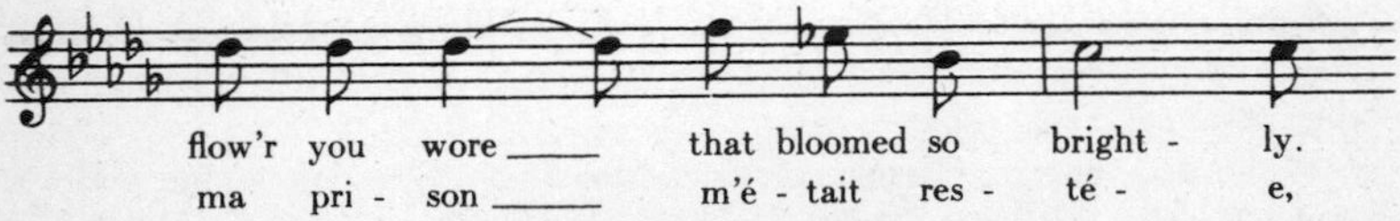
flow'r you wore ___ that bloomed so bright - ly.
ma pri - son ___ m'é - tait res - té - e,

[24] Allegretto moderato

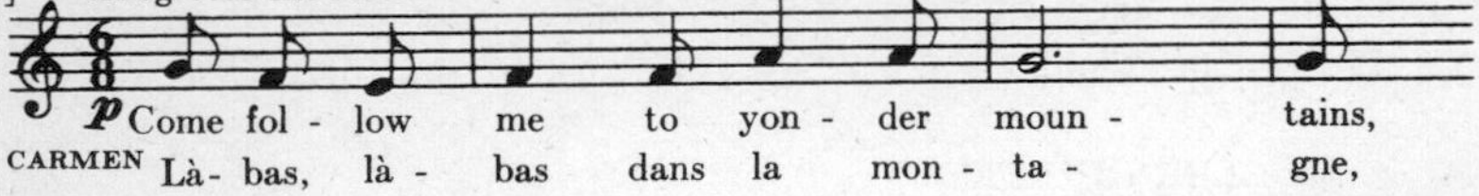
p
CARMEN
Come fol - low me to yon - der moun - tains,
Là- bas, là - bas dans la mon - ta - gne,

[25] Andantino, quasi allegretto

pp

[26] Allegretto moderato

pp

pleads with her, and forces her to listen to his protestations of love (Flower Song *La fleur que tu m'avais jetée:* "Here is the flow'r you gave so lightly") [23]. In vain Carmen tempts him to join the gypsies [24]. Just as he is leaving, Zuniga comes to visit Carmen. José, blind with jealousy, now forgets all army discipline and draws his saber. The smugglers, called in by Carmen, come forward to restrain the soldiers. With gentle words and a pair of pistols, Zuniga is persuaded to remain a prisoner for a few hours. José, after the fight with his captain, has no choice but to join the smugglers and their life of freedom [24].

Entr'acte: [25].

Act III: The gypsies on their march to the border are arriving at a resting-place in the mountains [26], talking about the dangers of their calling and extolling its joys.

José is thinking of his mother [11]. When Carmen, who by now has become tired of him, provokingly asks why he does not go back home, José's temper flares up [3a] and there remains no doubt that he would rather kill Carmen than leave her.

Frasquita and Mercédès bring out their cards (Card Trio *Mêlons, coupons:* "Shuffle, cut them") to read their fortunes [27] and are happy about the future promised them, but when Carmen tries her luck, the cards spell death, and she well knows that there is no escape (Aria *En vain pour éviter:* "If you consult the cards") [28].

Now the gypsies prepare to move on. They are confident that the girls

[27] CARD TRIO (Frasquita, Mercédès, Carmen)

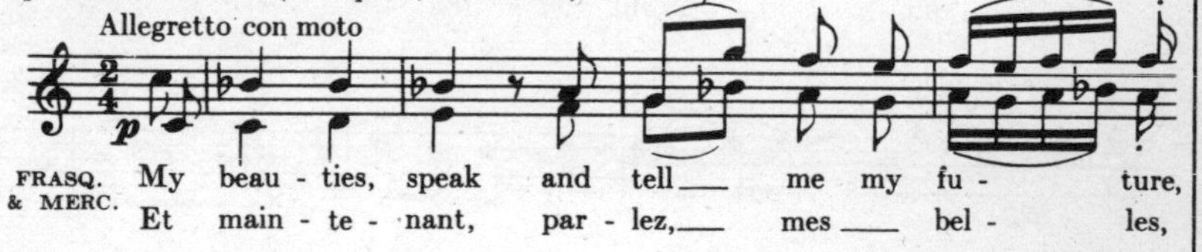
Allegretto con moto
p
FRASQ. & MERC.
My beau - ties, speak and tell me my fu - ture,
Et main - te - nant, par - lez, mes bel - les,

[28] ARIA *EN VAIN POUR EVITER* (Carmen)

Andante molto moderato
pp
If you con - sult the cards to learn a - bout your
En vain pour é - vi - ter les ré - pon - ses a -
fate, The cards re - ply to you;
mèr - es, En vain tu mê - le - ras,

[29] Allegro deciso

mf
Fear not, the guards are ea - sy prey!
Quant au doua - nier, c'est notre af - fai - re!

[30] ARIA *JE DIS* (Micaela)

Andantino molto

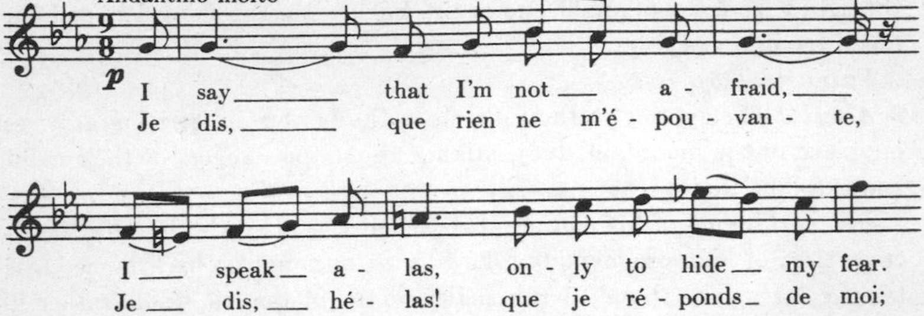
p
I say that I'm not a - fraid,
Je dis, que rien ne m'é - pou - van - te,
I speak a - las, on - ly to hide my fear.
Je dis, hé - las! que je ré - ponds de moi;

[31] Allegro molto moderato

mf
3
I shall face this dan - ger - ous girl
Je vais voir de près cet - te fem - me

[32] Moderato

f
JOSE
Though death be my part, I vow,
Dût - il m'en coû - ter la vi - e,

[33] Allegro vivo

pp

[34] Andantino, quasi allegretto

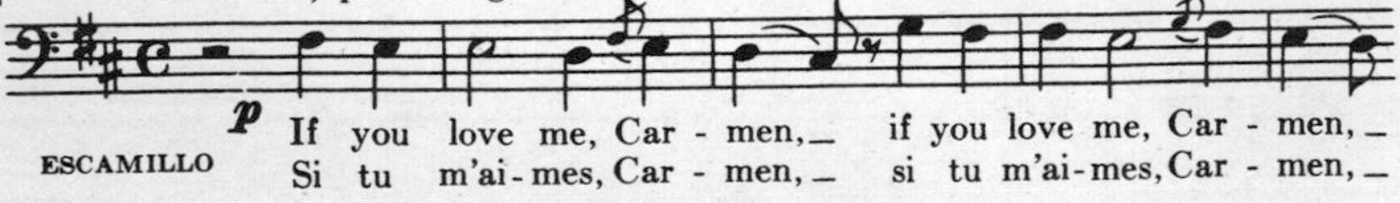
p
ESCAMILLO
If you love me, Car - men, if you love me, Car - men,
Si tu m'ai - mes, Car - men, si tu m'ai - mes, Car - men,

[35] Allegro moderato

mf
JOSE
But Car - men, I still a - dore, you
Mais moi, Car - men, je t'aime en - co - re

will be quite capable of handling the customs officers [29]. José is ordered to move to a rock from which he can guard the paths.

A guide brings Micaëla, who has come to find José (Recitative *C'est des contrebandiers:* "This is the smugglers' place"). She is trembling with fright, but she is firm in the faith that God will protect her (Aria *Je dis que rien ne m'épouvante:* "I say that I'm not afraid") [30] and will instill in her, courage to face the evil beauty [31] who has led to dishonor the man she once loved. As Micaëla spies José, he aims his rifle and fires, whereupon she hurriedly hides behind the rocks. But the bullet was meant for Escamillo, who now approaches unhurt. Unsuspectingly he asks José where to find Carmen, whom he professes to love madly. In another moment the two men are dueling, and Carmen appears just in time to save Escamillo's life. The toreador, flattered, invites "all who love him" to his next fight in Seville, and leaves [17]. Suddenly the smugglers, who have returned with Carmen, discover Micaëla. She asks José to return home [11]. Carmen tauntingly supports Micaëla's plea, but José swears that nothing but death will separate him from Carmen [32]. Only when Micaëla reveals that his mother is dying is José ready to leave Carmen; but he promises to return [3a]. Once more, when the toreador is heard singing in the distance [17], José turns to bar Carmen from rushing after her new love, before he follows Micaëla.

Entr'acte: The melody [33] is taken from a "Polo" (Andalusian dance) by Bizet's contemporary Manuel García.

Act IV: In front of the amphitheater in Seville, venders are offering their wares to the crowds. (A ballet to music of Bizet's *L'Arlesienne* is sometimes danced here.) Presently, to great acclaim, the various groups of fighters pass in solemn procession toward the arena [1; 1 with 2 major]. Last of all comes Escamillo [17], who exchanges tender vows of love with Carmen [34]. Frasquita and Mercédès warn her of José's presence, but Carmen insists on facing her destiny and waits for him while the spectators enter the amphitheater [1]. Now José approaches and begs Carmen to start life anew with him. But his pleading [35] is in vain. She would rather die in freedom than live with a man she no longer cares for. The crowds in the arena acclaim Escamillo [2 major with 1], whom Carmen proudly admits she loves, even in the face of death. Having sacrificed honor and all else for Carmen, José will not endure her scorn or her love for another man [3a]. When Carmen answers his last appeal by taking his ring off her finger and throwing it at him, he draws a knife, and as she tries to make her way past him into the arena, he stabs her to death. The spectators jubilantly issuing from the amphitheater [17] find a despairing José confessing to the murder of his adored Carmen [3a].

THEMES

[1] Andante sostenuto

[2] SICILIANA (Turiddu)

Andante

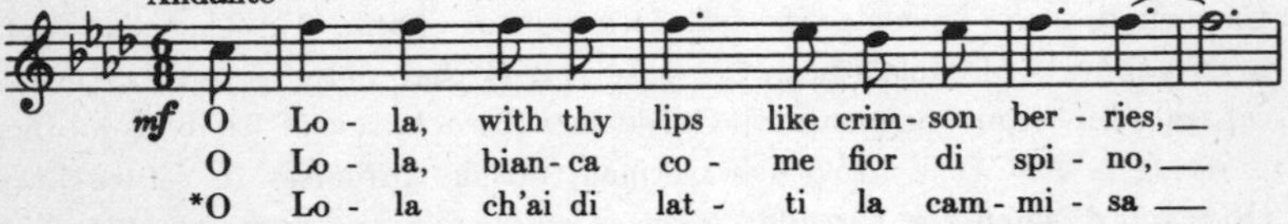
O Lo - la, with thy lips like crim - son ber - ries, —
O Lo - la, bian - ca co - me fior di spi - no, —
*O Lo - la ch'ai di lat - ti la cam - mi - sa —

[3] Allegro giocoso

[4] Allegro non troppo

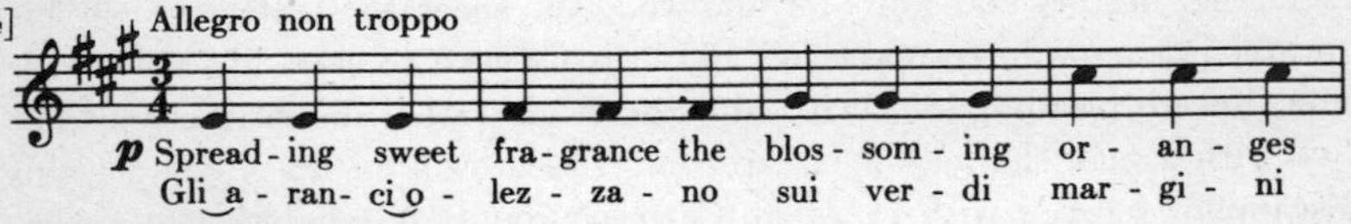
Spread - ing sweet fra - grance the blos - som - ing or - an - ges
Gli a - ran - ci o - lez - za - no sui ver - di mar - gi - ni

[5] Commodo

A - cross the field where gold - en wheat is blow - ing
In mez - zo al cam - po tra le spi - che d'o - ro

[6] Largo

*This is the commonly used Sicilian version of the text

Cavalleria Rusticana

RUSTIC CHIVALRY

Opera in one act by Pietro Mascagni. Libretto by G. Targioni-Tozzetti and G. Menasci, based on Giovanni Verga's short story. First performance: Rome, May 17, 1890.

Characters: SANTUZZA (soprano); TURIDDU (tenor); LUCIA, his mother (contralto); LOLA (mezzo-soprano); ALFIO, her husband (baritone).
A Sicilian village, in the nineteenth century.

Prelude: Beginning with a churchly melody[1]—the action takes place on Easter morning—the prelude continues with music from the duet between Santuzza and Turiddu [18, 19]. There is a sudden interruption, and the voice of Turiddu, accompanied by a harp, is heard behind the closed curtain as, risking the wrath of a wronged husband, he recklessly extols the charms of Lola (Siciliana *O Lola ch'ai di latti la cammisa:* "O Lola, with thy lips like crimson berries") [2]. The orchestra resumes with strains from the interrupted duet [19, 20, 17, 18] and ends quietly with a church cadence.

Scene 1: Peasants in a holiday mood [3] pass the church square in which Lucia's house and tavern are also located. Gaily singing of spring and love, groups of women [4] and men [5] meet to join their song [4 with 5, over 3 in the orchestra] and stroll off.

A shadow of tragedy falls over the scene [6] as Santuzza enters and hesitatingly knocks on the door of Lucia's house. When Lucia gruffly asks her business, Santuzza hints that Turiddu has not left town as he had said he would. Lucia invites her to come inside, but she refuses: she has been excommunicated and does not want to desecrate Lucia's house.

[7] ALFIO'S ENTRANCE SONG

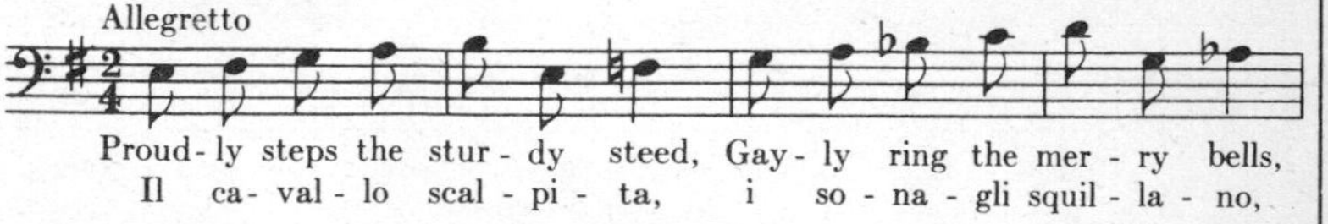
Allegretto
Proud- ly steps the stur - dy steed, Gay- ly ring the mer - ry bells,
Il ca- val - lo scal - pi - ta, i so - na - gli squil - la - no,

[8]

Allegretto
f
Oh to be a rov - er trav - el - ing all o - ver
O che bel me - stie - re fa - re il car- ret - tie - re

[9] EASTER HYMN

Moderato assai

CHO. Queen of the Heav - - ens, grief is end - ed!

Re - gi - na Coe - - li, lae - ta - re

[10] Largo maestoso

CHO. Let us sing Christ our Lord's won- drous sto - ry!

In - neg - gia - mo il Si - gnor non è mor - to!

[11] Moderato assai

SANT. Let us sing ______ Christ our Lord's won-drous sto - - ry

In - neg- gia - - mo il Si- gnor non è mor - - to

[12] ROMANZA *VOI LO SAPETE* (Santuzza)

Largo assai sostenuto *mestamente con semplicità*

Well do you know, good Mam-ma, ere to the war he de- part - ed

Voi lo sa - pe- te, o Mam-ma, pri- ma d'an-dar sol - da - to

[13] SANTUZZA'S JEALOUSY

Largo assai sostenuto

[14] Largo assai sostenuto

Life no long - er has

Pri - va dell' o- nor

mean - ing, hon - or and love are de - nied me.

mi - o, dell' o - nor mi - o ri - man - go.

[15] FROM DUET *TU QUI SANTUZZA* (Turiddu, Santuzza)

Andante *con forza*

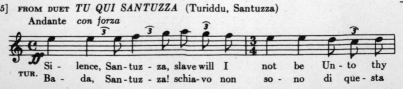

TUR. Si - lence, San-tuz - za, slave will I not be Un - to thy

Ba - da, San-tuz - za! schia- vo non so - no di que- sta

Alfio, the gay carter, appears [7] extolling his profession and the rewards on returning home to a faithful wife, and is spiritedly acclaimed by friends who have quickly gathered [8]. Unsuspecting, he mentions (Recitative) having seen Turiddu near his house early in the morning.

In the meantime, villagers have gathered in front of the church. As the organ starts to play, the carter goes about his affairs. The choir inside the church intones the Easter Hymn *Regina Coeli* [9], and the villagers, including Santuzza and Lucia, raise their voices exalting the risen Christ [10, 11].

After all have entered the church, Santuzza tells Lucia (Aria *Voi lo sapete, o mamma:* "Well do you know, good Mamma") [12] how Turiddu, on his return from the army, had found Lola, his former sweetheart, married, and had sought consolation in Santuzza's love. But now Lola has lured back Turiddu [13] and Santuzza is left dishonored and heartbroken [14]. She asks Lucia to pray for her in church [1] while she herself will remain in the square to talk to Turiddu once more.

Turiddu comes presently, and Santuzza accuses him of betraying her with Lola (Duet *Tu qui, Santuzza:* "You here, Santuzza"). Turiddu's resentment [15] is not soothed by her pleading, and it increases when Lola appears singing her ditty (Stornello *Fior di giaggiolo:* "My king of roses") [16] and, mocking both, goes on to church. All Santuzza's supplications [17, 18, 19, 20] are of no avail, and as she tries to bar Turiddu's way to the church, he throws her violently to the ground and follows Lola. Prostrate on the steps of the church, Santuzza shouts after him: "May the Bloody Easter come upon you."

Just then Alfio reappears [7], and when the girl in her fury reveals to him how his wife is betraying him with Turiddu [13], he swears vengeance [21]. Suddenly realizing the probable result of her raging, Santuzza tries

[15] *continued*

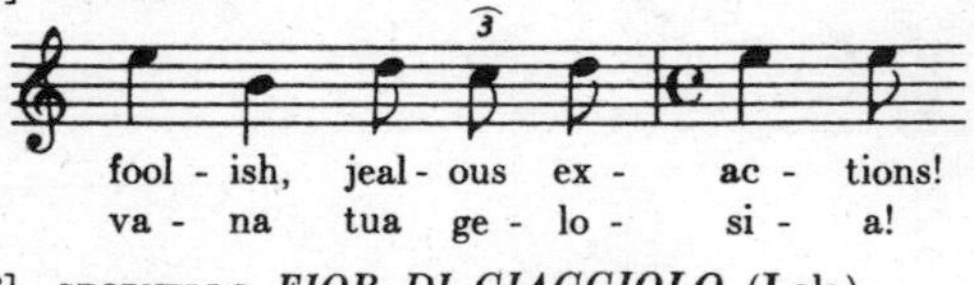

[16] STORNELLO *FIOR DI GIAGGIOLO* (Lola)

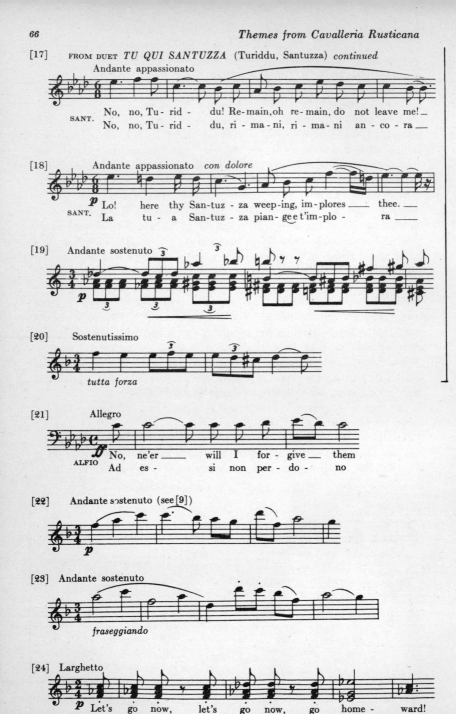

[17] FROM DUET *TU QUI SANTUZZA* (Turiddu, Santuzza) *continued*

Andante appassionato
SANT.
No, no, Tu - rid - du! Re-main, oh re-main, do not leave me! _
No, no, Tu - rid - du, ri - ma-ni, ri - ma-ni an - co - ra __

[18]

Andante appassionato *con dolore*
p
SANT.
Lo! here thy San-tuz - za weep-ing, im-plores ___ thee. ___
La tu - a San-tuz - za pian-ge e t'im-plo - ra ___

[19]

Andante sostenuto
p

[20]

Sostenutissimo
tutta forza

[21]

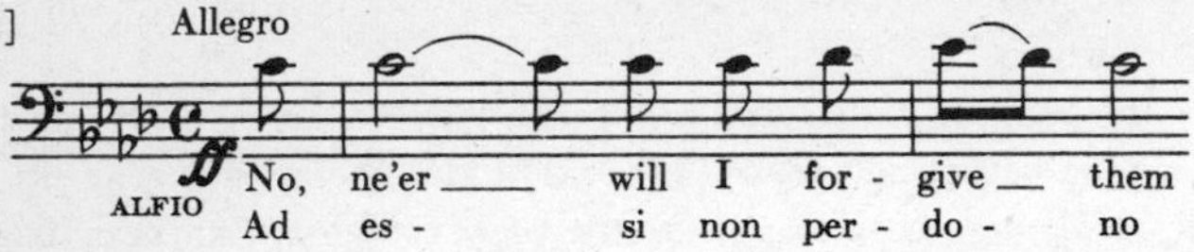
Allegro
ff
ALFIO
No, ne'er ___ will I for - give ___ them
Ad es - si non per - do - no

[22]

Andante sostenuto (see [9])
p

[23]

Andante sostenuto
fraseggiando

[24]

Larghetto
p
Let's go now, let's go now, go home - ward!
A ca - sa, a ca - sa, a - mi - ci!

in vain to shake Alfio's determination as she follows him from the square.

With the stage empty, the *Intermezzo* [22, 23] is now heard.

Scene 2: Gay crowds are leaving the church [3] for their homes [24]. Turiddu, accompanied by Lola, invites all to join him at the tavern in a toast to wine and love (Brindisi *Viva il vino spumeggiante:* "Hail the red wine richly flowing") [25, 26], but the merriment comes to an abrupt end with the appearance of Alfio. When Alfio refuses to accept a cup of wine from Turiddu, the women, foreseeing trouble, leave the square and take the frightened Lola with them. Turiddu bites Alfio's ear—the Sicilian challenge to a duel. Admitting his guilt and unworthiness (Aria *Lo so che il torto è mio:* "I'm guilty, I admit it") [27], Turiddu expresses nevertheless his fanatic will to be victorious, since he must remain alive for the sake of Santuzza. Stolidly Alfio leaves [8 moderato] for the dueling-place.

Turiddu, remaining alone in the square, calls his mother from the house and haltingly asks for her blessing (Turiddu's Farewell *Mamma, il vino è generoso:* "Mamma, too potent is our wine"). In case he should not return, he begs her to be a mother to Santuzza [28]. With a last kiss he leaves the bewildered woman, who is presently joined by a disconsolate Santuzza [14]. As people gather around them, a voice is heard screaming "Turiddu has been killed," and Santuzza falls senseless to the ground [6].

[25] BRINDISI *VIVA IL VINO SPUMEGGIANTE* (Turiddu)

Larghetto
Hail! the red wine rich - ly flow - ing,
Vi - va il vi - no spu - meg - gian - te,

[26]

Larghetto
rit.
a tempo
Hail to wine — for - ev - er flow - ing
Vi - va il vi - no ch'è sin - ce - ro

[27]

Largo
TUR.
I'm guilt - y, I ad - mit it
Lo so che il tor- to è mi - o

[28] FROM TURIDDU'S FAREWELL TO HIS MOTHER

Andante con moto *molto sentito*
Ah, — to poor San- tuz- za, I pray — you, be a moth - er!
Voi — do- vre- te fa - re da ma - - dre a San - ta,

THEMES

[1] **PRELUDE**

Maestoso
ff

[2] **THE DEVIL**

Allegro poco moderato
a
b
f
marcato
c
tr

[3] ARIA *DANS LES ROLES* (Lindorf)

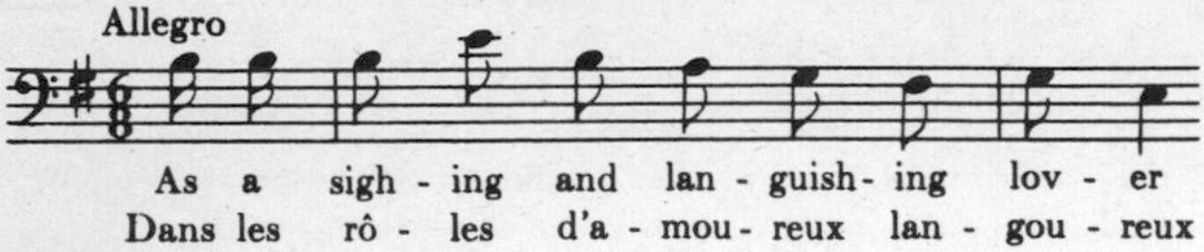
Allegro
As a sigh - ing and lan - guish - ing lov - er
Dans les rô - les d'a - mou - reux lan - gou - reux

[4] **DRINKING SONG**

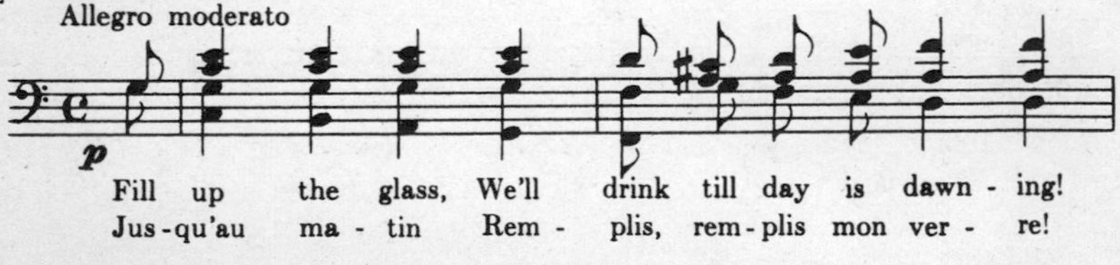
Allegro moderato
p
Fill up the glass, We'll drink till day is dawn - ing!
Jus - qu'au ma - tin Rem - plis, rem - plis mon ver - re!

[5]

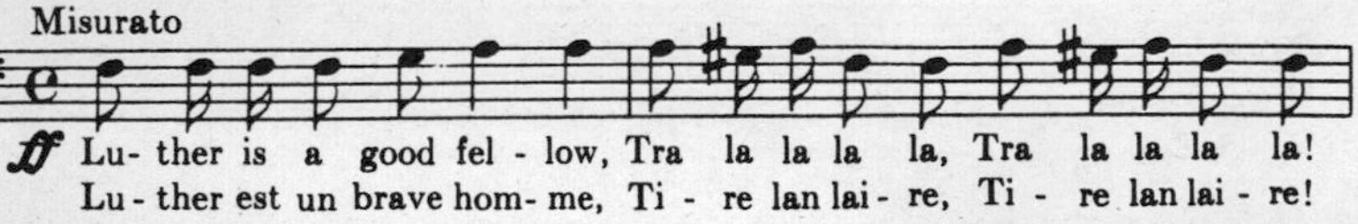
Misurato
ff
Lu - ther is a good fel - low, Tra la la la la, Tra la la la la!
Lu - ther est un brave hom - me, Ti - re lan lai - re, Ti - re lan lai - re!

[6] **THE LEGEND OF KLEINZACK** (Hoffmann)

Allegro non troppo
Oh, once up - on a time at the court of Ei - se - nach
Il é - tait u - ne fois à la cour d'Ei - se - nach

Les Contes D'Hoffmann

THE TALES OF HOFFMANN

Fantastic opera in four acts * by Jacques Offenbach. Libretto by Jules Barbier, from the writings of E. T. A. Hoffmann. First performance: Paris, February 10, 1881.

Characters: HOFFMANN, a poet (tenor); NICKLAUSSE, his friend (mezzo-soprano);

Act I and Act IV, Scene 2: STELLA, opera singer † (soprano); ANDRÈS, her servant § (tenor); LINDORF, councillor ‡ (bass or baritone); LUTHER, tavern keeper (bass or baritone);

Act II: OLYMPIA, a mechanical doll † (soprano); COPPELIUS, an inventor ‡ (bass or baritone); SPALANZANI, a scientist (tenor); COCHENILLE, his servant § (tenor);

Act III: GIULIETTA, a courtesan † (soprano); DAPPERTUTTO, her companion ‡ (bass or baritone); PITICHINACCIO § (tenor) and SCHLEMIL (bass or baritone), her admirers;

Act IV, Scene 1: ANTONIA, an invalid † (soprano); DR. MIRACLE, physician ‡ (bass or baritone); CRESPEL, Antonia's father (bass or baritone); FRANTZ, his servant § (tenor); A VOICE (mezzo-soprano).

The elegant Councillor Lindorf [2 minor] enters with Andrès, Stella's servant, and buys from him the letter which he has been ordered to deliver to the poet Hoffmann. It contains a key to Stella's dressing room, and Lindorf, who, according to his own claims (Aria *Dans les rôles d'amoureux langoureux:* "As a sighing and languishing lover") [3], is old but still quite game and endowed with a satanic power of fascination, is determined to make use of it.

Luther enters and prepares the place for the customers expected during the intermission of the opera that is played in the same building. Presently the tavern fills with students who sing their drinking song [4] and extemporize spontaneous ditties [5]. They also sing a toast to Stella, the great success of the evening's opera. Hoffmann, arriving with his young friend Nicklausse, is greeted with a resounding *vivat* by the students. But Hoffmann is in a somber mood and violently stops Nicklausse, who ventures an operatic tune (see *Don Giovanni* [5]). However, eventually Hoffmann is prevailed upon to sing the legend of Kleinzack, a freakish dwarf

* Prologue, three acts, and epilogue in the cut version.

† Stella, Olympia, Giulietta, and Antonia can be sung by the same artist.

§ The three servants, Andrès, Cochenille, and Frantz—and Pitichinaccio—can be sung by the same artist.

‡ Lindorf, Coppelius, Dappertutto, and Dr. Miracle—various manifestations of Hoffmann's ubiquitous and eternal antagonist—can be sung by the same artist.

[7] STELLA

Animato assai

[8] Moderato

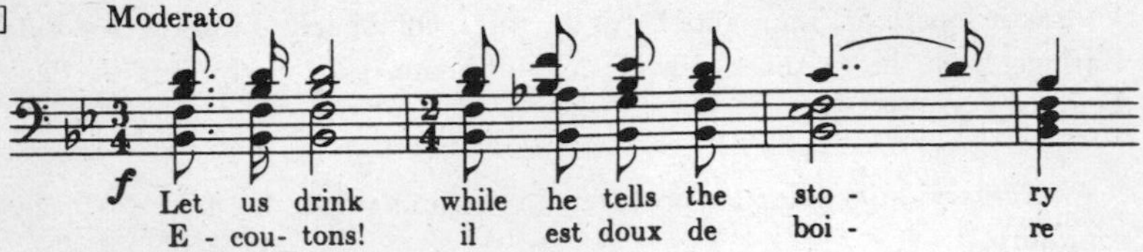

[9] THE MINUET

Moderato

[10] Andante

[11] COUPLETS *UNE POUPEE* (Nicklausse)

Allegro

[12] Moderato

[13] CHANSON *J'AI DES YEUX* (Coppelius)

Allegro

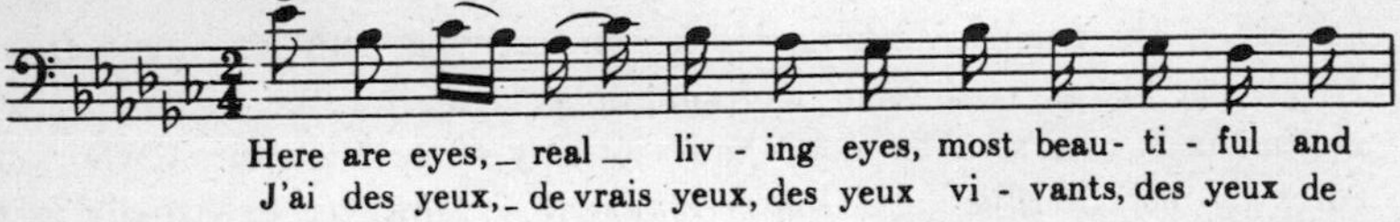

(Couplets *Il était une fois à la cour d'Eisenach:* "Once upon a time at the court of Eisenach") [6] whose creaking limbs went click-clack and crick-crack. The face? Ah, the face was charming, Hoffmann continues, losing himself in a dream of love [7], but eventually he returns to his senses and adds a few more characteristic touches to the little monster of Eisenach [6]. As Luther prepares the punch, the students honor him by repeating one verse of the ditty about him [5]. Hoffmann exchanges some well-studied insults with Lindorf, who, as Hoffmann claims, always brings him bad luck. However, the theme of love has gripped the company, and even Luther's announcement that the curtain for the next act of the opera is about to rise has no effect on them. They prefer [8] to drink and to listen to Hoffmann, who has offered to relate the story of his three loves. The name of the first one was Olympia, he announces. Everybody settles down to listen [8].

Entr'acte: The festive minuet [9].

Act II: Spalanzani, scientist and inventor, after a last look at Olympia, drops the curtain separating his cabinet from her room. She will regain for him the money he has lost in the bankruptcy of the Jew Elias—unless the crooked Coppelius [2b] makes further claims. Hoffmann enters and is promised that he will meet Spalanzani's lovely daughter, thanks to science! Hoffmann is somewhat puzzled by this pronouncement, but presently Spalanzani leaves and Hoffmann, alone, lifts the curtain to see the beauty on whose account he has decided to study science with Spalanzani—after seeing her only once through a window. How sweet life would be were he united with her in love [10]! Nicklausse joins his friend and, warning him not to be carried away so fast, he sings a song about two mechanical puppets in love (Couplets *Une poupée aux yeux d'émail:* "I had a doll of porcelain") [11], but is ignored by the poet. Coppelius comes in [2] and, noticing that Hoffmann is fascinatedly regarding what Coppelius calls "our Olympia," introduces himself [12] and offers his wares, among them life-like, even life-giving, eyes and magic glasses (Chanson *J'ai des yeux:* "Here are eyes") [13]. Hoffmann takes a pair of charmed spectacles, which, he finds, make Olympia look even prettier than before. When Spalanzani returns, Coppelius attempts to extort more money from him for supplying the eyes for Olympia. In exchange for a note relinquishing all rights to the girl, Spalanzani pays him with a draft on the Jew Elias. The "friends" embrace, and Coppelius leaves [2].

The guests invited for Olympia's coming-out party arrive [9]. Olympia's entrance on the arm of her "father" is greeted with approving whispers, and now she performs the "Chanson of Olympia" (*Les oiseaux dans la charmille:* "All the birds above are singing") [14, 15]. When suddenly her voice begins to falter, Cochenille, Spalanzani's servant, puts his hand on her back and a whirring sound is heard, whereupon she completes her song to the delight of the guests. Now Spalanzani invites everybody to supper,

[14] THE DOLL SONG

Moderato

mp
All the birds a- bove are sing - - - ing
Les oi-seaux dans la char-mil - - - le

[15] Moderato

rit.
So now you have heard the bal - - - lad
Voi - là la chan-son_gen-til - - - le

[16] THE WALTZ

Tempo di Valse

8va
p

[17] Tempo di Valse

mf

[18] Moderato

f
CHO.
Ha ha ha, the bomb is burst - ing!
Ah! ah! ah! la bombe é - cla - te!

[19] THE BARCAROLLE (Giulietta, Nicklausse)

Moderato

p
NICKL.
Shin-ing night, O night_ of love, Thy beam - ing beau - ty bles- ses!
Bel - le nuit, ô nuit_d'a-mour, Sou-ris_ à nos i - vres- ses!

[20] COUPLETS *AMIS, L'AMOUR TENDRE* (Hoffmann)

Allegretto poco maestoso

mf
My friends, love that preys on the mind is blind_
A - mis, l'a-mour ten- dre et rê - veur, Er- reur!_

[21] ARIA *SCINTILLE, DIAMANT* (Dappertutto)

Andante poco mosso

p
My_ dia - mond, shine bright_
Scin - til - le di - a - mant_

but permits Hoffmann to remain with Olympia. Spalanzani guides her to a chair and makes her sit down. After the guests have left [9], Hoffmann talks to Olympia, who says *"Oui, oui!"* whenever he touches her shoulder; but when he presses her hand she stiffly rises, zig-zags about the room, and eventually runs off. Nicklausse comes with rumors that Olympia is not a living being, but Hoffmann, as if under a spell, rushes after her and Nicklausse follows.

Coppelius returns, furious over having been swindled, and slips into Olympia's room. To the sounds of a waltz [16, 17] the guests return, and Hoffmann begins to dance with Olympia. She twirls faster and faster. Nicklausse is jostled in a vain effort to stop her, and Hoffmann collapses in a dizzy spell before Spalanzani with a light tap abruptly stops his "daughter." Now she retires singing the waltz [16] as the guests admire her accomplishments. Hoffmann's spectacles are shattered, but he is unhurt and just regaining his senses when a loud noise of breaking springs is heard inside and Coppelius enters triumphantly, announcing that he has broken Olympia. Now, finally, Hoffmann realizes that Olympia was an automaton. His despair is greeted with great mirth by the company [18].

Act III: At the palace of Giulietta in Venice, overlooking the Grand Canal, the guests are listening in luxurious relaxation to the approaching voices of the hostess and Nicklausse (Barcarolle *Belle nuit, ô nuit d'amour:* "Shining night, O night of love") [19]. The singers arrive, and Hoffmann, discontent with the languid Barcarolle, pleads for a love that is more exciting (Couplets Bachiques *Amis, l'amour tendre et rêveur, Erreur!:* "My friends, love that prays on the mind is blind") [20]. Schlemil and Pitichinaccio, jealous of each other and of Hoffmann, exchange sarcastic remarks, so Giulietta quickly invites all to the gaming rooms. Nicklausse warns Hoffmann not to fall in love with a courtesan like Giulietta; Hoffmann maintains that no devil can make him commit such folly, and the friends follow the others. Dappertutto [2bc] has come in time to overhear the conversation, but he thinks that Giulietta's eyes can deliver Hoffmann to him just as easily as they succeeded in obtaining Schlemil's shadow. Taking a big diamond ring from his finger, he holds it out conjuringly to attract Giulietta (Aria *Scintille, diamant:* "My diamond, shine bright") [21]. When she obediently appears, he gives her the ring and demands from her the reflection of Hoffmann. The poet approaches, and Dappertutto quickly withdraws. Giulietta hysterically professes to love Hoffmann, but begs him to leave for today, on account of Schlemil's jealousy. However, from tomorrow on she will be his forever. Hoffmann is vanquished [22]. He even agrees to give her his mirror reflection as a keepsake until the morrow that both ardently await [23].

Schlemil and the rest of the company return unexpectedly [13], and Giulietta whispers to Hoffmann that it is Schlemil who has the key to her room. Dappertutto, as if inadvertently, demonstrates to Hoffmann the

[22] Largo

HOFF. O heav'n with what de - light ___ my heart is all a - light ___
O Dieu de quelle i - vresse ___ em - bra - ses - tu mon â - me

[23] Allegretto agitato

GIUL. & HOFF. Ah to - day, ah to - day ___ all is sor - row
Au - jour - d'hui, au - jour - d'hui ___ les ___ lar - mes

[24] SEPTET *HELAS! MON COEUR* (Hoffmann, Nicklausse, Dappertutto, Giulietta, Schlemil, Pitichinaccio, Chorus)

Andante

HOFF. A - las! ___ My heart, where do you lead ___ me! ___
Hé - las! ___ mon coeur s'é - gare en - co - - re! ___

[25] ROMANCE *ELLE A FUI* (Antonia)

Andante

He has flown, my pret - ty tur - tle dove
Elle a fui, la tour - te - rel - le!

[26a] FRANTZ

Allegretto

[26b] COUPLETS *JOUR ET NUIT* (Frantz)

Allegretto

Night and day I must go and come
Jour et nuit je me mets en quatre

[27] DUET *C'EST UNE CHANSON D'AMOUR* (Hoffmann, Antonia)

Allegretto

HOFF. Ah! 'tis a bal - lad of love and of fol - ly, Love and fol - ly
C'est u - ne chan - son d'a - mour qui s'en - vo - le, Triste et fol - le

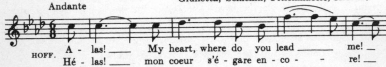

frightening fact that he makes no reflection in the mirror. Still (Septet *Hélas! mon cœur s'égare encore:* "Alas my heart, where do you lead me?") [24] the poet cannot tear himself away from Giulietta, who now facetiously confesses that she stole his reflection in order to earn a diamond ring. Nicklausse pities him, Dappertutto and Pitichinaccio deride him, and Schlemil swears to kill him. Giulietta announces that the gondolas are waiting [19], and leaves. Hoffmann demands the key from Schlemil (spoken dialogue with [19]), who refuses it, and in the ensuing duel Hoffmann kills him with a sword borrowed from Dappertutto. He takes the key from the body and rushes to Giulietta's room. Having found it empty, he quickly returns to look for Giulietta and discovers her in a gondola just leaving the palazzo. Laughing in his face, she nonchalantly resigns his life to Dappertutto and takes Pitichinaccio in her arms. When the guards approach, Nicklausse rushes toward Hoffmann and drags him from the scene of the murder.

Act IV, Scene 1: In the house at Munich where her father has moved to separate her from Hoffmann, Antonia sits at the harpsichord, sadly singing to her distant beloved (Romance *Elle a fui, la tourterelle!:* "He has flown, my pretty turtle-dove") [25]. Her father, Crespel, enters, and forbids her to sing, although her voice reminds him of that of her famous mother [motive 30]. Antonia promises to sing no more [25], yet Crespel again notices her unnaturally flushed cheeks and curses Hoffmann, who had encouraged Antonia's singing. When Frantz, the nearly-deaf old servant, enters [26a] and misunderstands everything, Crespel leaves in a rage. Frantz consoles himself with singing (Couplets *Jour et nuit je me mets en quatre:* "Night and day I must go and come") [26b], although he knows his technique is wrong—and with dancing, although he lands on his well-polished floor.

Presently Hoffmann enters. He is happy that he has found the Crespels' new home and sends Frantz for Antonia. Sitting down at the harpsichord, he sings a few measures [27]. Soon Antonia rushes in and they embrace passionately [28]. Antonia complains that her father does not want her to sing, and she is happy that Hoffmann does not mind listening to her. Together they intone their favorite love song (Duet *C'est une chanson d'amour qui s'envole:* "Ah, 'tis a ballad of love and of folly") [27]. Suddenly Antonia presses her hands to her heart, but she insists that nothing is wrong. Just then they hear the voice of Crespel. Antonia flees to her room and Hoffmann hides, curious to find out why Antonia has been forbidden to sing.

Crespel enters and Frantz comes in [26a] to announce Dr. Miracle [29a]. Crespel wants to shut the door on "the murderer who, after my wife, would kill my daughter," but the doctor [29a] with his clinking phials [29b] is suddenly here. Cynically he asks after Antonia's health and makes a commanding gesture toward her room. Apparently unassisted, the door

[28]

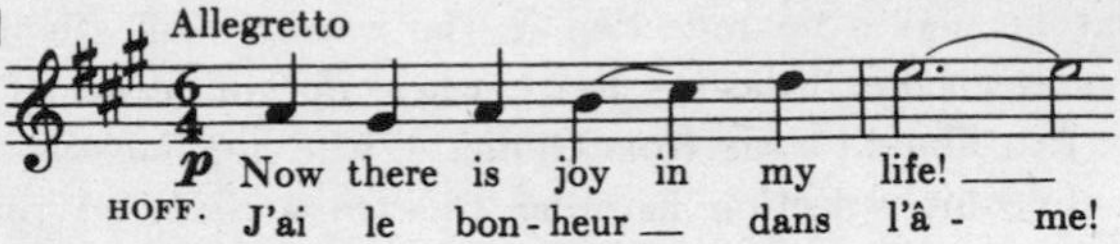
Allegretto
p
HOFF.
Now there is joy in my life!
J'ai le bon-heur dans l'â - me!

[29]

Marcato
b THE VIALS
f
f
a DR. MIRACLE

[30] TRIO *CHERE ENFANT* (The Voice of Antonia's Mother, Antonia, Dr. Miracle)

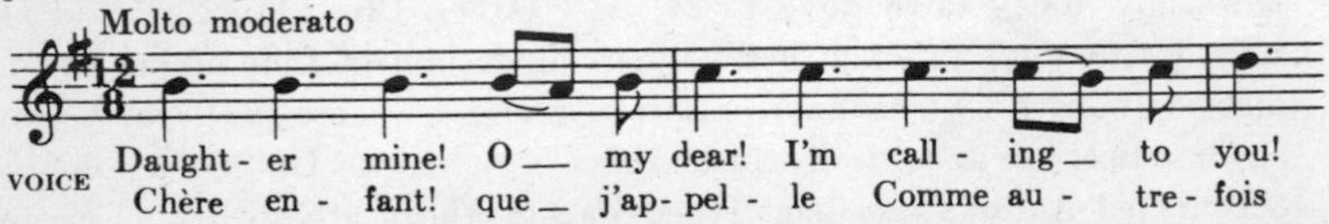
Molto moderato
VOICE
Daught - er mine! O my dear! I'm call - ing to you!
Chère en - fant! que j'ap - pel - le Comme au - tre - fois

[31] THE DEVIL'S FIDDLE TUNE

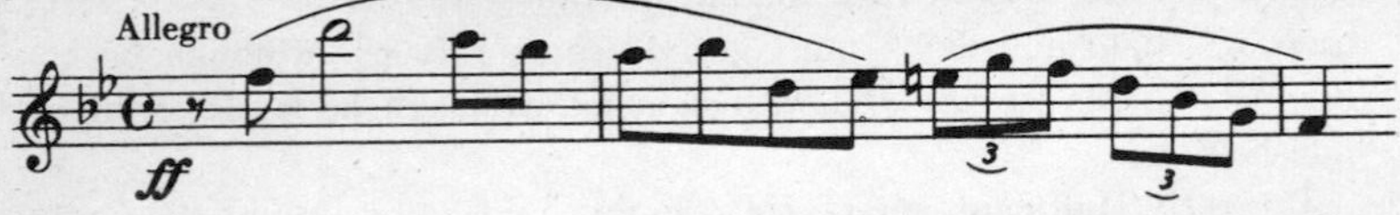
Allegro
ff

[32]

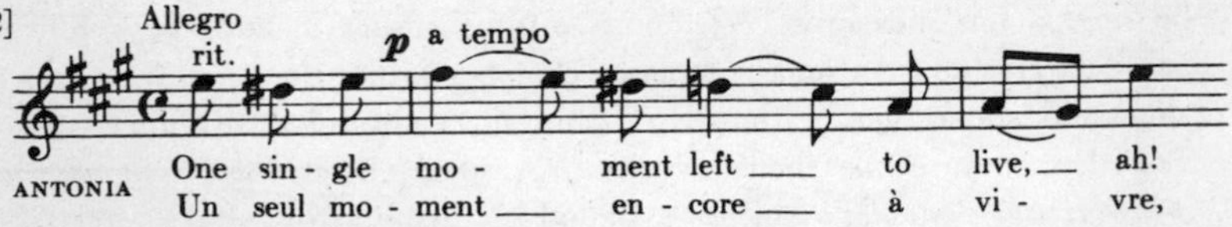
Allegro
rit.
p a tempo
ANTONIA
One sin - gle mo - ment left to live, ah!
Un seul mo - ment en - core à vi - vre,

opens and Miracle guides an Antonia, visible only to him, to a chair, takes her pulse (irregular beats in the orchestra), and asks her to sing. Antonia's voice is heard in a quickly fading cadenza. According to Miracle's dramatic description, her cheeks now redden, her eyes glow feverishly, and, pressing her hands to her heart, she retires to her room. The door closes again. While Crespel threatens and curses, and Hoffmann resolves to do what he can for Antonia, the doctor [29a] obstinately keeps offering his remedies (Trio). Crespel chases him outside.

Hoffmann leaves his hiding-place. He asks the returning Antonia to follow her father's wish that she sing no more. Having received her reluctant promise, he tenderly takes his leave [27]. Antonia sinks into a chair. Suddenly Dr. Miracle stands behind her [2abc] and in a sinister whisper demands that she not waste the talents given her by heaven merely because she is in love. As, in her torment, she calls on her dead mother for help, her mother's voice seems to be talking to her from a portrait (Trio *Chère enfant que j'appelle:* "Daughter mine, oh my dear") [30], while Miracle keeps urging her to sing. Now he grabs a fiddle and plays a frenetic melody [31]. Antonia can resist no longer [32]. She sings, but soon falls exhausted to the ground. The portrait again becomes lifeless, and Miracle disappears with a wild laugh.

Crespel enters to find Antonia dying and ready to join her mother [30], but her last thought belongs to Hoffmann [27]. When he enters with Nicklausse and calls for a doctor, Miracle materializes [29] and pronounces Antonia dead.

Entr'acte: After a reprise of the Barcarolle [19] (usually omitted), theme [8] of the first act is used to prepare the return to Luther's Tavern.

Act IV, Scene 2: Just as Hoffmann finishes his stories, enthusiastic shouts acclaiming Stella are heard from outside. Lindorf leaves with a murmured remark of relief at seeing Hoffmann too drunk to move. Nicklausse guesses that Hoffmann's three loves are in reality only three aspects of his beloved Stella.

The poet strives only for drunken oblivion. The glasses are refilled [4] and then all leave Hoffmann and go singing into an inner room.

The Muse of Poetry appears (this episode is often omitted) and asks Hoffmann to belong to her who loves him, and he breaks ecstatically into his love song [22] before he collapses in a drunken stupor.

Stella enters, tenderly looking for Hoffmann. When Nicklausse tells her that he is drunk beyond hope and introduces to her the just returning Lindorf, she leaves with the Councillor. The gay songs of the students [4, 5] are heard from the back room.

THEMES

[1] OVERTURE
Andante

[2] Andante

[3] Molto allegro

[4] Molto allegro

Don Giovanni

Opera in two acts by Wolfgang Amadeus Mozart. Libretto by Lorenzo da Ponte. First performance: Prague, October 29, 1787.

Characters: DON GIOVANNI (baritone); LEPORELLO, his servant (bass); THE COMMANDANT (bass); DONNA ANNA, his daughter (soprano); DON OTTAVIO, her fiancé (tenor); DONNA ELVIRA (soprano); MASETTO, a peasant (bass); ZERLINA, his bride (soprano).
In and near Seville, in the seventeenth century.

Overture: Opening with the fateful sounds that also accompany the appearance of the "stone guest" near the end of the opera [1, 2], the overture is based on two allegro themes [3, 4] not found elsewhere in the opera.

Act I, Scene 1: In front of Donna Anna's house Leporello is waiting for Don Giovanni, disgruntled (Aria *Notte e giorno faticar:* "Rest I've none by night or day") [5] that he has to pace up and down while, inside, his master is "amusing himself." Presently, Don Giovanni appears at the door, hiding his face behind his cloak and fighting to free himself from the grip of Donna Anna. She keeps calling for help, while trying in vain to uncover his face. Leporello, observing them from a dark niche, contributes a stream of half frightened, half caustic remarks (Trio). Aroused by the commotion, the Commandant appears with drawn sword, and Anna rushes off for help. Don Giovanni, forced to fight, transfixes the old man, who slowly sinks back and dies (Trio). Don Giovanni and his servant hurry away.

Anna returns with Don Ottavio and servants (Recitative). When she finds her father dead, she is so distraught that for a moment she mistakes her fiancé for her aggressor (Duet *Fuggi, crudele:* "Cruel, why art thou near me?") [6]; but soon she regains her senses, and both swear to avenge the murder [7].

[5] ARIA *NOTTE E GIORNO FATICAR* (Leporello)
Molto allegro

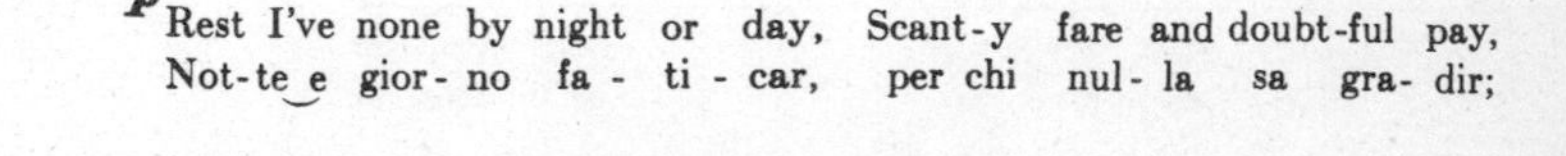

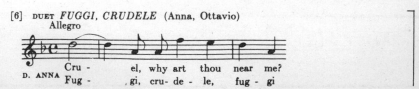

[6] DUET *FUGGI, CRUDELE* (Anna, Ottavio)
Allegro

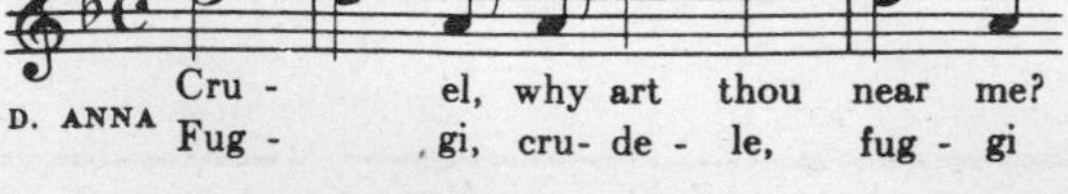

[7] DUET *FUGGI, CRUDELE* (Anna, Ottavio) *continued*

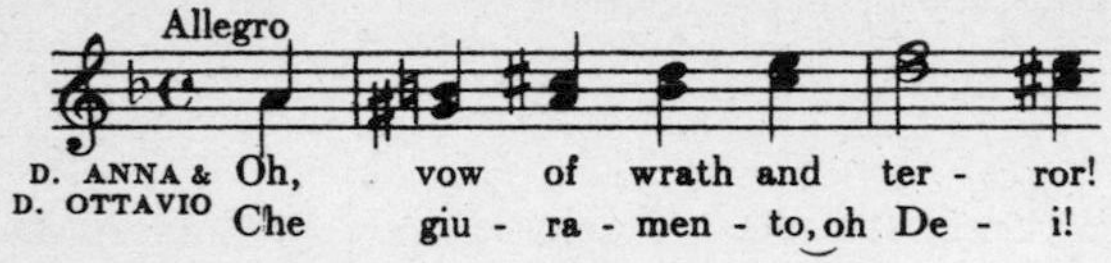
Allegro
D. ANNA & D. OTTAVIO
Oh, vow of wrath and ter - ror!
Che giu - ra - men - to, oh De - i!

[8] TRIO *AH! CHI MI DICE MAI* (Elvira, Giovanni, Leporello)

Allegro
f
p
ELVIRA
Where shall I find a to - ken to
Ah! chi mi di - ce ma - i, quel

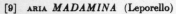

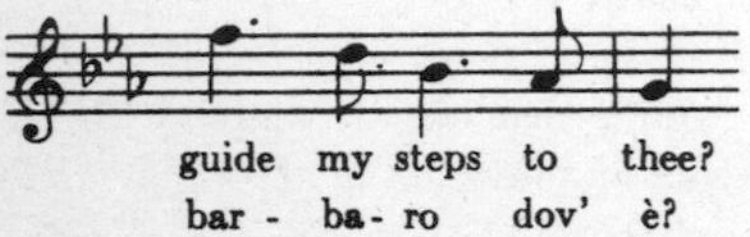
guide my steps to thee?
bar - ba - ro dov' è?

[9] ARIA *MADAMINA* (Leporello)

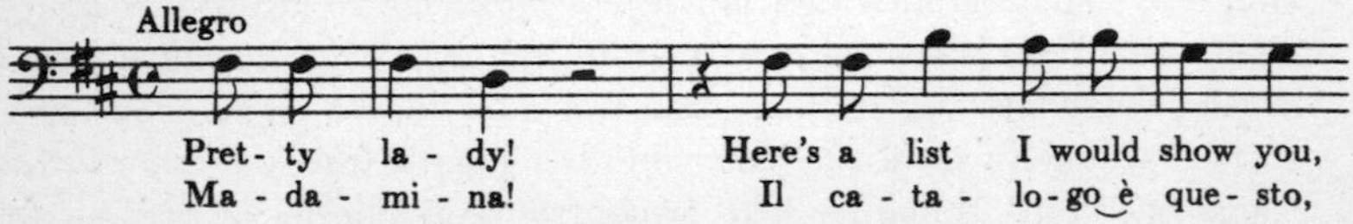
Allegro
Pret - ty la - dy! Here's a list I would show you,
Ma - da - mi - na! Il ca - ta - lo - go è que - sto,

[10]

Andante con moto
Is a maid - en fair and slen - der
Nel - la bion - da e - gli ha l'u - san - za

[11]

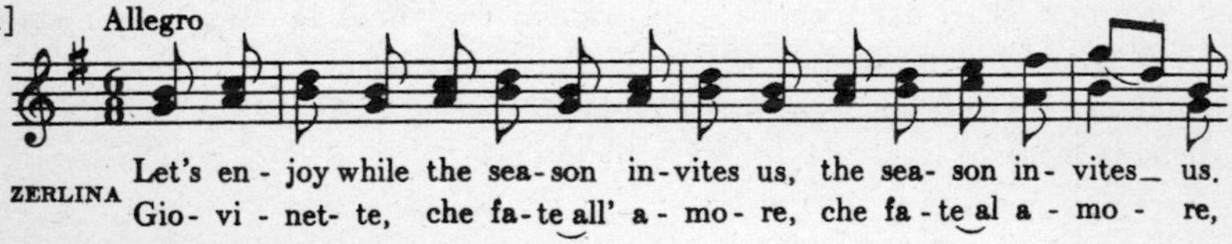
Allegro
ZERLINA
Let's en - joy while the sea - son in - vites us, the sea - son in - vites us.
Gio - vi - net - te, che fa - te all' a - mo - re, che fa - te al a - mo - re,

[12] ARIA *HO CAPITO* (Masetto)

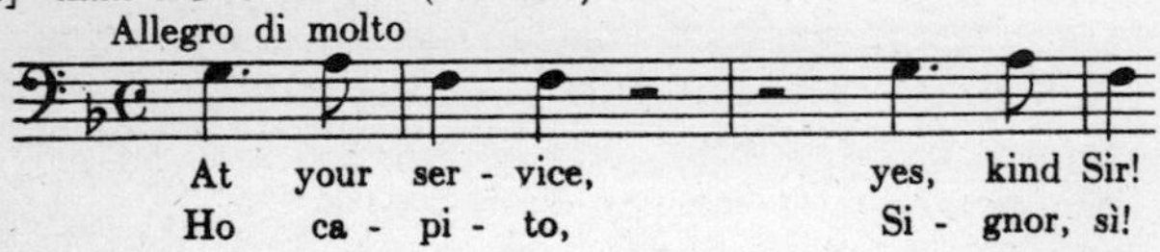
Allegro di molto
At your ser - vice, yes, kind Sir!
Ho ca - pi - to, Si - gnor, sì!

[13]

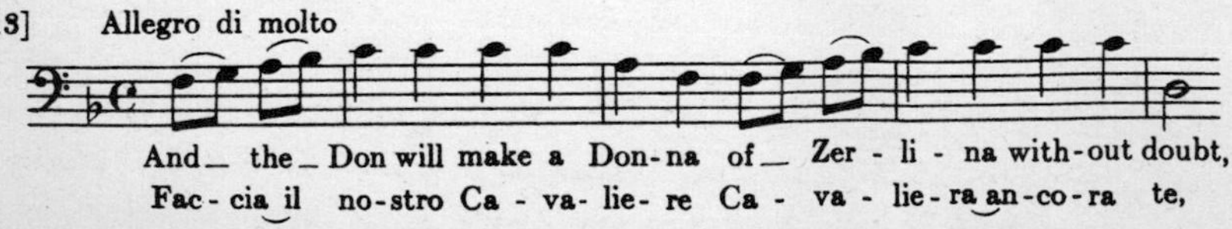
Allegro di molto
And the Don will make a Don - na of Zer - li - na with - out doubt,
Fac - cia il no - stro Ca - va - lie - re Ca - va - lie - ra an - co - ra te,

Act I, Scene 2: As Don Giovanni walks through the town with Leporello and plans future adventures, a lady in distress arrives and complains about her lover, who has run away (Trio *Ah! chi mi dice mai:* "Where shall I find a token") [8]. The Don who has been unable to see her face, approaches her, only to find that she is Donna Elvira, whom he has jilted and who is here precisely for the purpose of finding him. Leaving Leporello to make his excuses, he nimbly disappears. Leporello finds that the best means of consoling the beautiful young lady is to inform her about the other exploits of his master. Taking from his pocket a notebook, he reads off a long list (Aria *Madamina:* "Pretty lady") [9] of Don Giovanni's conquests in several countries. In Spain alone, there are already one thousand and three of them, of all ranks and professions, and of all ages, shapes, and complexions [10]. Impudently mocking Elvira—who, he implies, ought to know exactly how Don Giovanni behaves—Leporello leaves her angry and contemplating revenge. (Occasionally the aria *Mi tradì:* "Cruel heart" [36] is sung here; see end of Act II, Scene 2.)

Act I, Scene 3: In the country, Zerlina and Masetto, surrounded by boys and girls, are celebrating their wedding [11] when Don Giovanni and Leporello happen upon them. Don Giovanni, finding the bride attractive, invites the whole company to be his guests, and instructs Leporello to take the groom and the others along with him. Masetto does not take kindly to the idea of leaving his new bride alone with a "Signor" (Aria *Ho capito, Signor, sì!:* "At your service, yes, kind Sir!") [12] and sarcastically suggests that she may yet become a "Signora" [13], but at last the Don is left alone with Zerlina. He asks the girl, who is only half resisting, to follow him to his castle (Duet *Là ci darem la mano:* "Give me your hand, Zerlina") [14], but just as they have reached an agreement [15] Donna Elvira charges in, violently denounces the cavalier (Aria *Ah! fuggi il traditor!:* "The traitor means deceit!") [16], and leads off Zerlina.

Presently Don Ottavio and Donna Anna approach. Don Giovanni (Recitative) finds out, to his relief, that he has not been recognized as the murderer of the Commandant, and hypocritically he offers his assistance, but

[14] DUET *LA CI DAREM LA MANO* (Giovanni, Zerlina)

Andante
p
Give me your hand, Zer - li - na; An - swer your lov- er's plea;
D. GIOVANNI
Là ci da - rem la ma - no, là mi di - rai di sì;

[15]

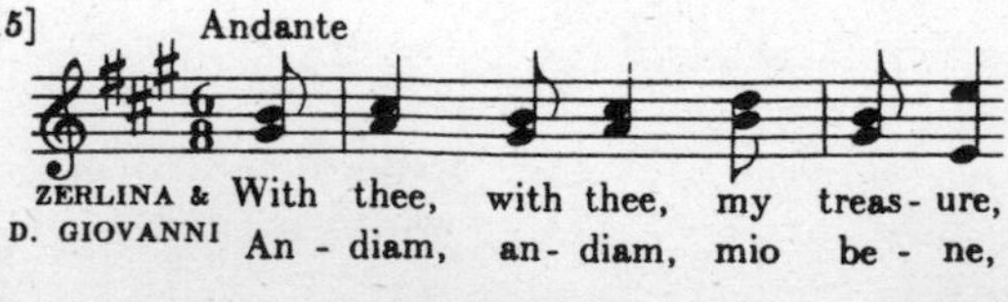
Andante
ZERLINA & D. GIOVANNI
With thee, with thee, my treas - ure,
An - diam, an - diam, mio be - ne,

[16] ARIA *AH! FUGGI IL TRADITOR!* (Elvira)

Allegro

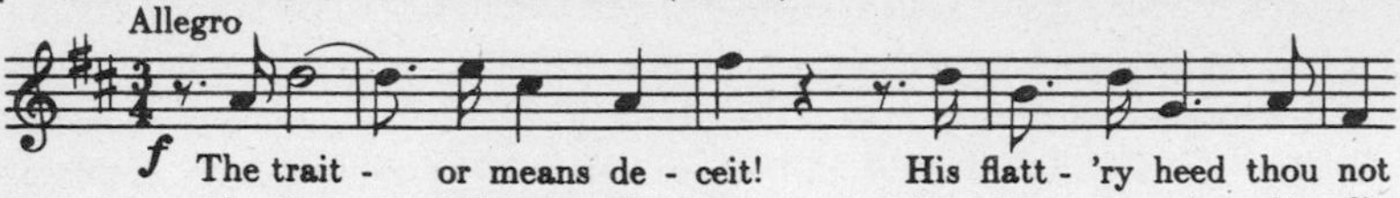

The trait - or means de - ceit! His flatt - 'ry heed thou not
Ah! fug - gi il tra - di - tor! Non lo la- sciar più dir;

[17] QUARTET *NON TI FIDAR* (Elvira, Anna, Ottavio, Giovanni)

Andante

Oh,___ do not trust this e - vil soul,
ELVIRA Non ___ ti fi - dar, o mi - se - ra,

[18] ARIA *OR SAI, CHI L'ONORE* (Anna)

Andante

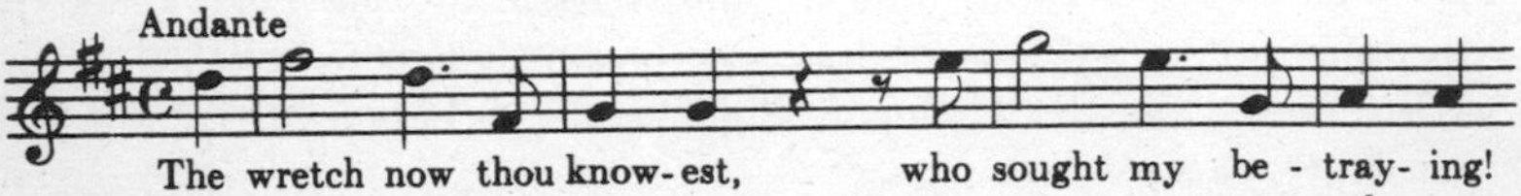

The wretch now thou know-est, who sought my be - tray- ing!
Or sai, chi l'o - no - re ra - pi - re a me vol - se,

[19] ARIA *DALLA SUA PACE* (Ottavio)

Andantino sostenuto

She is the meas - ure of all_ my_ glad - - ness,
Dal - la sua pa - ce la mia_ di - pen - - de,

[20] ARIA *FINCH' HAN DAL VINO* (Giovanni)

Presto

Let's have a par - ty, hap - py and heart - y,
Finch' han dal vi - no cal - da la te - sta,

I'm in the mood for laugh - ter and wine!
u - na gran fe - sta fa pre - pa - rar!

[21] ARIA *BATTI, BATTI* (Zerlina)

Andante grazioso

Beat me, beat me, dear Ma- set - to, beat your poor, de-spised Zer-li - na;
Bat- ti, bat-ti, o bel Ma-set- to, la tua po- ve- ra Zer-li - na;

[22] Andante grazioso

Peace and joy___ once more___ shall bless us
Pa - ce, pa - ce, o vi - ta mi - a!

Elvira returns and (Quartet *Non ti fidar, o misera:* "Ah, do not trust this evil soul") [17] launches another tirade against the Don. Anna and Ottavio do not quite know what to believe, although Don Giovanni whispers to them that Elvira is crazy. (Each of the singers here retains his characteristic melodic line, Elvira excited, Anna and Ottavio dignified, Giovanni an easy, cavalier chatter.) Eventually Don Giovanni succeeds in making Elvira leave, whereupon he, too (Recitative), quickly departs.

However, by his last words and gestures Donna Anna has recognized him as the man who the other night had come into her room and tried to assault her and, after being put to flight, had murdered her father. Now that Don Ottavio knows the murderer, she imperiously bids him avenge her (Aria *Or sai, chi l'onore:* "The wretch now thou knowest") [18] and leaves. Ottavio, hardly believing his ears, decides he will disprove Donna Anna's suspicions, or else comply with her wishes. Her peace of mind, he declares, is the foundation of his happiness (Aria *Dalla sua pace:* "She is the measure") [19], and he follows her into the house.

Leporello meets Don Giovanni and reports (Recitative) that the peasants, including Zerlina, are in the castle, while he has been able to lock out Donna Elvira. Don Giovanni, wishing to give the evening a fitting conclusion, bids Leporello gather all the girls he can find and prepare a rousing feast (Aria *Finch' han dal vino:* "Let's have a party") [20], so that by morning Leporello can add a dozen new names to his list.

Act I, Scene 4: In the garden on the castle grounds Zerlina tries to convince Masetto that the Don "hasn't even touched the tips of her fingers," and asks him to make peace with her, even if he feels he must beat her first (Aria *Batti, batti:* "Beat me, beat me") [21]. Just when she has inveigled him into forgiving her [22], they hear the voice of Don Giovanni. Masetto, moved by jealous curiosity, quickly hides in an arbor (*Presto, presto, pria ch'ei venga:* "Quickly, quickly, ere he sees me") [23] and leaves the frightened Zerlina in the path of their host. As it is getting dark, the guests move into the house. Don Giovanni finds Zerlina and tries to pull her into the arbor, but he is suddenly confronted by Masetto. After only a moment's surprised hesitation, the Don offers an arm to both bride and groom, and leads them inside to the dance.

Donna Elvira, Donna Anna, and Don Ottavio appear masked, resolved to find out what they can about Don Giovanni [24]. Leporello opens a window (the strains of the minuet [25] are heard from the inside) and invites the masks to join the festivities. They invoke the help of heaven

[23]

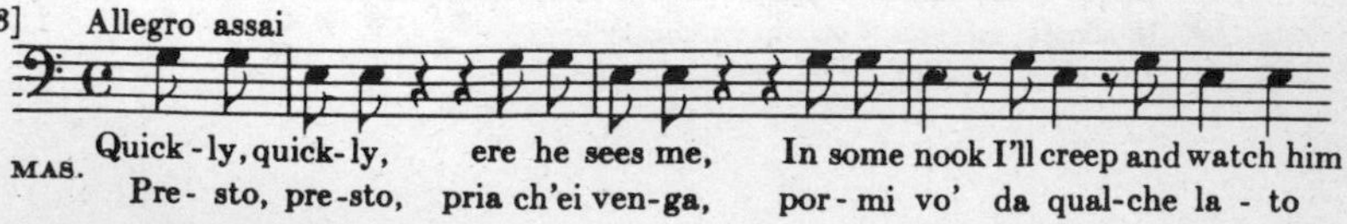
Allegro assai
MAS.
Quick-ly, quick-ly, ere he sees me, In some nook I'll creep and watch him
Pre-sto, pre-sto, pria ch'ei ven-ga, por-mi vo' da qual-che la - to

[24] Allegretto

And now let's be cou - ra - geous; by just re - sent - ment gui - ded,
ELVIRA Bi - so - gna a - ver co - rag - gio, o ca - ri a - mi - ci mie - i!

[25] THE MINUET
Tempo di minuetto

[26] TRIO OF THE MASKS (Anna, Ottavio, Elvira)
D. ANNA & D. OTT. Thou pow'r a - bove be near us,
Pro - teg - ga il giu - sto cie - lo,
Adagio

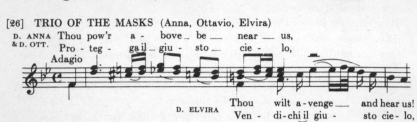

Thou wilt a - venge and hear us!
D. ELVIRA Ven - di - chi il giu - sto cie - lo,

[27] DUET *EH VIA BUFFONE* (Giovanni, Leporello)
Allegro assai

What's all the non - sense, what's all the non - sense, Sure - ly, you'll stay
D. GIOVANNI Eh via, buf - fo - ne, eh via, buf - fo - ne, non mi sec - car!

[28] TRIO *AH, TACI, INGIUSTO CORE* (Elvira, Giovanni, Leporello)
Andantino

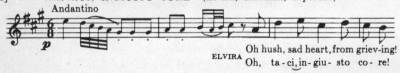

Oh hush, sad heart, from griev - ing!
ELVIRA Oh, ta - ci, in - giu - sto co - re!

[29] DON GIOVANNI'S SERENADE
Allegretto

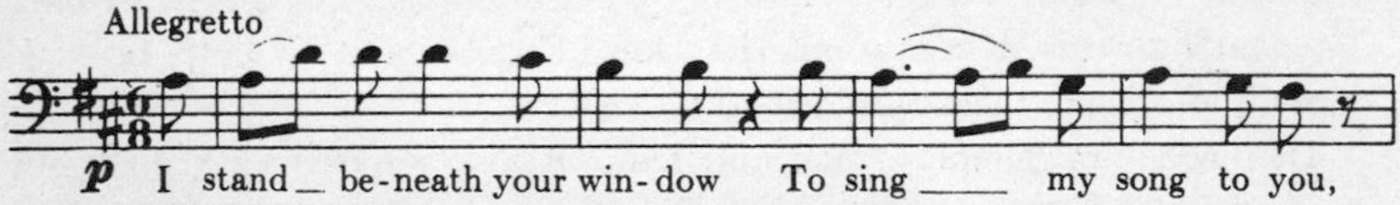

I stand be - neath your win - dow To sing my song to you,
Deh vie - ni al - la fi - ne - stra, o mio te - so - ro,

[30] ARIA *META DI VOI QUA VADANO* (Giovanni)
Andante con moto

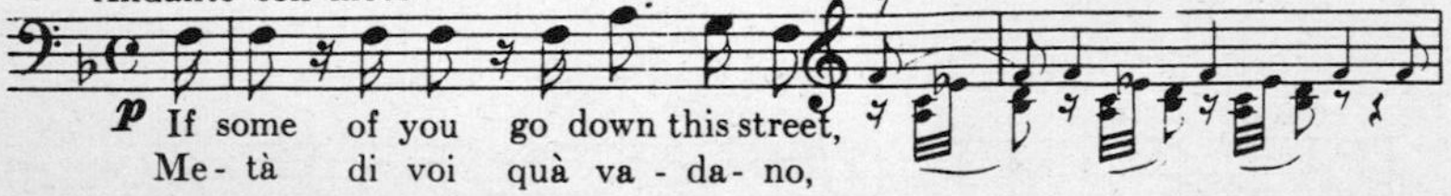

If some of you go down this street,
Me - tà di voi quà va - da - no,

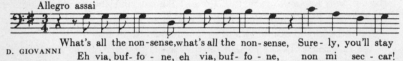

(Trio of the Masks *Protegga il giusto cielo:* "Thou, pow'r above, be near us") [26] and enter the castle.

Act I, Scene 5: In the brilliantly lighted ballroom of the castle, the host and Leporello circulate among the guests, and Don Giovanni pays special attention to Zerlina. When the three masks enter, they are cordially welcomed. Now, to the sounds of the palace string orchestra—or, rather, orchestras (three, each playing a different dance: the minuet [25] is the main tune)—Don Giovanni dances with Zerlina, the noble guests with one another, while Leporello forces Masetto to dance with him. Zerlina has been trying to escape from her host, but he catches up with her near a door and leads her off. Sensing trouble, Leporello hurries after them. Suddenly, a scream is heard from inside. It is Zerlina's voice. The entire company rushes toward the door to break it down. Don Giovanni appears pushing Leporello in front of him and threatening him, pretending that it was his servant who had molested Zerlina, but nobody believes him. Donna Anna, Donna Elvira, and Don Ottavio unmask and denounce the surprised Don Giovanni. All threaten him, and Don Ottavio draws his sword, but eventually master and servant escape.

Act II, Scene 1: It is evening. Don Giovanni and Leporello are walking along the street, carrying on an argument. Leporello wants to leave his master, but a purse persuades him to stay on. (Duet *Eh via, buffone:* "What's all the nonsense") [27]. They have now arrived at the house of Donna Elvira, and Giovanni makes Leporello change clothes with him so that he can woo Elvira's maid in more suitable garb. Elvira appears at the window (Trio *Ah, taci, ingiusto core:* "Oh hush, sad heart, from grieving!") [28], and Don Giovanni, hidden behind Leporello—who is wearing the Don's clothes—renews his vows of love for Elvira, at the same time forcing Leporello to make the appropriate gestures. Elvira can hardly believe her ears, while Leporello is constrained to laugh out loud at this comedy. Soon Donna Elvira comes outside (Recitative) and rushes into the arms of Leporello, who impersonates his master so successfully that the embrace seems never-ending to the impatient Don. Hiding his face behind his cloak, Giovanni leaps at them with a shout and startles them into flight. Now that Elvira has gone, he can sing his serenade to her maid (Canzonetta—accompanied by plucked strings and mandolin—*Deh vieni alla finestra:* "I stand beneath your window") [29]. Suddenly Masetto appears with a group of armed peasants (Recitative), looking for Don Giovanni with the intention of killing him. The Don, who, in the darkness, has been careful to mimic Leporello, sends the men in pursuit of "Don Giovanni," some in one direction, some in another (Aria *Metà di voi quà vadano:* "If some of you go down this street") [30], till he remains alone with Masetto. Now he tricks Masetto into giving him his weapons (Recitative), beats him up thoroughly, and leaves him sobbing on the ground. Zerlina finds

[31] ARIA *VEDRAI, CARINO* (Zerlina)

Grazioso
I have a cure for you, cer - tain and sure for you
Ve - drai, ca - ri - no, se sei buo - ni - no,

[32] SEXTET *SOLA, SOLA* (Elvira, Leporello, Ottavio, Anna, Zerlina, Masetto)

Andante
All a - lone I stand in dark - ness and — my —
ELVIRA
So - la, so - la in bu - jo lo - co pal - pi -
fright - ened heart is trem - bling,
tar il cor mi sen - to,

[33]

Andante
Good friends, oh spare — me! — you are mis - ta - ken! —
LEPORELLO
Per - don, per - do - no! — Si - gno - ri mie - i! —

[34] ARIA *AH, PIETA! SIGNORI MIEI!* (Leporello)

Allegro assai
Ah, have mer - cy on my soul, Ah, I beg of you, have
Ah, pie - tà! Si - gno - ri miei! Ah pie - tà, pie - tà, pie -
mer - cy, friends, oh spare my life!
tà, pie - tà, di me, pie - tà

[35] ARIA *IL MIO TESORO* (Ottavio)

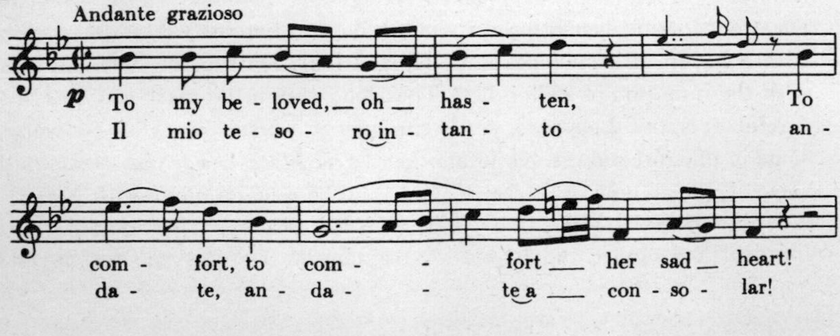
Andante grazioso
p
To my be - loved, — oh — has - ten, To
Il mio te - so - ro in - tan - to an -
com - fort, to com - fort — her sad — heart!
da - te, an - da - te a — con - so - lar!

him, consoles him, and invites him to leave with her, promising an excellent remedy for all his ills (Aria *Vedrai, carino:* "I have a cure for you") [31]. Gently she leads him away.

Act II, Scene 2: Meanwhile, Leporello and Elvira have come to a dark courtyard. He tries to escape her there (beginning of Sextet *Sola, sola in bujo loco:* "All alone I stand in darkness") [32], but just as in the darkness he finds the door, Don Ottavio enters trying to comfort Donna Anna, who clings, weeping, to his arm. Again Leporello tries to reach the door, but this time he is intercepted by Masetto and Zerlina, who enter at this moment. As Leporello is still wearing his master's cloak and hat, all mistake him for Don Giovanni and demand his death. Only Elvira pleads for pardon; however, her intercession is of no avail, so Leporello decides to show his face and to beg for mercy for himself [33]. To his grief, he discovers that he is judged as guilty as his master by his captors. Plaintively he appeals to each one of them separately (Aria *Ah, pietà! Signori miei!:* "Ah, have mercy on my soul") [34] and then, unexpectedly, makes good his escape. Don Ottavio asks those present to go after Donna Anna, who has left sometime earlier, and to console her (Aria *Il mio tesoro:* "To my beloved, oh hasten") [35] while he, finally convinced that Don Giovanni is the murderer and attacker, will go to notify the police and prepare for revenge.

Zerlina, a razor in hand (this episode is usually omitted), brings back Leporello and ties him to a chair, in spite of his pleading (Duet *Per queste tue manine:* "I beg you, I conjure you"), but again, as soon as Zerlina has gone, he manages to free himself and to get away. Elvira, returning with Zerlina, confesses that, abandoned, she yet feels pity for Don Giovanni (Recitative *In quali eccessi, o Numi:* "In what abysses of error"; aria *Mi tradì quell' alma ingrata:* "Cruel heart, thou hast betrayed me" [36], occasionally sung at the end of Act I, Scene 2).

Act II, Scene 3: Don Giovanni and Leporello meet late at night at the cemetery (Recitative). When Don Giovanni finishes a ribald story in a burst of loud laughter, a voice (accompanied by trombones) warns him to respect the dead and to leave them in peace. Looking about, Don Giovanni discovers the statue of the Commandant and proceeds to amuse himself by ordering the frightened Leporello to invite the statue for dinner (Duet *O statua gentilissima:* "O thou, most noble monument") [37]. To the sur-

[36] ARIA *MI TRADI* (Elvira)

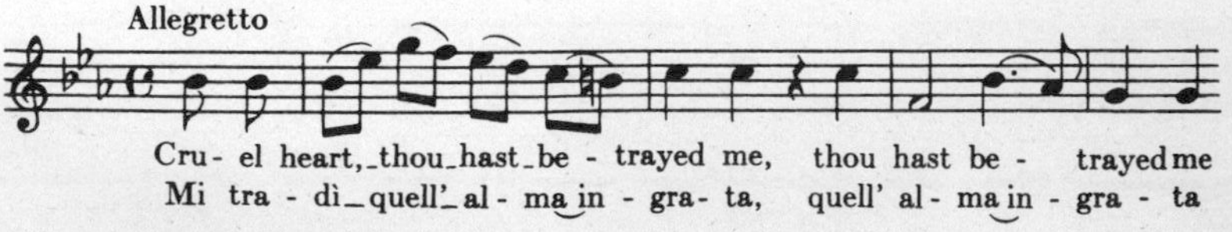
Allegretto
Cru- el heart, thou hast be - trayed me, thou hast be - trayed me
Mi tra - dì quell' al - ma in - gra- ta, quell' al - ma in - gra - ta

[37] Allegro

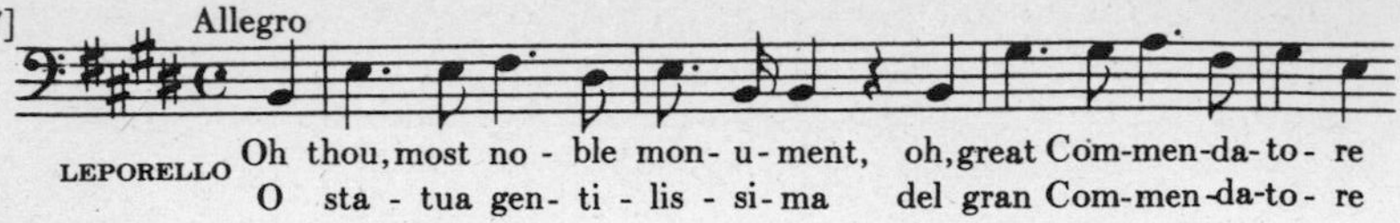
LEPORELLO
Oh thou, most no - ble mon - u - ment, oh, great Com-men-da-to - re
O sta - tua gen - ti - lis - si - ma del gran Com-men-da-to - re

[38] ARIA *NON MI DIR* (Anna)

Larghetto

Tell me not, oh thou be - lov'd one,
Non mi dir, bell' i - dol mi - o,

[39] Allegro vivace

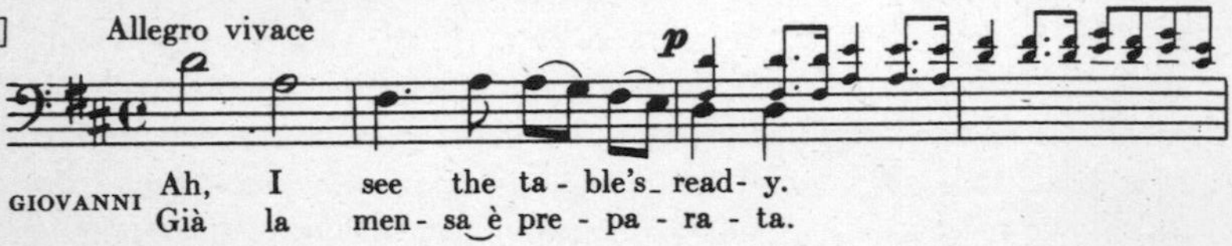
p
GIOVANNI
Ah, I see the ta - ble's ready - y.
Già la men - sa è pre - pa - ra - ta.

[40] Allegro assai

ELVIRA
Love guides me to you, love that's un - self - ish,
L'ul - ti - ma pro - va dell' a - mor mi - o,

[41] Allegro assai

p

[42] Allegro assai

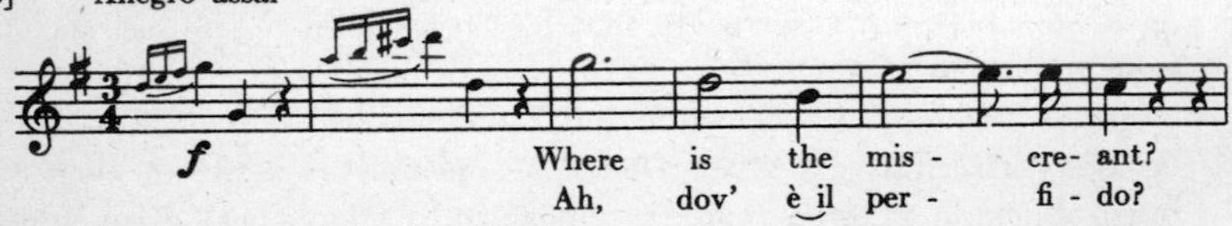
f
Where is the mis - cre - ant?
Ah, dov' è il per - fi - do?

prise of both men, the statue accepts with a loud *"Si"*: yes. They hurry away to prepare the feast.

Act II, Scene 4: Donna Anna, seated in her room, refutes Ottavio's contention that she keeps cruelly putting off their wedding (Recitative *Crudele? Ah no, mio bene:* "Beloved, don't think me cruel"; aria *Non mi dir:* "Tell me not") [38].

Act II, Scene 5: In a splendid hall in his castle Don Giovanni is served dinner by Leporello [39]. In excellent spirits, the Don orders his band to play. While they play three contemporary selections (contemporary with Mozart, that is, and one of them from Mozart's own *Figaro:* see *Le nozze di Figaro* [15]), the Don, displaying an excellent appetite, catches his servant in an attempt to stuff his own stomach while there is still some food left.

Donna Elvira enters in agitation and tries for the last time to make Don Giovanni relinquish his villainous ways [40], but he merely laughs at her [41]. Elvira leaves, but as she opens the door she utters a horrified scream, closes it again, and rushes off through a side entrance. Now Leporello goes to look outside, but he, too, quickly shuts the door and haltingly tells his master that the statue of the Commandant is approaching. Don Giovanni himself answers the ominous knock at the door. The marble statue enters [1], and while Leporello stammers hysterically as in a fever, the statue asks Don Giovanni to accept a return invitation for dinner [2]. Don Giovanni accepts with a handshake, only to find his hand clasped in an icy vise; yet he steadfastly refuses the command to repent. Suddenly the statue disappears. Flames rise from the ground and swallow Don Giovanni.

Donna Elvira, Donna Anna and Don Ottavio, Zerlina and Masetto (this episode is often omitted) enter in search of Don Giovanni [42] and are informed by Leporello of what has happened. Donna Anna promises to marry Ottavio after one year; Donna Elvira resolves to retire to a convent; Zerlina and Masetto decide to go quickly home for dinner. But presently all unite to proclaim the moral: "As one has lived, so shall he die."

THEMES

[1] Andante maestoso

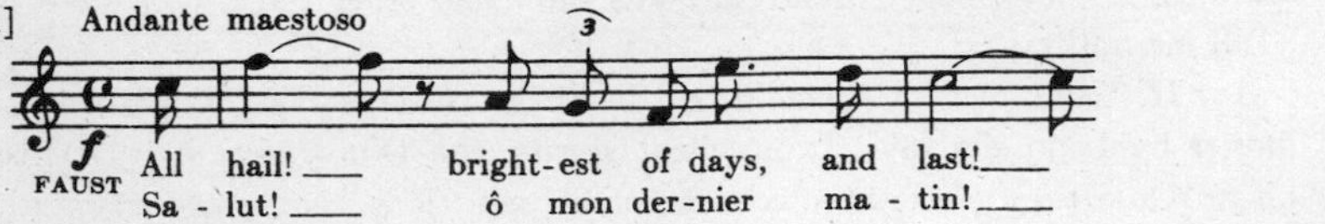
f
FAUST
All hail! ___ bright-est of days, and last! ___
Sa - lut! ___ ô mon der-nier ma - tin! ___

[2] Allegretto

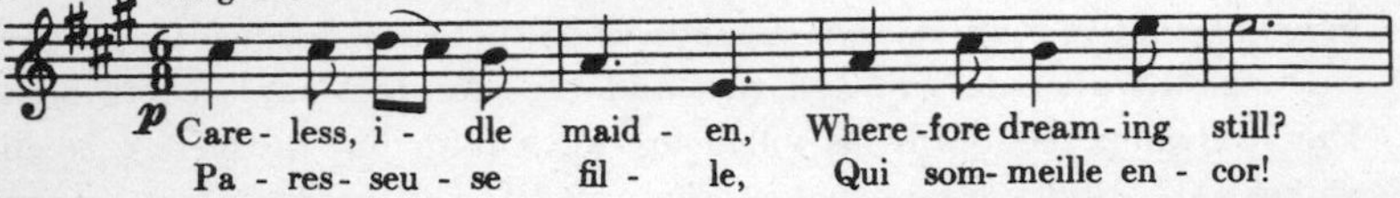
p
Care - less, i - dle maid - en, Where-fore dream-ing still?
Pa - res- seu - se fil - le, Qui som-meille en - cor!

[3] Allegretto

p
To fields the ear - ly morn - ing calls us, ___
Aux champs l'au - ro - re nous rap - pel - le, ___

[4] Allegro ben marcato

FAUST
Be mine ___ the de - light ___ Of Beau - ty's ca - ress - es,
A moi ___ les plai- sirs, ___ Les jeu - nes maî - tres- ses!

[5] THE SPINNING WHEEL

Andante

pp

[6] Allegretto

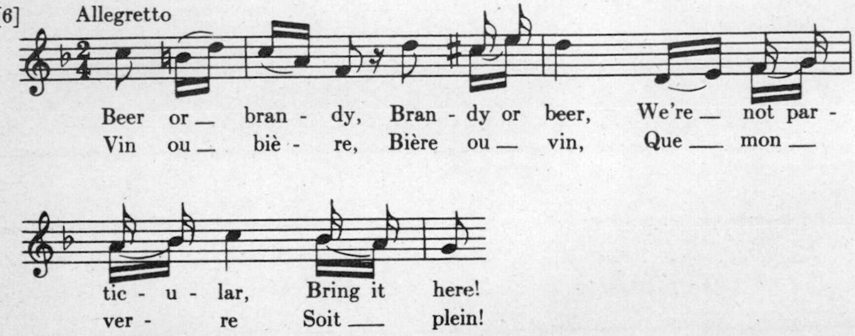
Beer or ___ bran - dy, Bran - dy or beer, We're ___ not par -
Vin ou ___ biè - re, Bière ou ___ vin, Que ___ mon ___
tic - u - lar, Bring it here!
ver - re Soit ___ plein!

Faust

Opera in five acts by Charles Gounod. Libretto by Jules Barbier and Michel Carré after Goethe. First performance: Paris, March 19, 1859.

Characters: DR. FAUST (tenor); MEPHISTOPHELES (bass-baritone); MARGUERITE (soprano); VALENTIN, her brother (baritone); MARTHE SCHWERLEIN, her neighbor (mezzo-soprano); SIEBEL, a youth (soprano or mezzo-soprano); WAGNER, a student (baritone).
Germany, during the sixteenth century.

Introduction: After a short, sober opening, the orchestra presents the main section of Valentin's aria [motive 7].

Act I: The aged Dr. Faust sits brooding at the desk in his somber study. He despairs of ever penetrating the secrets of nature. The approach of a new dawn [motive 2] only disgusts him. Rather than live another day, he fills a cup with poison and offers a last salute to the rising sun [1]. As he raises the goblet to his lips, the voices of happy maidens are heard as they sing a gay pastoral song to the morning [2]. Faust's hands begin to tremble. He hesitates. Now he hears the peasants on their way to the fields singing the praise of God [3]. At the sound of the Lord's name Faust, in a sudden outburst, curses faith, earthly pleasures long beyond his grasp, hope, and patience. He calls for Satan. Immediately the Evil Spirit appears, handsomely dressed as a nobleman. Gripped by sudden disgust, Faust tries to send him away, but is mockingly asked to reconsider. He is offered gold, glory, and power, but that is not enough for Faust: he wants youth and its joys [4]. Satan will be glad to oblige and to serve him on earth with whatever he desires if, in exchange, Faust will serve *him* "later." While the doctor hesitates, Mephistopheles magically calls up the vision of a lovely young maiden (Marguerite) at a spinning wheel [5, with love music from Act III 20, 21], and Faust eagerly signs the contract. Now, at Satan's bidding, he drains the goblet and is instantly transformed into a young man. Mephistopheles promises the joyous Faust to lead him to Marguerite (Duet) [4].

Act II: At the village fair at Leipzig all are in a happy mood [6] except

[7] ARIA *AVANT DE QUITTER CES LIEUX* (Valentin)

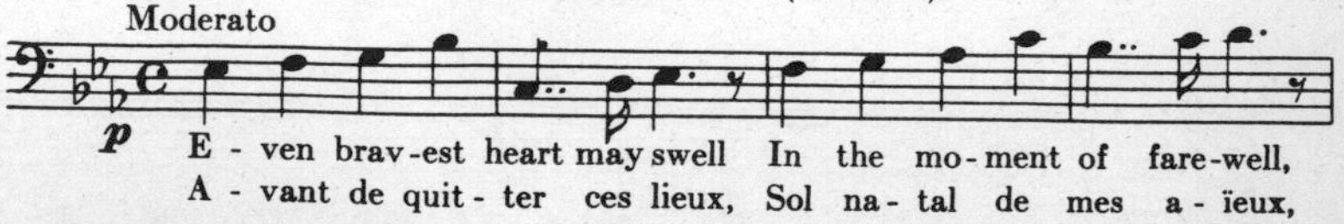
Moderato
p
E - ven brav-est heart may swell In the mo-ment of fare-well,
A - vant de quit - ter ces lieux, Sol na - tal de mes a - ïeux,

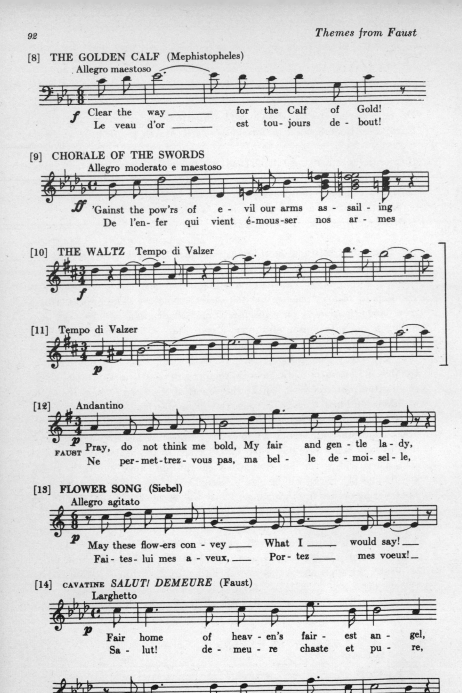

[8] THE GOLDEN CALF (Mephistopheles)

Allegro maestoso

Clear the way ______ for the Calf of Gold!
Le veau d'or ______ est tou- jours de - bout!

[9] CHORALE OF THE SWORDS

Allegro moderato e maestoso

'Gainst the pow'rs of e - vil our arms as - sail - ing
De l'en- fer qui vient é-mous-ser nos ar - mes

[10] THE WALTZ Tempo di Valzer

[11] Tempo di Valzer

[12] Andantino

FAUST Pray, do not think me bold, My fair and gen - tle la - dy,
Ne per-met-trez- vous pas, ma bel - le de - moi- sel - le,

[13] FLOWER SONG (Siebel)

Allegro agitato

May these flow-ers con - vey ____ What I ____ would say! ____
Fai- tes- lui mes a - veux, ____ Por- tez ____ mes voeux! ____

[14] CAVATINE *SALUT! DEMEURE* (Faust)

Larghetto

Fair home of heav - en's fair - est an - gel,
Sa - lut! de - meu - re chaste et pu - re,

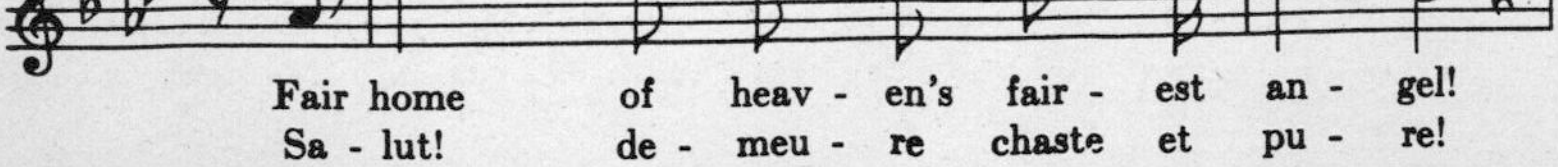

Fair home of heav - en's fair - est an - gel!
Sa - lut! de - meu - re chaste et pu - re!

Valentin, a young soldier, who is worried about his sister, Marguerite. He is going to war, and she will remain alone. Solemnly he prays to God that He may protect her in his absence (Aria *Avant de quitter ces lieux:* "Even bravest heart may swell") [7]. The soldiers start to drink and sing, but are interrupted by Mephistopheles, who suddenly appears and offers the "Rondo of the Golden Calf," a lively ditty about the power of gold, through which Satan rules a world of genuflecting followers (*Le veau d'or est toujours debout:* "Clear the way for the Calf of Gold!") [8]. Now Mephistopheles reads death in the hand of Valentin, and reveals to young Siebel that flowers plucked by his hand will wilt before he can offer them to Marguerite. With wine drawn mysteriously from a figure of Bacchus, Mephistopheles offers a toast to Valentin's lovely young sister. The outraged brother attacks him with drawn sword—but the sword breaks in mid-air. All the soldiers take their swords at the blades and, banning the sorcerer with the cross-shaped hilts (Chorale of the Swords *De l'enfer qui vient:* " 'Gainst the pow'rs of evil") [9], they leave the square.

While the burghers are dancing (The Waltz) [10, 11] and singing a gay chorus as a countermelody to the dance tune, Faust appears and asks Mephistopheles to guide him to Marguerite. She passes by, and Faust's offer to accompany her [12] is humbly if decisively refused. But Mephistopheles promises his aid. As he leaves with Faust, the townspeople continue their frolic [10, 11].

Act III: Young Siebel, arriving in the garden before Marguerite's house, asks the flowers to be his messengers of love (Couplet *Faites-lui mes aveux:* "May these flowers convey") [13], and starts to pluck one. It wilts—just as the sorcerer has predicted; but when Siebel dips his hand into holy water, the spell is broken. He gathers a bouquet and deposits it near Marguerite's door [13]. Faust and Mephistopheles arrive just in time to see Siebel leave, and Mephistopheles goes to produce a treasure that will outshine Siebel's flowers. Faust remains alone. He is overcome by emotion at the sight of the house of his beloved (Cavatine *Salut! Demeure chaste et pure:* "Fair home of heaven's fairest angel") [14]. Mephistopheles returns with a casket

[15] **THE KING OF THULE** (Marguerite)

[16] THE JEWEL SONG (Marguerite)

Allegretto
tr
p
f
Ah! ___ I see ___ beau-ty that is
Ah! ___ Je ris ___ de me voir si
smil - ing back at me!
belle en ce mi - roir,

Moderato
Ah, in - deed, I fear ___
Je ne vous crois pas ___
MARG.
MARTHE
p
Where - for do you fear? ___ Sir, you do not hear,
Lais - se - moi ton bras, ___ Vous n'en-ten-dez pas,
FAUST
MEPH.
Do not be se - vere
Ne m'ac - cu - sez pas

[17]

[18]

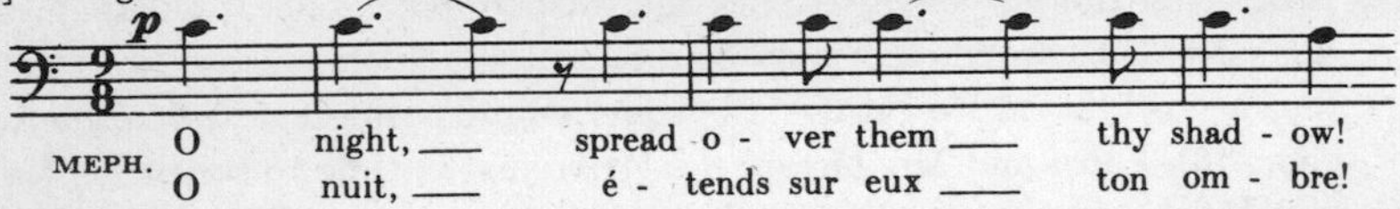
Adagio
p
MEPH.
O night, ___ spread o - ver them ___ thy shad - ow!
O nuit, ___ é - tends sur eux ___ ton om - bre!

[19] LOVE DUET (Faust, Marguerite)

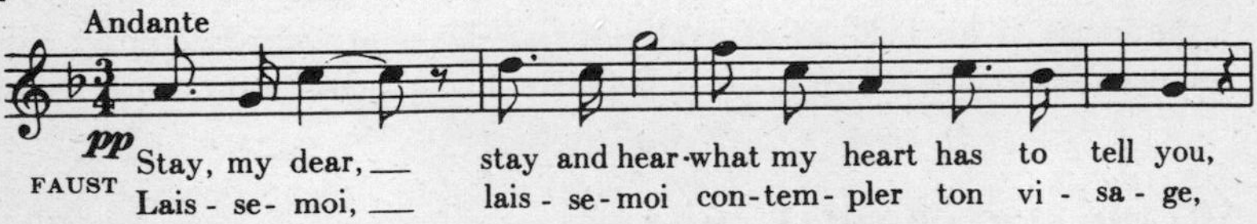
Andante
pp
FAUST
Stay, my dear, ___ stay and hear-what my heart has to tell you,
Lais - se- moi, ___ lais - se-moi con-tem- pler ton vi - sa - ge,

[20]

Andante
p
FAUST
O star of love, ___ se-rene and bright, ___ Shine down and
O nuit d'a - mour! ___ ciel - di - eux! ___ O dou-ces
hold ___ us in the still
flam - mes! Le bon - heur

and places it next to Siebel's flowers; then he and Faust quickly leave as Marguerite returns.

She is still wrapped in thoughts of the handsome nobleman whom she has encountered at the fair (Recitative *Je voudrais bien savoir:* "How I should like to know"). As she sits down at her spinning wheel, she sings the old ballad of the "King of Thule" (Chanson *Il était un roi de Thulé:* "Once a King in Thule of old") [15], interrupted occasionally by thoughts of Faust. She finishes her spinning, and on her way into the house she discovers Siebel's bouquet—and then the casket. In great excitement, she opens it and, giving vent to her joyous agitation in a succession of gay trills, runs, and roulades, she takes out the jewels and tries them on (The Jewel Song *Ah, je ris:* "Ah, I see") [16].

Marthe, her neighbor, comes by and gushingly admires the jewels. Now Mephistopheles enters with Faust, informing Marthe nonchalantly of the death of her husband. While Faust tenderly converses with Marguerite, Satan, with mock sincerity, makes love to the old neighbor [Quartet 17]. When he notices Faust and Marguerite strolling away, he escapes from the love-sick Marthe and solemnly invokes the powers of nature to cast a spell over the young couple so that they may succumb to their desires [18].

Faust and Marguerite, returning from their walk through the garden, feel the magic enchantment of night and love (Love Duet *Laisse-moi:* "Stay, my dear") [19]. Soon their lips are expressing their tender feelings [20, 21]. Nearly swooning, Marguerite asks Faust to leave, and eventually he bows before her innocence [14]. But as Marguerite flees into the house and Faust turns to go, Mephistopheles blocks his way. He mockingly per-

[21] LOVE DUET (Faust, Marguerite) *continued*

Andante
pp
MARG.
Take all my love, I lay my heart here be - fore you!
Je veux t'ai - mer et te ché - rir! Parle en - co - re!

[22]

Larghetto
8
pp dolcissimo

[23] ARIA *SI LE BONHEUR* (Siebel)

Andante
p
When all was young and pleas - ant May was bloom - ing,
Si le bon - heur à sou - ri - re t'in - vi - te,

[24] MARGUERITE'S PRAYER

Religioso

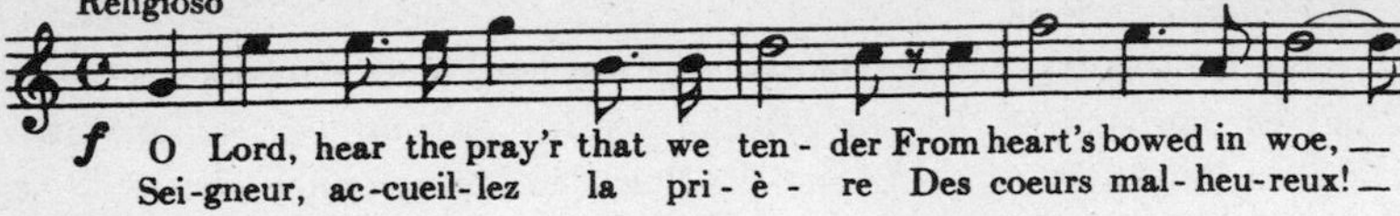
f
O Lord, hear the pray'r that we ten - der From heart's bowed in woe, —
Sei-gneur, ac-cueil-lez la pri - è - re Des coeurs mal-heu-reux! —

[25] SOLDIERS' CHORUS

Tempo marziale

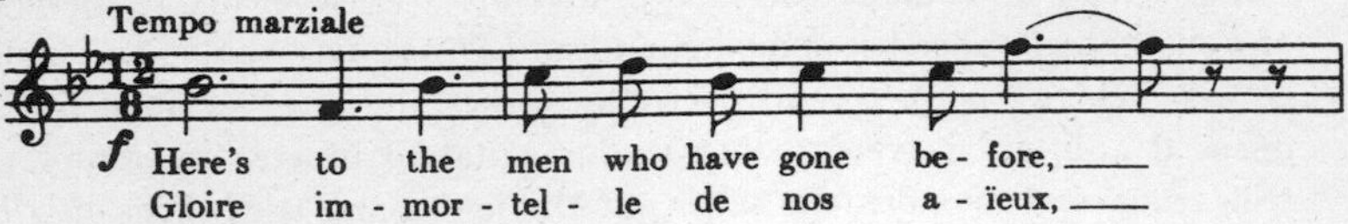
f
Here's to the men who have gone be - fore, —
Gloire im - mor - tel - le de nos a - ïeux, —

[26] MEPHISTOPHELES' SERENADE

Allegretto

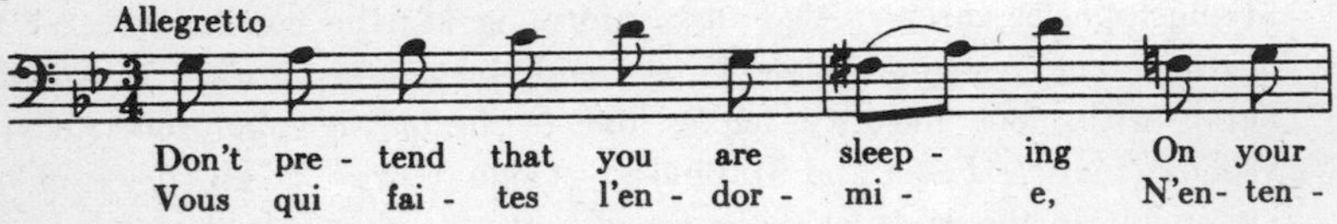
Don't pre - tend that you are sleep - ing On your
Vous qui fai - tes l'en - dor - mi - e, N'en - ten -

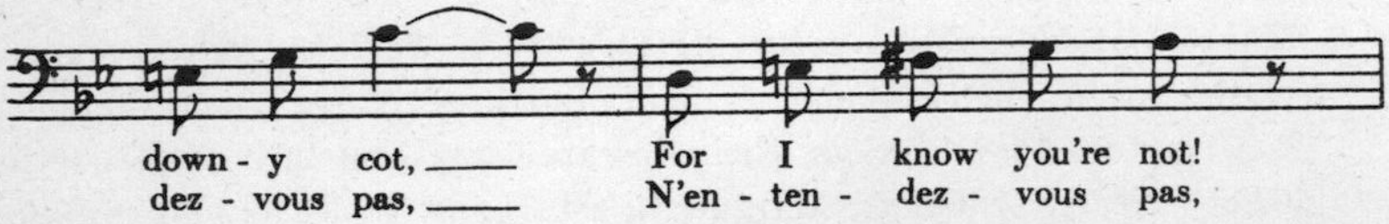
down - y cot, — For I know you're not!
dez - vous pas, — N'en - ten - dez - vous pas,

[27] BALLET

Allegretto, tempo di Valzer

p

[28] Adagio

p

[29] Allegretto

8
p

[30] Moderato maestoso

f

suades him to stay another moment and to observe Marguerite as she opens her window [22] and prays that her lover may soon return. Faust rushes into her arms [22 *ff*]—to the great satisfaction of Mephistopheles.

Act IV, Scene 1 (usually omitted): Marguerite is mocked by her former playmates for having been deserted by her gallant. Sadly she takes up her spinning and, to the accompaniment of the buzzing wheel [5], sings her sad aria *Il ne revient pas:* "He is not returning." Siebel comes to console her (Aria *Si le bonheur:* "When all was young") [23]. Marguerite thanks him for his compassion, and prepares to go to church to pray for Faust and for the child she is expecting.

Act IV, Scene 2: The severe sound of the organ fills the church as Marguerite kneels to pray. She hears the voice of Satan calling for the evil spirits, whose presence is depicted by furious passages in the orchestra. Recalling her days of innocence with unholy ridicule, the Devil tries to distract her from prayer. Adding to her soul's torment, the choir intones the "*Dies Irae,*" the chant of Judgment Day. Yet Marguerite manages to say a short prayer [24] before she hears the voice of the Evil One pronouncing her damnation. Thereupon, with a desperate outcry, she falls fainting to the ground.

Act IV, Scene 3: The soldiers are returning (Soldiers' Chorus) [25], and Valentin is informed by Siebel that all is not well with Marguerite. In terrible anger he enters his house. Mephistopheles comes with Faust and sings a mocking serenade in front of Marguerite's door (*Vous qui faites l'en-*

[31] BALLET *continued*

Moderato con moto

[32] Allegretto

[33] Allegro vivo

[34] Allegro non troppo

MARG.
Yes, — 'tis thou, I love thee, yes, 'tis thou, I love thee
Oui, — c'est toi, je t'ai - me, Oui, c'est toi, je t'ai- me

[35] TRIO *ANGES PURS* (Marguerite, Faust, Mephistopheles)

Moderato maestoso

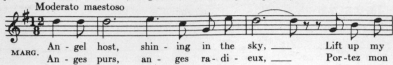

MARG.
An - gel host, shin - ing in the sky, — Lift up my
An - ges purs, an - ges ra- di - eux, — Por-tez mon

soul to God on high! —
âme au sein des cieux! —

[36] EASTER CHORALE

Moderato maestoso

ff
Christ is a - ris'n a - gain! —
Christ est re - sus - ci - té! —

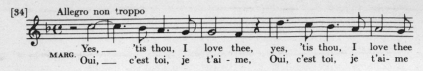

dormie: "Don't pretend that you are sleeping") [26]. Outraged, Valentin comes from the house and demands satisfaction. He duels with Faust, who transfixes him as Mephistopheles deflects Valentin's blade.

As the murderers flee, an excited crowd gathers around the dying Valentin. When Marguerite approaches, he violently denounces her. Deaf to her pleading, he curses her and bravely dies.

Act V, Scene 1 (usually omitted): Faust and Mephistopheles visit the Brocken Mountain for the Walpurgis Night, the Witches' Sabbath. There they meet some of history's most talked-about women (Ballet) [27, 28, 29, 30, 31, 32, 33]. A vision of Marguerite with a red line around her neck compels Faust to ask Mephistopheles that they return to her.

Act V, Scene 2: With the help of Mephistopheles, Faust gains entry to Marguerite's prison cell to free her on the eve of her execution. The half-crazed murderess of her child joyously recognizes her lover's voice. They exult in their reunion [34], and Marguerite recalls their first encounter at the fair [11, 12] and their tender meetings in the garden [21]. But she is deaf to his entreaties that she fly with him, and when the Devil comes to urge them to hurry, Marguerite is overcome with horror. Seeking refuge with the powers of heaven (Trio *Anges purs, anges radieux:* "Angel host shining in the sky") [35], she renounces Faust and dies.

Mephistopheles dramatically exclaims: "She is judged!" but voices from on high proclaim her "Saved" [22], and to the sound of the heavenly hosts singing "Christ is risen" [36] Marguerite is seen ascending to heaven.

THEMES

[1] THE GRAIL

Adagio
a
p
see 12

[2] THE KING'S TRUMPETS

Allegro non troppo
3
f

[3] THE KING'S ADDRESS

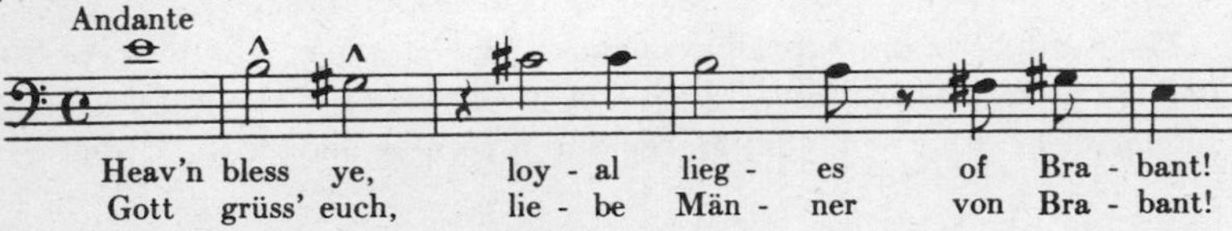
Andante
Heav'n bless ye, loy - al lieg - es of Bra - bant!
Gott grüss' euch, lie - be Män - ner von Bra - bant!

[4]

Un poco lento
f
a
b

[5] FRIEDRICH'S NARRATION

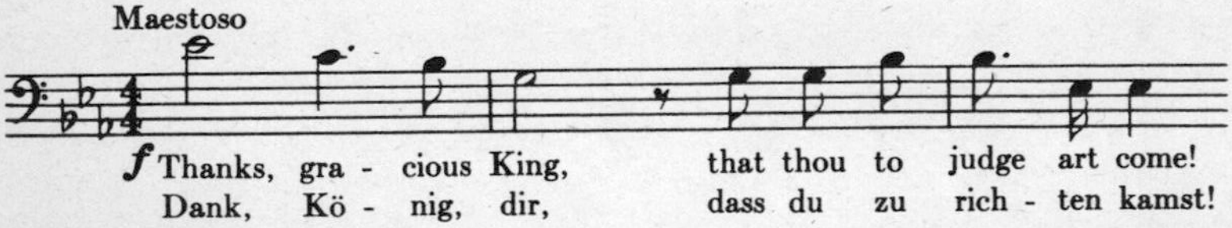
Maestoso
f Thanks, gra - cious King, that thou to judge art come!
Dank, Kö - nig, dir, dass du zu rich - ten kamst!

[6]

Andante moderato
p

[7] LOHENGRIN, THE DELIVERER

see 12
Andante moderato dolcissimo

Lohengrin

Opera in three acts by Richard Wagner. Libretto by the composer. First performance: Weimar, August 28, 1850.

Characters: LOHENGRIN (tenor); ELSA VON BRABANT (soprano); FRIEDRICH VON TELRAMUND (baritone); ORTRUD, a heathen sorceress, his wife (soprano or mezzo-soprano); KING HENRY THE FOWLER (bass); THE HERALD (bass). *Antwerp, in the first half of the tenth century.*

Prelude to Act I: As if the Holy Grail were descending from heaven, appearing to mortals in all its radiance, and slowly vanishing again, motive [1] starts *pianissimo* in the highest registers of the violins, builds up to a *forte* in the brasses, and ends the Prelude again *pianissimo* in the regions where it started.

Act I: In a grove by the banks of the Scheldt River near Antwerp, on a throne under the Judgment Oak, sits King Henry, surrounded by his Saxon nobles. The trumpets sound the King's call [2], and his herald bids the assembled Brabantians listen to their sovereign. The King greets them (The King's Address *Gott grüss' euch:* "Heav'n bless ye") [3] and asks them to join him in the imminent fighting against the Hungarians. Then he calls on Count von Telramund to explain to him the dissension in Brabant. The Count steps forward [4a] and relates (Friedrich's Narration *Dank, König, dir:* "Thanks, gracious King") [5] how the late Duke had assigned to him the guardianship of his children, Elsa and Gottfried, and how the heir had disappeared while walking one day in the woods with his sister. Telramund goes on to say that Elsa returned alone and, under his suspicious inquiry, made a full confession. Thereupon he renounced the right to her hand and married Ortrud, a princess of Friesland, who at this introduction comes forward and bows before the King. Telramund now charges Elsa with fratricide [4ab] and asks to be given sovereignty over Brabant. When all express horror at his accusation, he reveals his suspicion that Elsa, who had rejected him, has a secret lover with whom, having removed her brother, she hopes to rule over the land.

The King commands that Elsa be called. He hangs up his shield on the oak [2], indicating that he will hold court, and all the men bare their swords. Elsa comes [6, 7], appearing to everyone the very image of purity and innocence. Her thoughts seem to be far away, but eventually she re-

[8] **ELSA'S DREAM**

Andante

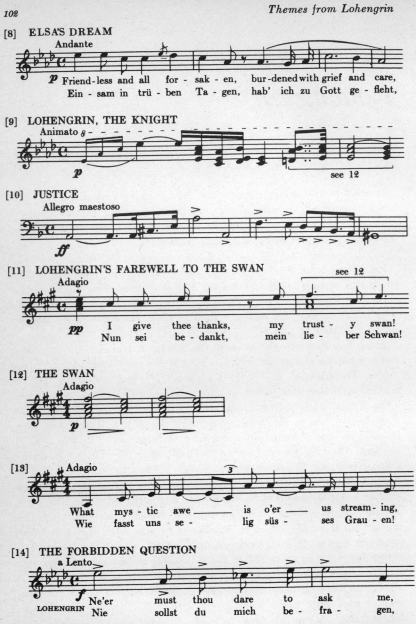

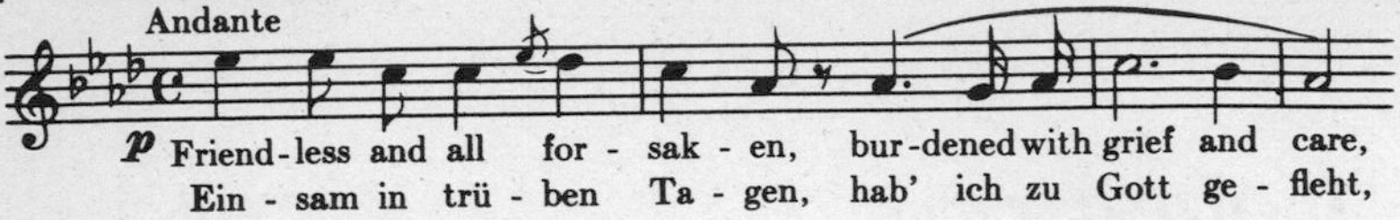
p
Friend-less and all for - sak - en, bur-dened with grief and care,
Ein - sam in trü - ben Ta - gen, hab' ich zu Gott ge - fleht,

[9] **LOHENGRIN, THE KNIGHT**

Animato

8
p
see 12

[10] **JUSTICE**

Allegro maestoso

ff

[11] **LOHENGRIN'S FAREWELL TO THE SWAN**

Adagio

see 12
pp
I give thee thanks, my trust - y swan!
Nun sei be - dankt, mein lie - ber Schwan!

[12] **THE SWAN**

Adagio

p

[13] Adagio

3
What mys - tic awe ___ is o'er ___ us stream - ing,
Wie fasst uns - se - lig süs - ses Grau - en!

[14] **THE FORBIDDEN QUESTION**

a Lento

f
LOHENGRIN
Ne'er must thou dare to ask me,
Nie sollst du mich be - fra - gen,

b Lento

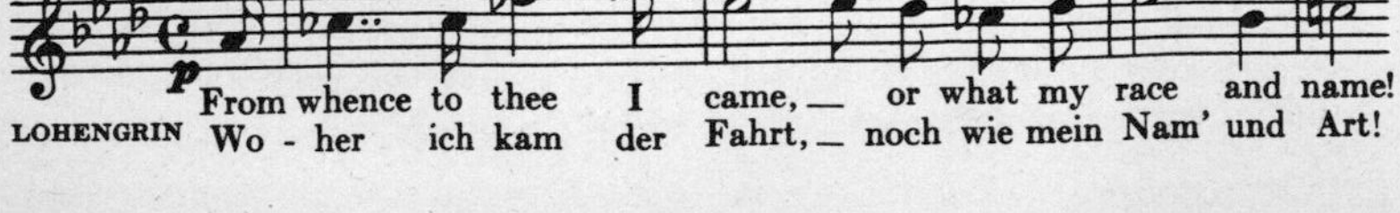
p
LOHENGRIN
From whence to thee I came, ___ or what my race and name!
Wo - her ich kam der Fahrt, ___ noch wie mein Nam' und Art!

plies to the King's gentle urging (Elsa's Dream *Einsam in trüben Tagen:* "Friendless and all forsaken") [8]: One day as she was praying to the Lord, one of her sighs seemed to be carried far away through the air. Then, as if in a trance, she saw a most noble knight [1, 9] a golden horn at his side and leaning on his sword, approach her from the air to comfort her [7]. This knight shall be her defender.

To the King's doubts of Elsa's guilt, Friedrich answers that producing his witness would be beneath his dignity, and the King decides that right shall be determined through mortal combat [10] by which God will make His judgment known. Elsa, asked by the King whom she will choose to fight for her cause, declares that she will wait for her knight [7], and offers him her lands and her hand. The herald calls twice for Elsa's defender to appear, but no one answers. Elsa sinks to her knees and prays God to send her defender [7]. Suddenly the men near the river shout in excitement that they see a knight [9] approaching on the river in a boat drawn by a swan. All realize that they are witnessing a miracle and greet the knight with bared heads. The knight, who has been standing motionless, a golden horn at his side, and leaning on his sword, now steps from the boat and turns to the swan [1a] to bid it a tender farewell (Farewell to the Swan *Nun sei bedankt:* "I give thee thanks") [11]. The swan slowly turns back [12] and Lohengrin * looks after it while all admire the knight's noble and handsome appearance [13]. Now he greets the King and declares that he has been sent [1a] to fight for a maiden in distress. Turning toward Elsa, he asks if she wants to put her fate in his hands and be his wife. She humbly offers her life to him [7]. Solemnly, he elicits her promise never to ask for his origin or name [14ab]. All watch, deeply moved [13], as he lovingly embraces her.

Now Lohengrin declares Elsa innocent and demands combat. The knights urge Telramund to desist, but he violently affirms the truth of his accusation and his hope for victory. Three Saxon and three Brabantian knights stake out the combat area, the herald exhorts all not to interfere in the battle [10], and the King prays (The King's Prayer *Mein Herr und Gott:* "Oh Lord and God") [15] that the Lord grant victory to the defender of truth [16]. All join his prayer [16] except Ortrud, who relies on Friedrich's strength and skill. The trumpets sound [2], the King strikes his shield three times with his sword, and the combat begins [10]. Soon Friedrich falls under a powerful blow from the unknown knight, but Lohengrin spares his life. Elsa sinks jubilantly on his breast [17] and there is general rejoicing [9, 17]. Only the perplexed Ortrud asks herself whether her power has come to an end before this mysterious knight.

Act II: Friedrich and Ortrud, dressed in paupers' clothes, are sitting on the steps of the cathedral, which faces the women's quarters of the palace. Motionless, they stare into the night, thinking somber thoughts [18, 19, 14].

* The knight's name is supplied here for convenience, though in the opera it is not revealed until the final scene.

[15] THE KING'S PRAYER

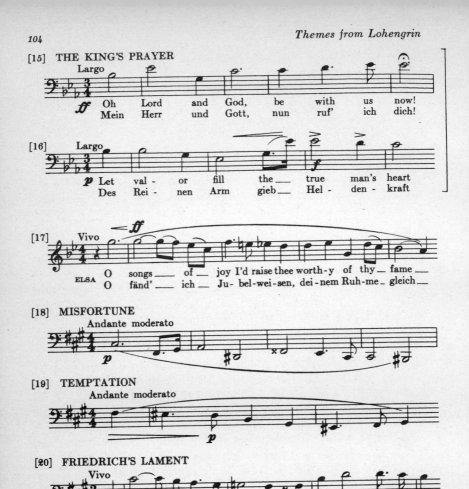

Largo
ff
Oh Lord and God, be with us now!
Mein Herr und Gott, nun ruf' ich dich!

[16]

Largo
p
f
Let val - or fill the __ true man's heart
Des Rei - nen Arm gieb __ Hel - den - kraft

[17]

Vivo
ff
ELSA
O songs __ of __ joy I'd raise thee worth-y of thy _ fame __
O fänd' __ ich __ Ju- bel-wei-sen, dei-nem Ruh-me _ gleich __

[18] MISFORTUNE

Andante moderato
p

[19] TEMPTATION

Andante moderato
p

[20] FRIEDRICH'S LAMENT

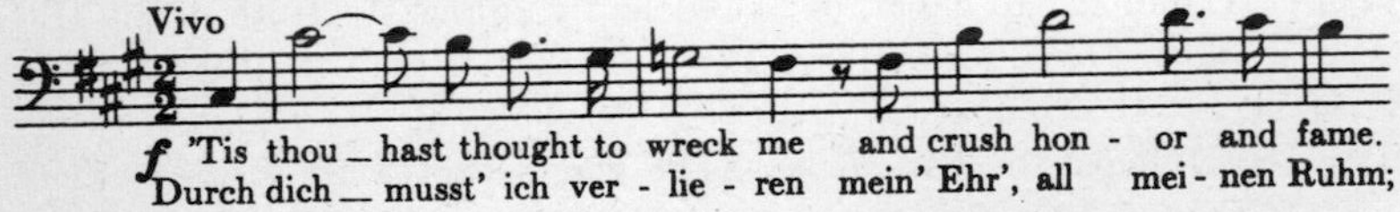
Vivo
f
'Tis thou _ hast thought to wreck me and crush hon - or and fame.
Durch dich _ musst' ich ver - lie - ren mein' Ehr', all mei - nen Ruhm;

[21] THE VOW OF REVENGE (Ortrud, Friedrich)

Moderato
p
ff
Dread pow'rs of ven - geance, I con - jure thee
Der Ra - che Werk sei nun be - schwo - ren

[22]

Andante moderato
p

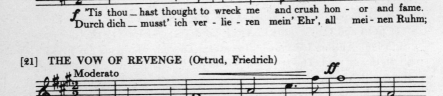

A fanfare and festive music [7] resound from within the men's quarters at the far end of the square, and Friedrich quickly rises to leave the country before daybreak, for, defeated by God's will in the duel, he is proscribed and banished. When Ortrud declares that she cannot leave while their enemies are joyous and triumphant, he furiously inveighs against her and laments the loss of his honor (Friedrich's Lament *Durch dich musst' ich verlieren:* " 'Tis thou hast thought to wreck me") [20], for was it not she who swore to him that she had observed Elsa drowning her brother in the lake? Ortrud, denying that she lied, also denies that her husband was beaten through the power of God, and claims instead [18, 19] that Friedrich's opponent deceived the court through the use of magic. This magic, she adds, can be dispelled if the stranger is forced to disclose his name and descent [14a]. Since apparently only Elsa has the power to force the knight to do so [18]—for he had demanded her vow that she would never inquire about his origin—Elsa must be slyly induced [19] to put the question to the stranger. Ortrud, well versed in magic arts, also claims that one has but to draw a drop of blood from a human being protected by magic powers to render those powers nil; this might be an alternate means for them to try. The thought that he may have been tricked into defeat by magic powers provokes an outburst of most bitter despair from Telramund, and, though angrily warning his wife not to deceive him again, he is persuaded to sit down next to her [18] and to join her in a vow of vengeance [21].

When Elsa appears on the balcony of the women's quarters [22] to thank the breezes for bringing her husband to her (Aria *Euch Lüften, die mein Klagen:* "Ye wand'ring breezes heard me") [23], Ortrud in a whisper, bids Friedrich hide. Calling to Elsa in feigned humbleness, she describes her "undeserved" fate in such mournful sounds [24] that Elsa asks her to wait until she comes down to admit her. Hardly has Elsa disappeared from the balcony when Ortrud triumphantly addresses her heathen gods and calls on them to favor her revenge (Aria *Entweihte Götter:* "Assist my vengeance") [25].

Elsa comes from the house and promises Ortrud, who kneels servilely at her feet, to ask her husband's mercy for Telramund. Ortrud thanks her by warning her of the future [19], which seems ominous to her, considering the fact that Elsa knows nothing about her betrothed [14ab]. However, Elsa's faith remains unshaken, and her superior confidence only spurs Ortrud's determination (Duet) [26]. As the women enter the house [26], Friedrich looks after them [18], hoping for the downfall of those who have caused his own ruin.

Trumpets from the towers announce the arrival of the day, and Friedrich finds a niche near the portal of the cathedral to hide him from view. The King's trumpets appear, and their call [2] assembles the inhabitants of the castle [27]. Again the trumpets sound [2], and the herald appears. He proclaims Telramund's banishment and announces, to the joyful acclaim of

[23] ARIA *EUCH LUEFTEN* (Elsa)

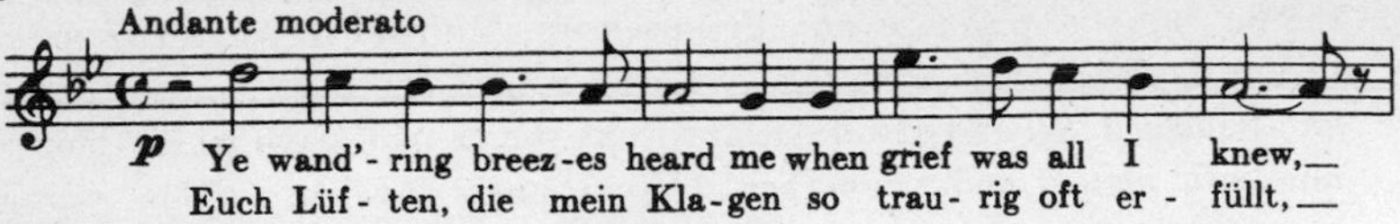
Andante moderato
p
Ye wand'-ring breez-es heard me when grief was all I knew,
Euch Lüf-ten, die mein Kla-gen so trau-rig oft er-füllt,

[24]

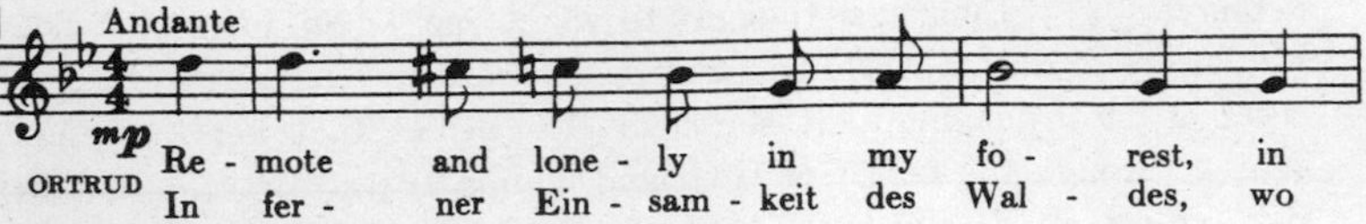
Andante
mp
ORTRUD
Re-mote and lone-ly in my fo-rest, in
In fer-ner Ein-sam-keit des Wal-des, wo

peace and qui-et-ude I dwelt,
still und fried-sam ich ge-lebt,

[25] ARIA *ENTWEIHTE GOETTER* (Ortrud)

Vivacissimo
f
As-sist my ven-geance, de-i-ties for-sa-ken!
Ent-weih-te Göt-ter! Helft jetzt mei-ner Ra-che!

[26] ELSA'S DEVOTION TO LOHENGRIN

Moderato
p

[27]

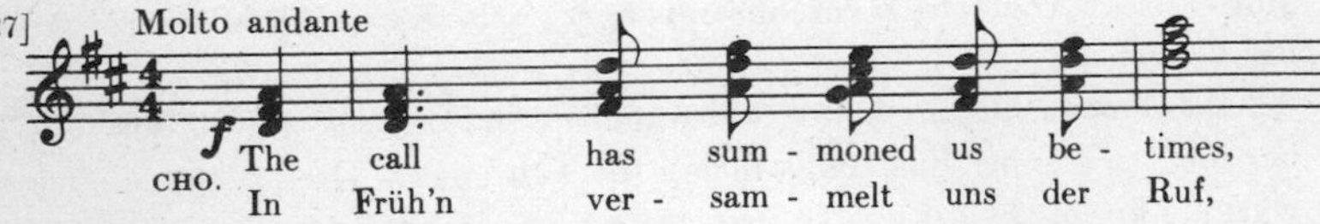
Molto andante
f
CHO.
The call has sum-moned us be-times,
In Früh'n ver-sam-melt uns der Ruf,

[28] THE BRIDAL PROCESSION

Largo
p

the people, the appointment of the God-sent stranger as ruler of Brabant. He furthermore brings from the new "Guardian of Brabant" an invitation to celebrate his wedding with him this day, and the call to follow him the next morning on the road to glory in the army of the King. All are eager for battle under such leadership [9]. Only four of Friedrich's former knights, who have gathered away from the crowd, question the new Duke's authority. Friedrich steps among them and informs them that he will accuse the stranger of sorcery, but they quickly rush him back into hiding.

Announced by four pages, the cortege of the bride moves in solemn procession [28] from the women's quarters around the square to the cathedral, and Elsa's appearance [22] is warmly greeted by all. Suddenly, as she is about to enter the cathedral, Ortrud, who has been walking among Elsa's attendants, steps in front of her, demanding precedence. Although her husband has been banished in consequence of what Ortrud denounces as a false judgment, his name was well known and honored in the land; but who knows about the nobility of Elsa's knight? Who knows whence he came, she asks, or when he may leave again? All present agree with Elsa that the nobility of her betrothed is beyond question, yet all listen attentively to Ortrud when she dares Elsa to dispel any doubt by asking the knight the source of his magic power. Just then the King [2], Lohengrin [9], and the Saxon knights appear in solemn procession from the men's quarters. Elsa explains Ortrud's presence and reports her accusations [18], and Lohengrin, promising defeat to Ortrud, proceeds with Elsa toward the church.

Now Friedrich steps forward and accuses Lohengrin of sorcery [10]. He demands an answer to the question which, by rights, should have been put to the stranger before the duel [10]: what is his name, race, rank? Lohengrin merely recalls his victory before God. He need not answer Telramund or anybody else, except Elsa if she wishes to question him [19, 14]. King and nobles gather around Lohengrin expressing their confidence. Elsa, left alone for a moment, is approached by Telramund. He will be close by at night, he promises, and at Elsa's call he can easily come and inflict an ever so slight wound upon her husband. This, he claims, would break the spell; she would know who he was, and he would never leave her [19]. Their whispered conversation is surprised by Lohengrin, who with thunderous voice commands the banned couple to leave his sight forever. Now he asks Elsa once more if doubt has entered her heart, and with a heroic effort to master her feelings she once more swears confidence. Lohengrin, amid the acclaim of her people, guides Elsa toward the King [28]. To the sound of the organ from the church and of gay fanfares from the towers, they ascend the cathedral steps. Once more Elsa glimpses Ortrud's menacing glance [14a] before the assembly enters the cathedral for the wedding ceremony.

Prelude to Act III: Exuberant music [29, 30] describes the wedding feast

[29] PRELUDE TO ACT III

Vivacissimo

[30]

Vivacissimo

[31]

Vivacissimo

[32] THE WEDDING MARCH

Andante
CHO.
Faith - ful and true, we lead ye forth,
Treu - lich ge - führt zie - het da - hin,
Where love tri - umph - ant shall crown ye with joy
wo euch der Se - gen der Lie - be be - wahr'!

[33]

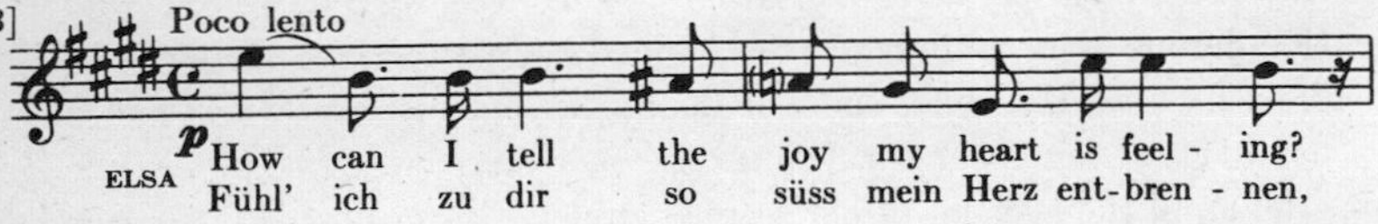
Poco lento
ELSA
How can I tell the joy my heart is feel - ing?
Fühl' ich zu dir so süss mein Herz ent-bren - nen,

[34] ARIA *ATHMEST DU NICHT* (Lohengrin)

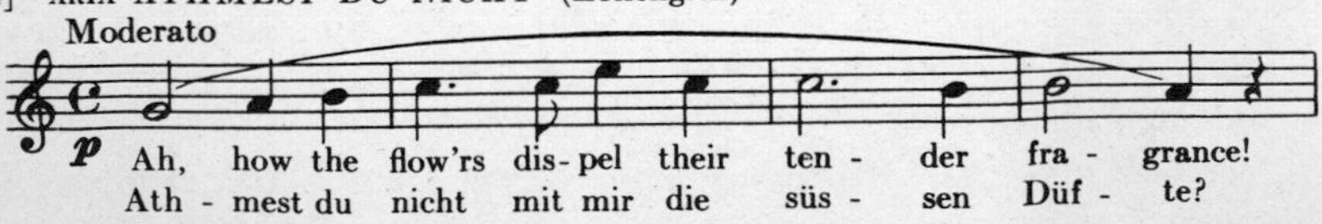
Moderato
Ah, how the flow'rs dis-pel their ten - der fra - grance!
Ath - mest du nicht mit mir die süs - sen Düf - te?

and its jubilant atmosphere, which, however, does not seem quite devoid of more gentle aspects [31]. [29] and [30] return and, subsiding, give way to the wedding march [32].

Act III, Scene 1: Lohengrin, guided by the King and the nobles, and Elsa, accompanied by the ladies, are conducted into the bridal chamber [32]. When the couple has met in the center of the room, the pages relieve them of their heavy ceremonial robes and the King gives them his silent blessing. Now the processions of nobles and ladies leave, their voices gradually disappearing in the distance [32].

Tenderly Lohengrin addresses his bride, and she happily confesses her love [33], which prompts a similar avowal from him [33]. He recalls the moment when he first saw her, and Elsa describes the delight she felt when he appeared in the boat just as she had seen him in her dream [9]. However, soon her longing to know his identity creeps into the conversation. At first Lohengrin asks her to accept the mystery surrounding him as one accepts the mysteries of nature, as one enjoys the fragrant breezes now blowing toward them from the garden (Aria *Athmest du nicht:* "Ah, how the flow'rs") [34], but her urge to know his secret [14a] becomes ever stronger. In vain Lohengrin reminds her of her vow (Aria *Höchstes Vertrau'n:* "Greatest of trust") [35], assures her of his love, and admonishes her to banish doubt [18, 14a]. He even admits that he is not of low origin, but of highest and noblest birth. Elsa, fearful that he may one day leave her [19], already sees in her mind's eyes the swan appearing [12] to take him away. Although Lohengrin sternly tries once more to dissuade her [14a], her hysterical fear can no longer be repressed, and she asks him the fateful question.

Just then Friedrich and his four knights rush in with drawn swords, but Lohengrin quickly takes the sword that Elsa holds out to him and with one mighty stroke fells Telramund. Telramund's companions fall on their knees before Lohengrin. He, after supporting the swooning Elsa to the couch [33], orders Telramund's men to bring their leader's body before the King's court [10]. When they have gone with their burden [18], Lohengrin rings for Elsa's maids and bids them lead her before the King and his court, where he will answer the question about his origin [14ba].

Scenic Transformation: For an instant the curtain closes, and fanfares, [1a] among them, are heard from the distance.

Act III, Scene 2: Into the grove by the bank of the Scheldt River descend the Brabantian counts with their followers [36], fully armed and ready to join the King's forces. The King arrives [2, 36] and happily greets the mighty assembly, but a hush falls over the grove when Telramund's men place a bier with a covered body before the King. The feeling of impending calamity is deepened when Elsa advances [14ab, 19] pale and with uncertain steps, unable to return the King's friendly greeting [7 minor].

Now Lohengrin arrives [9], warmly welcomed by King and warriors, but their joy quickly turns to astonishment when he reveals that he cannot

[35]

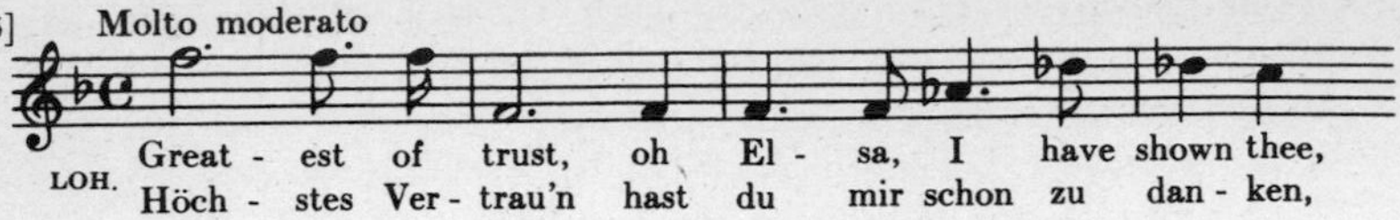
Molto moderato
LOH.
Great - est of trust, oh El - sa, I have shown thee,
Höch - stes Ver - trau'n hast du mir schon zu dan - ken,

[36]

Vivace
ff
see 13

[37] LOHENGRIN'S NARRATIVE

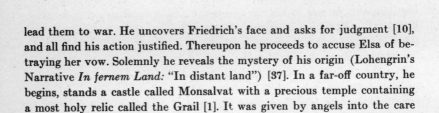

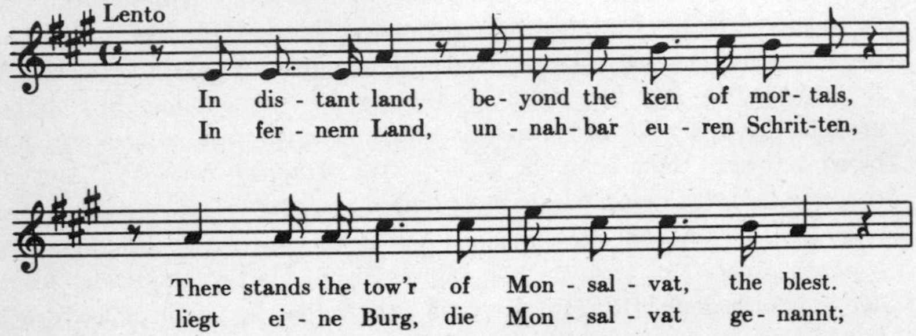
Lento
In dis - tant land, be - yond the ken of mor - tals,
In fer - nem Land, un - nah - bar eu - ren Schrit-ten,
There stands the tow'r of Mon - sal - vat, the blest.
liegt ei - ne Burg, die Mon - sal - vat ge - nannt;

lead them to war. He uncovers Friedrich's face and asks for judgment [10], and all find his action justified. Thereupon he proceeds to accuse Elsa of betraying her vow. Solemnly he reveals the mystery of his origin (Lohengrin's Narrative *In fernem Land:* "In distant land") [37]. In a far-off country, he begins, stands a castle called Monsalvat with a precious temple containing a most holy relic called the Grail [1]. It was given by angels into the care of the purest among men, and its powers are renewed yearly by a dove descending from heaven. The servants of the Grail are endowed with invincibility, which they retain on their journeys to succour the virtuous, but only as long as they remain unrecognized. When his holy nature is revealed, the Grail's messenger can no longer remain with the laymen, but must return. He himself has been sent by the Grail; he is the son of Parsival, King of the Grail, and his name is Lohengrin [9].

Lohengrin approaches Elsa and gently reproaches her for destroying their happiness, for now he must leave. This announcement is greeted by all with shouts of woe, and Elsa frantically begs Lohengrin to remain, if only to witness her repentance. In vain the knights entreat him to lead them into battle, but he foretells victory for the King and eternal freedom from Eastern domination for Germany.

Already the swan has appeared on the river [9 minor]. Filled with sorrow, Lohengrin turns toward it [12]. He would have been happier to see it in a different shape, he sighs, and, turning to Elsa, he reveals that her brother is alive and would have returned after only one year of their marriage. For him he leaves his horn, sword, and ring, whereupon he kisses Elsa passionately and goes toward the boat.

Ortrud arrives triumphantly and tells Elsa that the swan is none other than the Duke of Brabant, over whom she has cast a spell with the help of the gods who have been cast aside by the Brabantians. Hearing this, Lohengrin sinks in prayer on his knees [1]. When the white dove of the Grail appears, Lohengrin unties the swan's chain, and as the swan submerges, Gottfried, the young Duke of Brabant, appears in its place. Ortrud collapses with a desperate outcry. Gottfried bows before the King and greets Elsa. Lohengrin [9] meanwhile has stepped into the boat, which is immediately pulled away by the dove. When Elsa sees Lohengrin reappearing far away beyond the bend of the river, sadly leaning on his shield [9 minor], she sinks lifeless into her brother's arms. Lohengrin slowly disappears in the distance [1a].

THEMES

[1]

Allegro giusto
NORM.
Let us roam thro' these ru - ins de - sert - ed,
Per - cor - re - te le spiag - ge vi - ci - ne,
GUARDS
Let us roam ___ thro' these ru - ins de - sert - ed,
Per - cor - ria - - mo le spiag - ge vi - ci - ne,

[2] ARIA *CRUDA, FUNESTA SMANIA* (Enrico)

Larghetto
Tor - ments of hate and ven-geance,_ now in my heart a - wa - ken,
Cru - da, fu - ne - sta sma-nia ___ tu m'hai sve-glia-to in pet - to!

[3]

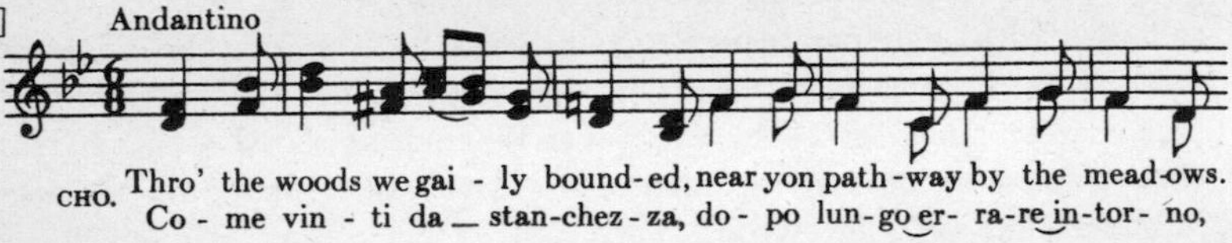
Andantino
CHO.
Thro' the woods we gai - ly bound-ed, near yon path-way by the mead-ows.
Co - me vin - ti da _ stan-chez-za, do - po lun-go er- ra-re in-tor- no,

[4]

Allegro moderato
ENRICO
If thou plead'st _ for _ her _ I scorn thee, Cast _ thee from me, then let me warn thee,
La pie- ta - de in _ suo _ fa - vo - re Mi - ti sen - si in - van mi det - ta,

[5] ARIA *REGNAVA NEL SILENZIO* (Lucia)

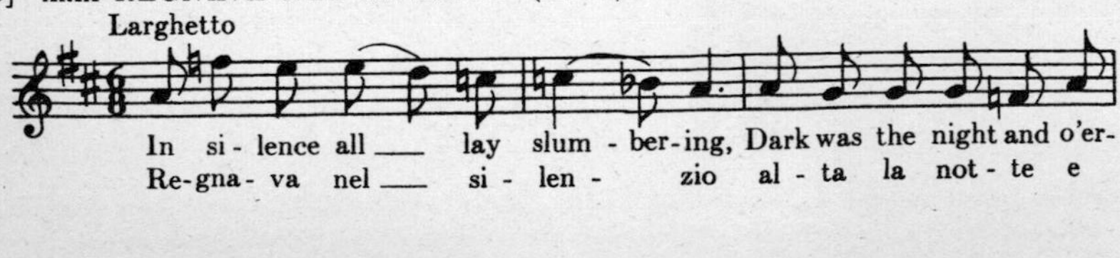
Larghetto
In si - lence all ___ lay slum - ber-ing, Dark was the night and o'er-
Re-gna - va nel ___ si - len - zio al - ta la not - te e

Lucia di Lammermoor

Opera in three acts by Gaetano Donizetti. Libretto by Salvatore Cammarano after Sir Walter Scott's novel *The Bride of Lammermoor*. First performance: Naples, September 26, 1835.

Characters: LORD ENRICO ASHTON (baritone); LUCIA, his sister (soprano); SIR EDGARDO DI RAVENSWOOD (tenor); LORD ARTURO BUCKLAW (tenor); RAIMONDO BIDEBENT, cleric, Lucia's tutor (bass); ALISA, Lucia's companion (mezzo-soprano); NORMANNO, Captain of the Guard (tenor).
Scotland, in the seventeenth century.

Prelude: The opera begins with a short, somber introduction; then, with the start of a lively hunting tune [motive 1] the curtain is raised.

Act I, Scene 1: On the grounds near the castle of Ravenswood, which now belongs to Lord Enrico Ashton, a group of his men are ordered by Normanno, Captain of the Guard, to cover the area [1] in search of the man who, it is said, secretly meets Lucia. Normanno tells Enrico that somebody recently has saved Lucia from a wild bull and since then has been seeing her daily, and he suspects that it is Edgardo, the mortal enemy of the Ashton family. Enrico is enraged (Aria *Cruda, funesta smania:* "Torments of hate and vengeance") [2]. When his men return and report [3] that they have indeed seen Edgardo but that he has fled, Enrico, despite Bidebent's intercession, swears revenge (Cabaletta *La pietade in suo favore:* "If thou plead'st for her, I scorn thee") [4].

Act I, Scene 2: Lucia, with her companion Alisa, enters the gardens of the castle. She is expecting to meet Edgardo so that she can warn him of her brother's anger. As they approach a fountain Lucia suddenly stops in horror and tells her companion about a ghostly apparition that has recently

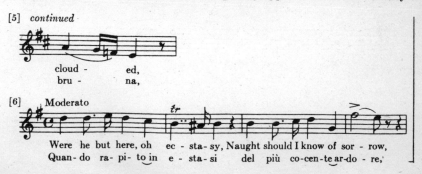

[5] *continued*

cloud - ed,
bru - na,

[6]

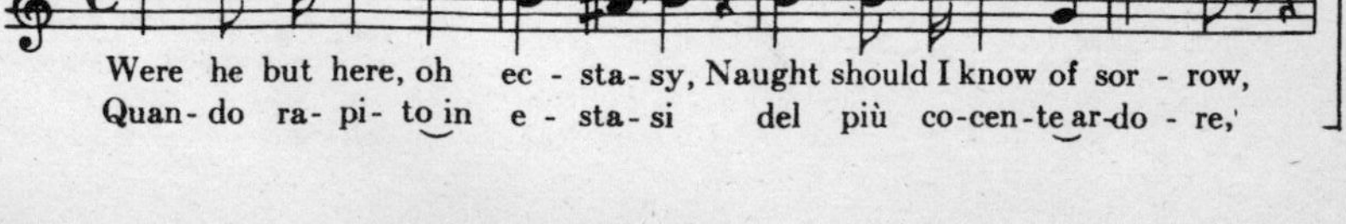
Moderato
tr
Were he but here, oh ec - sta- sy, Naught should I know of sor - row,
Quan- do ra- pi- to in e - sta- si del più co-cen-te ar-do - re,'

[7] Larghetto

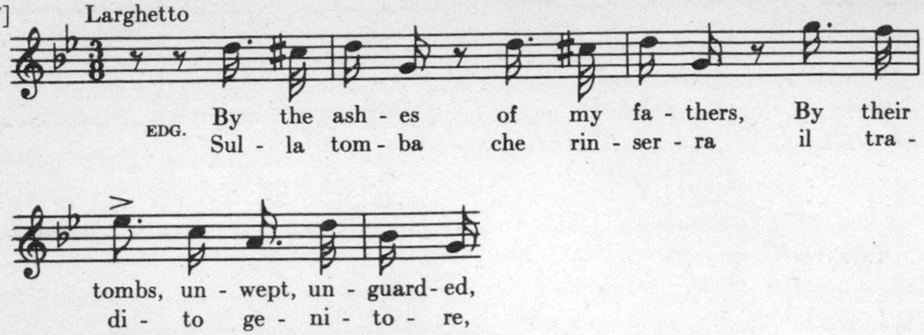
EDG.
By the ash - es of my fa - thers, By their
Sul - la tom - ba che rin - ser - ra il tra -
tombs, un - wept, un - guard - ed,
di - to ge - ni - to - re,

[8] Larghetto

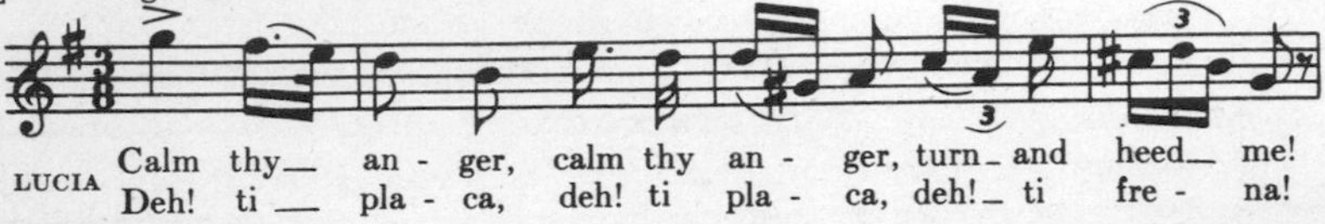
LUCIA
Calm thy_ an - ger, calm thy an - ger, turn_ and heed_ me!
Deh! ti _ pla - ca, deh! ti pla - ca, deh!_ ti fre - na!

[9] DUET *VERRANNO A TE* (Lucia, Edgardo)

Moderato assai

LUCIA
When twi - light shad - ows low - er, My
Ver - ran - no a te sul - l'a - u - re i
ar - dent pray'rs _ as - cend - ing,
miei so - spi - ri ar - den - ti,

[10] DUET *IL PALLOR FUNESTO* (Lucia, Enrico)

Moderato

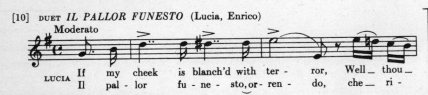

LUCIA
If my cheek is blanch'd with ter - ror, Well_ thou_
Il pal - lor fu - ne - sto, or - ren - do, che_ ri -
know - est my cause of griev - - - ing;
co - pre il vol - to mi - - - o,

[11] Larghetto

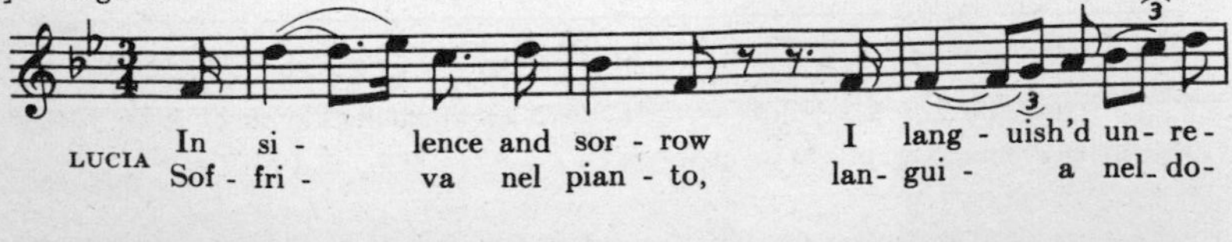
LUCIA
In si - lence and sor - row I lang - uish'd un - re -
Sof - fri - va nel pian - to, lan - gui - a nel_ do-

threatened her here (Aria *Regnava nel silenzio:* "In silence all lay slumbering") [5]. It was the specter of a woman killed on this spot by a jealous Ravenswood. The specter had beckoned Lucia toward the well where she herself had once found her watery grave. Despite Alisa's pleading and despite her warning that this vision is surely a bad omen, Lucia is determined to wait for Edgardo, whose love is her only consolation and joy (Cabaletta *Quando rapita in estasi:* "Were he but here, oh ecstasy") [6].

Edgardo comes, and Alisa retires to keep watch. He reveals that he must leave for France the following morning. On hearing that Enrico, filled with hatred, is searching for him, he threatens to revive his oath of revenge, broken only for Lucia's sake [7], and Lucia tries to calm his anger [8]. Then, before God, they complete a marriage ceremony by exchanging rings. Promising to write, they bid each other a tender farewell (Duet *Veranno a te sull' aure:* "When twilight shadows lower") [9].

Act II, Scene 1: In his apartments, Enrico is in conversation with Normanno. He is awaiting his sister with apprehension, as he has arranged for her to marry Lord Arturo Bucklaw this very day. Will Lucia dare oppose him? Normanno assures him that Lucia will not object. Has he not intercepted all Edgardo's letters so that Lucia has had no news from him since he left? Besides, the forged letter they have prepared should further spur a change of heart in the girl. As Lucia approaches, Enrico sends his captain to meet Arturo.

In great sadness Lucia enters and rebukes her brother for his cruelty (Duet *Il pallor funesto orrendo:* "If my cheek is blanched with terror") [10]. When Enrico proposes to let bygones be bygones and mentions the bridegroom, Lucia is forced to confess that she already is pledged to another. Enrico shows her the forged letter, which says that Edgardo has found a new love. This is a mortal blow for Lucia [11], but her brother claims it is her just reward for betraying her family [12].

Festive music is heard, heralding Arturo's approach. Enrico explains to Lucia that only her marriage to Arturo can save her family from ruin. If Lucia refuses, she will see her brother's threatening ghost forever before her eyes [13]. The hapless Lucia has no other means of resisting Enrico than asking God to take her life [13].

[11] *continued*

pin - ing,
lo - re,

[12] Larghetto

ENR.
Your love is per - fid - ious, Be - tray - ing your broth - er
Un fol - le t'ac - ce - se, un per - fi - do a - mo - re

[13] DUET *IL PALLOR FUNESTO* (Lucia, Enrico) *continued*

Vivace

ENRICO To my ru- in then con - sent - ing,
Se tra - dir - mi tu po - tra - i,

Cold and — si - lent, thou yet dost — brave me;
la mia — sor - te è già com - pi - ta;

[14] Moderato mosso

CHO Hail to the hap-py brid - al — day, Hence ev-'ry thought of sor - row,
Per te d'im-men-so giu - bi - lo tut - to s'av-vi-va in tor - no,

[15] Andante

[16] SEXTET *CHI MI FRENA* (Edgardo, Enrico, Lucia, Bidebent, Arturo, Alisa)

EDGARDO What from ven - geance yet re - strains me, Words suf-
Chi mi fre - na in tal mo - men - to? chi tron-

Larghetto

ENRICO What from ven - geance yet re - strains — me, Will he
Chi raf - fre - na il mio fu - ro - re, e la

fice not to up- braid thee;
cò del - l'i - re il cor - so?

mad - ly dare up - braid — her?
man che al bran - do cor - se?

[17] Larghetto

ENR. Ah, day — of wrath, — what will be — thy end - ing?
Ah! è — mio san - gue — l'ho — tra - di - ta!

Enrico leaves, and (this episode is generally omitted) Raimondo tells Lucia that he has sent one of her letters by a trusted messenger to Edgardo, yet there has been no answer. Therefore Lucia had better accept the marriage to Arturo (Aria *Cedi, cedi:* "Resist no longer").

Act II, Scene 2: Arturo is welcomed in the great hall of the castle (Chorus *Per te d'immenso giubilo:* "Hail to the happy bridal day") [14]. Before he can find out from Enrico whether there is any truth in the gossip he has heard about Edgardo, Lucia enters, pale and faltering [15], and the marriage contract is signed. At this moment Edgardo forces his way in—to the astonishment of all present. He and Enrico face each other threateningly, but the aspect of the fainting Lucia stops them (Sextet *Chi mi frena in tal momento:* "What from vengeance yet restrains me") [16, 17]. All feel deep concern and sympathy for Lucia, who seems closer to death than to life. Even Enrico suddenly feels himself a traitor. Edgardo confesses his love in spite of believing himself betrayed, and Lucia, realizing that she has been deceived, is crushed.

A fight is barely avoided through the intervention of Raimondo, and Edgardo is shown the marriage contract. When Lucia admits having signed it, Edgardo curses the hour he met her. The assembled wedding guests demand his immediate withdrawal [18]. As he bares his breast, asking to be slain as a fitting wedding sacrifice [19], Lucia, her voice joining his [19], prays that God may protect him. Eventually he is permitted to leave in safety.

Act III, Scene 1 (often omitted): A storm is raging outside as Edgardo, wrapped in thought, sits in a chamber of Wolfscrag Tower, a ruin on the Ravenswood estate. Enrico enters, and Edgardo warns him of the presence here of the vengeful spirits of Enrico's victims (Duet *Qui del padre ancor respira:* "Here avenging shades surround thee") [20]. The proud Ashton joyfully informs his enemy that the marriage ceremony has been completed, that the couple has been conducted to the bridal chamber, and

[18] Vivace

[19] Vivace

[20] DUET *QUI DEL PADRE* (Edgardo, Enrico)

Moderato

[21] Marziale

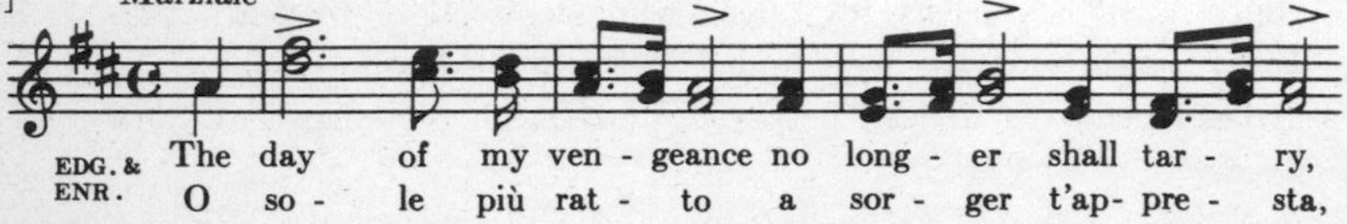

[22] Allegro vivace

[23] ARIA *DALLE STANZE* (Bidebent)

Moderato maestoso

[24] FROM THE MAD SCENE (Lucia)

Andante

[25] Andante

that he has ridden through the wild thunderstorm to challenge Edgardo to a duel. Both men are impatient to see the approach of dawn (Duet *O sole più ratto:* "The day of my vengeance") [21], when they will meet in mortal combat at the burial place of the Ravenswoods.

Act III, Scene 2: The wedding festivities at the castle are in full course [22] when Raimondo comes downstairs, horror in his eyes. The gaiety comes to an abrupt end as he falteringly tells (Aria *Dalle stanze:* "From the chamber") [23] how he had heard an agonized outcry in the bridal chamber and, on entering, found a demented Lucia with a bloody dagger in her hand and Arturo stabbed to death at her feet. Presently, to the consternation of the assembled guests, Lucia appears [24], unconscious of everyone about her (The Mad Scene *Il dolce suono mi colpì:* "I hear the breathing of his voice"). In her wandering mind she sees Edgardo sitting with her by the fountain [9]. The ghost separates them, but they succeed in fleeing to the altar. They are going to be married [25], and Lucia is jubilant. Now the wedding is celebrated (Aria *Ardon gl'incensi:* "The burning tapers") [motive 26] and they are finally united in happiness [26]. (In a passage generally omitted, Enrico returns to hear Lucia accuse him of cruelty and repeat her vows of love for Edgardo.) Sadly Lucia asks her beloved to weep over her remains [27]. She will meanwhile pray for him in heaven, which will hold no joys for her until he joins her. Exhausted, she falls in a swoon.

(In a concluding episode, generally omitted, Enrico orders Alisa to take Lucia away, and Raimondo accuses Normanno of being the author of all the misfortune.)

[26] FROM THE MAD SCENE (Lucia) *continued*

[27]

[28] ARIA *FRA POCO A ME RICOVERO* (Edgardo)

Larghetto

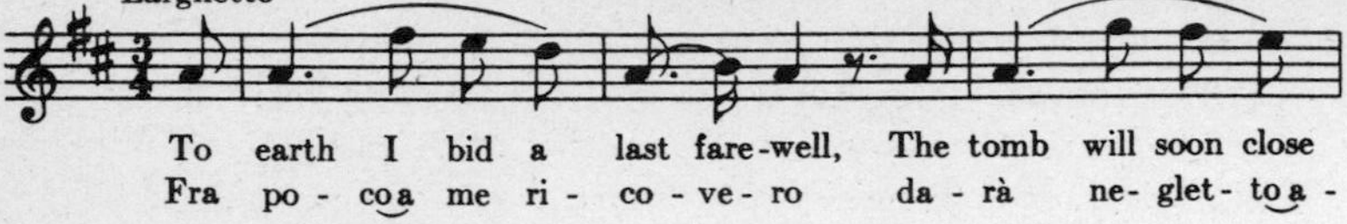
To earth I bid a last fare-well, The tomb will soon close
Fra po - co a me ri - co - ve - ro da - rà ne- glet - to a -

o - ver me;
vel - lo.

[29] Moderato

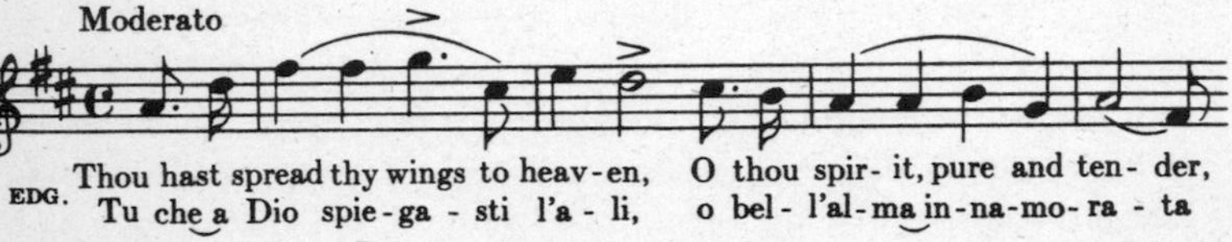
EDG.
Thou hast spread thy wings to heav-en, O thou spir- it, pure and ten- der,
Tu che a Dio spie-ga - sti l'a - li, o bel- l'al-ma in-na-mo-ra - ta

Act III, Scene 2: It is still night when Edgardo arrives dejectedly at the graveyard of his forebears. Ignorant of the events at the castle, he accuses Lucia of faithlessness and wishes only to die. Soon he will be forgotten in his grave (Aria *Fra poco a me ricovero:* "To earth I bid a last farewell") [28]. May Lucia forget him, too, but may she at least stay away from his tomb when, smiling on her husband's arm, she promenades through the grounds of Ravenswood Castle.

Suddenly a mournful procession is heard as it comes from the castle grieving over Lucia. Edgardo learns that, dying, she continually calls his name. Through the silent night the death knell rings out, and when Edgardo resolves to rush to the castle, Raimondo tells him that he is too late. Edgardo promises the soul that has preceded him to heaven that he will join her quickly [29]. Before anyone can prevent him, he stabs himself, hoping that he and Lucia, though separated on earth, will be together in another world [29].

THEMES

[1] Allegro *vigoroso*

[2] NAGASAKI

Allegro

[3] THE WEDDING GUESTS

Allegretto moderato

[4] SHARPLESS

Allegretto moderato

[5] ARIA *DOVUNQUE AL MONDO* (Pinkerton)

Allegro sostenuto con spirito

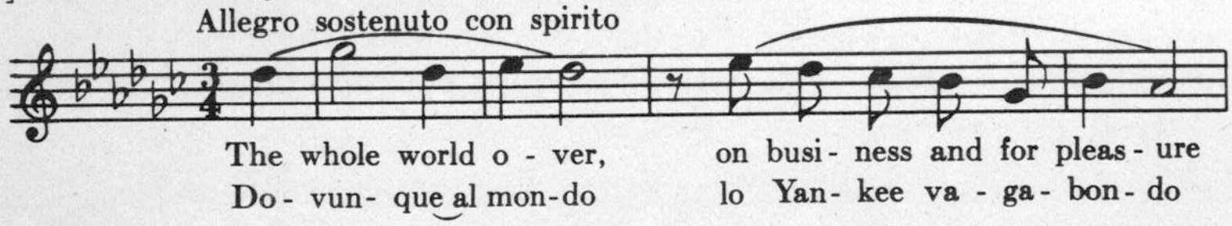

[6] ARIA *AMORE O GRILLO* (Pinkerton)

Allegretto moderato

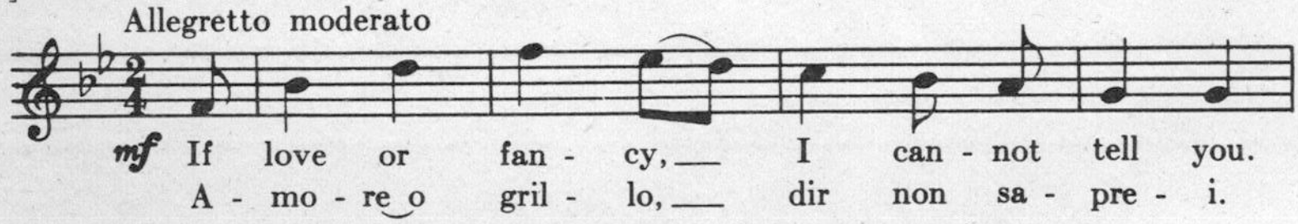

[7] Allegro moderato

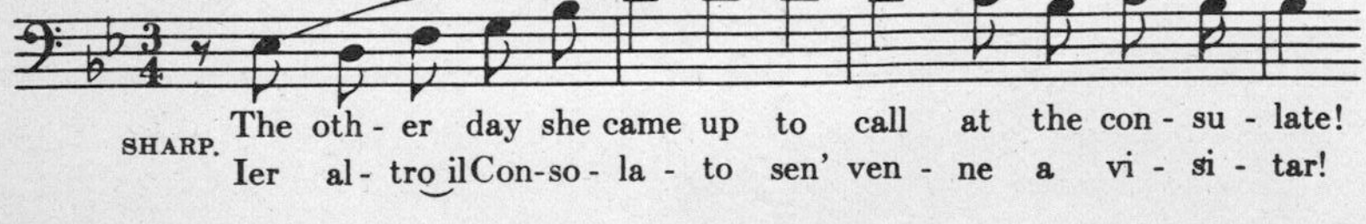

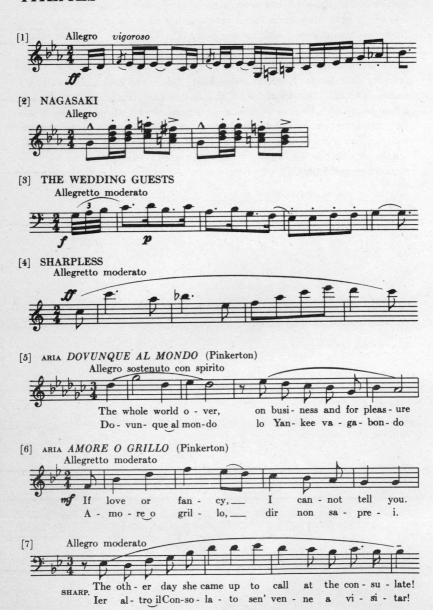

Quotations used by permission of G. Ricordi & Co.

Madama Butterfly

Opera in three acts by Giacomo Puccini. Libretto by G. Giacosa and L. Illica from the drama by David Belasco, after the story by John Luther Long. First performance: Milan, February 17, 1904.

Characters: CIO-CIO-SAN, called MADAMA BUTTERFLY (soprano); SUZUKI, her servant (mezzo-soprano); B. F. PINKERTON, Lieutenant, U.S. Navy (tenor); SHARPLESS, U.S. Consul (baritone); GORO, marriage broker (tenor); PRINCE YAMADORI (baritone); IL BONZO (THE BONZE) (bass); KATE PINKERTON (mezzo-soprano); DOLORE (SORROW OF TROUBLE), Cio-Cio-San's child (silent).
Nagasaki, at the turn of the century.

Introduction to Act I: The sections of the string ensemble, in fugal style, succeed one another in the presentation of theme [1], a vivid and erratic melody moving this way and that, somewhat like Goro but also somewhat like the sliding screens in Pinkerton's Japanese house. Then an exotic motive [2] is introduced, and the curtain rises.

Act I: Lieutenant Pinkerton, making last-minute arrangements for his wedding, is shown through his new house overlooking the harbor of Nagasaki by Goro. The marriage broker, who has provided the house as well as the bride, demonstrates how various sliding partitions can make rooms appear and disappear as if by magic [1, 2]. When Goro claps his hands, three servants appear and are introduced. The maid, Suzuki, is just warming up to a long speech on the wisdom of one Ocunama when Goro claps his hands again and the servants ceremoniously leave. The Lieutenant now learns who will attend the wedding [3]: the official registrar, the American Consul, the bride, and about two dozen of her relations.

Sharpless, the Consul, arrives [4]. As he sits down for a drink with Pinkerton, the young Lieutenant expounds the philosophy of the roving Yankee [5] who ventures forth boldly, expecting the fairest of every land as his reward. After a toast to the United States (in English, to the accompaniment of "The Star Spangled Banner"), the conversation turns to the bride. Goro praises her beauty, and Pinkerton sends him to fetch her. The mere thought of his bride moves Pinkerton to raptures (Aria *Amore o grillo:* "If love or fancy") [6], but the kindly Consul warns him not to betray a girl who, to judge from her behavior, takes this marriage very seriously [7]. As Sharpless offers a toast to the family of Pinkerton in the States, the Lieutenant drinks to his real marriage one day to an American

[8] ILL FORTUNE

a Allegro

f

b Allegro moderato

[9] BUTTERFLY, THE BRIDE

Largo

ppp

[10] LOVE

Largo

p sost.
a tempo
sost.
a tempo

[11] Andante cantabile *dolcissimo*

p
BUT. My fate I have to fol - low, and full of hum-ble_ faith
Io se-guo il mio de - sti - no e pie - na d'u - mil - tà

[12] THE DAGGER

Allegro moderato

p

[13] Moderato

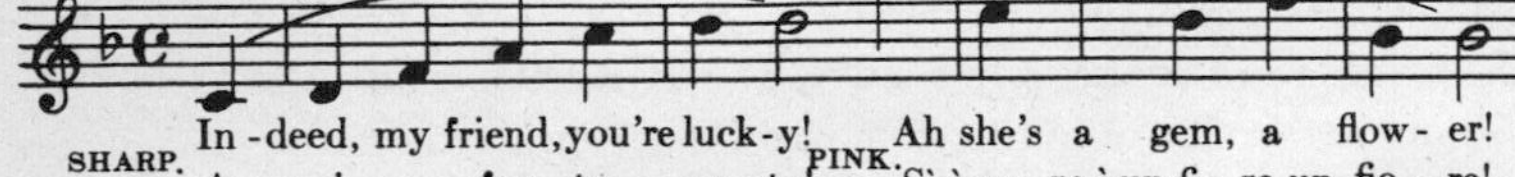
SHARP. In-deed, my friend, you're luck-y! Ah she's a gem, a flow- er!
A - mi- co for- tu - na- to! PINK. Sì è ve- ro,è un fio-re,un fio - re!

[14] Allegro molto moderato, mollemente

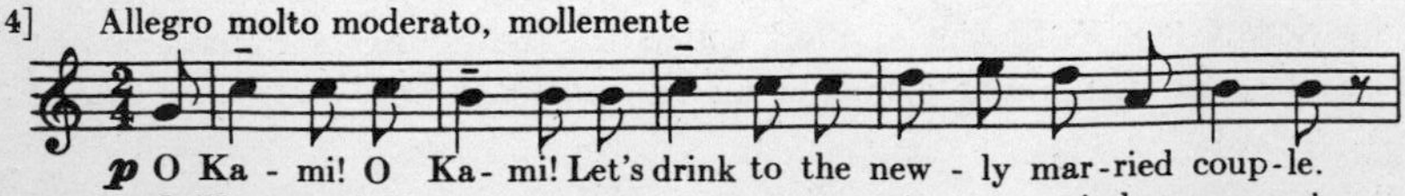
p O Ka - mi! O Ka - mi! Let's drink to the new - ly mar-ried coup-le.
O Ka - mi! o Ka- mi! Be-via- mo ai no- vis - si - mi le - ga - mi.

bride. Goro now returns, announcing the arrival of Butterfly and her companions. The girls can already be heard in the distance chattering gaily without a thought of the disaster which is beginning to unfold [8a]. Butterfly's voice [9] soars in rapture above those of her companions as, following the call of her heart, she approaches the threshold of love [10]. Now they have reached the house, and Butterfly is ready to start her new life [motive 11]. When the introductions are over, the bride tells Pinkerton that she comes from a once rich family that later met with ill-fortune [8a], whereupon she was forced to earn a living as a geisha. The Consul's friendly questions about details of her background [2] come to a painful interruption when he asks about her father. As all her friends fan themselves in embarrassment, Butterfly answers curtly, "Dead" [12]. Sharpless quickly changes the subject, and soon the officials and Butterfly's relations arrive [3]. If Pinkerton regards them facetiously, their opinion of him is by no means undivided praise [3]. Meanwhile, Sharpless and Pinkerton admire the bride [13], and the Consul again warns the Lieutenant that she is in earnest about the marriage.

Pinkerton approaches Butterfly [9], and she commences to unburden herself of her belongings, which she has been carrying in the sleeves of her kimono. Among them is something she does not want to show in front of all the people [8b], but Goro gives Pinkerton a whispered explanation: it is the dagger sent by the Mikado to her father with the order to commit hara-kiri [12]. Now Butterfly confides to Pinkerton that she has secretly embraced Christianity, so that her fate may be linked closer to that of her husband [11].

The marriage ceremony is performed. Then the officials, including the Consul [4], congratulate the groom and leave, the Consul not without returning once more to warn Pinkerton of the bride's deep devotion [13].

All are drinking a toast to the young couple [14] when suddenly a voice from the distance furiously calls and curses Cio-Cio-San [15]. It is her uncle, the Bonze, who has found out about her conversion. He arrives and commands all the relations to renounce Butterfly [15]. When Pinkerton finally intercedes, all leave [12], repeating the curse over and over [15].

Butterfly's despair quickly gives way to childlike happiness under Pinkerton's gentle words of love. A strange mumbling is heard, and Butterfly explains that it is Suzuki offering her evening prayers. Slowly night begins to fall (Love Duet *Viene la sera:* "Evening is falling") [16], and after the servants have closed up, the pair remains alone. Butterfly changes

[15] THE CURSE

[16] **LOVE DUET** (Pinkerton, Butterfly)

Andantino calmo

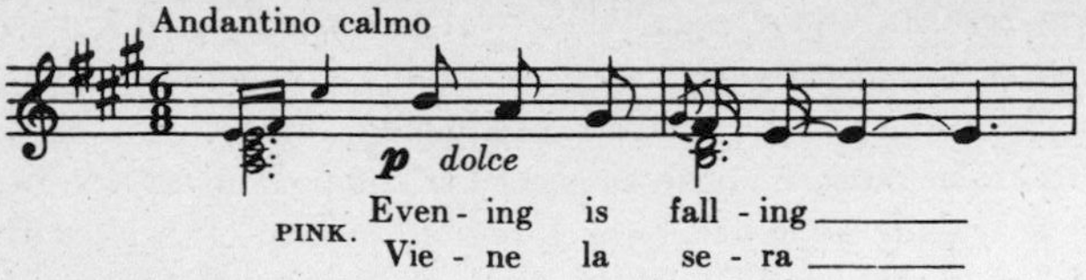
p dolce
PINK. Even - ing is fall - ing
Vie - ne la se - ra

[17] Andante lento *sostenendo, dolcissimo*

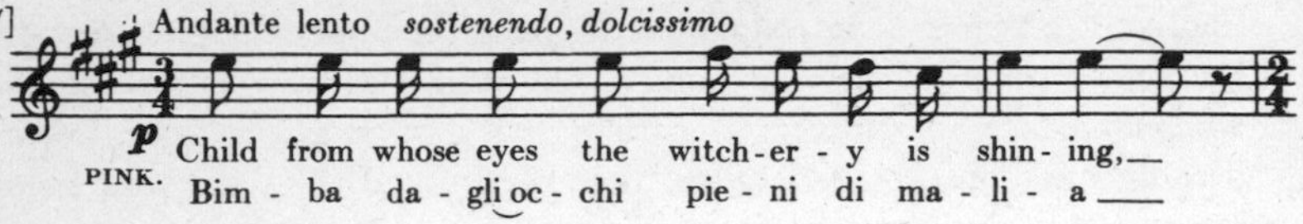
p
PINK. Child from whose eyes the witch-er - y is shin - ing,
Bim - ba da - gli oc - chi pie - ni di ma - li - a

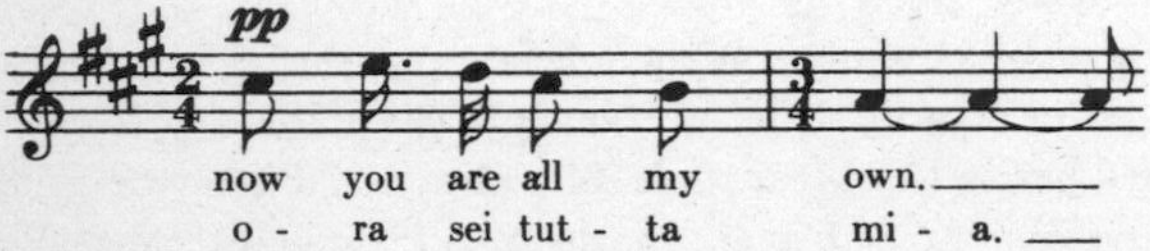
pp
now you are all my own.
o - ra sei tut - ta mi - a.

[18] Andante sostenuto

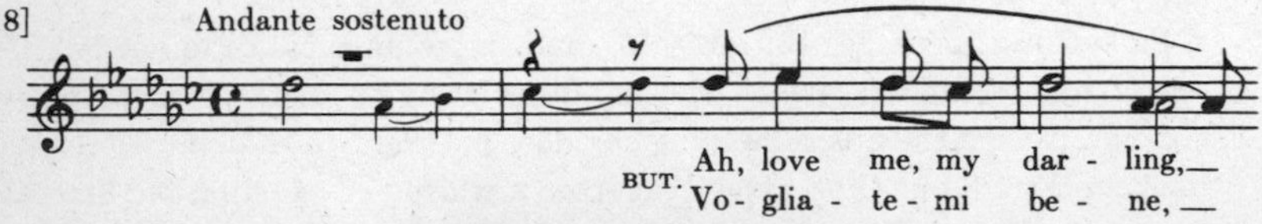
BUT. Ah, love me, my dar - ling,
Vo - glia - te - mi be - ne,

[19] ARIA *UN BEL DI* (Butterfly)

Andante molto calmo

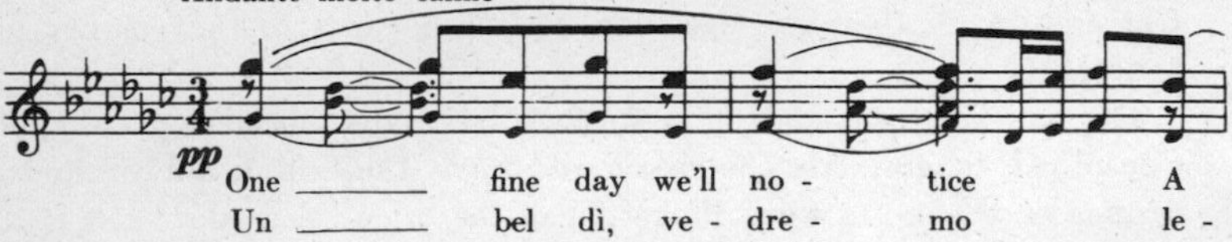
pp
One fine day we'll no - tice A
Un bel dì, ve - dre - mo le -

thread of smoke a - ris - ing
var - si un fil di fu - mo

[20] Andante molto calmo

rallentando un poco

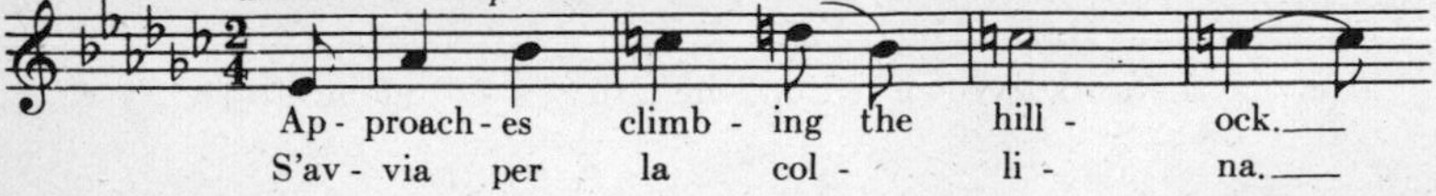
Ap - proach - es climb - ing the hill - ock.
S'av - via per la col - li - na.

[21] Allegro

ff

into a white gown, and her new husband gently approaches her and leads her onto the terrace as vows of love flow from their lips [17, 18]. Suddenly, when Pinkerton likens her to a real butterfly, she becomes frantic with fear lest she receive the treatment butterflies receive in America—being pierced by a needle and displayed pinned to a board [15]. But Pinkerton persuasively dispels all her fears, and love envelops them [9, 10] as they slowly move inside.

Act II: In a room of her house which looks into the garden and over the harbor, Butterfly stands rapt in thought [15] as Suzuki prays to her Japanese gods that they may stop the tears of her mistress. Butterfly is annoyed [8b]. She has more faith in the American God—but unfortunately He does not seem to know where Butterfly lives. Her money is just about gone, and a catastrophe is imminent [8b, 15, 1] unless Pinkerton returns soon. As he has had the Consul provide for her until now [motive 20, 4] Butterfly is sure that he will return [9]. Does Suzuki not believe it? Well, Butterfly knows how it will be (Aria *Un bel dì:* "One fine day") [19]: A wisp of smoke will appear on the horizon, and soon the white ship will be in port. Pinkerton, a tiny white dot at first, will slowly ascend from the city [20], calling "Butterfly." However, she will hide for an instant, partly to tease him, partly so that she will not die from excitement [19]. Then all will be again as it was when he first was here, and Butterfly's faith will be vindicated [19].

Sharpless [4], guided by Goro [2, 1], arrives at the house. Butterfly recognizes him [4] and, in her naïve joy [21], gives him at first no chance to fulfill the purpose of his visit: to read to her a letter he has received from Pinkerton. But she is delighted to hear that he is in good health, for he has stayed away much longer than she had expected. Hearing this, Goro bursts out laughing, and Butterfly indignantly tells the Consul how, during the three years since Pinkerton's departure, the marriage broker has continually offered her suitors [21]. At the moment it is an old fogy [8b]. It is Prince Yamadori, Goro interposes. He is very rich, and Butterfly is very poor, for all her relatives have renounced her [15]. The Prince himself now appears [21], but Butterfly merely makes sport of him [22].

[22]

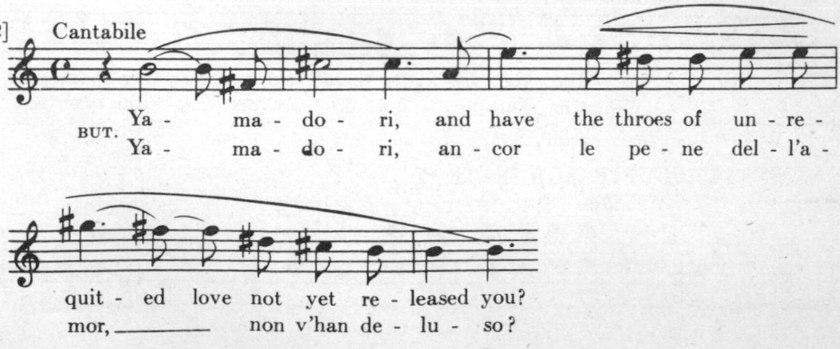

[23] Molto moderato quasi Valzer lentissimo

p dolce
ten.
ten.

[24] Andantino mosso

ppp

[25] **THE CHILD**

Allegro moderato

[26] ARIA *CHE TUA MADRE* (Butterfly)

Andante molto mosso

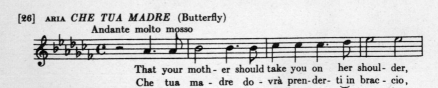

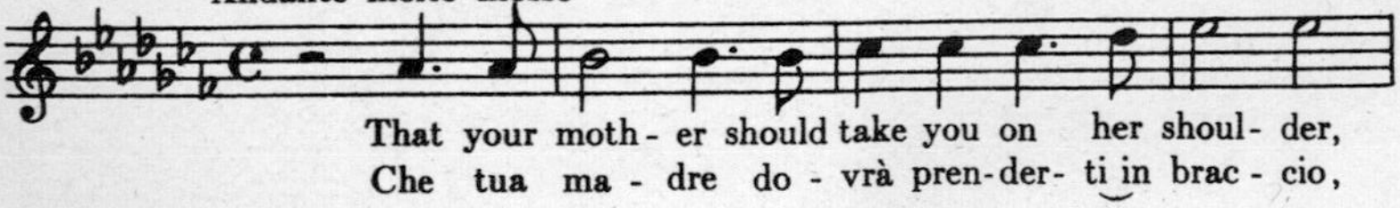
That your moth - er should take you on her shoul - der,
Che tua ma - dre do - vrà pren-der- ti in brac - cio,

[27] **BUTTERFLY'S TRAGIC FATE**

Andante

She claims that she is still married [8a], and that, according to American law ("Star Spangled Banner"), one cannot simply leave and forget his wife as one can do in Japan. Gaily [23] Butterfly asks Suzuki to serve tea, and Yamadori, after bidding Butterfly a reluctant farewell [21], takes his leave [22], followed by Goro.

At last Sharpless [4] can begin to read the letter [24], but when he reaches the critical words ". . . will you carefully prepare her . . ." Butterfly is so overjoyed that the Consul cannot bring himself to read on. With a curse for Pinkerton, he bluntly asks the girl what she would do if Pinkerton were never to return. Haltingly she stammers that she could be a geisha again, or better, she could die. When the Consul, filled with pity, suggests that she marry Yamadori, her first impulse is to ask him to leave, but suddenly she runs into an adjoining room and returns with a small child [25]. Can he forget this, she exclaims, this blue-eyed boy with blond curls? Will she have to carry him through rain and wind (Aria *Che tua madre:* "That your mother") [26], begging and dancing, a geisha again? Is this to be her fate [27]? No, this shall never be [26]. Rather than dance, she would die [27]. The Consul [4] asks the child's name. Butterfly answers that today his name is Sorrow, but that on his father's return [19] it shall be Joy. Deeply moved, Sharpless promises to tell Pinkerton about his son and takes his leave.

Goro is now dragged in by Suzuki. He has claimed that in America a child such as Butterfly's would be disgraced throughout his life [15]. Butterfly takes the dagger from above the shrine and is about to stab Goro, but Suzuki halts her. The marriage broker makes good his escape, and Suzuki leads the child away. Left alone, Butterfly promises her son [25] that his father will take them to his country.

At this moment the cannon of the harbor is heard firing [19], and Suzuki hurries in. Butterfly in great excitement looks through a telescope and recognizes Pinkerton's ship, the *Abraham Lincoln*. Everyone has been lying to her, she exclaims; Pinkerton is back, her love is triumphant ("Star Spangled Banner"). She orders Suzuki to gather the blossoms from their cherry tree (Flower Duet *Scuoti quella fronde di ciliegio:* "Shake that

[28] FLOWER DUET (Butterfly, Suzuki)

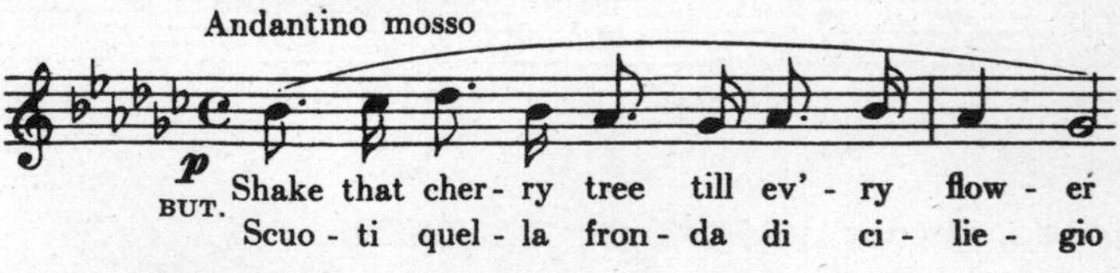

[29]

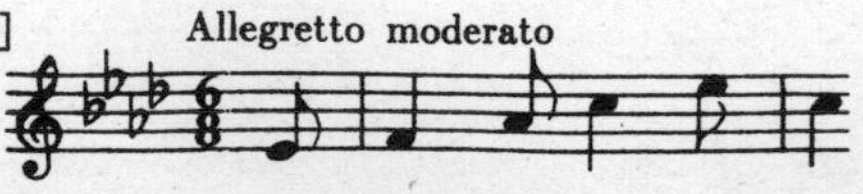

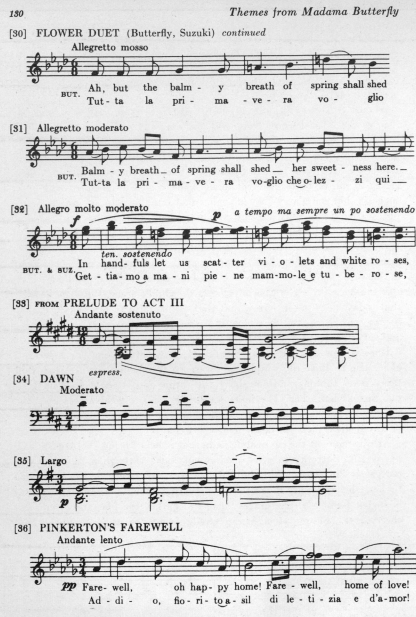

[30] FLOWER DUET (Butterfly, Suzuki) *continued*

Allegretto mosso

BUT.
Ah, but the balm - y breath of spring shall shed
Tut - ta la pri - ma - ve - ra vo - glio

[31] Allegretto moderato

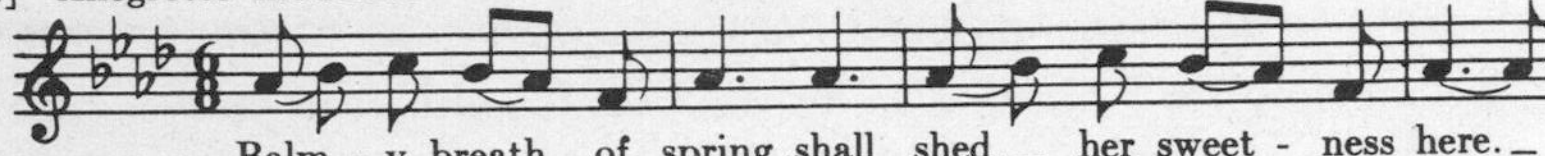
BUT.
Balm - y breath _ of spring shall shed _ her sweet - ness here. _
Tut-ta la pri - ma - ve - ra vo-glio che o- lez - zi qui _

[32] Allegro molto moderato

f
p
a tempo ma sempre un po sostenendo
ten. sostenendo
BUT. & SUZ.
In hand- fuls let us scat - ter vi - o - lets and white ro - ses,
Get - tia- mo a ma - ni pie - ne mam-mo-le e tu - be - ro - se,

[33] FROM PRELUDE TO ACT III

Andante sostenuto

espress.

[34] DAWN

Moderato

[35] Largo

p

[36] PINKERTON'S FAREWELL

Andante lento

pp
Fare- well, oh hap- py home! Fare - well, home of love!
Ad - di - o, fio - ri - to a - sil di le - ti - zia e d'a-mor!

[37] FROM BUTTERFLY'S FAREWELL TO HER CHILD

Andante sostenuto

f
My son, sent to me from Heav - en, straight from the throne of glo - ry,
O a me, sce - so dal tro - no del- l'al - to Pa - ra - di - so,

cherry tree till every flower") [28] and to bring in all the flowers from the garden [motive 30; 29] so that the house may be filled with the scent of spring [30, motive 31]. Reluctantly Suzuki obeys and then, with her mistress, proceeds to strew the blossoms all over the room [31, 30, 32]. Then Suzuki helps mother and child to dress in preparation for Pinkerton's arrival. What will all her relatives say [15], Butterfly muses, and Yamadori [21]! She puts on the robe she wore on her wedding night [16] and motions to Suzuki to close the screen that separates the room from the terrace. In the screen Butterfly makes three tiny holes through which they can observe the expected arrival of Pinkerton [15, 8b]. The light is fading as they gaze into the distance [Humming chorus 24].

Prelude to Act III: The motive of disaster [8a] precedes an extensive section based on [33] and coming to a climax with [10]. Then strains from the preceding act and the act that follows are interrupted by the distant shouts of sailors in the harbor.

Act III: Night is gradually receding before the new day [34], but Butterfly still stands motionless, her gaze fixed on the harbor [11]. Suzuki and the child have long since fallen asleep, but with the rising of the sun Suzuki awakes and rouses Butterfly from her rigid state. Butterfly assures her sleeping child [25] that Pinkerton will come, but for the moment she gathers him in her arms [25] and, following Suzuki's advice, retires for a brief rest.

Pinkerton and the Consul enter [35], and Suzuki shows them the flowers strewn about the room [29, 30]. Then she sees a lady in the garden and learns with horror that she is Pinkerton's wife, Kate. Sharpless asks Suzuki to comfort her mistress and to persuade her to give up her child to Kate (Trio) [35]. Pinkerton is overcome by his memories. Reproached by Sharpless [7] and crushed by remorse, he bids a tearful farewell to the past (Pinkerton's Farewell *Addio, fiorito asil:* "Farewell, O happy home!") [36] and departs, leaving to the Consul and to Kate the task of obtaining the child.

Butterfly rushes in, but does not dare ask the Consul about Pinkerton. Then she notices Kate and understands what is expected of her [25, 8b, 15]. Sadly she wishes Kate luck and promises to give the child to Pinkerton personally if he comes [20] in half an hour.

The Consul and Kate leave. Butterfly is, for a moment, near collapse [20]. Then she bids Suzuki close all doors and curtains [34 minor] and sends her out. She goes to the shrine [15], takes the dagger [12], and reads the inscription on the blade: "Death with honor is better than life with dishonor." As she raises the dagger, Suzuki sends in the child. Butterfly hugs him hysterically, then bids him a heart-rending farewell (Butterfly's Farewell to Her Child *O a me, sceso dal trono:* "My son, sent to me from Heaven") [37], blindfolds him, and gives him an American flag to play with. Again taking the dagger, she moves behind a screen. The knife is heard dropping. Butterfly tries to crawl toward the child as Pinkerton, ascending the hill [20], is heard calling her name. By the time he reaches the threshold, Butterfly is dead [27].

THEMES

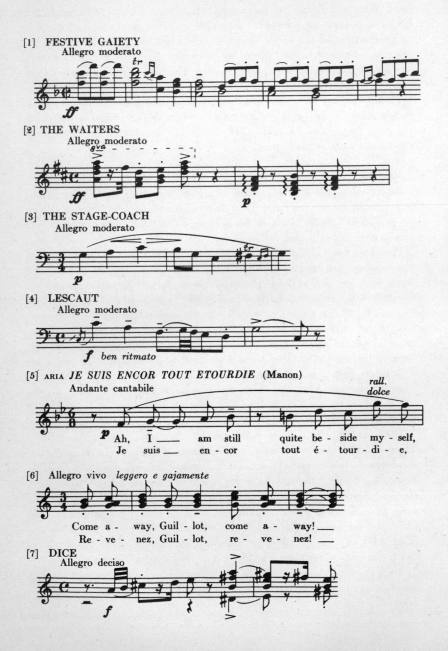

[1] **FESTIVE GAIETY**
Allegro moderato

tr
ff

[2] **THE WAITERS**
Allegro moderato

8va
ff
p

[3] **THE STAGE-COACH**
Allegro moderato

tr
p

[4] **LESCAUT**
Allegro moderato

f ben ritmato

[5] ARIA *JE SUIS ENCOR TOUT ETOURDIE* (Manon)
Andante cantabile

rall.
dolce
p
Ah, I ___ am still quite be - side my - self,
Je suis ___ en - cor tout é - tour - di - e,

[6] Allegro vivo *leggero e gajamente*

Come a - way, Guil - lot, come a - way! ___
Re - ve - nez, Guil - lot, re - ve - nez! ___

[7] **DICE**
Allegro deciso

f

Manon

Opera in five acts by Jules Massenet. Libretto by Henri Meilhac and Philippe Gille after the novel *Les Aventures du Chevalier des Grieux et de Manon Lescaut* by François Prevost d'Exiles (Abbé Prevost). First performance: Paris, January 19, 1884.

Characters: MANON LESCAUT (soprano); LESCAUT, her cousin, a soldier of the guard (baritone); THE CHEVALIER DES GRIEUX (tenor); THE COUNT DES GRIEUX, his father (baritone); GUILLOT MORFONTAINE, a rich nobleman (tenor); DE BRETIGNY, tax collector (baritone); POUSSETTE (soprano), JAVOTTE (mezzo-soprano), ROSETTE (contralto), actresses; INNKEEPER (bass). *Amiens, Paris, and on the road to Havre, in the 1720's.*

Prelude: The motive depicting the festive spirit of the Cours la Reine [1], when everyone pays homage at the feet of Manon, is contrasted with the song of the soldiers who conduct a chained Manon to Havre for deportation [motive 39]. The third theme used is that of Des Grieux's unconditional surrender to the charms of Manon [motive 36].

Act I: From the summerhouse of an inn at Amiens, Guillot and De Brétigny descend into the courtyard and call angrily, but in vain, for the innkeeper. Their three companions—the actresses Poussette, Javotte, and Rosette—join them in their efforts. Finally the innkeeper appears, and behind him the waiters, loaded down with delicacies which he proudly points out to his guests [2]. The guests now return to the summerhouse, followed by the waiters. The innkeeper notices that the townspeople are already gathering in expectation of the coach [3] which is about to arrive and in which the innkeeper has been asked by the Chevalier Des Grieux to reserve him a seat.

Lescaut appears with two other guardsmen. With a haughty wave of his hand [4] he bids them precede him into the inn, as he must wait for Manon, his cousin, who is to arrive in the coach. He will join them later for a gay drinking bout.

The coach arrives [3] and excited travelers get off in confusion, to the amusement of the onlookers. Lescaut spies Manon [motive 5] and swaggeringly [4] introduces himself. Manon (Aria *Je suis encore tout étourdie:* "Ah, I am still quite beside myself") [5] explains her excitement at her first trip [3] overland. She even forgot that she was bound for the convent!

There is much bustle among the passengers, who are now departing once

[8] Allegretto maestoso

mf
f
LESCAUT
Don't go a - stray, ___ Be good and kind. ___
Ne bron-chez pas, ___ Soy-ez gen- tille, ___

[9] Andantino lento

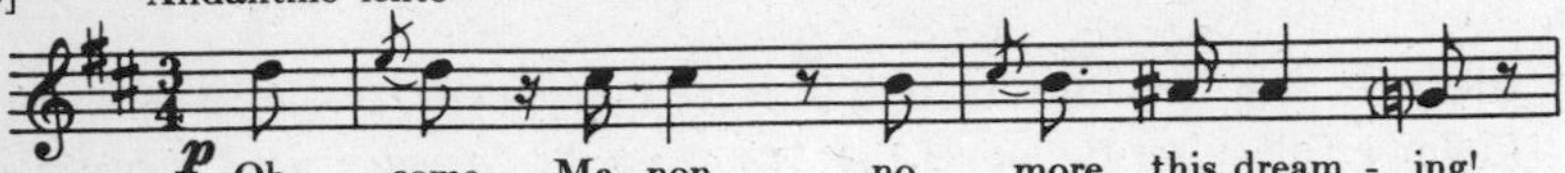
p
MANON
Oh come, Ma-non, no more this dream - ing!
Voy - ons, Ma-non, plus de chi- mè - res,

Dream - ing thus will not change thy fate. ___
Où va ton es - prit en rê - vant? ___

[10] DES GRIEUX
Andante molto tranquillo

mf *sost.*

[11] Andante cantabile *ben cantato, espr.*

DES G.
Love - ly en - chant - ress, With con - quer - ing art, ___
En - chan - te - res - se! Au char - me vain - queur! ___

[12] DUET *NOUS VIVRONS A PARIS* (Des Grieux, Manon)
Allegro

3
MANON
DES GRIEUX
p
DES G.
We shall go ___ to Pa - ree, You and I! You and I!
Nous vi - vrons ___ à Pa - ris, Tous les deux! Tous les deux!

[13] a Andantino tranquillissimo

p *leggero*
f

MANON THE FLIRT
b Allegro maestoso

f *ben marcato e ritmato*

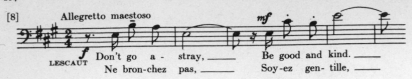

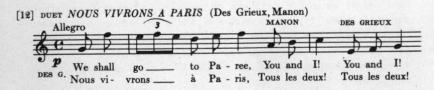

more. Lescaut goes after Manon's baggage, leaving her alone for a moment. Guillot reappears [2] and, fascinated by Manon's beauty [5], offers her all his riches for a word of love, but she breaks into loud laughter in which she is joined by Guillot's companions, who have come from the summerhouse in time to witness the scene. However, De Brétigny quite appreciates the find. The girls call back Guillot [6] and he delays only to inform Manon that a coach will come by soon which will be at her disposal—and afterwards . . . When Lescaut returns [4], Guillot beats a hasty retreat to his laughing companions [6]. Two guardsmen pass by and invite Lescaut to join them in a game [7]. He follows them after explaining to his cousin that he has to take care of some important business [7] and advising her on how to behave while waiting [8]. Manon tries to suppress some foolish thoughts that pass through her mind, but as she sits down on a bench [5], she suddenly notices the three actresses [6] and cannot help admiring their pretty dresses and rich jewelry. With a sigh she reminds herself [9] that she is bound for the convent.

Des Grieux [10] comes from the inn, wondering why he has hesitated to leave. When his eye falls on Manon, he is enchanted [motive 11] and asks her name [motive 14]. His feelings, finding an echo in Manon's heart, culminate in an enraptured declaration of love [11], but she wistfully tells him that the story of Manon is about to end in a convent [9]. Des Grieux swears [10] that he will not permit that to happen. As they plan to leave together, the coach ordered by Guillot arrives, and Manon suggests that they use it to flee to Paris (Duet *Nous vivrons à Paris:* "We shall go to Paris") [12].

From inside the summerhouse Poussette, Javotte, and Rosette are heard calling for Guillot [6], and after a last longing glance at them Manon turns to flee with Des Grieux [11]. Lescaut, having lost all his money [7], returns drunk, but quickly sobers up when he discovers that Manon is missing. He turns furiously against Guillot, who at that moment enters the courtyard [6], but their altercation suddenly takes a turn which the congregating villagers find rather amusing when the innkeeper informs them that Manon has left in Guillot's coach—but in the company of a young man. Lescaut is enraged over the loss of honor suffered by the family; Guillot swears revenge; and the villagers gleefully comment on the discomfiture of this roué.

Introduction to Act II: [motives 10 and 13a].

Act II: In their Paris apartment, Des Grieux [10], who has been writing a letter, gently reproaches Manon [13a] for reading over his shoulder. He has been writing to his father, and now they reread together the enthusiastic description that Des Grieux has given of Manon (Duet *On l'appelle Manon:* "And her name is Manon") [14]. Des Grieux declares he wants to marry Manon [11] and they embrace, but just as he is about to go out and mail his letter a bouquet of flowers catches his eye, and he stops to ask from where it came. With feigned indifference, Manon [13a] replies that someone had tossed it through the window. A noise is heard outside [4] and

[14] DUET *ON L'APPELLE MANON* (Manon, Des Grieux)

Andantino tranquillissimo

p
MANON
And her name is Ma-non; she is just now six - teen.
On l'ap- pel- le Ma-non, elle eut hi - er seize ans;

[15] DE BRETIGNY

Allegro appassionato

p
f

[16] ARIA *ADIEU, NOTRE PETITE TABLE* (Manon)

Andante

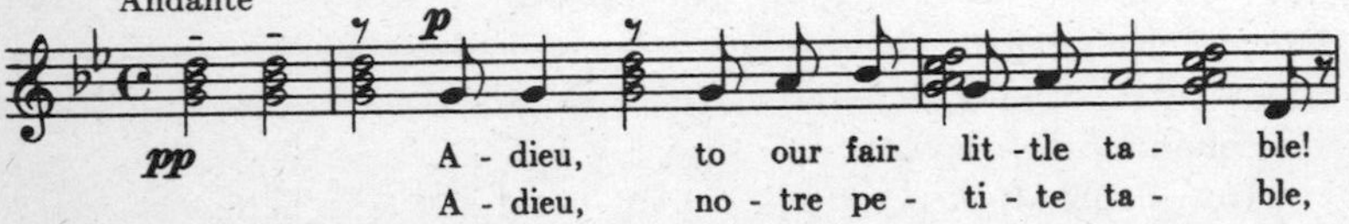
p
pp
A - dieu, to our fair lit -tle ta - ble!
A - dieu, no - tre pe - ti - te ta - ble,

mf
You have been our dear meet-ing - place. A - dieu,
Qui nous ré - u - nit si sou - vent! A - dieu,

[17] THE DREAM (Des Grieux)

Andante tranquillissimo

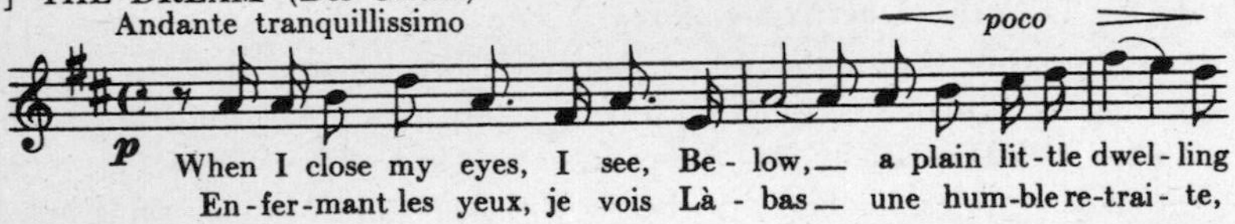
poco
p
When I close my eyes, I see, Be - low,— a plain lit-tle dwel-ling
En-fer-mant les yeux, je vois Là - bas— une hum-ble re-trai- te,

[18] MINUET

Allegretto

p

[19] Allegretto

p
sf

[20] Allegro moderato

p sostenuto
Oh how charm-ing prom-e - nad - - - ing!
POUSSETTE, JAVOTTE La char- man-te pro - me - na - - - de,

the maid announces two guardsmen, one of whom claims to be a relative of Manon. The other one, the girl whispers to Manon, is their neighbor, Monsieur De Brétigny, the tax collector who is in love with her, in disguise. De Brétigny and Lescaut enter [7] and the latter bombastically announces that he has caught the fine pair and that he is going to take revenge; but when he finds himself threatened by Des Grieux, he suddenly changes his tone and gladly follows De Brétigny's advice to try politeness. The visitors now declare that they regard Des Grieux a good fellow like themselves [4], whereupon the Chevalier, to prove his honorable intentions, shows Lescaut the letter he has just finished writing [10]. Lescaut takes this chance to draw Des Grieux away from the others, and De Brétigny [15] informs Manon that the Count Des Grieux will have his son kidnapped this very night in order to separate him from her. If she should warn him and prevent the abduction, the result will be poverty for her and her lover. On the other hand, if she keeps quiet, it will mean that she can have anything she desires.

As (Quartet) Lescaut keeps rereading the letter and the Chevalier reassures him of his sincere love for his cousin, Manon is deeply disturbed by De Brétigny's flattery and enticing promises [15]. Lescaut, apparently satisfied, now gives the young pair his exaggerated blessings [7] and leaves [4] with De Brétigny, who has accomplished his purpose. Manon and Des Grieux remain alone [15]. When he leaves to mail the letter, Manon tries to understand the contending feelings in her heart (Recitative *Allons! Il le faut!:* "Come, come! It must be!"): True, she loves Des Grieux, but she cannot forget [15] that through her beauty she may reign over Paris—as De Brétigny has promised her. Unbidden tears well up in her eyes [13a], and with sorrow she bids farewell to the place that witnessed her great happiness (Aria *Adieu, notre petite table:* "Adieu to our fair little table") [16]. Des Grieux returns [11] and sees tears in her eyes, but she quickly rallies [13a]. They sit down to dinner, and he tells about an enchanted vision he entertained (The Dream *En fermant les yeux:* "When I closed my eyes") [17]: He saw a little house in a landscape that was paradise, and yet it was not paradise, for it lacked Manon.

There is a knock [15] and Manon hysterically tries to prevent Des Grieux from going downstairs, but laughingly he descends to open the door [10]. At the sound of a struggle Manon rushes to the window. The rumble of a departing carriage is heard and, overcome with grief, Manon follows it with her eyes [15].

Entr'acte: Minuet [18, 19].

Act III, Scene 1: On the Cours la Reine in Paris, street venders are hawking their wares. Poussette and Javotte come from a dance hall [18, 19] and soon find two beaus whose company they enjoy—far from the watchful eyes of Guillot [20]. Rosette, too, is out to enjoy a little escapade. In the prevailing mood of festive gaiety [1], Lescaut, urged by the hawkers to choose from their wares, is ready to buy everything (Recitative *Choisir!:* "To

[21] ARIA *A QUOI BON L'ECONOMIE* (Lescaut)

Allegro moderato

f
Why-not-spend-it — if you're a - ble To-em-ploy three dice-in play —
A-quoi-bon-l'é - co- no - mi- e Quand on a trois dés-en main —

[22] THE CROWD

Allegretto brillante

f

a
3

[23] Allegro maestoso

MAN. A sov'- reign am I — in my way —
Je mar - che sur tous — les che-mins —

[24] THE GAVOTTE (Manon)

Moderato e leggero

Come and o - bey the voice that is call - ing
O - bé - is - sons quand leur voix ap - pel - le

[25] Moderato e leggero

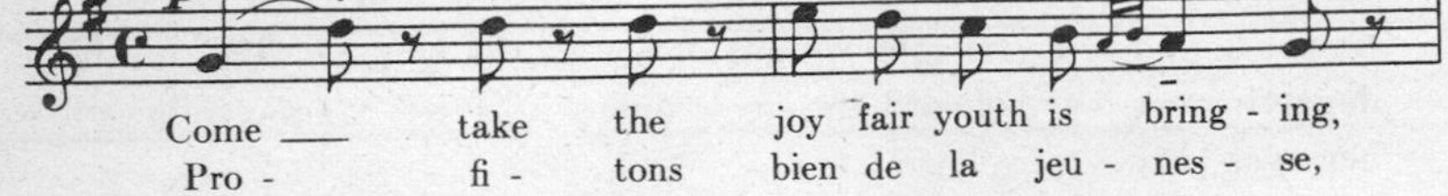
p
Come — take the joy fair youth is bring - ing,
Pro - fi - tons bien de la jeu - nes - se,

[26] DIVERTISSEMENT

Allegro deciso

choose!"; Aria *À quoi bon l'économie:* "Why not spend it if you're able?") [21] for his fair Rosalinde, he says. Poussette, Javotte, and Rosette rejoin the crowd [1], having returned from the dance hall where they had gone again [18, 19]. Discovered by Guillot, they run off. De Brétigny, who has just arrived, mockingly begs the furious Guillot not to console himself by taking Manon away from him [15]; but he admits that he has refused to engage the opera for a private performance for Manon, and Guillot immediately leaves, gaily murmuring to himself that he will yet steal Manon [1]. The crowd gazes at the passing beauties [22], but soon all eyes are attracted by the arrival of Manon leaning on the arm of De Brétigny. She is radiantly beautiful and enjoys the general reaction (Recitative *Je marche sur tous les chemins:* "A sov'reign am I in my way") [23, 13b] and reveals her philosophy of enjoying life, and adventure, and love, while one is young (Gavotte *Obéissons quand leur voix appelle:* "Come and obey the voice that is calling") [24, 25].

Now Manon leaves De Brétigny [15] to enter a shop, and the crowd slowly disperses [22a]. When she returns, she overhears the Count Des Grieux telling De Brétigny that his son has entered the seminary of St. Sulpice to become an abbé [10]. She approaches, sends off De Brétigny on an errand [19], and then, claiming to be a friend of Manon's, tries [18, 19] to learn from the Count how Des Grieux feels about her. To her despair, the Count claims that his son has forgotten Manon.

The crowds saunter back [22], and Guillot facetiously discloses to De Brétigny that he has engaged the ballet of the opera to dance for Manon right here at the Cours la Reine. Loudly acclaimed by the populace, the ballet arrives, the music starts [26], and the dancers perform four classic selections. During the last number Manon, who, rapt in thought, has seen and heard nothing, orders her coach to go to St. Sulpice. At her departure, Guillot is stunned, but the crowd is still in the gayest of holiday moods [1].

Act III, Scene 2: The organ plays the postlude that ends the service, and the ladies of the congregation enter the reception room of the seminary of St. Sulpice. They are excited [27] about the latest sermon of the Abbé Des Grieux, and they salute him with reverence as he enters. When they leave, Des Grieux is confronted by his father, who ironically congratulates him on his success. Does he really intend to make the church his career? When the young abbé expresses his disgust with the world [11], the Count advises

[27] THE LADIES

Allegretto animato

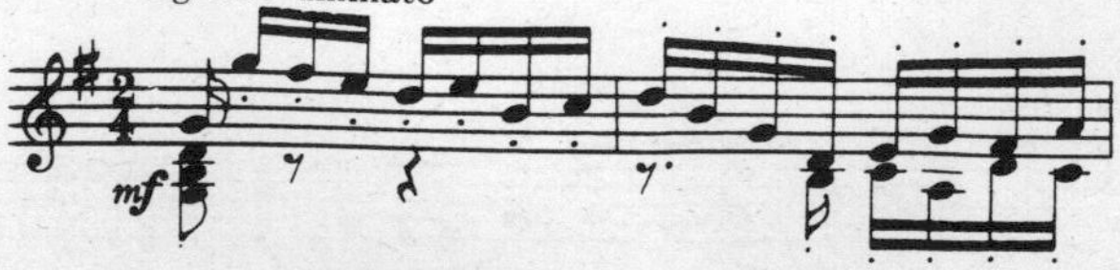

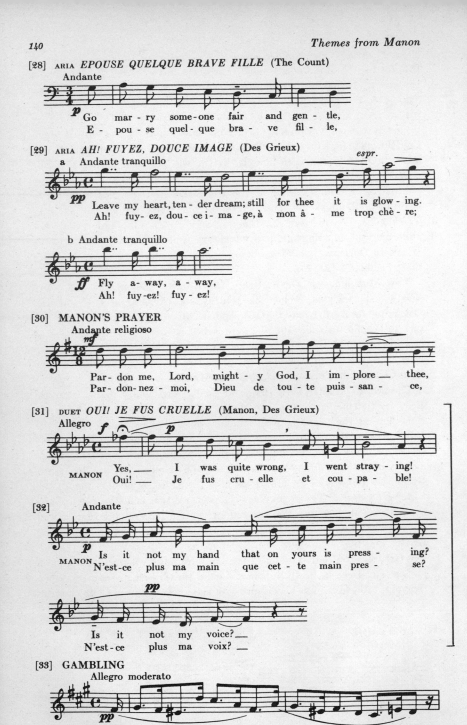

[28] ARIA *EPOUSE QUELQUE BRAVE FILLE* (The Count)

Andante

Go mar - ry some - one fair and gen - tle,
E - pou - se quel - que bra - ve fil - le,

[29] ARIA *AH! FUYEZ, DOUCE IMAGE* (Des Grieux)

a Andante tranquillo

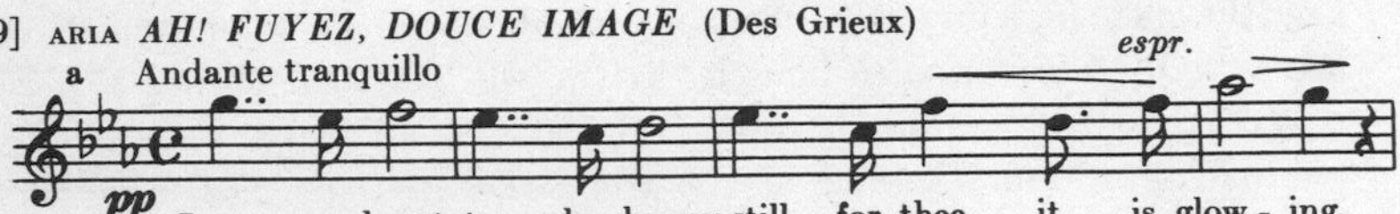

Leave my heart, ten - der dream; still for thee it is glow - ing.
Ah! fuy- ez, dou - ce i - ma - ge, à mon â - me trop chè - re;

b Andante tranquillo

Fly a- way, a - way,
Ah! fuy -ez! fuy - ez!

[30] MANON'S PRAYER

Andante religioso

Par- don me, Lord, might - y God, I im - plore — thee,
Par- don-nez - moi, Dieu de tou - te puis - san - ce,

[31] DUET *OUI! JE FUS CRUELLE* (Manon, Des Grieux)

Allegro

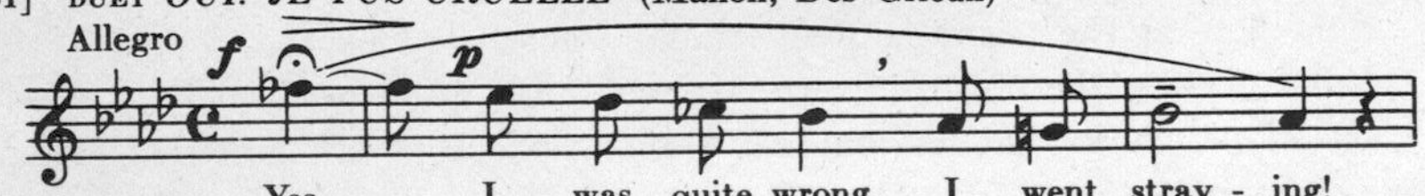

MANON
Yes, — I was quite wrong, I went stray - ing!
Oui! — Je fus cru - elle et cou - pa - ble!

[32] Andante

MANON
Is it not my hand that on yours is press - ing?
N'est-ce plus ma main que cet - te main pres - se?

Is it not my voice? —
N'est - ce plus ma voix? —

[33] GAMBLING

Allegro moderato

misterioso e sostenuto

that he get to know it better, get married to a decent girl (Aria *Épouse quelque brave fille:* "Go, marry someone fair and gentle") [28], and continue the family as have his fathers before him. However, the Chevalier's decision is immutable, and sadly the Count leaves [28]. Alone, Des Grieux confesses that his efforts to replace with religion the sweet image that is always before him have, so far, been in vain (Recitative *Je suis seul!:* "All alone"; Aria *Ah! fuyez, douce image:* "Leave my heart, tender dream") [29ab]. Hardly has he left for another service when Manon enters [27] and asks the porter to call Des Grieux [11]. Moved by the sounds of a "*Magnificat*" that reach her ear, Manon kneels to pray to the Lord for Des Grieux's love (Manon's Prayer *Pardonnez-moi, Dieu de toute puissance:* "Pardon me, Lord, mighty God, I implore thee") [30]. He comes and is taken aback when he recognizes Manon [29b]. Sternly he bids her leave. Manon, admitting her guilt, fervently pleads her love (Duet *Oui! Je fus cruelle et coupable!:* "Yes, I was quite wrong, I went straying") [31], but her contrition and her desperate appeals [11] are at first violently rejected. In a final effort, she asks whether her hands, her eyes, her voice no longer hold the charm they once possessed [32]. When the bells call to devotion, their sound pales before Manon's voice. No longer does Des Grieux want to do battle with his dreams [29b]. Throwing off all restraint, he once again confesses his love, and flees with Manon [11].

Act IV: In the gaming room of the Hotel Transylvanie considerable sums are rapidly changing hands [33], and the sharpers are not the ones to lose, they admit [34]. Also Poussette, Rosette, and Javotte claim that for pretty girls there is always something to gain among the gamblers. Lescaut, having won, confesses his love for the Queen of Spades in a little song [35], and Guillot, who has entered in time to hear the end of it, offers a bawdy ditty with pantomime about the Regent's affairs. (Both songs are often omitted.)

The arrival of Manon and Des Grieux causes a great deal of excitement [22], particularly in the still jealous and vengeful Guillot. Des Grieux has come against his better judgment, yet, incapable of resisting Manon's wishes [36], he is coaxed by her and Lescaut into gambling. Guillot offers his rival a game. As they begin to play [33], Manon succumbs to the excitement of the atmosphere and reveals her craving for beauty, love, and gold (Couplets *À nous les amours et les roses!:* "Let ours be sweet love and fair roses!") [37]. When Guillot continues to lose, he accuses the Chevalier of cheating. Des Grieux is barely kept from springing at him. Guillot leaves with a threat, and the assembled company decides [33] that Des Grieux must be

[34] GAMBLERS' SONG

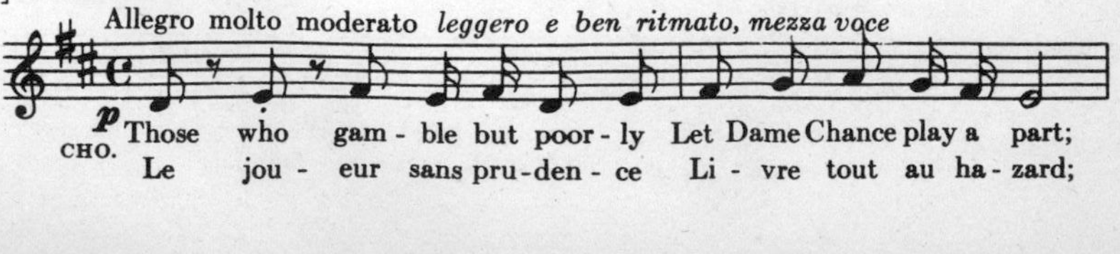

[35] Allegro

LESCAUT
It is here that she has her dwell - ing, Quite the fair - est
C'est i - ci que cel - le que j'ai - me A dai - gné — fi -

one I have known —
xer son sé - jour —

[36] Andante — *molto espressivo*

DES GRIEUX
Ma - non, sphinx of de - light, like a
Ma - non, sphinx é - ton - nant, vé - ri -

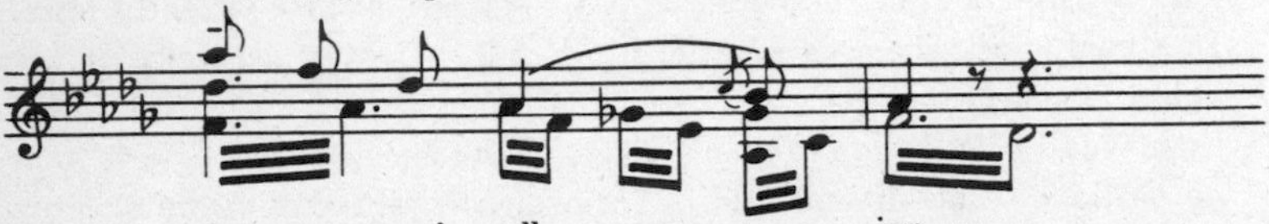

si - ren you're call - ing,
ta - ble si - rè - ne!

[37] COUPLETS *A NOUS LES AMOURS* (Manon)

Allegro brillante

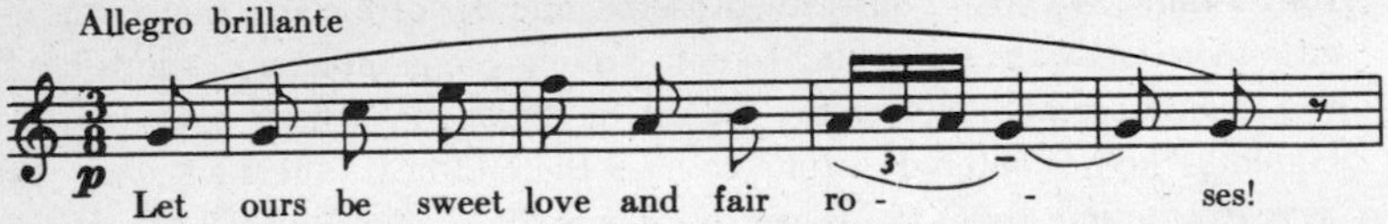

Let ours be sweet love and fair ro - - ses!
A nous les a - mours et les ro - - ses!

All things love - ly spring now dis - clos - - es.
Chan - ter, ai - mer, sont dou - ces cho - - ses!

[38] Andante cantabile

MANON
Oh, de - spair, fate will tear us a - sun - der,
O dou - leur! l'a - ve - nir nous sé - pa - re!

[39] SOLDIERS' SONG

Allegro moderato

Cap - tain fine and gay, Are you tired, I say, When we march all day? —
Ca - pi - taine, ô gué, Es - tu fa - ti - gué De nous voir à pied? —

a sharper. To dispel the suspicion, Des Grieux resists Manon's urgent entreaty to hurry away. There is a knock on the door. Guillot arrives with the police and points out Des Grieux and Manon to them. Gloatingly he informs the pair that he has accomplished his revenge. The Count appears in time to prevent his son from committing violence against Guillot, and he berates him for heaping dishonor on himself and his family [motive 38]. Toward Manon the Count is as inflexible as Guillot himself, although all others share Manon's sorrow [38]. The Chevalier is arrested, while his father whispers to him that he will soon be freed, and the hapless Manon is led off by the guards to be dealt with "as other such women are dealt with."

Act V: On the road to Havre, Des Grieux, disheartened, is waiting for Manon to pass under guard [motive 39], with other undesirable females, toward the port for embarkation to Louisiana. Lescaut arrives and miserably confesses that he does not have the promised men with him to attack the guards, who already can be heard approaching [39]. With difficulty he prevents Des Grieux from attacking them with his sword; instead, he bribes the sergeant in charge to let him talk with Manon "for a while." As the soldiers move on and Lescaut leads aside the guard who was left behind with Manon, Des Grieux remains alone with her. Apparently very ill, she had crept along apathetically. When she looks up and recognizes Des Grieux, she is overjoyed. Then her tears flow as she heaps reproaches on herself for the manner in which she treated Des Grieux in spite of her undying love for him [40]. However, he has forgiven her, and in rapture they apostrophize the love that unites them [41]. Happy, they recall former days [11, 14]; but when they prepare to leave, Manon finds herself too weak to move [41] and only offers her lover a parting kiss before dying [11]. In vain he tries to revive her with memories of the past [32]; she knows that the story of Manon Lescaut has reached its end [9]. As she dies, Des Grieux falls over her body with a cry of despair [32].

[40] Andante espressivo

pp
p
sf

[41] DUET *AH, JE SENS UNE PURE FLAMME* (Manon, Des Grieux)

Andante
mf
MANON
Ah, I feel pur - est love a - flam - ing with - in
Ah, je sens u - ne pu - re flam - me M'é - clai -
3
f
me and il - lu - min - ing my heart with heav'n - ly joy.
rer de ses feux; Je vois en - fin les jours heu - reux.

THEMES

[1] THE MASTERSINGERS

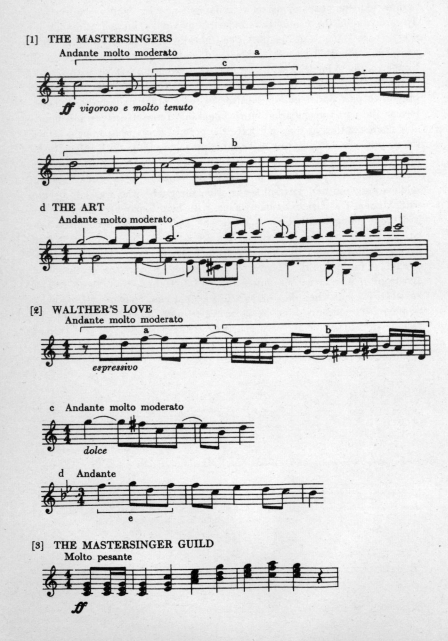

Andante molto moderato

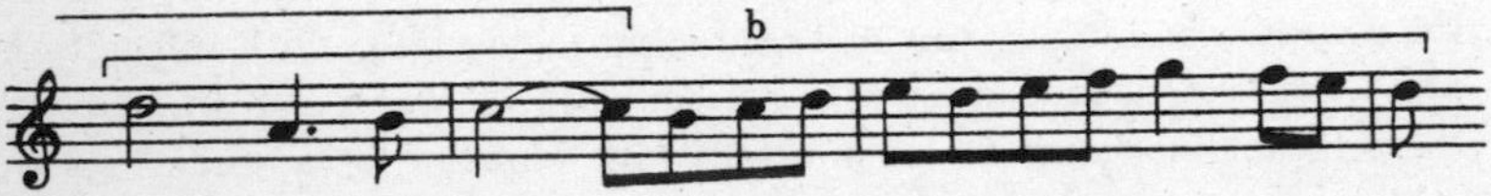

d THE ART

Andante molto moderato

[2] WALTHER'S LOVE

Andante molto moderato

c Andante molto moderato

d Andante

[3] THE MASTERSINGER GUILD

Molto pesante

Die Meistersinger von Nürnberg

THE MASTERSINGERS OF NUREMBERG

Opera in three acts by Richard Wagner. Libretto by the composer. First performance: Munich, June 21, 1868.

Characters: Mastersingers: HANS SACHS, shoemaker (bass-baritone); VEIT POGNER, goldsmith (bass); SIXTUS BECKMESSER, town clerk (bass); FRITZ KOTHNER, baker (bass); KUNZ VOGELGESANG, furrier (tenor); KONRAD NACHTIGALL, tinsmith (bass); BALTHASAR ZORN, pewterer (tenor); ULRICH EISSLINGER, grocer (tenor); AUGUSTIN MOSER, tailor (tenor); HERMANN ORTEL, soap-boiler (bass); HANS SCHWARZ, stocking-weaver (bass); HANS FOLTZ, coppersmith (bass);

WALTHER VON STOLZING, a young knight from Franconia (tenor); DAVID, Sachs' apprentice (tenor); EVA, Pogner's daughter (soprano); MAGDALENE, Eva's nurse (soprano or mezzo-soprano); A NIGHT WATCHMAN (bass). *Nuremberg, about the middle of the sixteenth century.*

Prelude: The motive of the Mastersingers [1ab] is followed by that of Walther's love [2ab], thus immediately establishing the main dramatic conflict of the opera.* The motive of the Mastersinger Guild [3] is introduced; then the motive of conventional art [1d] is set off against that of youthful fervor [4]. Motives of love [5abc] and of passion [6ab] are succeeded by the sprightly ones of the apprentices [1ab in double time], by [6a] in a lively version, and by the motive of gaiety [7]. In various forms and combinations —at one time [1ab, 3, and 5abc] are played simultaneously—these motives bring the Prelude to a climax with [1a] and [7]. Without interruption in the music the curtain opens.

Act I: While the congregation in church sings the final chorale [8], Walther and Eva exchange glances of love [2ab, 6ab, 5ab]. When the service ends and the people leave, Walther stops Eva to ask her if she is already promised in marriage. Eva asks her companion to reply for her, but Magdalene, noticing that everyone has left the church, is anxious to get away. However, encouraged when she notices the arrival of her sweetheart, David, Hans Sachs' apprentice [1b in double time], she explains that tomorrow the judges will award Eva as prize to the Mastersinger who wins the song contest. Eva blurts out that she hopes it will be Walther. Magdalene calls David [9], who has started to prepare for the meeting of the Mastersingers

* The battle of Walther against the Mastersingers is a lightly disguised version of Wagner's own fight for recognition by the musicians of his time.

[4] YOUTHFUL FERVOR

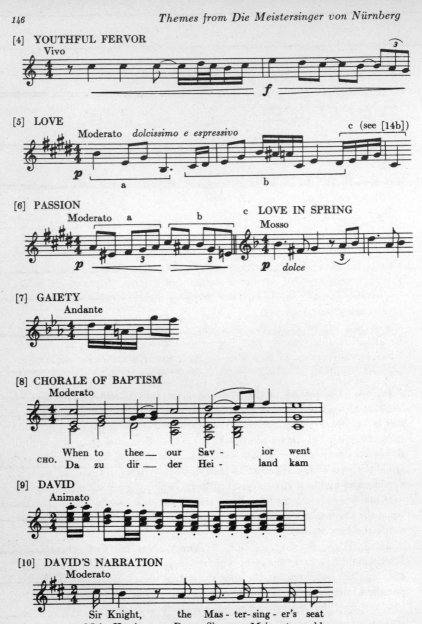

Vivo

[5] LOVE

Moderato *dolcissimo e espressivo*

[6] PASSION

Moderato

c LOVE IN SPRING

Mosso

[7] GAIETY

Andante

[8] CHORALE OF BAPTISM

Moderato

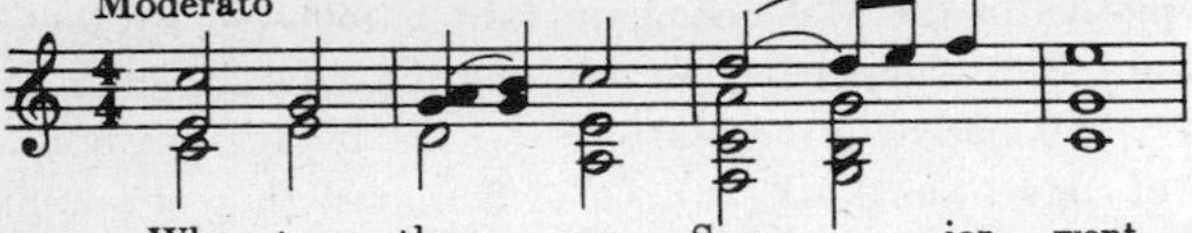

CHO. When to thee— our Sav - ior went
Da zu dir — der Hei - land kam

[9] DAVID

Animato

[10] DAVID'S NARRATION

Moderato

Sir Knight, the Mas - ter- sing - er's seat
Mein Herr! Der Sin - ger Mei - ster- schlag

[11] WORK

Con vigore

[3], and promises him the leftovers from the kitchen [9] if he helps Walther to become a Mastersinger [3]. The knight tells Eva that he will come to see her in the evening [4] and assures her that he will try with all his powers [5b] to win her [2c, 5ab]. Eva and Magdalene leave.

Apprentices, who meanwhile have entered and are busy arranging furniture for the meeting, call David to help them, but he is busy explaining to Walther (Aria *Mein Herr! Der Singer Meisterschlag:* "Sir Knight, the Mastersinger's seat") [10] how, together with shoemaking [11], he has been studying the basic rules of the singer's art. He goes on to enumerate and to demonstrate the various admitted tunes ("The Tunes" *Der Meister Ton und Weisen:* "The Masters' tones and tunes diverse") [12], and he explains the rules for handling the voice in singing them. For a whole year Hans Sachs has been teaching him [11], and he still makes mistakes, whereupon Sachs gives him a good whipping [motive 28ab]. He isn't even a "pupil" as yet, David continues, and one must be a "singer" and a "poet" before one can become a Master [3] capable of inventing a new tune to original rhymes. Looking for a moment past the undaunted Walther [2a] toward the apprentices, David [9] discovers that they have prepared the wrong booth for the "Marker" [18a], who, David tells Walther, will sit hidden behind curtains and chalk up every mistake a singer makes. Only seven errors are permitted before the singer is disqualified. Mockingly, David wishes the noble knight good luck in his attempt to gain the Mastersinger's wreath [13].

The apprentices start a dance around Walther [13], but retire quickly when Pogner arrives for the meeting [14ab] accompanied by Beckmesser, whom he promises to support in his suit for Eva's hand. Walther approaches Pogner and claims that he has come to Nuremberg mainly out of love for music [14ab with 5c] and that he would like to become a Mastersinger immediately [2c]. Pogner is amazed, but gladly promises to propose his name at the meeting. Beckmesser looks suspiciously at the young knight.

Meanwhile, more Masters have arrived, and Kothner calls the roll [14ab]. Pogner asks for the floor (Pogner's Address *Das schöne Fest, Johannistag:* "The Feast of John, Midsummerday") [15]: The Mastersingers celebrate St. John's Day every year with an outdoor singing competition before the townspeople, and Pogner, to disprove the reputation of the burghers as merely gold-seekers, and to demonstrate the high value they set on art [1c, 14b], offers as prize for tomorrow's competition [15 with 14ab], together with all his possessions, Eva, his only daughter, in matrimony. He adds the provision that Eva must give her consent, but if she refuses, she must forever remain unmarried, for only a Mastersinger [1ab] shall be her husband.

Sachs proposes that for once the untutored people, more likely to be in accord with the girl, should be the judges. Also, it would be wise thus to test the soundness and continued freshness of the Mastersinger rules [14b, 1c], by trying them on those who are ignorant of them. The apprentices

[12] DAVID'S NARRATION *continued*
THE TUNES

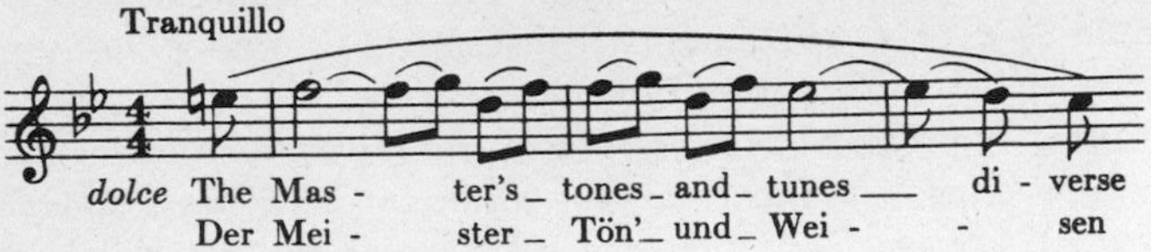
Tranquillo
dolce The Mas - ter's tones and tunes di - verse
Der Mei - ster Tön' und Wei - - sen

[13] THE APPRENTICES' DITTY

Commodo dolce
p The silk - en chap - let of flow - ers bright,
Das Blu - men-kränz - lein aus Sei - den fein,

[14] THE GUARDIANS OF THE RULES

Moderato
a
b

[15] ST. JOHN'S DAY

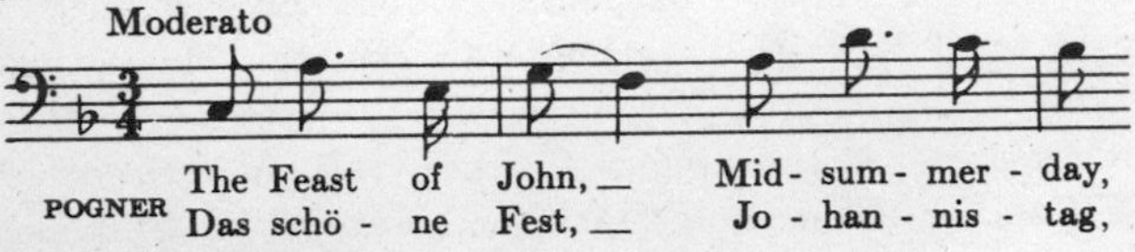
Moderato
The Feast of John, Mid - sum - mer - day,
POGNER Das schö - ne Fest, Jo - han - nis - tag,

[16] THE KNIGHT

Molto moderato

[17] ARIA *AM STILLEN HERD* (Walther)

Moderato
p In snow - bound hall at win - ter time,
Am stil - len Herd in Win - ters - zeit,

[18] BECKMESSER

Ben tenuto
a
p

[19] SPRING

Mosso
p dolce

applaud the idea [13], but the Masters decline energetically [1d], and Beckmesser accuses Sachs of being merely a cheap ballad-monger [13]. Pogner's offer [15] is accepted as proposed [14ab with 15]—while Beckmesser and Sachs exchange taunts regarding their qualifications as suitors for the girl.

Now Pogner introduces Walther as a candidate, and he steps forward [16] to subject himself to the scrutiny of the Masters. When at last they ask him where he has studied singing, he calls on Love for inspiration [2e] and answers (Aria *Am stillen Herd:* "In snowbound hall") [17] that in wintertime he perused a book by Walther von der Vogelweide,* while in spring [17] he listened to the singing of the birds. He is asked to sing, and Beckmesser is appointed Marker. Beckmesser [18] facetiously informs Walther [16 minor] about the duties of the Marker, and with a mocking "God help you" to the knight [16], he closes the curtain of his booth. Kothner reads—or, rather, sings—the rules to be followed in the composition of a mastersong [1a]: a mastersong comprises a number of strophes, each consisting of two stanzas several lines in length, rhymed, and following the same melody, plus an "aftersong," also several lines long but set to a different tune.

Beckmesser from his booth calls: "Now begin!" and Walther sings (Aria *Fanget an!:* "Now begin!") a song of love [6a] and spring [19, 6c], frequently interrupted by the Marker's screeching chalk. Before he can finish his second stanza he is stopped [16] by the triumphant Beckmesser [20ab], who emerges from his booth, his board covered with marks, and charges Walther with violation of every rule in the book. Most of the Masters agree that the knight's performance could hardly be called singing [6ab]. However, Sachs [21a] finds the tune orderly even though it might not accord with the rules of the Mastersingers. When Beckmesser makes facetious remarks about Sachs' hack tunes [20a], Sachs accuses him of bias against a rival [1c, 15]. Thereupon, the Marker tells Sachs to stick to his workbench and to finish his new shoes for him [22] for St. John's Day. Sachs promises to make the shoes after he has heard Walther to the end, but the Masters decide that they have heard enough. Nevertheless, encouraged by Sachs, Walther finishes his song [19, 6ca] over the loud discussion in progress among the Masters. His song ended, he proudly leaves, breaking through the delighted band of apprentices [13]. The excited Masters follow.

Sachs, oblivious to the noisy apprentices, who are busy restoring the furniture to its original position [13], is for a while absorbed in his own thoughts [6c]; then, with a shrug of the shoulders, he follows the other Masters [1ab].

Act II: After a short introduction [15] the curtain rises. Along the street, on which Sachs' and Pogner's houses stand opposite each other, the apprentices are putting up the window shutters for the night. David hums the apprentices' ditty [13]. Magdalene comes with a basket full of food for him, but when she hears of Walther's failure [motive 28a] she violently takes it

* A famous thirteenth-century Minnesinger.

[20] MALICIOUSNESS

a Molto vivace

fp *staccato*

b Molto vivace

[21] SACHS' KINDNESS

a Moderato

b Piuttosto mosso

[22] THE COBBLERS

Con vigore

ff

[23] NUREMBERG

Molto moderato

tenuto

[24] EVA

a Moderato

b

p *dolce*

[25] MIDSUMMER-NIGHT

Moderato

p *dolce*

back. David, teased by the other apprentices, is on the point of starting a fight when Sachs appears and stops him [22]. They go inside, and David puts Beckmesser's shoes on the last [11]. Pogner strolls down the street with Eva and spies a light in Sachs' shop [motive 28a]. He is about to go in for a talk, but decides against it. Worried about the happenings of the day, he talks to Eva about the morrow when, before all Nuremberg [23], she will crown the winning Mastersinger with the wreath, thereby accepting him as a husband [2d]. However, to Eva's cautious inquiry after Walther, he remains uncommunicative. Finally she persuades him to go into the house. Magdalene appears at the door, and from her Eva hears the bad news about Walther. Eva decides to go and sound out her friend Sachs later [24a].

Sachs sends David to bed and sits down to work [22] in the open doorway of his shop, but the fragrance of the lilac bush distracts him [6c, 19] (Monologue *Was duftet doch der Flieder:* "The lilac's scent surrounds me"). He tries to resume his work [motive 28], but his thoughts return to Walther's song [6c, 4], so familiar and yet so strange [6ab], created like a bird's song from the fullness of the heart [5a], yet well and orderly composed. No matter what the other Masters thought about this song, he, Sachs, liked it.

He is happily surprised when Eva comes to see him [24b]. Is she worried about the shoes she will wear tomorrow as a bride? Whose bride, Eva would like to know [24a]. Oh, suggests Sachs, maybe Beckmesser's, whose shoes he is just readying. This is an odious prospect for Eva, and she asks [24a] whether Sachs will make no effort at all to win her. Tenderly they recall what they have meant to each other ever since Eva was a little girl, and Sachs regretfully declares himself too old to become her husband. Craftily he turns the conversation to the events of the afternoon [16] and tells Eva [24a] that Walther's case is hopeless, for one born a Master will always have the hardest position among Masters. Let the knight go wherever he may [22, 20b] without bothering and upsetting the Masters of the Guild. Eva is called home by Magdalene, but she remains long enough to vent her frustration [20b] by expressing the hope that the knight may find people elsewhere more kind-hearted [6c] than a certain unfeeling and malicious cobbler of her acquaintance [22].

Sachs, now certain of Eva's love for Walther, wonders what to do about it. Meanwhile, Magdalene takes Eva across the street and gives her a message from Beckmesser: he will serenade her later this evening [20b]. Eva asks Magdalene to appear at the window in her stead, and then, seeing Walther approaching [16], she leaves her companion to explain her absence to her father and rushes to meet her beloved [24a]. Whatever hopes she has left are quickly shattered when Walther tells about his failure, and how her father had sworn that she will marry only a Mastersinger [1ab]. He had put all his love into his song [6c], but those Masters! As in a nightmare he sees himself beleaguered by their grimacing faces [20b] while he is

[25] *continued*

[26] NIGHT-WATCHMAN'S SONG

Adagio

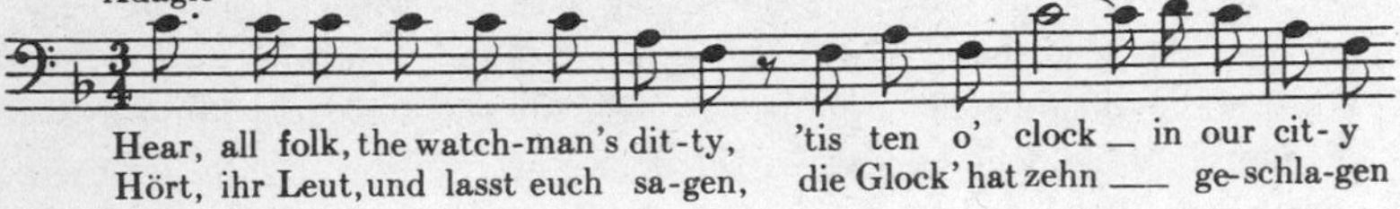
Hear, all folk, the watch-man's dit-ty, 'tis ten o' clock _ in our cit-y
Hört, ihr Leut, und lasst euch sa-gen, die Glock' hat zehn ___ ge-schla-gen

[27] THE LUTE (see [31])

Moderato

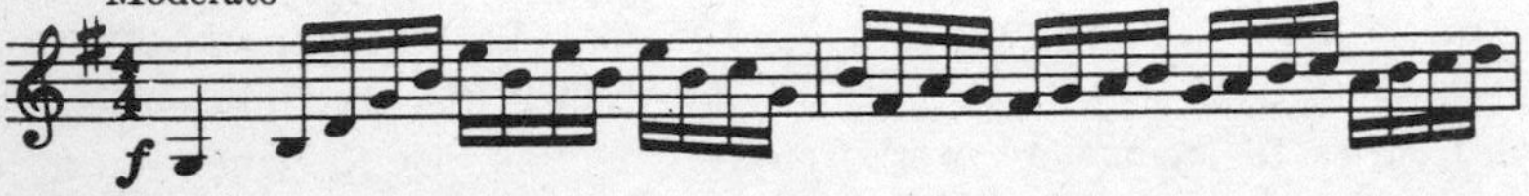
f

[28] COBBLER'S SONG (Sachs)

Con vigore (see [22])

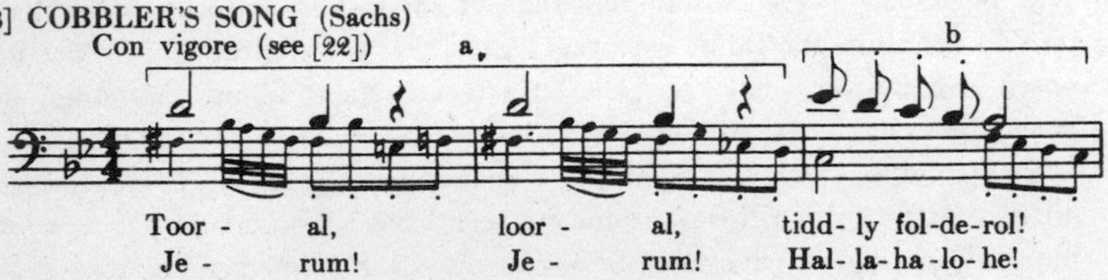
a
b
Toor - al, loor - al, tidd- ly fol-de-rol!
Je - rum! Je - rum! Hal- la- ha -lo- he!

[29] Con vigore

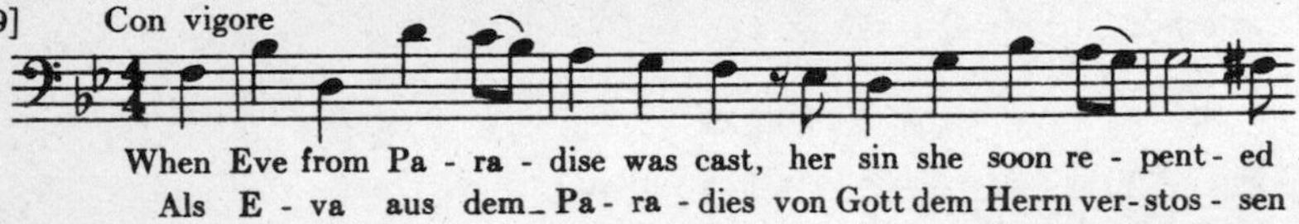
When Eve from Pa - ra - dise was cast, her sin she soon re - pent - ed
Als E - va aus dem_ Pa- ra -dies von Gott dem Herrn ver-stos - sen

[30] BECKMESSER'S SERENADE

Moderato

a
b
I see _ the day - light dawn-*ing*, with great pleas-*úre* I do
Den Tag_ seh' ich_ er - schei- *nén*, der mir wohl *gé*-fall'n thut.

[31] RIOT

Vivace

a
b
f e staccato

stuck in the glue of their rules. As the only way out, he urges Eva to flee with him, but just then the horn of the Night Watchman is heard. In a frenzy Walther clutches at his sword, but Eva gently calms him [25] and asks him to hide for the moment under the linden tree. When Magdalene calls her into the house, she leaves, but not without assuring Walther of her love and determination [motive 37a].

The Night Watchman passes by, calling the hour [26]. When he has disappeared, Sachs [22], who has listened to Walther's and Eva's conversation from behind his slightly open door, now opens it a little wider, intent on preventing an elopement [25].

Eva returns, dressed in Magdalene's clothes, and throws herself into Walther's arms [motive 37ab]. Just when they are ready to flee, Sachs opens his door wide and lets the light of his lamp fall full on the street [22]. The two lovers must now retire again into the shade of the linden tree [25]. Their relief when the shoemaker withdraws his lamp is short-lived because now, as the crafty Sachs is well aware, Beckmesser with his lute [27] is barring their way. With difficulty Eva dissuades Walther from killing the Marker. Meanwhile, Sachs has silently put his workbench right in the open doorway, and at the moment when Beckmesser is ready to begin his serenade, Sachs turns the light of his lamp onto the street again and commences to hammer loudly and to sing (Cobbler's Song *Jerum, jerum, halla-hallohe* [28ab, 29, 11]. Eva feels the sting in the song, which deals with the expulsion from Paradise and the trouble Eva gives the heavenly shoemakers, and Walther tries not to listen. Beckmesser is at first stunned, then angry, and finally furious, but two verses have passed and then a third one [29 with 32a] before he can interrupt Sachs for any appreciable length of time. Meanwhile Magdalene, dressed in Eva's clothes, has opened the window, and Beckmesser must, at all costs, stop Sachs and sing his song. Strumming his lute [27] to keep "Eva's" attention, he tells Sachs that he does not care about the shoes any more and that he wants him to listen to his composition for the contest so he may benefit from Sachs' fine and erudite criticism. But Sachs repeats all Beckmesser's taunts at the meeting: isn't he, after all, just a common writer of hack tunes [13]? He starts the fourth verse of his song, but is interrupted by a wild tirade ending with the vow that as long as Beckmesser has something to say in the Guild, the envious cobbler [22] shall never become Marker [1c]. However, eventually they agree that Beckmesser shall sing his song while Sachs tries to learn the Marker's art [1c], "marking" with his hammer on the last [28a, 31a]. Against their will, Walther and Eva follow the weird scene with fascination [25]. At last Beckmesser, who through all this has kept strumming loudly on the lute [27], actually begins to sing his badly composed and silly serenade (Beckmesser's Serenade *Den Tag seh' ich erscheinen:* "I see the daylight dawning") [30ab]. After the first lines he remonstrates with Sachs about his hammering, but, finding himself balked, he just keeps on singing,

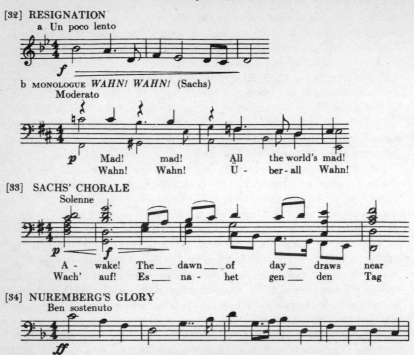

[32] RESIGNATION

a Un poco lento

b MONOLOGUE *WAHN! WAHN!* (Sachs)

Moderato

Mad! mad! All the world's mad!
Wahn! Wahn! Ü - ber - all Wahn!

[33] SACHS' CHORALE

Solenne

A - wake! The dawn of day draws near
Wach' auf! Es na - het gen den Tag

[34] NUREMBERG'S GLORY

Ben sostenuto

blindly and furiously, while Sachs relentlessly and with relish marks away and after awhile triumphantly shows Beckmesser the finished shoes [28a, 29]. Now Sachs adds a song of his own to the town clerk's serenade.

Gradually the windows along the street have opened and the neighbors start complaining about the noise. When David awakens and notices somebody serenading Magdalene, he jumps out of the window and starts to beat him up [31ab]. This is the signal for a free-for-all in which apprentices, journeymen, and even Masters gradually join [31ab with 30ab]. At last the women, who have been shouting from the windows, marshal all available containers and, at a signal, pour cold water on the hotly fighting mob below. This and the sound of the Night Watchman's horn close by at that very same instant puts everyone to wild flight. Walther, his sword drawn, is about to force his way through the crowd, but Sachs, who has kept a watchful eye on the lovers, now strides from his workshop [22], grabs Walther's arm, pushes "Magdalene" toward Pogner, who has come from his house to look for her [25], shoves David before him, and pulls Walther after him into his house.

The Watchman appears and, puzzled by the suddenly silent row of closed doors and windows, shakily intones his call [26]. Slowly he walks up the empty street [25, 31ab, 30a] and rounds the corner.

Prelude to Act III: Between strains developed from [32], the chorale "Awake" * [33] is introduced by the orchestra, interrupted by excerpts from

* Words by Hans Sachs.

the Cobbler's Song and [6a]. Without interruption in the music the curtain opens [9].

Act III, Scene 1: Unnoticed by Sachs, who is absorbed in reading a voluminous tome, David [9] steals into the workshop from the street. However, his bad conscience, the result of last night's fight, forces him to address his master [32] and to give a detailed account of the events leading up to the riotous scene [25, 27, 31ab]. Finally Sachs, who up to now has been apparently quite unaware of his surroundings [32], notices David [9] and the charming flowers he has brought [24a]. He asks his apprentice to sing the St. John's Day Chorale, and David, after a false start—he sings the words of the chorale to the tune of Beckmesser's serenade [30a]—acquits himself well, and is told to put on his finery to accompany Sachs to the song fest [3].

Alone, Sachs (Monologue *Wahn! Wahn!:* "Mad! mad!") [32b] passionately decries man's unconquerable folly. Not even peaceful Nuremberg [23, 34] is spared its share of it [31ab] when a meddling cobbler acts to prevent calamity. However, St. John's Eve [25, 31ab] is past, and now on St. John's Day [15] Hans Sachs must try to guide folly so that it may accomplish a noble end [23, 2d, 15].

Walther, entering from the adjoining room, is greeted kindly by Sachs [21b]. The knight has had a lovely dream [2d], and Sachs encourages him [21b] to use it as the theme for a mastersong [2c], for he still hopes the knight will succeed. Sachs explains that a mastersong contains the spirit of youth [35] and spring [6c] and ardor [6a] within the framework of mature experience. Then he takes paper and pen [21b, 35] to write down the words as Walther sings of his vision of paradise (The Dream Song *Morgenlich leuchtend in rosigem Schein:* "Bathed in the sunlight at dawn of the day") [36, 2a, 37ab]. Sachs is deeply moved by the song [32]. After Walther has completed two strophes, Sachs bids him [21b] keep the tune well in mind should he be called upon to sing it publicly [23], but for the present Walther had better come with him and get dressed for their undertaking [16, 23; 23 with 34; 37a, 21a].

Beckmesser [30a minor, 31ab] enters the shop [32, 18], obviously still quite sore in mind and limb from the adventures of the past night [22, 27, 31a, 30a, 31b, 16]. Suddenly he notices Walther's song on the desk [36], but just then Sachs returns, and Beckmesser quickly hides it in his pocket. Sachs greets him cordially [22], but Beckmesser declares [18] that he knows now what Sachs has in mind. Furiously [38], he calls him a vicious dowry-hunter who had tried to shout him down the previous night [28a] and, when he failed to do so, had sent his boy to beat him up [31ab]. Sachs calmly states that he will not compete in the singing contest, and when Beckmesser shows him the poem [37a] as proof of the contrary, Sachs makes him a gift of it [21b]. Beckmesser is overjoyed and extols Sachs' poetry and his friendship. But, just to be sure [18], he makes Sachs vow that he will never claim authorship of the poem [21b]. Now Beckmesser feels safe

[35] YOUTH

Moderato

[36] DREAM SONG (Walther)

Moderato

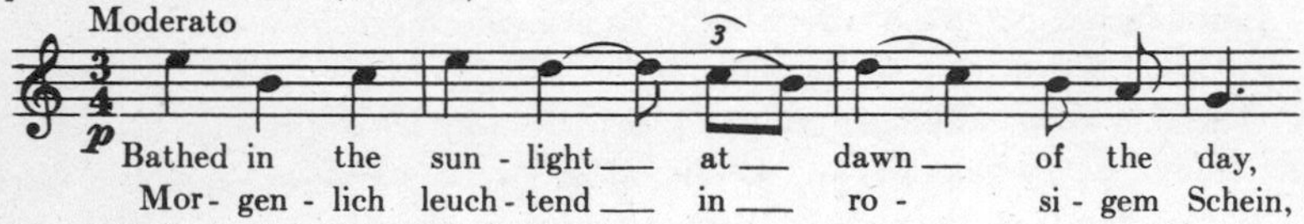

[37] Moderato (see 5)

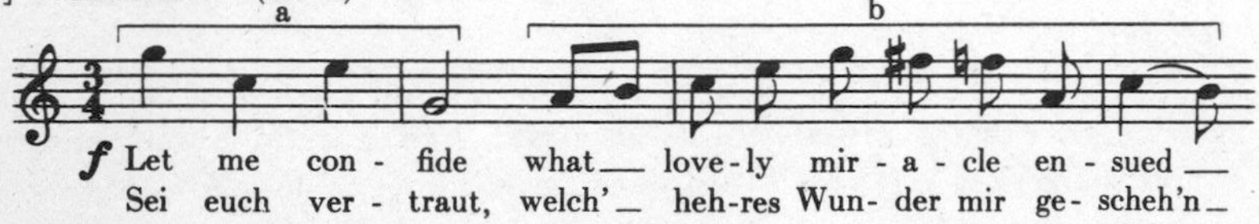

[38] RAGE

Molto allegro

[39] ARIA *O SACHS! MEIN FREUND!* (Eva) (see [32])

Molto vivace

and fully recompensed for the hardships he has suffered. He is altogether confused, though, by the words of the poem [31b] and must hurry home to memorize them. Already at the door, he promises to vote for Sachs for Marker [13]. He runs off [31b], and Sachs looks musingly after him, quite content with the turn events have taken [22, 23 with 2d].

Eva comes in [24b] to have her new shoes adjusted [22]. When Walther re-enters [25] she is overwhelmed and stands as if transfixed. Sachs seems not to notice anything, but when he mentions that he would like a song while he is working, Walther, in rapture, sings a third strophe to his dream song, extolling Eva and expressing confidence that he will win her [2b, 36, 37ab]. Eva, deeply moved, hides her head on Sachs' chest [32a]. Reluctantly he tears himself away [32a] and starts grumbling about the troubles of a cobbler [28b; 29 with 32a; 11], for which, in the end, he is repaid with insults [20b]. Fervently and tenderly Eva embraces Sachs [39 with 32] and confesses that all she is she owes to his love [40a] and that she would love only him, were it not for a force beyond her control. Sachs, leaving her in Walther's arms, soberly congratulates himself on having avoided the doubtful happiness of King Marke * [40b] by finding the right husband for her just in the nick of time.

Now Magdalene appears, and Sachs calls David and proceeds solemnly to baptize the new mastersong [8, 1a]. However, for such an occasion an apprentice will not do as a witness; consequently, with the traditional box on the ear, he raises David to the status of journeyman [1d]. Eva, called upon to say the blessing, prays that the song may win the prize (Quintet *Selig, wie die Sonne:* "Brightly as the sun") [41, 36]. Walther joins his hopes to hers; David and Magdalene are occupied with their own expectations; and Sachs' renunciation is as tender as it is philosophical. The ceremony over [36, 37a], Sachs bids everyone repair to the celebration, and goes ahead with Walther [23].

Scenic Transformation: Behind the closed curtain the scene is changed to an open meadow by a small river; in the foreground, to one side, a platform has been erected for the Mastersingers and guests of honor. The music, which flows on without interruption, prepares for the festive scene with motives [23, 34, 1d] mingled with a gay fanfare [42].

Act III, Scene 2: The shoemakers' guild makes its formal entrance [28ab], followed by the town musicians [42], the journeymen with toy instruments [13], the tailors bleating like goats,† and the bakers. They all plant their banners on the platform and then disband. When a boatload of girls arrives [15], the apprentices and David dance with them to the music of the town pipers [43]. Now the Mastersingers arrive [1d, 42], and the apprentices hurry to the river to meet them [1a in double time]. The Mastersingers start their procession [1ab], led by Kothner carrying their banner [3]. Directly behind him come Pogner and Eva. When they have ascended the platform [42], the apprentices ask the cheering crowd for silence [3]. Sachs steps forward and all join spontaneously in singing his chorale (Chorale *Wach' auf!:* "Awake!") [33] and hail him enthusiastically [1d, 3]. Humbly he thanks them for their ovation (Sachs' Address *Euch macht ihr's leicht:* "Words light to you") [32, 21b]. What he has to say, he informs them, will bring honor to his art [14ab], for one Master has offered to the winner of the singing contest [14ab with 15] his only daughter and all his possessions. But, Sachs adds, he must exhort the eligible Masters [14a, 1c] to consider the prize involved [2c] and to act in such a manner that the girl may never have reason to regret that Nuremberg [23] is honoring art with its highest treasures.

With deep emotion Pogner thanks Sachs [23 with 34; 14a with 15]. Then Sachs turns to Beckmesser, who admits that he has difficulties with the poem [18] but will not heed Sachs' advice to withdraw from the competition. Now Kothner calls on the oldest competitor first, and the apprentices [1a in double time] lead the town clerk to a mound in front of the platform. When the crowd sees Beckmesser stumbling and nearly falling off,

* See *Tristan und Isolde.*
† The symbol of their guild.

[40] SACHS' LOVE FOR EVA

a Molto vivace

b (see ***Tristan und Isolde*** [2])

Molto moderato

f
(see b)
pp

[41] BAPTISMAL BLESSING

Andante ma non troppo

p
Bright - - ly as the sun
Se - - lig, wie die Son - ne

[42] FESTAL FANFARE

Moderato

f

[43] DANCE OF THE APPRENTICES

Tempo di Valzer moderato

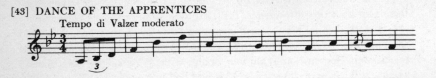

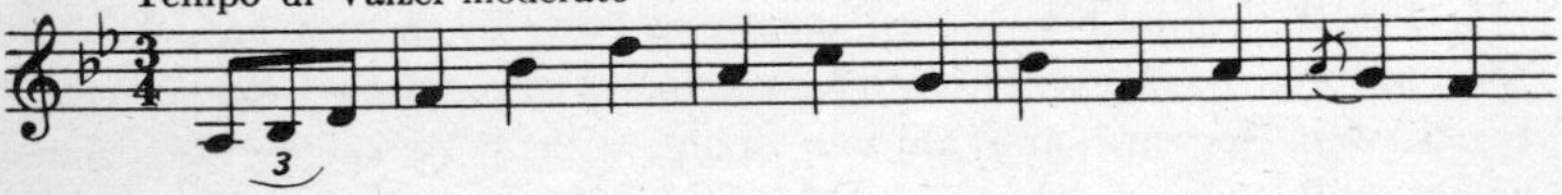
3

they mockingly [7 with 1d] express their doubts regarding his qualifications as a bridegroom. The apprentices call for silence [3], and Beckmesser [18], after preluding nervously on his lute [27], starts his song, a hopeless and ridiculous distortion of Walther's poem (Beckmesser's Contest Song *Morgen ich leuchte in rosigem Schein:* "Bathing in sunlight at dawning of day") [30a minor, 27]. The listeners are at first stunned [18], but Beckmesser continues with mounting desperation until the entire gathering breaks out in thunderous laughter. The furious [38] Town Clerk declares that the poem was written and forced on him by Sachs, and rushes off. To everybody's amazement, Sachs calmly declares [21b] that he never could write so beautiful a poem. He asks if there is anyone present who might act as his witness and sing the song as it was originally written, proving that the song really is beautiful and establishing at the same time that he is its author and well worthy of the title of Mastersinger [1b]. Walther steps forward [5a, 16]. Introduced by Sachs [24a], he ascends the mound [2d) and, to the delight and acclaim of people and Mastersingers, sings a more elaborate version of his dream song (The Prize Song *Morgenlich leuchtend in rosigem Schein:* "Bathed in the sunlight at dawn of the day") [36, 2a, 37ab]. Eva crowns him with the wreath [37a], but when Pogner comes to bestow the golden chain of the Mastersinger on him [3, 2d] Walther declares that he wants his bliss [41] without mastersinging. After a moment of general perplexity Sachs soberly advises Walther (Sachs' Exhortation *Verachter mir die Meister nicht:* "Do not disdain our Masters' art") [1a] not to scorn the men and the art immediately responsible for his present happiness [5abc with 1ab]. It is the Masters [3], he continues, who have taken over German art [1d] in all its greatness from the courts and preserved it, a standard about which to rally in the days ahead when grave danger from without will face the nation. Sachs' plea to revere and honor the German Master and German art [22 with 34; 3 with 5ab and 1ab] is fervently repeated by the people [3, 1d]. Eva adorns him with the wreath taken from Walther's brow, and Sachs hangs the golden chain around Walther's neck. Masters and folk pay homage to their great Sachs [1a, 7].

THEMES

[1] OVERTURE

Presto
pp

[2]

Presto
p

[3]

Presto
p
3

[4] DUET *CINQUE, DIECI* (Figaro, Susanna)

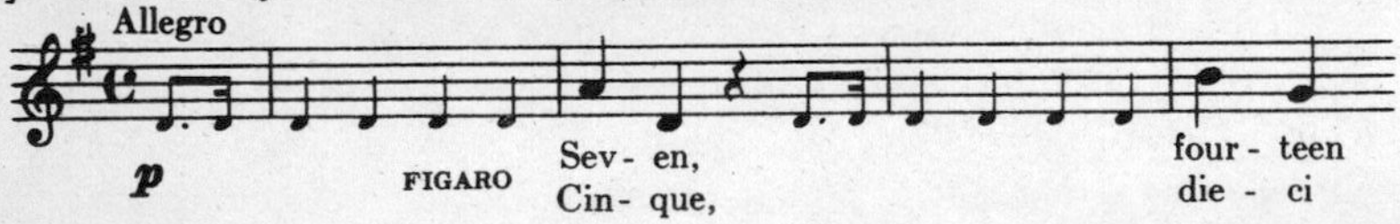
Allegro
p
FIGARO
Sev- en, four - teen
Cin - que, die - ci

[5]

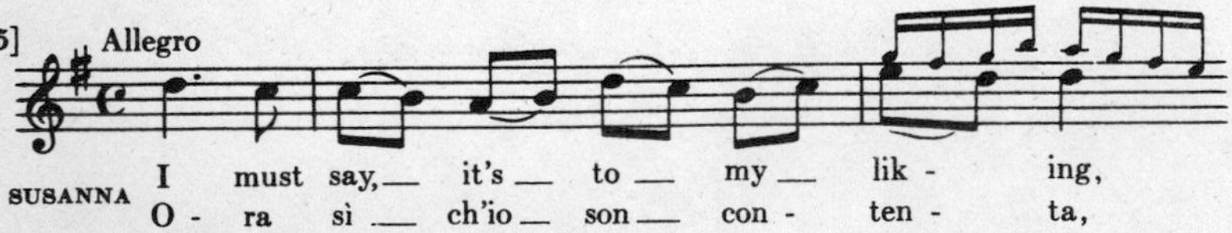
Allegro
SUSANNA
I must say,— it's — to — my — lik - ing,
O - ra sì — ch'io — son — con - ten - ta,

[6]

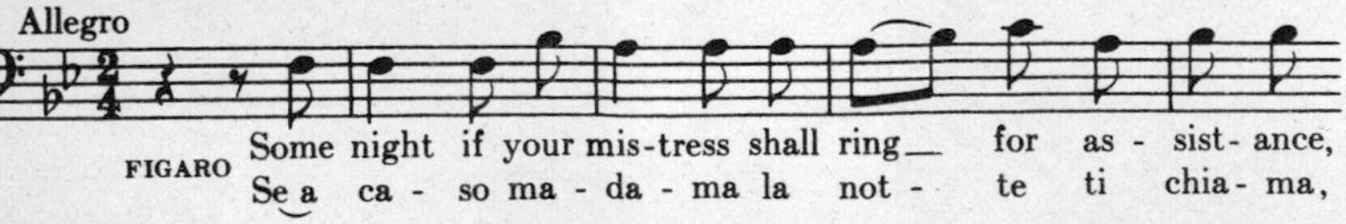
Allegro
FIGARO
Some night if your mis-tress shall ring — for as - sist - ance,
Se a ca - so ma - da - ma la not - te ti chia - ma,

[7] ARIA *SE VUOL BALLARE* (Figaro)

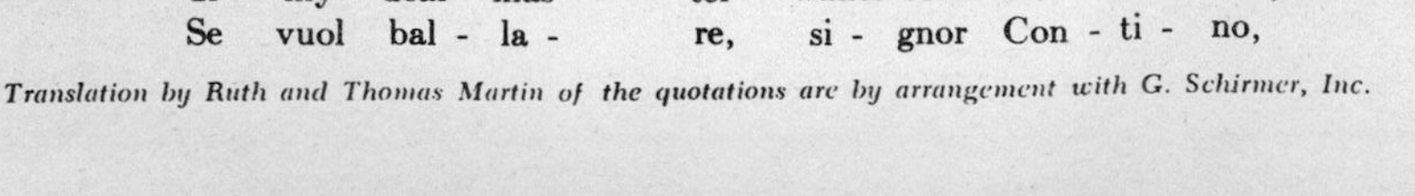
Allegretto
If my dear mas - ter wants some di - ver - sion,
Se vuol bal - la - re, si - gnor Con - ti - no,

Translation by Ruth and Thomas Martin of the quotations are by arrangement with G. Schirmer, Inc.

Le Nozze di Figaro

THE MARRIAGE OF FIGARO

Opera in four acts by Wolfgang Amadeus Mozart. Libretto by Lorenzo da Ponte, based on the play by Beaumarchais. First performance: Vienna, May 1, 1786.

Characters: COUNT ALMAVIVA (baritone); FIGARO, his valet (bass); COUNTESS ALMAVIVA (soprano); SUSANNA, her maid (soprano); DR. BARTOLO (bass); MARCELLINA, his former servant (mezzo-soprano); CHERUBINO, a page (soprano or mezzo-soprano); DON BASILIO, a music master (tenor); DON CURZIO, a judge (tenor); ANTONIO, a gardener (bass); BARBARINA, his daughter (soprano).
The Count's castle at Aguas-Frescas near Seville, in the latter half of the eighteenth century.

Important parts of this opera are cast in the form of recitative accompanied solely by the harpsichord. These "secco recitatives" are indicated in the text by (Recitative).

Overture: A sprightly presto movement [1, 2] containing a lovely lyric melody [3].

Act I: In a room located between the apartments of the Count and those of the Countess, Figaro is measuring the floor (Duet *Cinque, dieci:* "Seven, fourteen") [4] while Susanna is trying on, and showing off to him, the bonnet she has made for herself [5]. She intends to wear it for their marriage, which the Count has promised to perform that day. When Susanna learns (Recitative) that Figaro is trying to find the best location for the bed that the Count is giving to them, she is not pleased. Unquestionably, Figaro's claim that this is a most convenient room is correct (Duet *Se a caso madama:* "Some night if your mistress") [6]. Whenever the master or mistress rings for service, they can, with a few steps, be right there—but, Susanna reminds her bridegroom, the Count could just as quickly be here "with a few steps." And in the absence of Figaro . . . ? Would Figaro like to hear more without getting excited? Basilio, her music master, she continues (Recitative), keeps talking to her about the Count's affection for her and—— Just then the Countess rings and Susanna must be off.

Ah, so the Count wants to amuse himself, comments Figaro bitterly; well, it is to Figaro's tune he will be dancing (Cavatina *Se vuol ballare, signor Contino:* "Should my dear master want some diversion") [7]. No means will remain untried [8] till the Count's plans have been brought to naught. Figaro leaves, and Marcellina enters with Dr. Bartolo (Recitative). She

[8] ARIA *SE VUOL BALLARE* (Figaro) *continued*

Presto

Subt - ly out - wit - ting, in - no - cent seem - ing,
L'ar - te scher - men - do, l'ar - te a - do - pran - do,

[9] ARIA *LA VENDETTA* (Bartolo)

Allegro con spirito

Tak - ing ven - geance, yes, tak - ing ven - geance!
La ven - det - ta, oh, la ven - det - ta!

[10] Allegro con spirito

Al - ways pro - ceed - ing with ut - most le - gal - i - ty,
Se tut - to il co - di - ce do - ves - si vol - ge - re,

[11] ARIA *NON SO PIU* (Cherubino)

Allegro vivace

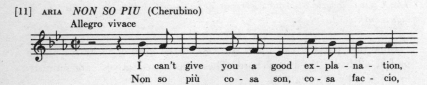

I can't give you a good ex - pla - na - tion,
Non so più co - sa son, co - sa fac - cio,

[12] TRIO *COSA SENTO* (Count, Basilio, Susanna)

Allegro assai

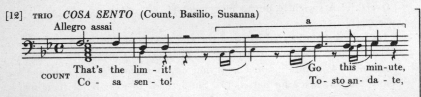

COUNT That's the lim - it! Go this min - ute,
Co - sa sen - to! To - sto an - da - te,

[13] Allegro assai

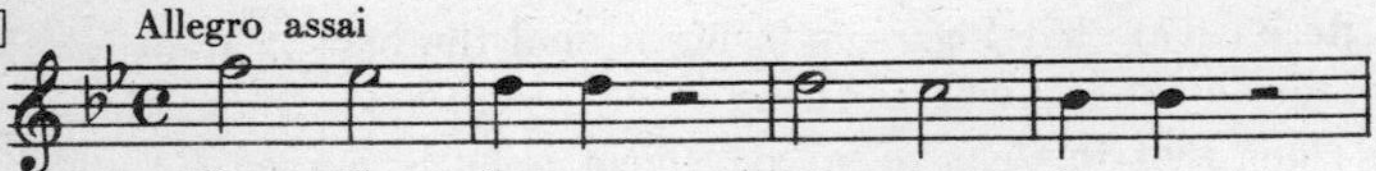

BASILIO How ill cho - sen was my sto - ry,
In mal pun - to son qui giun - to;

[14] Allegro

CHO. Come, — lads and las - ses, flow - ers humb - ly strew - ing
Gio - va - ni lie - te, fio - ri spar - ge - te

[15] ARIA *NON PIU ANDRAI* (Figaro)

Vivace

From now on, my ad - ven - tur - ous lov - er,
Non più an - drai, far - fal - lo - ne a - mo - ro - so,

shows him a contract that commits Figaro to marry *her* rather than Susanna. The doctor promises his aid. He would be delighted, he murmurs to himself, to see Figaro married to his former housekeeper—if only to get even with him for his betrayal. For it was Figaro who helped the Count steal and marry Bartolo's ward, Rosina.* Yes, Bartolo exclaims, revenge is sweet to a man of culture (Aria *La vendetta:* "Taking vengeance") [9]. Slyly, and using every trick of the lawyer's trade [10], Dr. Bartolo will subdue the scoundrel Figaro. He leaves Marcellina in high spirits; thus, when Susanna enters, the older woman engages her in a little name-calling bout (Duettino *Via resti servita:* "To greet you, my lady"), but Susanna, by referring to Marcellina's ripe age, triumphantly achieves her rival's hasty retreat.

Presently she is joined by the mercurial young page Cherubino, who complains (Recitative) that the Count has just caught him alone with Barbarina and has dismissed him. If the lovely Countess, Cherubino's godmother, cannot obtain his pardon—— Suddenly he notices one of the Countess' ribbons in Susanna's hand. He quickly snatches it from her and gives her in exchange the manuscript of a love song he has just written. May she sing of his love to every female in the castle, for love is driving him insane (Aria *Non so più cosa son, cosa faccio:* "I can't give you a good explanation") [11].

Suddenly a voice is heard outside, and Cherubino has barely time to hide behind the big armchair before the Count enters. The lord of the manor has scarcely installed himself comfortably in the chair and favored Susanna with a declaration of his deep affection (Recitative) when Basilio's voice is heard outside. Now it is the Count's turn to hide behind the chair, while Cherubino, shielded from the Count's view by Susanna, sneaks around the chair and curls up tightly in it. Susanna covers him quickly with a dress. Basilio enters, asking whether Susanna has seen the Count. He is also looking for Cherubino, who has been seen in this vicinity this morning. He mentions the page's glances of love toward the ladies in general and especially toward the Countess. On hearing this, the Count comes forward in high dudgeon (Trio *Cosa sento:* "That's the limit") [12]. Basilio makes oily excuses [13] for having arrived at such an inopportune moment, and Susanna, trembling with fright, nearly swoons. The two men support her to the chair, but she recovers just before being deposited on top of Cherubino. Now the Count, while dramatically telling about his discovery at Barbarina's, at the same time discovers the page in the armchair. He rages against the desperate Susanna [12a], and the delighted Basilio in mock dejection takes back his now-proved accusations against Cherubino [13]. The Count realizes to his dismay (Recitative) that Cherubino has heard his entire conversation with Susanna.

Figaro enters with a group of peasants, who sing the Count's praises [14].

* See *Il Barbiere di Siviglia.*

[16] ARIA *NON PIU ANDRAI* (Figaro) *continued*

Vivace

p
Up the ston - y moun- tains wheez-ing,
Per mon - ta - gne, per val - lo - ni,

[17] ARIA *PORGI, AMOR* (Countess)

Larghetto

Pour, O love, _ sweet con - so - la - tion
Por - gi, a - mor, _ qual- che ri - sto - ro

[18] CANZONE *VOI, CHE SAPETE* (Cherubino)

Andante con moto

You know the an- swer, you hold _ the _ key,
Voi, che sa - pe - te che co - sa è a - mor,

[19] ARIA *VENITE, INGINOCCHIATEVI* (Susanna)

Allegretto

p
Come here and kneel in front of me,
Ve - ni - te, in- gi - noc-chia-te- vi,

[20] Allegretto

If wo - men fall in love with him, they know _ the _ rea- son why! _
Se l'a - ma- no le fe - mi- ne, han cer - to il lor per- chè! _

[21] TRIO *SUSANNA, VIA SORTITE* (Count, Countess, Susanna)

Allegro spirituoso

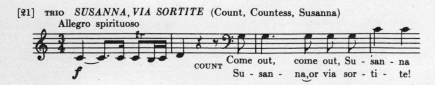

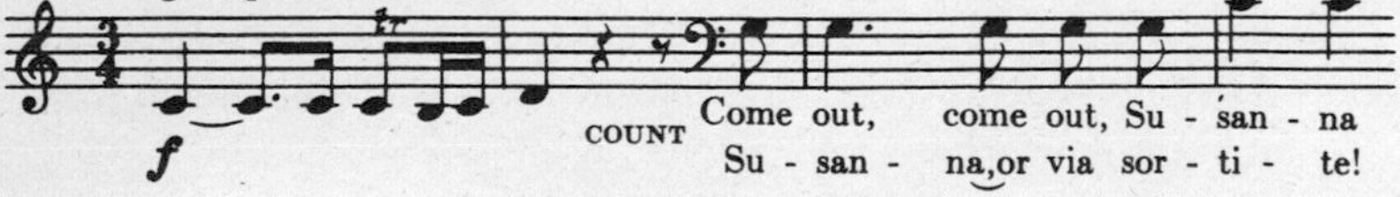
f
COUNT
Come out, come out, Su - san - na
Su - san - na, or via sor - ti - te!

[22] DUET *APRITE, PRESTO APRITE* (Susanna, Cherubino)

Allegro assai

pp
SUSANNA
Un- lock the door and hur - ry! It's I, it is Su - san- na,
A- pri- te, pre- sto a- pri - te, a- pri- te, è la Su - san- na,

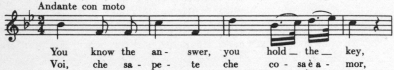

He especially thanks his master (Recitative), somewhat ironically, for giving up the master's traditional right over his maidservants on their wedding nights. Will the Count therefore place the white veil, symbol of virtue, on the bride's head? The Count is forced to smile graciously, and he promises to perform the ceremony—a little later, for he secretly hopes that Marcellina will meanwhile put in her bid. The peasants leave.

The Count, blackmailed by Cherubino, who slyly indicates his willingness to forget what he has heard, agrees to forgive the page. Moreover, he makes him captain of a regiment in Seville, with orders to report there immediately. Most satisfied with this brilliant solution, the Count leaves, and Basilio with him. Figaro, with pantomimic assistance from Susanna, gives Cherubino a gay send-off (Aria *Non più andrai:* "From now on") [15], previewing for him in good-natured raillery the less pleasant, though more glorious, aspects of military life [16].

Act II: In her boudoir, the Countess prays for the restoration of her husband's love (Aria *Porgi amor:* "Pour, O love") [17]. Susanna joins her, and they discuss (Recitative) the Count's shameless behavior toward each of them. Now Figaro comes and proposes placing a letter in the Count's hands informing him of a supposed secret rendezvous between the Countess and a lover this evening. This will keep the Count too busy, Figaro hopes, to plot against his and Susanna's marriage. Figaro also reveals that he has persuaded Cherubino to stay at the castle, for he has yet another plan: Susanna should promise her master a nocturnal meeting in the gardens, but the Count should be met instead by Cherubino dressed as a girl. This tender rendezvous should then be discovered by the Countess, and the embarrassed Count will need little persuasion to abandon his designs on Susanna and to comply with the Countess'—and Figaro's—wishes. This agreed upon, Figaro leaves to find the page and send him here to try on the disguise.

Soon Cherubino enters and, asked to sing the *canzone* whose manuscript he had left with Susanna earlier, shyly performs his latest love song (Canzone *Voi, che sapete:* "You know the answer") [18]. Now Susanna starts to dress Cherubino in female apparel (Aria *Venite, inginocchiatevi:* "Come here and kneel in front of me") [19]. If only he would stop turning his head to send adoring glances after Madame [motive 20]! Susanna bids him trip across the room, and finds him so fetching that she thinks it no wonder all the women are in love with him [20]. With this pointed remark —pointed toward the Countess, that is—Susanna goes into her room for a ribbon.

The Countess notices Cherubino's travel orders (Recitative), and observes that the official seal is missing. Cherubino takes advantage of their being alone and is about to declare his love when there is a loud knock and the voice of the Count demands that the door be opened. Cherubino locks himself in the Countess' dressing room, and the Countess, her pulse beating rapidly, admits her husband. There is a loud noise from the dressing room,

[23] TRIO *ESCI OMAI* (Count, Countess, Susanna)

Allegro

COUNT *f* Out you come, don't waste a moment,
E - sci o - mai, gar- zon mal - na - to;

[24] Allegro

COUNTESS Ah, his ear — is — deaf to rea - son,
Ah! la cie - ca — ge - lo - si - a,

COUNT I shall kill him!
Mo - ra, mo - ra!

[25] Molto andante

SUSANNA Your Lord - ship!
Si - gno - re!

[26] Allegro

FIGARO Dear Mas - ter, just lis - ten, the mu - sic is sound - ing,
Si - gno - re, di fuo - ri son già i suo - na - to - ri,

[27] Andante

COUNT Kind - ly tell me, mis - ter Fi - ga - ro, did you ev - er see this note?
Co - no - sce - te, si - gnor Fi - ga - ro, que - sto fo - glio chi ver - gò?

[28] Andante

[29] Allegro assai

MARCELLINA, BASILIO, BARTOLO Lord, our case de - mands a hear - ing,
Voi, si - gnor, che giu - sto sie - te,

[30] DUET *CRUDEL? PERCHE FINORA* (Count, Susanna)

Andante

COUNT But why, why make me suf - fer, long - ing for your re - ply?
Cru - del! per - chè fi - no - ra far - mi lan - guir co - si?

and the Count, who has already received Figaro's anonymous letter, does not believe the Countess when she claims that Susanna is in there. (Actually Susanna has just re-entered and, seeing the Count, has quickly hidden behind a screen.) An argument ensues (Trio *Susanna, via sortite:* "Susanna, what's the matter") [21] as to whether or not it would be proper for Susanna to come out of the dressing room and show herself to the Count—while Susanna from behind the screen gives vent to her fears. At length (Recitative) the count decides to take his wife along while he goes for tools to force the lock of the dressing-room door, since the Countess is unwilling to hand over the key. As a precaution, he first locks all the doors still remaining open, then ceremoniously offers his arm to his wife and leaves, locking the hall door behind him.

Quickly Susanna comes from her hiding-place and calls for Cherubino to come out (Duet *Aprite, presto aprite:* "Unlock the door and hurry") [22], and the page, after embracing her hurriedly, jumps out the window. Susanna locks herself in the dressing room in his place. Re-entering, the Countess confesses to the Count (Recitative) that it is really Cherubino who is in her dressing room. The Count, in a fury, commands Cherubino to come out (Trio *Esci omai garzon malnato:* "Out you come, don't waste a moment") [23]. Deaf to the Countess' explanations, he draws his sword [24]—but when the door opens it is Susanna who calmly emerges from the room [25]. The Count entreats pardon for his jealousy and suspicion, and the Countess, who herself is most relieved to learn from Susanna what has actually happened, forgives him after he promises in turn to forgive Figaro for writing the letter.

Figaro comes [26] and reports that everything is ready for the marriage ceremony, but there is still a little matter of an anonymous letter which the Count would like to have cleared up [27]. Ignoring the Countess' and Susanna's urgings to confess, Figaro disclaims all knowledge of such a letter, and the Count is about to give up when Antonio, the drunken gardener, staggers in. He complains, despite Figaro's efforts at distracting him, that he saw someone, probably Cherubino, jump from the window and trample his flowers. Quickly Figaro claims that it was he who jumped because he did not want to meet the Count just then. However, Antonio produces a paper [28] that he has found beneath the window, and the Count snatches it from him before Figaro can see it. The Count opens the sheet and then asks his valet sarcastically what he has lost. While Figaro squirms, the Countess, behind her husband's back, sees that it is the page's orders. This information is unobtrusively relayed to Figaro by way of Susanna, and Figaro answers accordingly. The Count now wants to know what Figaro was doing with Cherubino's orders, and the Countess remembers that the seal was missing from the document. This, too, is relayed to Figaro, who is most relieved to find an explanation. Quickly the Count checks and finds, to his astonishment, that Figaro is correct. He is again checkmated, and

[31] DUET *CRUDEL! PERCHE FINORA* (Count, Susanna) *continued*

Andante
COUNT
p The sweet ___ prom - ise you gave ___ me
Mi sen - to ___ dal con - ten - to
rais - es my hope ___ so ___ high. ___
pie - no di gio - ja il ___ cor. ___

[32] ARIA *VEDRO MENTR'IO SOSPIRO* (Count)

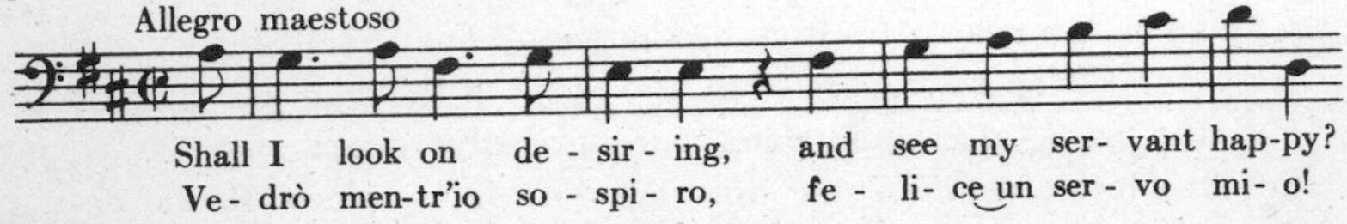
Allegro maestoso
Shall I look on de - sir - ing, and see my ser- vant hap-py?
Ve- drò men-tr'io so - spi - ro, fe - li- ce un ser - vo mi- o!

[33]

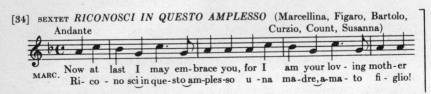

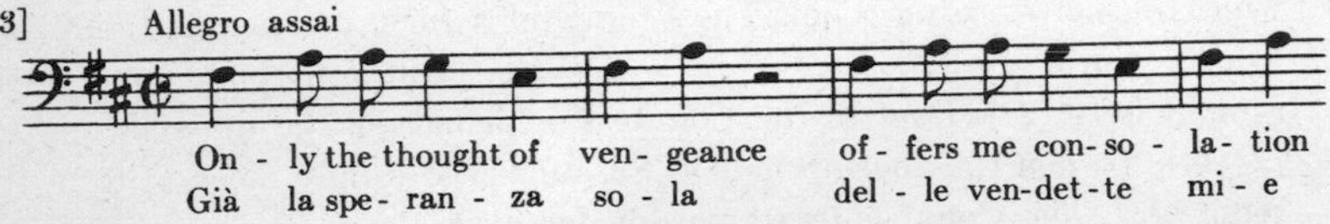
Allegro assai
On - ly the thought of ven- geance of - fers me con- so - la- tion
Già la spe - ran - za so - la del - le ven-det-te mi - e

[34] SEXTET *RICONOSCI IN QUESTO AMPLESSO* (Marcellina, Figaro, Bartolo, Curzio, Count, Susanna)

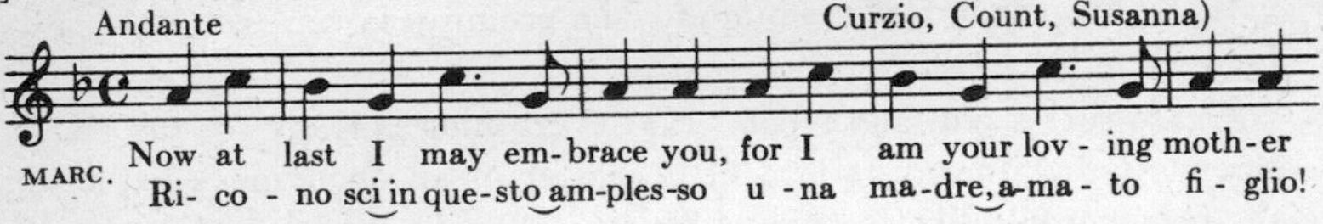
Andante
MARC.
Now at last I may em- brace you, for I am your lov - ing moth- er
Ri- co - no sci in que-sto am-ples-so u - na ma-dre, a-ma - to fi - glio!

the other three are breathing somewhat more easily, but now Marcellina arrives with Bartolo and Basilio [29]. She presents to the Count the contract in which Figaro has promised to marry her if he cannot repay some money she lent him. The Count promises an early judgment, and while the Countess, Figaro, and Susanna are desperate and in confusion, the others gloatingly enjoy their triumph.

Act III: In a hall of the castle the Count paces to and fro, thinking over (Recitative) all the recent strange events he still cannot explain. Apart, the Countess tells her maid to arrange a tryst with the Count for the night, a tryst that the Countess herself will attend. As she leaves, Susanna approaches her master and tells him that she will be at his service. They make a rendezvous in the garden (Duet *Crudel! perchè finora:* "But why, why make me suffer") [30]. The Count is overjoyed [31], while Susanna secretly expresses the hope that all lovers will forgive her for lying. As she leaves, she carelessly whispers to Figaro outside the door that their case is already won. The Count overhears this, and in mounting anger he repeats her words (Recitative *Hai già vinto la causa!:* "You have won the decision!"). Mad with jealousy, he swears that he will not suffer torment and ridicule from his servants (Aria *Vedrò, mentr'io sospiro:* "Shall I look on desiring") [32]. He will prepare a triumphant revenge, and this thought in itself gives him comfort and consolation [33].

The Judge enters with Figaro, Marcellina, and Bartolo (Recitative), and sentence is pronounced: "Pay up, or marry." However, Figaro claims he cannot marry without the consent of his parents: he declares that he is a nobleman, kidnapped by robbers, and an emblem on his arm is proof of his nobility. By the emblem Marcellina recognizes him as "Rafaello," and identifies herself and Bartolo as his parents (Sextet *Riconosci in questo amplesso:* "Now, at last, I may embrace you,") [34]. When Figaro and Marcellina embrace, the Count and the Judge give up their case as lost. Just then Susanna enters with money (given her by the Countess) to redeem the contract and sees Figaro in the arms of Marcellina. Outraged, Susanna slaps Figaro's face. All present barely manage to convince her that Marcellina and the doctor are her future in-laws [35]. After the Count leaves in a huff, followed by the Judge, Bartolo consents (Recitative) to marry Marcellina this very day at the same ceremony that will unite Figaro and Susanna. As wedding presents Figaro receives from Marcellina the contract, from Susanna the money she has brought, and from his father another purse. Then, laughing at the Count's fury, they all leave happily.

Barbarina, passing through the hall with Cherubino, decides to take him home with her and dress him as a girl, so that he can join the village maidens in the presentation of flowers to the Countess.

The Countess enters musing (Recitative *E Susanna non vien:* "And Susanna is late"). She is worried about the outcome of Figaro's plot, yet she must take the risk. Instead of Susanna, she herself, dressed in her maid's clothes, will keep the rendezvous with the Count. To what a state have things come, she laments, and where are the days of love's delight (Aria *Dove sono:* "Are they over") [36]? Sadly she returns to her rooms.

The Count passes through with his gardener, who informs him (Recitative) of his discovery that Cherubino, still at the castle, has been dressed up as a girl by Barbarina.

Now the Countess returns with Susanna and they compose a letter to the Count specifying the pine grove in the gardens as the place for their assignation (Letter Duet *Che soave zefiretto:* "When the breeze is gently blowing") [37]. Susanna seals the note with a pin and, as a joke, adds a postscript asking that the seal be returned.

The village girls come and present their flowers, and Cherubino is discovered by Antonio and the Count (Recitative). This time the page—and with him the Countess—is saved by Barbarina, who ingenuously reveals the Count's advances toward her. Now the wedding march is heard [38], and as the Count and the Countess ascend their thrones, the wedding

[35] SEXTET *RICONOSCI IN QUESTO AMPLESSO continued*
(Marcellina, Figaro, Bartolo, Curzio, Count, Susanna)

Andante — BARTOLO: His moth-er! / Sua ma-dre! — COUNT: His moth-er! / Sua ma-dre!

SUSANNA: His moth-er? / Sua ma-dre? — SUS.: His moth-er? / Sua ma-dre?

CURZIO: His moth-er! / Sua ma-dre! — MARC.: His moth-er! / Sua ma-dre!

SUS.: His moth-er? / Sua ma-dre? — SUSANNA: His moth-er! / Sua ma-dre!

[36] ARIA *DOVE SONO* (Countess)

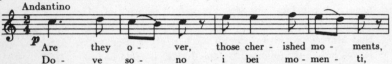

Andantino

Are they o- ver, those cher- ished mo- ments,
Do- ve so- no i bei mo- men- ti,

[37] LETTER DUET (Countess, Susanna)

Allegretto

COUNTESS: When the breeze is gent- ly blow- ing,
Che so- a- ve ze- fi- ret- to,

[38] WEDDING MARCH

Marcia

[39] FANDANGO

Andante

[40] CAVATINA *L'HO PERDUTA* (Barbarina)

Andante

I have lost it, heav- en help me! I have lost the lit- tle pin!
L'ho per- du- ta, me me-schi- na! ah chi sa do-ve sa- rà,

[41] ARIA *APRITE UN PO' QUEGL' OCCHI* (Figaro)

Moderato

O fel- low man be smart- er, don't be a blind- ed mar- tyr.
A- pri- te un po' quegl' oc- chi, Uo- mi- ni in- cau- ti e scioc- chi.

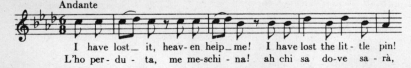

guests enter and the principals advance in solemn procession. As Susanna kneels before the Count to receive the veil, she gives him her letter. At the same time Marcellina receives her veil from the Countess. Now, while a fandango is danced [39], the Count secretly opens Susanna's letter and pricks his finger with the pin, an incident laughingly noted by Figaro. The Count invites all to return for a big celebration that night, and they leave, praising their noble master.

Act IV: As night is falling over the gardens of the castle, Barbarina is looking for a pin (Cavatina *L'ho perduta:* "I have lost it") [40]. To Figaro and Marcellina, who happen to pass by, she explains (Recitative) that she is looking for the "pin of the pines" which the Count gave her to take to Susanna. Figaro, remembering what he has observed at the wedding, rushes off "to avenge all husbands." Alone, Marcellina complains (Aria *Il capro e la capretta:* "The birds and bees are able"—usually omitted) about the hard lot of the female of the species, before she rushes off to warn Susanna. Barbarina returns and enters an arbor where she expects to meet Cherubino (Recitative). Figaro meets Basilio and Bartolo and assigns them strategic positions, there to await his signal, then leaves for further preparations. Basilio explains to Bartolo his most unheroic philosophy of unconditional acquiescence (Aria *In quegli anni:* "Youth is headstrong"—usually omitted) before they hide in the vicinity. Figaro returns (Recitative *Tutto è disposto:* "It won't be long now"), ready to deal with a faithless wife who was betraying him at the very moment of the wedding ceremony. O foolish men, look at women and see what they are really like, he exclaims (Aria *Aprite un po' quegli occhi:* "O fellow man, be smarter") [41], before he, too, takes his post behind the shrubbery.

Darkness has set in. The Countess and Susanna appear, disguised in each other's clothes. They are joined by Marcellina, who informs them in a whisper that Figaro is listening. Susanna asks to be left alone and takes pleasure in regaling her eavesdropping husband with a tender romance about the joys awaiting her in the arms of her lover (Recitative *Giunge alfin il momento:* "This at last is the moment"; Aria *Deh, vieni, non tardar:* "Beloved, don't delay") [42]. Now she relinquishes the place to the Countess.

Unexpected and unwelcome, Cherubino arrives [18] and, mistaking the Countess for her maid, tries to make love to "Susanna" [43], as the real Susanna and Figaro watch unseen. Soon the Count approaches [43] and as Cherubino attempts to kiss "Susanna" he steps between them. He intends to slap Cherubino, but the page has already fled into the arbor. In his stead, the Count, without noticing it in the darkness, slaps Figaro, who, in his curiosity, has stepped forward and now hastily retreats. The Count enjoys a few moments in the company of the charming girl he believes to be Susanna, but when he leads her toward one of the arbors, loud steps and voices in the vicinity, originating with Figaro, cause him to let her go ahead while he, for the moment, moves in another direction.

[42] ARIA *DEH VIENI* (Susanna)

Andante

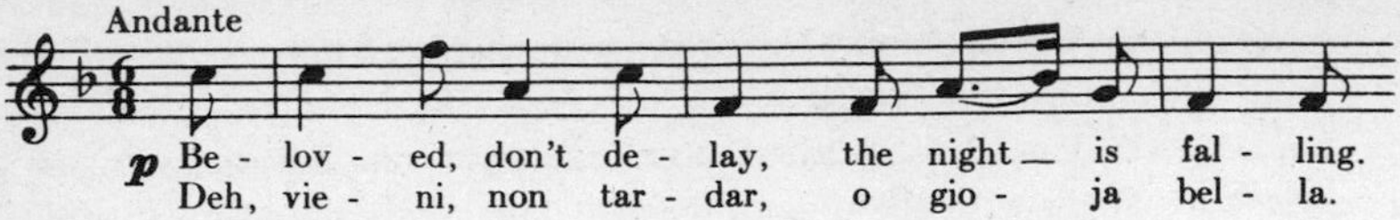
p
Be - lov - ed, don't de - lay, the night — is fal - ling.
Deh, vie - ni, non tar - dar, o gio - ja bel - la.

[43] Andante

p
sfp
CHERUBINO
On my tip - toes_I go near - er,
Pian, pia-nin_ le an-drò più pres - so,

[44] Andante

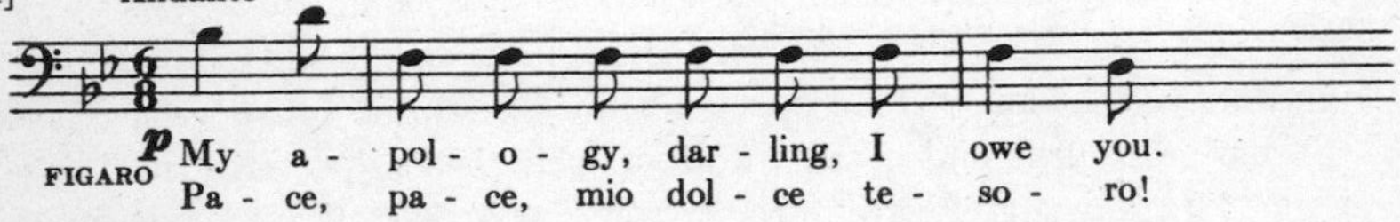
p
FIGARO
My a - pol - o - gy, dar - ling, I owe you.
Pa - ce, pa - ce, mio dol - ce te - so - ro!

Figaro, leaving his hiding-place and fearing the worst for Susanna, is now joined by the "Countess"; but soon, and to his great relief, he recognizes her voice, and now enjoys his own little game by expressing his most fervent love for the "Countess." Furious, Susanna slaps his face again and again, but the misunderstanding is quickly cleared up [44], and for the benefit of the presently returning Count the two repeat their love scene. The Count seizes Figaro and calls for assistance. When Basilio, Bartolo, Don Curzio, and Antonio appear, the Count accuses Figaro of betraying him with the Countess. From the arbor into which Susanna has just run, he drags, one after another, Cherubino, Barbarina, and Marcellina—and finally the "Countess." In vain the "Countess" and Figaro ask the furious Count's mercy; in vain all the others join them in their supplications. However, the Count's rage quickly changes into mortification when "Susanna" appears from the other arbor and, taking off her veil, asks her husband whether perhaps *her* intercession might obtain a pardon. All are perplexed. The Count, humbly begs for forgiveness, which is lovingly granted by his wife, and contentment reigns everywhere.

THEMES

[1] Allegro agitato

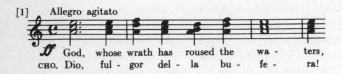

ff God, whose wrath has roused the wa - ters,
CHO. Dio, ful - gor del - la bu - fe - ra!

[2] Allegro agitato

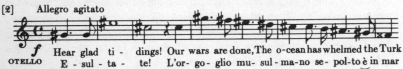

f Hear glad ti - dings! Our wars are done, The o-cean has whelmed the Turk
OTELLO E - sul - ta - te! L'or- go- glio mu- sul - ma-no se- pol-to è in mar

[3] Allegro assai moderato

p A frag - ile vow of a la - dy fair
IAGO Se un fra - gil vo - to di fem - mi - na

[4] BRINDISI

Allegro con brio

IAGO Then let ___ me the can - na - kin clink. A
I - naf - fia ___ l'u - go - la! ___
sol - dier's but a man,
trin - ca, tra - can - na

[5] Allegro con brio

IAGO Who once has kissed it, ___ this ___ mag - ic brink, ___
Chi al- l'e-sca ha mor - so ___ del ___ di - ti - ram - bo

[6] LOVE DUET (Othello, Desdemona)

Cantabile

OTELLO Dark is the night and si - lent, All bla - tant clam-ors cease;
Già nel- la not - te den - sa s'e-stin- gue o-gni cla - mor,

Quotations used by permission of G. Ricordi & Co.

Otello

Opera in four acts by Giuseppe Verdi. Libretto by Arrigo Boïto, based on Shakespeare's drama. First performance: Milan, February 5, 1887.

Characters: OTELLO, general in the Venetian army, a Moor (tenor); DESDEMONA, his wife (soprano); IAGO, an ensign (baritone); EMILIA, his wife and maid of Desdemona (mezzo-soprano); CASSIO, a captain (tenor); RODERIGO, a Venetian gentleman (tenor); LODOVICO, Ambassador of the Republic of Venice (bass); MONTANO, predecessor of Otello as Governor of Cyprus (bass); A HERALD (bass).
Cyprus, at the end of the fifteenth century.

Act I: In front of a tavern outside the castle that overlooks the port, Montano, Cassio, Roderigo, and Iago, among a crowd of Cypriots, are scanning the ocean for a sign of the fleet. Commanded by Otello, the Venetians are fighting the Turks, the thunderstorm, and the waters which the howling winds have turned into a wild inferno. Otello's boat is sighted by the excited watchers, and at one moment it appears so hopelessly at the mercy of the elements that the horrified spectators suddenly join in a great cry to heaven for help [1]. However, the ship is brought safely into port, and the Moor, hailed by the people, appears briefly on the quay to announce proudly the defeat of the enemy [2].

Iago approaches Roderigo, who is standing apart from the jubilant crowd, and promises the unhappy young man that he will help him win Desdemona, Otello's wife [3]. For, in spite of appearances, Iago hates the Moor for promoting Cassio to captain instead of him.

Meanwhile, the people have built victory fires along the quay and gaily watch them burn down to ashes. Iago persuades the reluctant Cassio to drink (Brindisi *Inaffia l'ugola!*": "Then let me the cannakin clink!") [4, 5], and when he is drunk, Iago incites Roderigo—to whom he has pictured the Captain as a rival for the love of Desdemona—to provoke him. Montano tries to stop the argument, but is assaulted and wounded by the drunken Cassio. Iago, having sent Roderigo to sound the alarm, now incites the stirred-up crowd to call for help.

Otello, attracted by the commotion, appears from the castle and imperiously calls for a halt to the fighting. "Honest Iago," called upon to explain the fracas, only professes sorrow over having been unable to prevent it. When Otello learns that Montano is wounded and sees Desdemona ap-

[7] **LOVE DUET** (Othello, Desdemona) *continued*

Un poco sostenuto

OTELLO
You loved me for the hard-ships I had suf - fered,
E tu m'a - ma - vi per le mie sven - tu - re

[8] Cantabile

p
con espressione
p
f
ppp

[9] THE *CREDO* (Iago)

Allegro

a
fff
Go then!
Van - ne;
cupo
Well thy fate I de - scry.
la tua me - ta già ve - do.

[10] Allegro sostenuto

col 8va
a
ff
tr
f
Cru - el is he, the God
Cre - do in un Dio cru-del
col 8va

[11] Allegro sostenuto

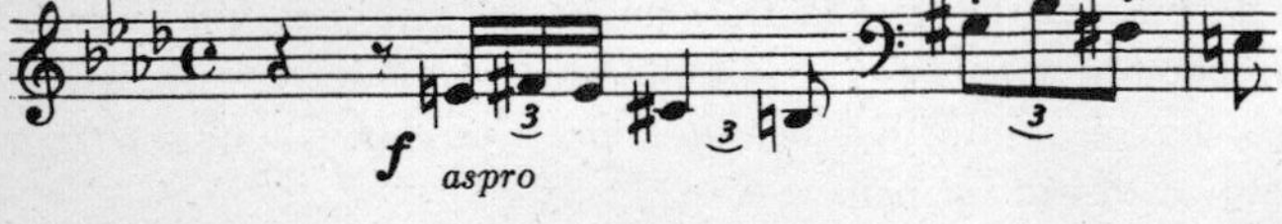
f
aspro

[12] Moderato *cupo e legato*

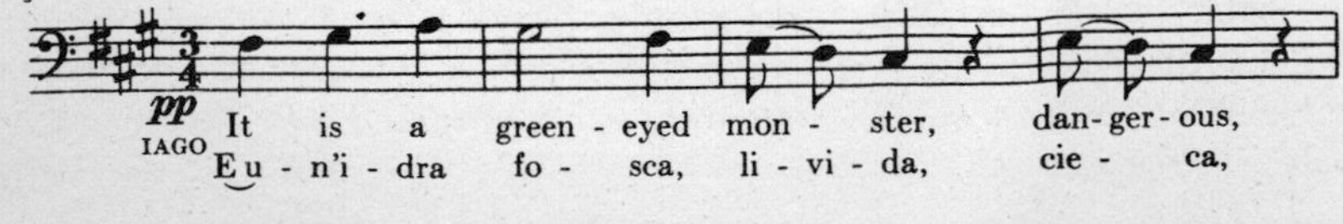
pp
IAGO
It is a green - eyed mon - ster, dan - ger - ous,
E u - n'i - dra fo - sca, li - vi - da, cie - ca,

proaching, aroused from her sleep, he demotes Cassio. He sends the secretly triumphant Iago to restore peace in the city, and bids all return to their homes.

Otello remains alone with Desdemona. One embrace of hers, he whispers, outweighs all the hardships of all the battles in the world (Duet *Già nella notte densa:* "Dark is the night and silent") [6], and Desdemona recalls the times he told her of these hardships and awakened fond pity in her. Yes, they agree, it was his adventures that made Desdemona love Otello, and it was her compassion that made him love her [7]. Their happiness is boundless, and they pray that it may last forever. Trembling with love, he begs a kiss of her [8], and with a look at Venus resplendent in the sky, they re-enter the castle [6].

Act II: In a hall of the castle which overlooks a spacious garden, the plotting Iago [9a] advises Cassio to beg Desdemona to intercede for him with Otello. Cassio goes to the garden to await her, and Iago feels that his plot is well on its way (Recitative *Vanne!:* "Go then!") [9]: a demon called Iago, he muses, is shaping the fate of Cassio, while Iago himself is driven by his own demon, by his God, supreme and relentless. He believes (The Credo *Credo in un Dio crudele:* "Cruel is he, the God") [10] in a cruel God who has created him cruel [11] in his own image, out of the primordial dirt, and with the destiny to create evil. He believes further that the honest man is, in all his good deeds, nothing but a hypocrite, and that man is the plaything of evil forces from his cradle to his worm-eaten grave. And thereafter [10a]? Why, all is over, for heaven is but an old wives' tale [11]!

Now Iago sees Desdemona arriving in the garden, and Cassio joining her in a pleasant conversation. As he goes to look for Otello, the Moor, by good fortune, is just approaching, and Iago cleverly plants in him the seed of suspicion. Apparently revealing his thoughts only reluctantly, he advises Otello not to be jealous of Cassio, for jealousy is a wicked monster [12]. When the Moor demands proof for Iago's suspicions, he merely advises careful observation.

Cassio has meanwhile left Desdemona, and she is now surrounded by local women, children, and sailors who pay her homage with flowers and other presents [13]. When they have left, Desdemona, accompanied by Emilia, enters the hall and immediately asks Otello to forgive Cassio [14]. When in irritation he refuses and complains about a headache, she attempts to tie her handkerchief around his head, but he violently throws it to the ground. Patiently and humbly Desdemona asks his forgiveness for whatever she may have done to offend him [15], but Otello (Quartet), convinced of her infidelity, sees all his dreams suddenly ended. He asks himself whether his lack of sophistication, his age, or his color is to blame. Meanwhile, Iago forces his reluctant and suspicious wife, Emilia, to relinquish to him Desdemona's handkerchief, which Emilia had retrieved from the floor, and airs his joy as he sees his intrigue progressing.

[13] Allegro moderato *dolce*

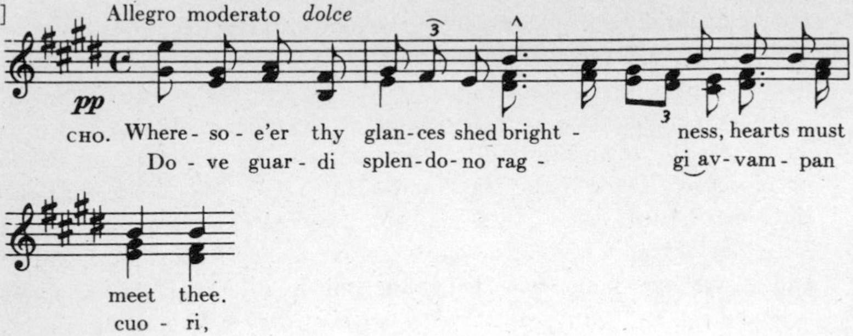
pp
CHO. Where-so-e'er thy glan-ces shed bright-ness, hearts must meet thee.
Do-ve guar-di splen-do-no rag-gi av-vam-pan cuo-ri,

[14] Allegro moderato

DESD. A man who late-ly has a-roused your an-ger, asked for my in-ter-ces-sion
D'un uom che ge-me sot-to il tuo di-sde-gno la pre-ghie-ra ti por-to.

[15] Largo

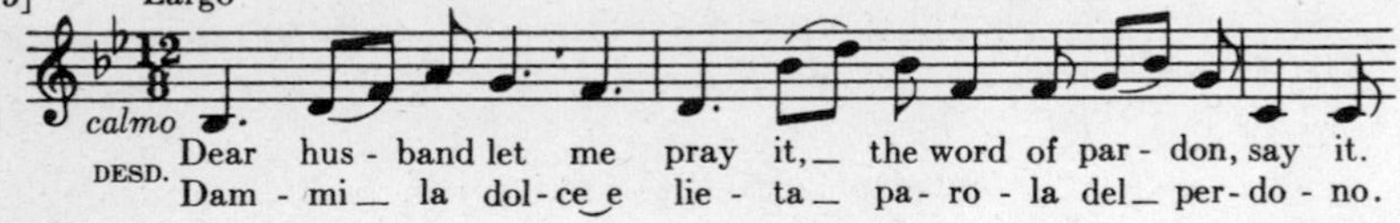
calmo
DESD. Dear hus-band let me pray it, the word of par-don, say it.
Dam-mi la dol-ce e lie-ta pa-ro-la del per-do-no.

[16] ARIA *ORA E PER SEMPRE ADDIO* (Otello)

Allegro assai ritenuto *larga la frase*

a
p
And now for-ev-er fare-well, ye sa-cred mem'-ries
O-ra e per sem-pre ad-dio san-te me-mo-rie,

[17] THE DREAM (Iago)

Andantino

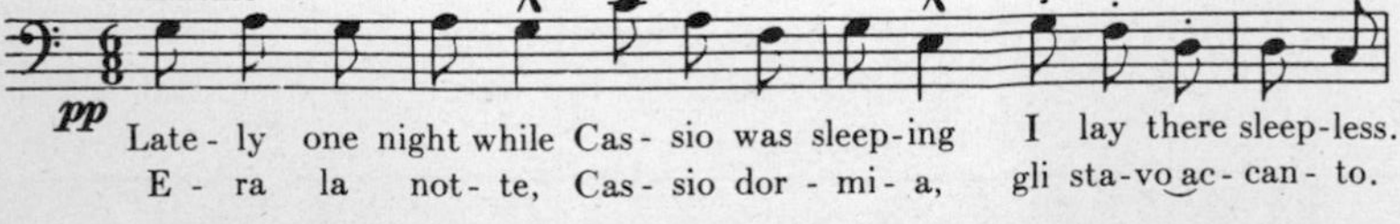
pp
Late-ly one night while Cas-sio was sleep-ing I lay there sleep-less.
E-ra la not-te, Cas-sio dor-mi-a, gli sta-vo ac-can-to.

When Desdemona again asks forgiveness [15], Otello wildly commands all to leave, but Iago remains hidden for one moment to witness Otello's despair. Then he approaches him again, ostensibly to console him. Otello, infuriated, claims that Iago has robbed him of all life's joys forever [16]. Violently he assaults him, asking for proof of his accusations if he wants to live [16a]. As though offended, Iago threatens to resign and makes as if to leave. Called back by Otello, who knows no longer whom to believe, or whom to doubt, Iago offers, if not proof, at least some circumstantial evidence. He claims that he has heard Cassio talking most tenderly to Desdemona in his sleep, and in a whisper Iago creates a scene, hair-raising in its detail, of the sleeping Cassio as he called Desdemona by name and with sighs and kisses bemoaned the fate that had given her to the Moor (The Dream *Era la notte:* "Lately one night") [17]. Iago also claims that he saw in Cassio's hands a very rare and delicate handkerchief which Otello easily identifies as his first gift to Desdemona. Otello rages against Cassio and, violently divorcing himself from all feelings of love, he vows bloody revenge (Duet *Sì, pel ciel marmoreo giuro:* "Witness yonder marble heaven") [18]. His "ever faithful" ensign eagerly joins his vow.

Prelude to Act III: The short introduction is built on the motive of jealousy [12].

Act III: A herald enters the great hall of the castle and announces to Otello, who has been in conversation with Iago, that the ambassadors from Venice are about to arrive. When he has left, Iago continues to outline his plan: he will bring Cassio here and make him talk while Otello, hidden on the terrace, can listen.

Seeing Desdemona approaching, Iago leaves after counseling his master to hide his feelings and to remember the handkerchief. Desdemona enters, greeting Otello warmly [19], but he manages only with difficulty to play the loving husband [19]. When Desdemona again mentions Cassio, he again complains of a sudden headache and asks for Desdemona's handkerchief, but the one she proffers is not that which she had received from Otello. That handkerchief, he warns her with suppressed fury, has a magic spell woven into its cloth, a spell which would cause destruction if the handkerchief were lost or given away. She must find it immediately. Desdemona smilingly intimates [20] that Otello just wants to distract her mind from Cassio, and Otello, barely able to contain himself, asks her to swear that she has been faithful. Perplexed and unable to understand her husband's rage, she protests her innocence, but he does not believe her and shouts that she is merely a strumpet. When she cries out against such an accusation, Otello, with cutting irony, makes amends [19] as he leads his wife to the door and then, suddenly, with one motion of his arm, pushes her out. In a choked voice he cries that he could have borne misery and defeat in calm submission, but now he has been robbed of the core of his existence, of the life-sustaining rays of Desdemona's smile [21]. However, he has made his decision: Desdemona must confess and die.

[18] **OATH OF VENGEANCE** (Otello, Iago)

Molto sostenuto

OTELLO
Wit - ness yon - der mar - ble heav - en
Sì, pel ciel mar- mo - reo giu - ro

[19] Allegro moderato

DESD.
Joy be with you, my hus - band, My heart's sole lord — and
Dio ti gio-con - di o spo - so, del - l'al- ma mia — so -

mas - - ter!
vra - - no.

[20] Andantino *con eleganza*

DESD.
I can see you are jest - ing, Sir!
Tu di me ti fai gio - co,

[21] Adagio *cantabile*

OTELLO
But, but there a - las! Gone the
Ma, o pian - to, o duol! m'han ra -

fount of my be - ing
pi - to il mi - rag - gio

[22] Allegro moderato

[23] Allegro brillante

IAGO
This is a spi - der's web, where your poor heart ———
Que- sta è u - na ra - gna do - ve il tuo cuor ———

Iago returns and quickly leads Otello to the terrace so that he may observe from there Iago's colloquy with the approaching Cassio. Slyly, Iago involves the Captain in a subdued conversation of which Otello can hear only certain key words spoken loudly by Iago, and ribald, loud laughter [22] that his poisoned mind interprets in its own way. Eventually Iago makes Cassio produce the handkerchief—which the ensign had planted in his room—and waves it again and again in the direction of the terrace so that Otello can clearly recognize it. At the same time Iago jokingly—or apparently so—warns Cassio against the cloth that looks so much like a spider web, for Cassio may be caught by the spider [23]. Unconcerned, the Captain admires the handkerchief's delicate workmanship while the hapless Moor is crushed by the "proof" of his wife's infidelity.

Trumpet calls, a cannon shot, and *evviva's* outside announce the arrival of the Venetian delegation. Hastily Cassio takes his leave. Otello and Iago now decide that the Moor will strangle Desdemona in her "bed of sin," while Iago will take care of Cassio. Otello promotes his ensign to captain.

Lodovico enters, and with him dignitaries, ladies and gentlemen, and guards, as well as Desdemona and Emilia. Otello receives from Lodovico a parchment from the Doge of Venice, and while he reads it, Lodovico asks after Cassio. When Desdemona repeatedly expresses the hope that Cassio, of whom she is very fond, will be forgiven by Otello, the Moor makes a movement as if to strike her. Although he is stopped by Lodovico, everyone is horror-stricken.

Otello sends for Cassio and, when he arrives, reveals that the Doge has selected the Captain to be Commandant on Cyprus. Otello, recalled to Venice, will leave with his wife and the ambassadors the following day. In a violent outbreak, he suddenly throws Desdemona to the ground, and she, trembling and terrified, laments the passing of her happiness [24] as everyone around her expresses compassion (Ensemble) and Otello is goaded by Iago to strike this very night. To Roderigo, who has lost all hope of winning Desdemona now that she will be leaving Cyprus, Iago explains that she would stay here with Otello if by chance some accident should befall Cassio. Roderigo is persuaded to bring about such an accident before the dawn of the next day.

With stentorian voice Otello now commands everyone to leave, and when Desdemona attempts once more to address him, he sends her off with a curse. When he is alone, his excitement overpowers him. Trembling, he becomes convulsed and delirious, and collapses in a faint. Iago, who has observed him with satisfaction from a distance, now comes forward, and as the crowds outside hail "Otello, the Lion of Venice," he triumphantly plants his heel on the inert body: "Behold the Lion!"

Act IV: In her bedroom, Desdemona, attended by Emilia, prepares for

[24]

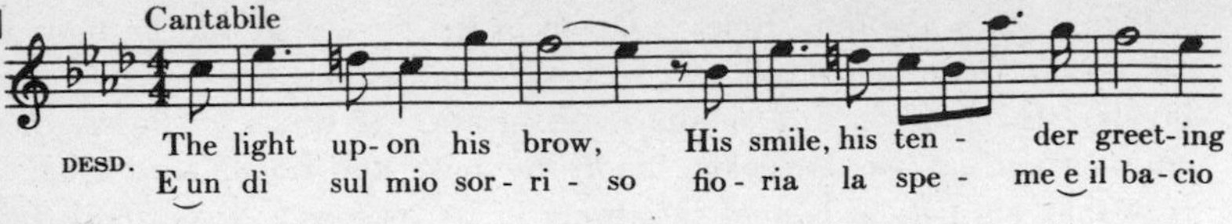
Cantabile
DESD.
The light up-on his brow, His smile, his ten - der greet-ing
E un dì sul mio sor-ri - so fio-ria la spe - me e il ba-cio

[25]

Andante mosso
p con espressione

[26] THE WILLOW SONG (Desdemona)

Andante mosso
p

[27]

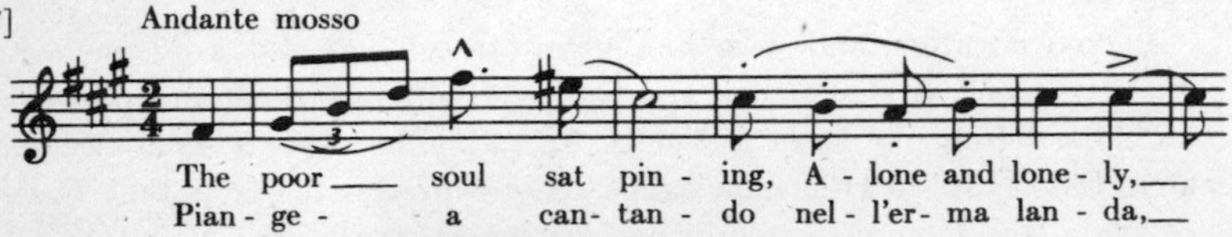
Andante mosso
The poor soul sat pin - ing, A - lone and lone - ly,
Pian - ge - a can - tan - do nel - l'er - ma lan - da,

[28] FROM THE *AVE MARIA* (Desdemona)

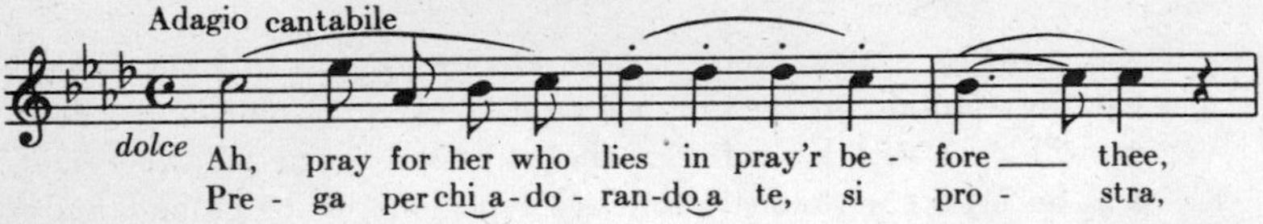
Adagio cantabile
dolce
Ah, pray for her who lies in pray'r be - fore thee,
Pre - ga per chi a - do - ran - do a te, si pro - stra,

[29] OTELLO'S GRIEF

Andante sostenuto
pp

[30] MURDER

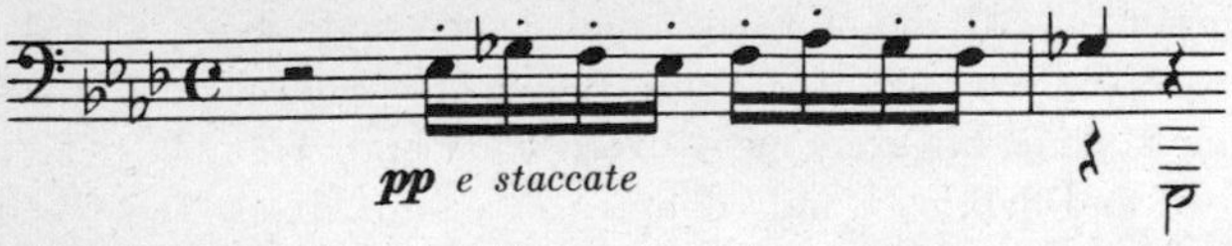
Andante sostenuto
pp e staccate

[31]

Sostenuto
pppp
OTELLO
None need fear me, Though I still have a weap - on.
Niun mi te - ma, se an - co ar - ma - to mi ve - de.

bed, but somber thoughts occupy her mind [motive 27; 25]. She is expecting Otello and asks Emilia to lay on the bed the robe which she wore on her wedding night; but her thoughts keep revolving about death, and the song her mother's servant Barbara used to sing will not leave her mind (Recitative *Mia madre aveva una povera ancella:* "My mother long ago had a poor servant"). While Emilia is combing her hair, she sings it (The Willow Song *Piangea cantando:* "The poor soul sat pining") [26, 27]. The song, Desdemona adds, always ended like this: "He was born to live in glory, and I, to love him and to die." She bids Emilia good night [26], but as the maid is about to leave, Desdemona calls her back once more for a last, desperate farewell.

Alone with her forebodings [25], she kneels on the prayer bench and begins to say her *Ave Maria,* and soon her prayer takes on an intense fervor [28]. She says a second *Ave Maria,* audible only in part, then goes to bed and falls asleep.

Otello enters, his sorrow over the loss of Desdemona [29 major] momentarily subdued by his determination to murder her [30]; but after putting his sword on the table, he pulls back the bed curtain and sadly gazes once more on his beloved [29]. When he kneels and kisses her passionately [8], she awakes. Sternly [30] he asks whether she has said her prayers, for she must die. There will be no mercy, for Cassio has been her lover. Cassio had her handkerchief, and for that he has already died. All Desdemona's protestations of innocence are of no avail [30]. Otello strangles her until her scream ends in silence.

Emilia knocks loudly on the door and, admitted by Otello, informs him that Cassio has just killed Roderigo. From her bed, Desdemona with her last breath vows that she is innocent and claims that she has killed herself, but Otello shouts that it was he who killed her, for she has been—Iago knows it, too—Cassio's strumpet. Emilia runs to the door calling for help, and Lodovico, Cassio, and Iago enter with shouts of horror at the sight of Desdemona. Emilia demands an explanation from Iago, and when Otello mentions the handkerchief, she reveals, despite her husband's threats, that Iago had taken it from her by force. Cassio adds that one day he had found it mysteriously in his room.

Now Montano enters with guards to arrest Iago, for the dying Roderigo has revealed to him the Ensign's vile machinations, but Iago quickly flees.

When Otello, with a wild outburst, reaches for his sword, Lodovico bids him yield it. Stunned and broken, Otello contemplates the course of his star, which is about to set [31]. Sadly he laments the unjust fate that has brought death to the innocent Desdemona. Then he quickly draws his dagger and stabs himself. With a final effort he moves to Desdemona's bed [29] and, dying, kisses her for the last time [8].

THEMES

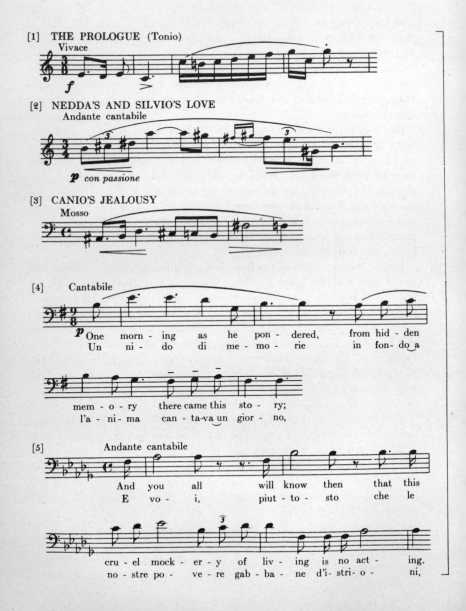

[1] THE PROLOGUE (Tonio)

Vivace
f

[2] NEDDA'S AND SILVIO'S LOVE

Andante cantabile
p con passione

[3] CANIO'S JEALOUSY

Mosso

[4]

Cantabile
p One morn - ing as he pon - dered, from hid - den
Un ni - do di me - mo - rie in fon - do a
mem - o - ry there came this sto - ry;
l'a - ni - ma can - ta-va un gior - no,

[5]

Andante cantabile
And you all will know then that this
E vo - i, piut - to - sto che le
cru - el mock - er - y of liv - ing is no act - ing.
no - stre po - ve - re gab - ba - ne d'i - stri - o - ni,

Pagliacci

Opera in two acts and a prologue by Ruggiero Leoncavallo. Libretto by the composer. First performance: Milan, May 21, 1892.

Characters: CANIO, also PAGLIACCIO (tenor); NEDDA, also COLOMBINA (COLUMBINE), his wife (soprano); TONIO, also TADDEO (baritone) and BEPPE, also ARLECCHINO (HARLEQUIN) (tenor), members of Canio's troupe; SILVIO, a villager (baritone).
Near Montalto, Calabria, in the late 1860's.

Prologue: Theme [1] is interrupted by melodies that describe the tragedy of the clown [motive 17], Nedda's and Silvio's love [2], and Canio's jealousy [3]. The first theme [1] returns and comes to a climatic stop as Tonio steps before the curtain (The Prologue *Si può:* "Permit me") to explain the author's intentions: the play to be performed, he states, is not fiction, but is written from the remembrance of actual happenings which still brings a tear to the writer's eye [4]. It treats of real love [2] and real hatred and sorrow [3]. "Therefore," the prologue addresses the audience, "do not look at our theatrical make-up alone, but at our souls [5], for we are, after all, people of flesh and blood just like you." His explanations completed, Tonio now calls to the players on stage to start the show. The orchestra resumes with the main theme of the prologue [1] and brings it to a sparkling close.

Act I: As a trumpet and a big drum are heard heralding the arrival of Canio's troupe of players, the townspeople gather in front of a little outdoor stage near the village to greet them [6, 7]. Canio, from the top of his cart,

[6] Marziale deciso

[7] Marziale un poco sostenuto

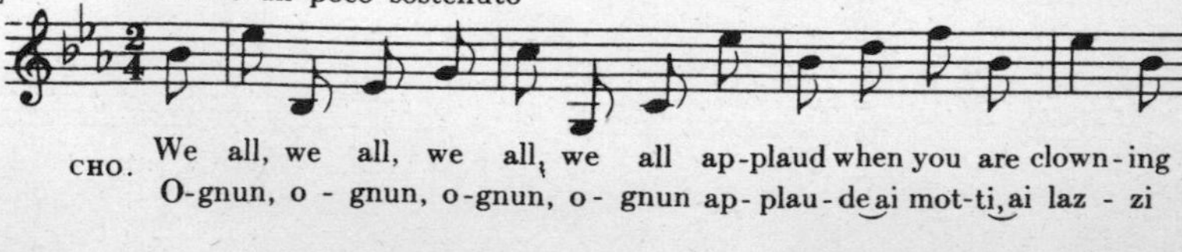
CHO.
We all, we all, we all, we all ap-plaud when you are clown-ing
O-gnun, o - gnun, o-gnun, o- gnun ap- plau-de ai mot-ti, ai laz - zi

[8] ARIA *UN TAL GIOCO* (Canio)

Adagio molto

If you're jok - ing, I'm warn- ing you,___
Un tal gio - co, cre- de - te- mi, ___

[9] BELL CHORUS

Andantino grazioso

Ding dong,__ 'tis the ves- per bell, come girls come a -
Din, don,__ suo-na ve - spe- ro, ra - gaz - ze e gar -

long!______ Ding dong! ________
zon,______ din, don! ________

[10] BALLATELLA *STRIDONO LASSU* (Nedda)

Vivace

How they sing on high,__ hap - py in free - dom,
Stri - do- no las- sù,__ li - be - ra- men - te

[11] Vivace *con anima e passione* *allargando la frase e ben cantato*

On - ward they fly__ in search of un- known coun-tries,
Van - no lag- giù__ ver - so un pa - e - se stra - no

[12] ARIA *SO BEN CHE DIFFORME* (Tonio)

Cantabile sostenuto

I know I am ug - ly, I know I'm mis-shap - en;
So ben che dif- for - me, con - tor - to son i - o;

[13] TONIO'S HATRED

Moderato

[14] ARIA *DECIDI IL MIO DESTIN* (Silvio) *poco rit.*

Andantino amoroso *a tempo*

Cantabile con garbo

p You must de - cide my fate, Ned - da! Ned-da, stay with me!
De - ci - di il mio de - stin, Ned - da! Ned-da ri - ma - ni!

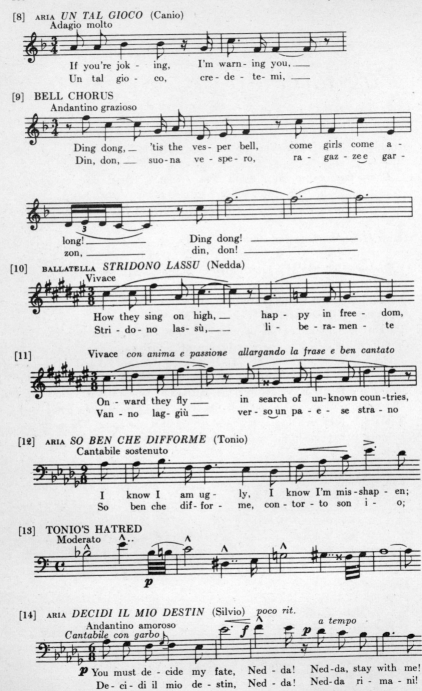

invites all to this evening's performance. Tonio, attempting to help Nedda from the cart, receives a slap from his master and retires, promising revenge. A villager invites the players to join him for a drink, and all but Tonio accept. Someone jokingly suggests that Tonio wants to remain alone with Nedda, but to Canio this sort of a joke is not funny (Aria *Un tal gioco:* "If you're joking") [8]. True, the crowds are amused when, in the comedy, Pagliaccio is made a fool of by Columbine [22], but if Canio in real life were deceived by Nedda, the story would take a different turn [3]. Therefore, he concludes, nobody should ever jokingly arouse a husband's jealousy. Now, in an instant, he shakes off his somber mood, and fondly kisses his wife, before he leaves for the tavern. The villagers follow (Bell Chorus)[9].

Nedda remains alone, fearful (Recitative *Qual fiamma avea nel guardo:* "His raging made me shiver") that Canio may discover her secret love [2]. But yet the sun is smiling down on her as on the birds which with shrill cries (Balatella *Stridono lassù:* "How they sing on high") [10] fly recklessly toward the goal of their dreams [11] as her own thoughts fly toward her beloved.

Unnoticed, Tonio has been listening to her singing. Now he comes forward and confesses how he is tortured by love for her, in spite of his being deformed and ugly (Aria *So ben che difforme:* "I know I am ugly") [12]. Nedda, with biting irony, advises that he save his ardor for the performance later on [23]. When Tonio forcibly tries to kiss her, she is terrified and, cornered, she strikes him with a whip. Ablaze with hatred [13], he retreats, swearing revenge. Presently Silvio [2] arrives, and she tells him what has just happened. He pleads with Nedda not to move on with the comedians, but to remain with him (Aria *Decidi il mio destin:* "You must decide my fate") [14]. As Nedda begs him not to upset her life, Tonio, unseen, observes them from a distance [13], then disappears in the direction of the tavern. When Silvio recalls the hours of bliss they have spent together [15], Nedda can no longer restrain her passion [2]. As they embrace, Tonio returns [13], followed by Canio, who arrives in time to hear the pair planning an elopement at midnight [2], but too late to recognize the lover, who flees at Canio's violent outcry. While Canio, pushing Nedda out of his way, runs in pursuit of her lover, Tonio expresses his satisfaction with the initial damage he has done [13]. Canio, returning from the vain chase, demands from Nedda the name of her lover [3], and as she steadfastly refuses to divulge it [2], he rushes at her with bared dagger. Beppe, returning at this moment, disarms him. He tries to calm Canio and asks him to prepare for the imminent performance, and Tonio convinces his master that he must go on with the show so that they will be able to catch the lover, who will surely attend and will give himself away.

Left alone, Canio bitterly laments the tragic lot of the clown (Recitative *Recitar! Mentre preso dal delirio:* "Play the clown! While my mind is

[15] ARIA *E ALLOR PERCHE* (Silvio)

Andante appassionato

p
Then tell me why, why — did you be- witch me,
E al - lor per- chè, di', — tu m'hai stre- ga - to

[16] ARIA *VESTI LA GIUBBA* (Canio)

Adagio

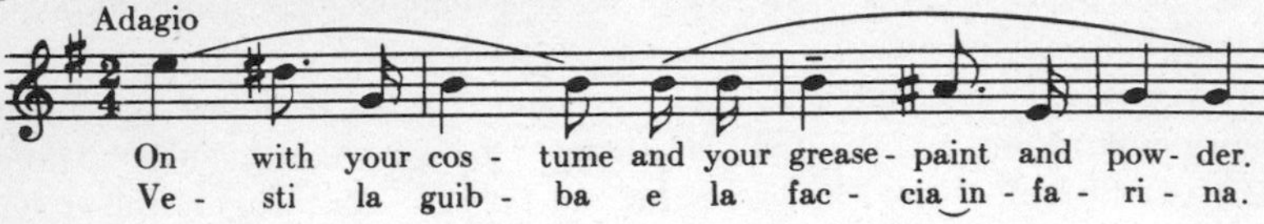
On with your cos - tume and your grease- paint and pow- der.
Ve - sti la guib - ba e la fac - cia in - fa - ri - na.

[17] Adagio

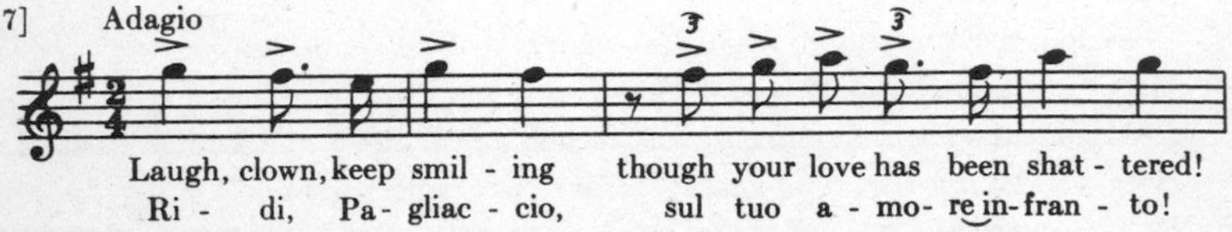
Laugh, clown, keep smil - ing though your love has been shat - tered!
Ri - di, Pa- gliac - cio, sul tuo a - mo- re in- fran - to!

[18] Marziale deciso

[19] THE COMEDY

Tempo di minuetto

sf

[20] Tempo di minuetto

[21] HARLEQUIN'S SERENADE (Beppe)

Allegretto un poco moderato

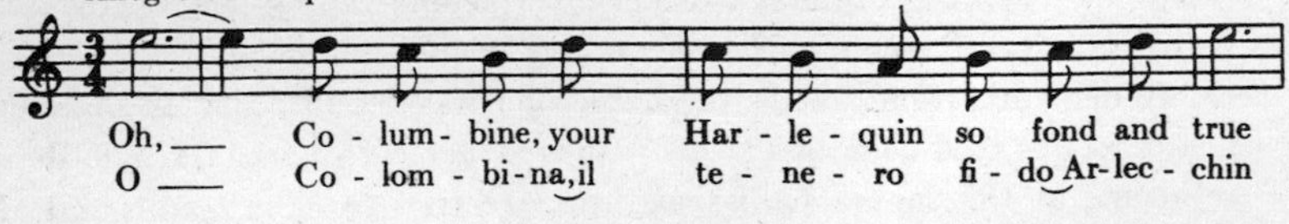
Oh, — Co - lum- bine, your Har - le - quin so fond and true
O — Co - lom - bi- na, il te - ne - ro fi - do Ar- lec - chin

[22] Andantino sostenuto assai

delirious"), the clown who must get into his costume (Aria *Vesti la giubba:* "On with your costume") [16] and, to satisfy the audience, must make merry—even though his heart may be breaking [17].

Intermezzo: Mainly themes [4] and [5].

Act II: At the call of Beppe's trumpet and Tonio's big drum, the villagers approach, fighting for the best seats [18] and impatiently waiting for the show to start [6, 7]. Finally a bell rings, and the curtain of the little stage rises for the comedy. Colombina (played by Nedda) is not expecting her husband until very late [19, 20]. Arlecchino (Beppe) is heard serenading her [21], and she signals to him through the window that the coast is clear. But Taddeo (Tonio) comes in first, and in proper comedy style tries to declare his love, ironically praising Colombina's—or Nedda's?—virtue [23 with 12]. Meanwhile, Arlecchino has entered, and he turns out the would-be lover with a well-aimed kick. Arlecchino and Nedda daintily embrace and sit down to dine [24]. Just as he gives her a flask of poison to be administered to her husband, Taddeo rushes in, comically trembling, to announce Pagliaccio's arrival. Arlecchino climbs through the window and an elopement at midnight is being planned [2] just as Pagliaccio (Canio) enters. He makes a desperate effort to go through with the comedy [25]. He accuses Colombina—or Nedda?—of infidelity, but Taddeo, called as a witness, swears that she is pure—yes, pure and truthful [25 with 13]. The mirthful reaction from the audience throws Canio into a fury. He demands from Nedda the name of her lover [3]. When she mockingly calls him "Pagliaccio," his anguish wells up beyond endurance. "Pagliaccio no longer," he cries out over a turbulent accompaniment of strings (Aria *No, Pagliaccio non son:* "No, I'm not just a clown") [26]. He is only a fool who has loved and married a poor and fatherless wretch, he exclaims; and the audience senses that this is no longer part of the standard comedy. He has hoped,

[23] THE COMEDY *continued*

Sostenuto assai

[24]

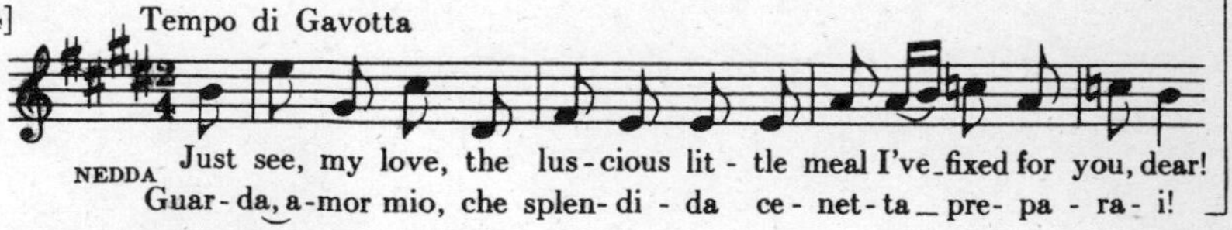
Tempo di Gavotta
NEDDA
Just see, my love, the lus-cious lit-tle meal I've fixed for you, dear!
Guar-da, a-mor mio, che splen-di-da ce-net-ta pre-pa-ra-i!

[25]

Andantino
f
p

[26] ARIA *NO, PAGLIACCIO NON SON* (Canio)

Allegro moderato

No, I'm not just a clown;
No, Pa- gliac - cio non son;

[27] Cantabile espressivo

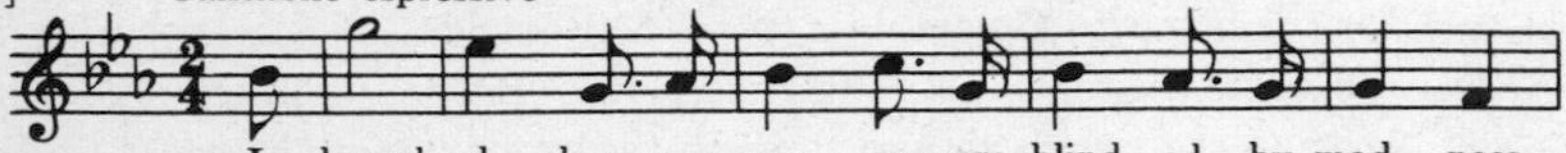
I hoped, oh, how my sens - es were blind- ed by mad - ness,
Spe - rai, tan - to il de - li - rio ac - ce - ca - to m'a - ve - va

Canio continues, at least for gratitude and loyalty from Nedda in return [27], but now she is worthy only of contempt. Calling her a wanton, he again demands the name of her lover.

Nedda, numb with fright, desperately tries to resume the comedy [24], but Canio will have none of it. With uncontrollable passion he demands either the name of the lover or her life, but Nedda will brave death rather than betray her lover [2]. While Tonio restrains Beppe from interfering, Canio snatches a knife from the table and stabs Nedda. With her dying breath she calls her lover's name. Silvio rushes toward the stage, and Canio, shouting "So it's you? Welcome!", buries the knife in his heart [3]. As the people clamor for his arrest, Canio brokenly informs them that "The comedy is ended" [17].

THEMES

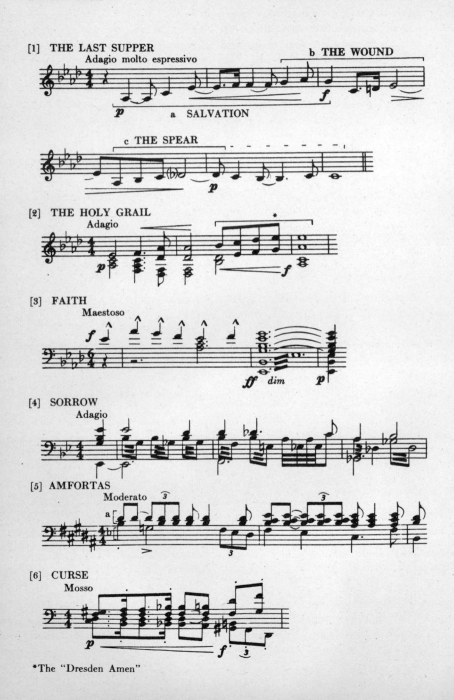

[1] THE LAST SUPPER

Adagio molto espressivo

b THE WOUND
p
f
a SALVATION

c THE SPEAR
p

[2] THE HOLY GRAIL

Adagio

*
p
f

[3] FAITH

Maestoso

f
ff
dim
p

[4] SORROW

Adagio

[5] AMFORTAS

Moderato

a
3
3
3

[6] CURSE

Mosso

p
f
3

*The "Dresden Amen"

Parsifal

Religious festival play in three acts by Richard Wagner. Libretto by the composer. First performance: Bayreuth, July 26, 1882.

Characters: AMFORTAS, King of the Grail (baritone); TITUREL, his father (bass); GURNEMANZ, aged knight of the Grail (bass); PARSIFAL (tenor); KLINGSOR, a sorcerer (baritone); KUNDRY, servant for the Grail (soprano or mezzo-soprano).
In and near the Castle of Monsalvat, in the realm of the Grail in the mountains of Spain, in the Middle Ages.

Prelude: The solemn music of the Prelude uses the motives of the Last Supper [1], the Holy Grail [2], and Faith [3] in succession. Returning to motives [1cab] interwoven with [4] and [19b], the Prelude fades away *pianissimo* to mystical heights.

Act I, Scene 1: Gurnemanz, one of the older knights, and two young esquires are asleep in a clearing in the woods belonging to the realm of the Grail. As the morning call [1a, 2] is sounded, Gurnemanz awakens and rouses the esquires to join him in silent prayer [3]. Presently he sends them to prepare the bath for the ailing King Amfortas [5ab], two of whose knights are already preceding him to the lake. They report that the herb brought by the knight Gawan has given no relief, and Gurnemanz sadly murmurs that there is but one person who can heal the King [motive 9]. The esquires, looking excitedly toward the woods, describe the approach of a wild-looking woman on a galloping horse [6], and, having dismounted, Kundry [7] rushes in. Apparently at the end of her endurance, she gives Gurnemanz a balm for the King; then, exhausted, she throws herself down on the ground.

Amfortas [5ab] is carried in on a stretcher and enjoys the beauty of the forest in the morning [8]. Healing, he knows, can come only from "The Blameless Fool made wise through pity" [9]. Nevertheless, he accepts from Gurnemanz the balm brought by Kundry [7] before he continues toward the lake [5ab, 8].

Some of the young esquires start a discussion about the mystery that is Kundry [2, 10, 7]. Gurnemanz admits that she may be a heathen, or even under a magic spell, but surely, if she is doing penance [1] for sins in a former life [7] by helping the knights of the Grail, she does a service both to them and to herself [3]. Strangely, whenever she has stayed away, he continues, misfortune has befallen the servants of the Grail, ever since Titurel, the first King and builder of the castle found her in the woods lifeless and numb [10]. Gurnemanz himself had found her in the same con-

[7] KUNDRY

Mosso
ff

[8] FOREST

Molto moderato
p

[9] THE BLAMELESS FOOL

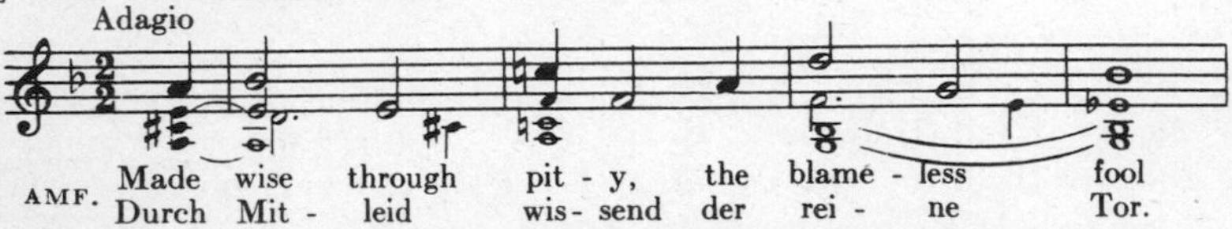
Adagio
AMF.
Made wise through pit - y, the blame - less fool
Durch Mit - leid wis- send der rei - ne Tor.

[10] MAGIC

Moderato
pp
pp

[11] GURNEMANZ' NARRATIVE

Moderato
Ti - tu - rel, the gal - lant Saint
Ti - tu - rel, der from - me Held

[12] MIRACLE

Maestoso
pp

[13] KLINGSOR

Con vigore
a
p
b

dition just recently, following the disaster [1b] in which he saw the Spear [1c] carried off by the evil magician Klingsor. It all happened when Amfortas, attacking the magician's castle, was bewitched [10] by a beautiful woman. Suddenly Gurnemanz had heard the King cry out in agonized pain [7] and, rushing to his aid, had found Amfortas with a wound [1bc] in his side, a wound that never ceases to bleed.

Two esquires return from the lake [5ab] and report that at the moment Amfortas is feeling better [8]. When Gurnemanz' companions beset him with more inquiries about the Grail's history, he starts at the beginning (Gurnemanz' Narrative *Titurel, der fromme Held:* "Titurel, the gallant Saint") [11]. Angels, he relates, appeared one night to Titurel [12] and committed to his care the cup [2] from which the Lord drank at the Last Supper [1]—the Grail [2] that also received the blood from the Lord's wound [1b]—and the Holy Spear [1c] that caused the wound. Thereupon Titurel built the temple [2] on ground inaccessible to sinners. Klingsor [13], who lived across the mountain, wished to join the holy order. However, unable to master his lusts, he had mutilated his body in an effort to turn from sin. Therefore Titurel refused him entrance, and Klingsor turned to black magic [10, 7]. Out of the desert he created a garden whose flowers are women of devilish beauty [14]. Many knights have been lost to him, for all who succumb to his women belong thereafter to Klingsor. In the effort to stop this danger Amfortas, who by then had succeeded Titurel as King of the Grail [2], lost the Holy Spear [1c] to the magician [10, 13], but when he lay praying before the shrine [2, 1b] a vision foretold his salvation [1a] through a "Blameless Fool made wise through pity" [9].

Suddenly a swan pierced by an arrow [15], flutters dying to the ground, and Parsifal is brought in amid threats. He proudly admits having shot the bird [15]. When Gurnemanz points out the beauty of the swan as it flew

[14] CHORUS OF THE FLOWER MAIDENS

Grazioso
p

[15] PARSIFAL

Allegro vivo
f
3

[16] THE SWAN (see *Lohengrin* [12])

Moderato
p

[17] **HERZELEIDE**

[18] **THE BELLS OF MONSALVAT**

[19] **SINNER'S TORMENT**

over the peaceful woods [8, 16] Parsifal is moved by remorse [4], and in violent disgust he breaks his bow. Gurnemanz asks Parsifal for information about himself [15], but all the youth knows is the name of his mother: *Herzeleide* (German for "Sorrowful Heart") [17]. Gurnemanz sends the knights to look after the King [5ab], while others ceremoniously carry off the dead swan [16 minor]. It is Kundry who now supplies more information about Parsifal: Herzeleide brought him up in solitude in the wilderness so that he should not die an untimely death in battle as had his father, Gamuret. But one day, Parsifal interrupts, he ran after some men in glittering garb [6]. Thus he caused his mother to die of grief, adds Kundry. Only Gurnemanz' quick action restrains Parsifal [15] from harming her, and as the youth, now accepting Kundry's news [17], is about to faint, she quickly brings water to restore him [6, 7]. Then, as if gripped by a spell [10] that she tries in vain to resist [7], Kundry feels sleep overcoming her. She murmurs that her time has come [13ab], and sinks to the ground behind a bush.

It is noon [18]. This is the hour, says Gurnemanz, to go to the temple of the Grail [2] for the annual unveiling of the Holy Cup. Since nobody may enter the Grail's realm unbidden, he reasons, this must be Parsifal's destination.

Scenic Transformation: Slowly Gurnemanz and Parsifal have begun walking [18], and the scene gradually changes into the vaulted temple of the Grail [19ab, 1c, 18].

Act I, Scene 2: Entering the temple [2], Gurnemanz leaves Parsifal near the door. Knights and esquires arrive in procession [18 with 20 and 21] and take their places at the long tables [2]. Amfortas is brought in on his stretcher, while invisible voices sing about Christ's suffering for the sinner [19ab]. The shrine containing the Grail is put on a table in front of Amfortas, and voices from the height of the dome proclaim the living faith and invite the knights to partake of the bread and wine [3].

From the far end of the hall the voice of the ancient Titurel is heard as he asks Amfortas to unveil the life-preserving Grail. Thereupon the King in desperation [19a] begs his father to conduct the service, but Titurel, too weak to serve, orders Amfortas to begin [2]. However, when the pages attempt to open the shrine, Amfortas turns against them with a wild outcry [7]. He describes the woes of his soul, exceeding even those of his body (Amfortas' Lament *Wehvolles Erbe:* "Ah, woeful birthright") [22, 3, 7, 19a]. He describes his longing to see the sacred cup [2 with 5a], and the sudden agony when, at the sight of the Grail's holy light [1], his own sinful blood revolts [5b, 10] and pours from the wound [1b, 19ab]. He, the King of the guardians of the holiest of relics [2], a sinner doomed to unending penance [7, 10, 13b], now asks the Lord for mercy and for deliverance from his sinful life [4]. As he feebly sinks back, the invisible voices intone the prophecy of hope [9].

Again the knights and Titurel ask that the Grail be unveiled [2], and Amfortas painfully prepares [1b] to officiate. As mysterious voices sound from above [1], the hall becomes dark; the Holy Grail commences to glow and is devoutly lifted by Amfortas and waved in blessing over the assembly and over the bread and wine [4, 19b], whereupon it pales again and is restored to its shrine. Normal light returns [18], and all partake of the blessed bread and wine. The ceremony comes to an end [2] and, preceded by Amfortas, all leave the temple [3, 19ab, 18, 21). Parsifal still stands motionless near the entrance [9, 4]. In horrified fascination he has stared at Amfortas, but the compassion he felt in his heart would not find its way to his lips and he fails to ask for the cause of Amfortas' suffering. Gurnemanz, disappointed, walks toward him and gruffly shows him the door [9, 15]. Soft voices of hope are heard from above [9, 2].

Introduction to Act II: Themes [13ab] and [10] are combined with [19a] and [7]. Finally the motive of Kundry [7] alone remains and, descending, dies away. The curtain rises.

Act II, Scene 1: In the tower of his castle Klingsor [10], looking in a magic mirror, sees the "fool" [9] approaching his realm. With flames and magic herbs he calls on Kundry [7], the eternal princess of evil, to arise [10, 13ab]. She appears still asleep [19a], but soon she awakens with a horrible scream [7], unwilling to serve Klingsor [19ab], yet powerless to resist.

[20] CHORALE OF THE KNIGHTS

Maestoso

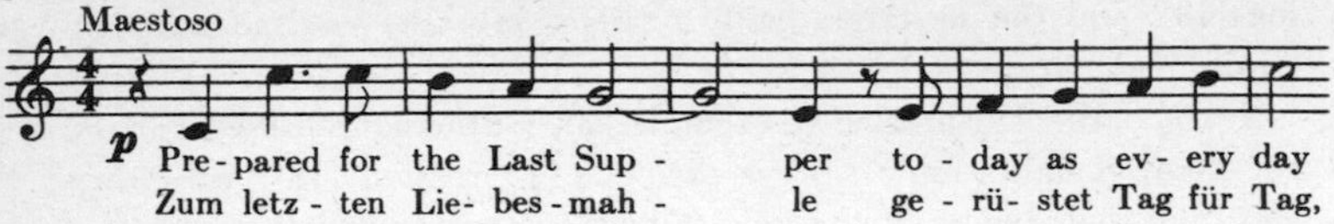
Pre-pared for the Last Sup - per to - day as ev - ery day
Zum letz - ten Lie- bes - mah - le ge - rü - stet Tag für Tag,

[21] PROCESSION OF THE KNIGHTS

Maestoso

[22] AMFORTAS' LAMENT

Molto mosso

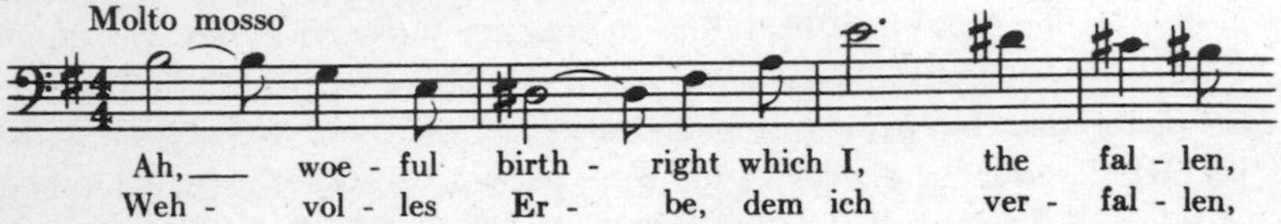
Ah, woe - ful birth - right which I, the fal - len,
Weh - vol - les Er - be, dem ich ver - fal - len,

[23] FLOWER MAIDENS' PLAINT

Vivace

[24] FLOWER-MAIDENS' JEALOUSY

Grazioso

[25] KUNDRY'S NARRATIVE

Molto tranquillo

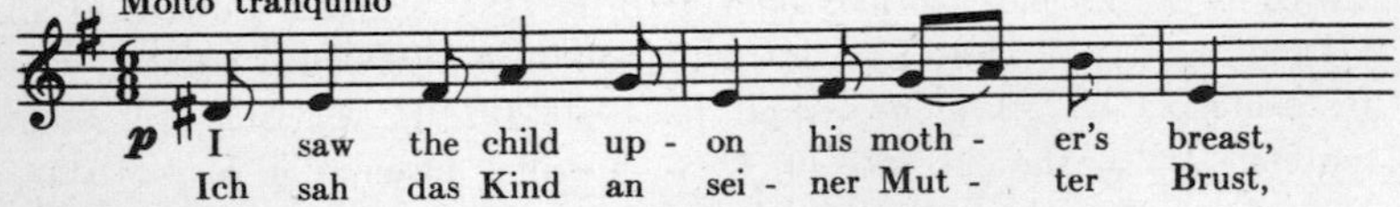
I saw the child up - on his moth - er's breast,
Ich sah das Kind an sei - ner Mut - ter Brust,

[26] ANGUISH

Molto sostenuto

[27] KUNDRY'S SUPPLICATION (see [19a])

Allegro molto vivace

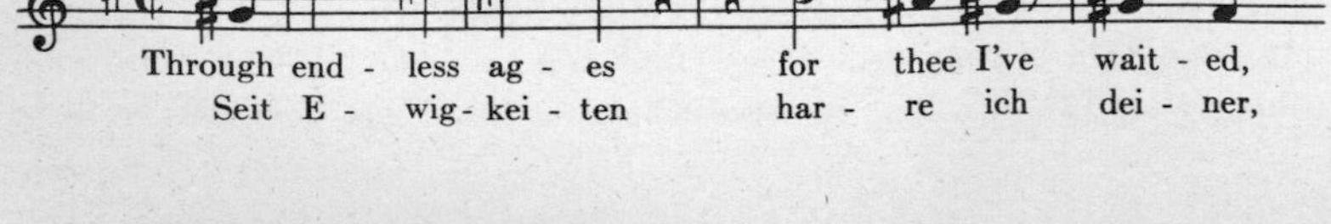
Through end - less ag - es for thee I've wait - ed,
Seit E - wig - kei - ten har - re ich dei - ner,

She has delivered to him the master of the Grail, says Klingsor, and now she must deliver the "fool" [9], and thereby enable him, Klingsor, to defeat Amfortas [5ab] and to rule over the Grail [2]. Kundry violently revolts against continuing her work of ruin, but he reminds her that whoever resists her tempting will free her from her curse. Looking in his mirror again, Klingsor sees Parsifal [15] scaling the wall and slashing at Klingsor's knights who jealously try to prevent the intruder from entering the garden. Parsifal emerges victorious [15, 9]. As Klingsor turns back to Kundry, she has already disappeared to prepare Parsifal's doom [9].

Act II, Scene 2: The tower vanishes [13ba] and in its place there appears, alongside the corner of a superb castle, a beautiful tropical garden. From one point of its wall Parsifal [15] surveys it in amazement. Lovely flower maidens are running about [23], bewailing the sudden departure of their lovers. Discovering Parsifal and finding him friendly, they adorn themselves with flowers and invite him to play with them [14]. But when they start to fight over him [24] and he is about to leave in disgust, Kundry, now lovely, and beautifully clothed, appears and addresses him as "Parsifal." At the sound of his long-forgotten name, he stops, and Kundry sends away the reluctant flower maidens [23, 24]. She informs him that he was named Parsi-fal, "Blameless Fool" [9], by his dying father, and she [10] goes on to tell (Kundry's Narrative *Ich sah das Kind an seiner Mutter Brust:* "I saw the child upon his mother's breast") [25] about his mother, Herzeleide [17], and how she finally died of sorrow [26] when he ran off. When Parsifal is overcome with remorse [26], Kundry proceeds to console him [10, 7], but when their lips meet [10], an abrupt and terrifying change takes place in Parsifal [1a, 19a]. He tears himself away from Kundry. He feels in his own flesh the terrible wound of the King of the Grail, and in choking anguish he cries out "Amfortas!" [7, 5b]. Suddenly he understands the torment of the soul [19a], the searing longing of the senses [10], the stark glance with which Amfortas [5a] looked at the Holy Grail [2, 1]. He hears the voice of the Savior crying out for delivery from sin-stained hands [1c, 19ab, 1] and he asks His mercy [4] for running off foolishly in search of adventure.

Again Kundry tries to approach Parsifal, but now he has seen through the wiles that ruined Amfortas [7 with 5a], and vehemently he pushes her away.

In a passionate transport Kundry now declares that for endless ages she has been waiting for him (Kundry's Supplication *Seit Ewigkeiten:* "Through endless ages") [27] to deliver her from the curse [7] which has haunted her ever since she saw the Savior's Martyrdom [1a, 30a] and laughed [5a, 7]. Then [19ab] His glance had met hers, and from that hour she has been trying desperately to find Him again [19b]. Yet, whenever He seems close [2] and forgiveness imminent, the laughter returns to convulse her [7] as another sinner sinks into her arms [5b]. Once more

[28] THE GRAIL'S BEREAVEMENT

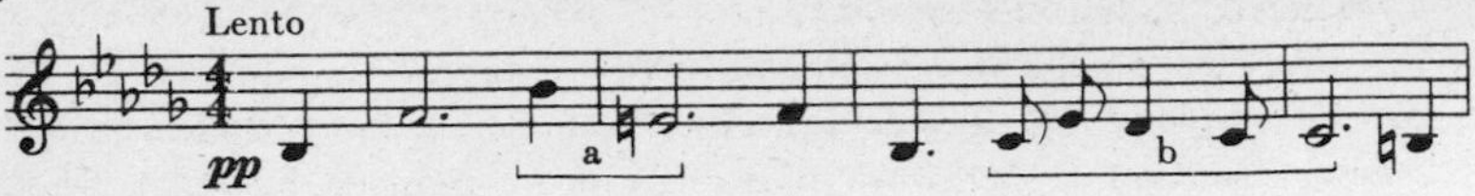
Lento
pp
a
b

[29] ERRING

Mosso
p
3
8va bassa

[30] GOOD FRIDAY

a AGONY
Adagio
sf
p

[31] ARMOR

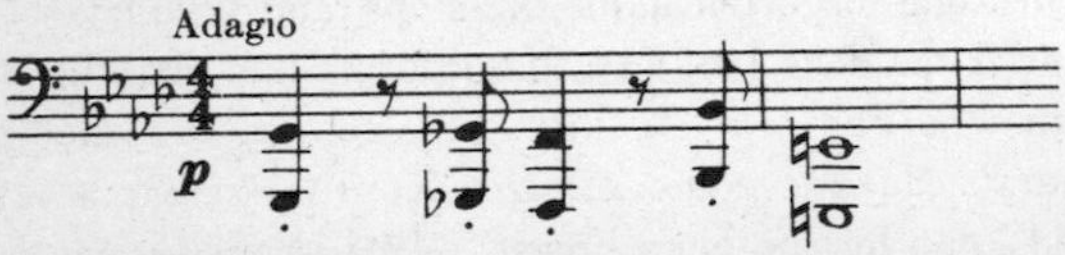
Adagio
p

[32] BENEDICTION

Andante maestoso
p

[33] FUNERAL MARCH

Maestoso
ff

she begs Parsifal for deliverance in his embrace, but Parsifal [9] knows the road Kundry must travel to gain salvation from sin [19a, 3]. When Kundry repeats her appeal for redemption after her own fashion [23], Parsifal promises love and salvation [15, 2] if she will show him the way to Amfortas. Never, Kundry cries out [7], shall he find the Grail. In wild excitement she alternately threatens and begs [23], and finally puts a curse [6, 13b] on all the paths leading to the Grail.

Klingsor appears on the rampart of the castle [7, 13b] and hurls the Holy Spear [1c] at Parsifal, but it remains suspended over Parsifal's head. He grasps it and solemnly makes the sign of the cross with it [2]. The castle is swallowed up, and the garden returns to wilderness. Parsifal turns to the prostrate Kundry [23]: "You know where you can find me." She raises her head a trifle to look after him [19a] as he slowly disappears.

Introduction to Act III: The music describes the state of desolation reigning in the realm of the Grail [28] and the errings [29] of Parsifal, who finally returns, bearing the Holy Spear [9 with 1c].

Act III, Scene 1: Gurnemanz, much aged and dressed in hermit's garb, comes from his poor hut in the woods. He is searching for the source of the mournful sounds he has been hearing [23, 10, 13ab]. In a thicket he finds Kundry, in a death-like stupor. Under his care she slowly awakens [23], realizes where she is [2], and rises with an outcry [7]. Wildly dressed, as in the first act, she silently prepares to resume her duties as a servant, but Gurnemanz remarks that there is no longer work for her here. Messengers to distant places are no longer needed, for the knights remain in the realm, living quietly on roots and herbs they gather themselves. To his surprise, Gurnemanz discovers that all wildness seems to have left Kundry's features this Good Friday morning [30, 1ab, 34a].

As he looks up, he sees a strange knight approaching [15 minor], his visor closed [31] and spear in hand. Gurnemanz greets the knight, who answers only by signs, and he bids him honor the holy day and remove his armor [2, 30, 1b]. As the knight does so [15 minor with 31), Gurnemanz and Kundry recognize him. Parsifal looks up in devotion at the Spear [1c, 4, 1], and Gurnemanz recognizes the weapon as well. Parsifal, his prayer over [30, 2], now greets Gurnemanz, happy that his wanderings [29] have come to an end in these woods [8] so that he can bring Amfortas [5] salvation [9] and return the Holy Spear [2].

Gurnemanz, after his rapture at this miracle [1, 30a, 12], tells Parsifal about the great need of the Grail folk [19b, 28]. Amfortas [5b, 19a, 7], seeking death, has refused to execute the holy rites. The knights now have to live on common food and, weak as any mortals, are no longer called upon [18] to do battle in faraway countries. Titurel [2], deprived of the strength-preserving sight of the Grail, has died [28b].

Parsifal, feeling that all this misery is his fault [9], is about to faint, but is supported by Kundry and Gurnemanz, who guide him to the holy spring [32, 2]. There he is relieved of the rest of his armor while Gurnemanz tells him about the impending service in commemoration of Titurel's death [33]. When Kundry [19a] has bathed Parsifal's feet, Gurnemanz sprinkles his head with water to purify him [32]. Now Kundry pours oil over his feet, and Gurnemanz, anointing his head [15], blesses him [9] as his king [2]. Thereupon Parsifal takes water from the spring and baptizes Kundry [3], who seems to be weeping silently [19ab]. Parsifal becomes aware of the special beauty of forest and meadow and admires it in calm delight [34ab, the Good Friday Spell]. Gurnemanz explains that, unlike mourning mankind [1, 30a], nature rejoices on Good Friday [34abc] and, not comprehending the Lord's suffering [1ac], joins only in man's joy over salvation [34abc].

[34] GOOD FRIDAY SPELL

a Molto tranquillo

b Molto tranquillo

c Molto tranquillo

[35] LAMENT FOR TITUREL

Largo

Parsifal remembers flowers of a different kind [23] that now might languish [19ab] for salvation, and tenderly he kisses Kundry on the forehead.

The noonday bells are heard [18], and Gurnemanz humbly offers to guide his master to the castle [33 with 18]. He throws his knight's cape over Parsifal's shoulders and leads the way, as Parsifal [15], bearing the Spear, and Kundry solemnly follow.

Scenic Transformation: The change of scene is similar to the first-act transformation [33, 26, 28a, 18].

Act III, Scene 2: Two processions enter the temple from opposite sides [28 with 33], one escorting the Holy Grail [3] and Amfortas, the other carrying the coffin with Titurel's body and relating the circumstances of his death. The knights following the King explain that he will once more, and for the last time [28, 28b], preside over the ceremony of the Grail in atonement for his father's death. Amfortas ruefully admits his guilt [19a, 28, 28a], and when Titurel's coffin is opened, Amfortas mourns over his father [35] and asks Titurel to implore the Savior in His glory [12] that the sight of the Grail [1a, 2] may bring him death and peace. When the knights press Amfortas to perform his office [18 with 5a], he tears open his shirt and in wild ecstasy asks the knights to kill the sinner [5b, 5ab, 13b, 10], whereupon the Grail will surely shine for them of itself [2].

Parsifal, with Gurnemanz and Kundry, has entered the temple. Now he touches Amfortas' wound with the Spear to close it [1c], and blesses his suffering [5ab] for it has brought compassion and wisdom to the "fool" [9]. Solemnly [15] he presents the Spear to the assembly [1c, 12] and proceeds to perform the Grail ceremony [2, 1a, 3, 9]. When the Holy Dove appears over Parsifal's head, Kundry sinks lifeless to the ground. Parsifal raises the Grail in blessing [3] as Amfortas and Gurnemanz kneel down to pay homage to their new King.

THEMES

[1] THE BALL

Allegro con brio

[2] Allegro con brio

[3] Allegro con brio

[4] Allegro con brio

[5] ARIA *QUESTA O QUELLA* (Duke)

Allegretto
con eleganza

In my heart all ___ are e - qual-ly cher - ish'd, Ev'- ry

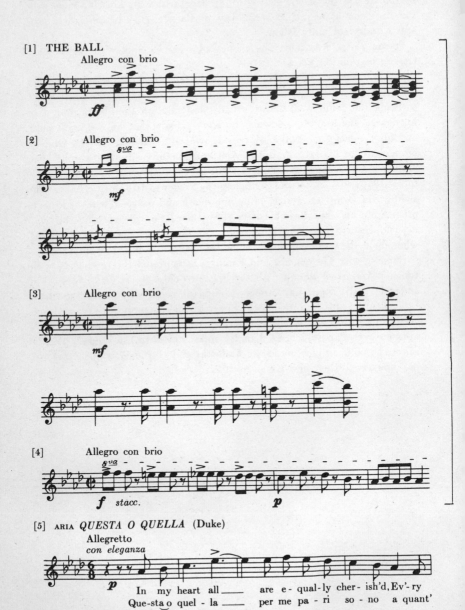

Que-sta o quel - la ___ per me pa - ri so - no a quant'

Rigoletto

Opera in three acts by Giuseppe Verdi. Libretto by Francesco Maria Piave after Victor Hugo's *Le Roi s'amuse*. First performance: Venice, March 11, 1851.

Characters: THE DUKE OF MANTUA (tenor); RIGOLETTO, court jester (baritone); GILDA, his daughter (soprano); GIOVANNA, Gilda's nurse (mezzo-soprano); SPARAFUCILE, an assassin for hire (bass); MADDALENA, his sister (contralto); COUNT MONTERONE (baritone); COUNT CEPRANO, courtier (bass); COUNTESS CEPRANO, his wife (mezzo-soprano); MARULLO (baritone) and BORSA (tenor), courtiers.
Mantua, in the sixteenth century.

Prelude: The central theme of the opera, the curse of an outraged father called down upon another father, is somberly set forth in the short introduction by trumpets and trombones [motive 8].

Act I, Scene 1: Gay festivities at the ducal palace are highlighted by brilliant dance music [1, 2, 3, 4] played by a band in the inner rooms. The Duke talks of his intention of bringing to a fitting conclusion his adventure with a pretty but unknown young girl. However, for the moment he has his sights set on the lovely Countess Ceprano. As he explains it (Ballata *Questa o quella:* "In my heart all are equally cherished") [5], his love will not be fettered to one woman. He joins the Countess while his jester, Rigoletto, makes sport of her furious husband. Meanwhile, Marullo secretly tells his fellow courtiers about a startling discovery: the hunchback Rigoletto has a sweetheart. The courtiers, after a further insult by the hated jester, seize

[5] *continued*

thought — of ex - clu - sion ___ with- in me I smoth - er,
al - tre d'in - tor - no, ___ d'in- tor- no mi ve - do,

[6] Allegro con brio

DUKE
Come hith - er, thou fool, — of thy jests — we are wear - y.
Ah! sem - pre tu spin - gi lo scher - zo al - l'e - stre - mo.

[7] Vivace *sotto voce assai*

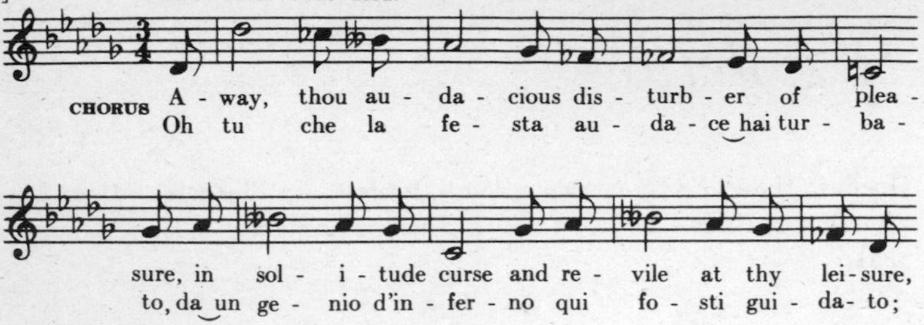
CHORUS
A - way, thou au - da - cious dis - turb - er of plea -
Oh tu che la fe - sta au - da - ce hai tur - ba -
sure, in sol - i - tude curse and re - vile at thy lei - sure,
to, da un ge - nio d'in - fer - no qui fo - sti gui - da - to;

[8] THE CURSE
Andante sostenuto

p
RIG.
He laid a fa - ther's curse on me.
Quel vec - chio ma - le - di - va mi.

[9] Andante mosso

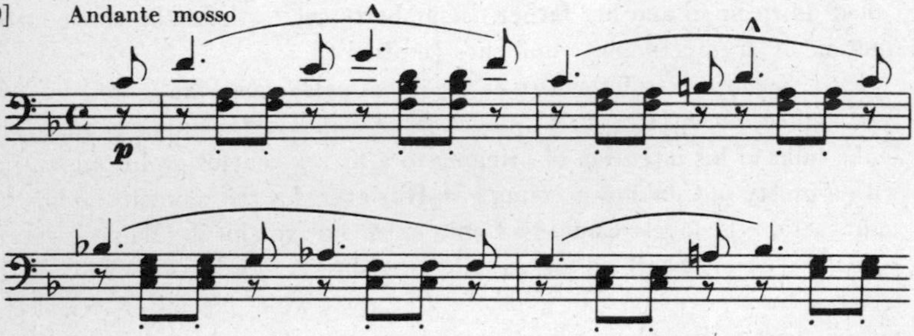
p

[10] DUET *FIGLIA–MIO PADRE* (Rigoletto, Gilda)
Allegro vivo

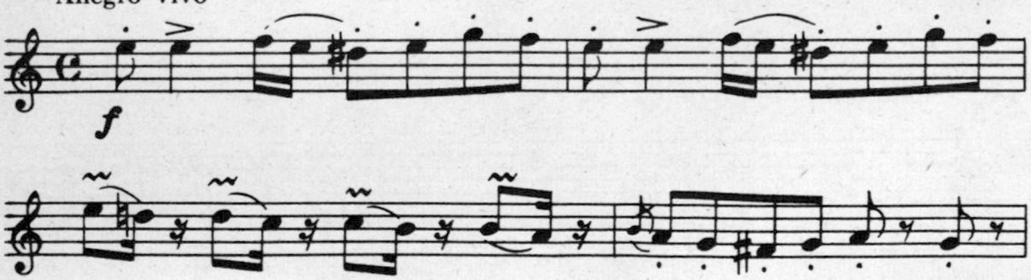
f

[11] Andante *con espressione*

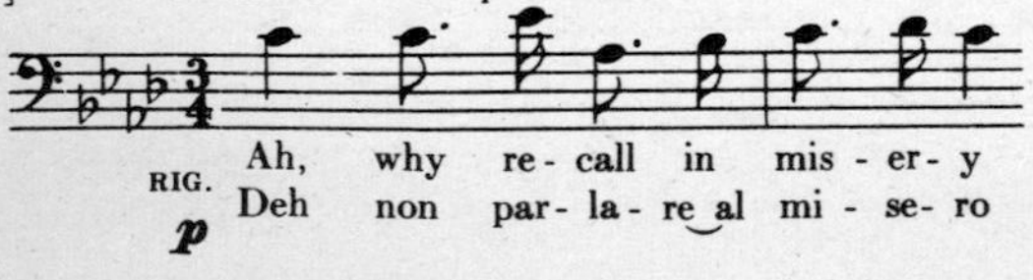
RIG.
Ah, why re - call in mis - er - y
Deh non par - la - re al mi - se - ro
p

upon the news concerning his private life and plot a long-awaited revenge; but Rigoletto feels safe under the protection of his master, who lightheartedly rebukes him for going too far with his jokes [Ensemble 6].

At the entrance of Monterone, whose daughter is also numbered among the Duke's victims, the dance music comes to an abrupt end. Rigoletto, walking about with grotesque movements, teases him for coming "to reclaim his daughter's honor," and at first only smiles at Monterone's curse. But when Monterone singles him out for laughing at a father's grief, he is stricken with horror. All are taken aback [7] by the daring of Monterone, who is arrested and led away, still repeating his curse.

Act I, Scene 2: Rigoletto's house stands in a garden surrounded by a wall, which, however, permits a view of the second story from the street. A corner of Ceprano's palace occupies the other side of the street through which Rigoletto now approaches, Monterone's curse still on his mind [8]. As he prepares to unlock the door leading into his garden, he is approached by Sparafucile [9], who proudly introduces himself as an assassin for hire and offers his services, intimating that Rigoletto might have a rival for the affections of the girl who lives in his house. In astonishment, Rigoletto learns how Sparafucile's sister lures the prospective victims to his house, where they succumb to a well-aimed sword thrust. Horrified, he refuses Sparafucile's offer. Nevertheless, he makes sure that he can find the assassin should the need arise.

Alone again, Rigoletto compares himself to Sparafucile (Recitative—generally known as "Aria"—*Pari siamo:* "Equals are we"): what the jester does with words, he muses, the killer does with the sword; both are assassins. Rigoletto curses his deformity, which forces him to be a vile and ever laughing jester, ready at any hour to amuse his master, and he curses the sneering courtiers as the authors of his depravity; but all somber thoughts [8] are discarded at the sight of his home.

As he enters the garden, his young daughter, Gilda, in town only a short time since leaving a convent, comes to greet him (Duet *Figlia!—Mio Padre!:* "Daughter!—My Father!") [10]. She begs him to tell her about their family and station, but, refusing to speak about his profession, he talks lovingly about Gilda's dead mother [11]. While Gilda tries to console him [12], he tells her that she is the sole loved one he has left on earth. He calls the nurse, Giovanna, and asks her to watch carefully over his daughter [13], but he is interrupted by a noise at the gate. When he opens it to look out, the Duke, disguised as a student, slips past him, unseen also by Gilda. Throwing a purse to Giovanna, the Duke hides. Rigoletto once more admonishes Giovanna to be watchful [13] and leaves.

While Gilda talks to her nurse about the unknown young man who has been following her on her way to church, the Duke—who is this very man—motions Giovanna to leave and comes forward. Extolling the powers of

[12] DUET *FIGLIA–MIO PADRE* (Rigoletto, Gilda) *continued*

Andante *con agitazione*
GILDA
Stay, oh say no more, oh say no more! my ___
Oh quan - to do- lor! quan- to do- lor! che ___
words ___ have ___ wa - ken'd thy hid - den fount of tears!
spre - me - re ___ sì a - ma - ro pian - to può!

[13]

Allegro moderato assai *affettuoso*
RIG.
Ah! watch, I pray ___ thee, o'er this flow - er,
Ah! ve- glia, o don - na, que - sto fio - re
In its in - no - cence con - fid - ed
che a te pu - ro con - fi - da - i;

[14] LOVE DUET (Duke, Gilda)

Andantino *cantabile*
DUKE
Sun of the soul, a di - vine in - spi - ra - tion
E il sol dell' a - ni - ma, la vi - ta è a - mo - re,

[15]

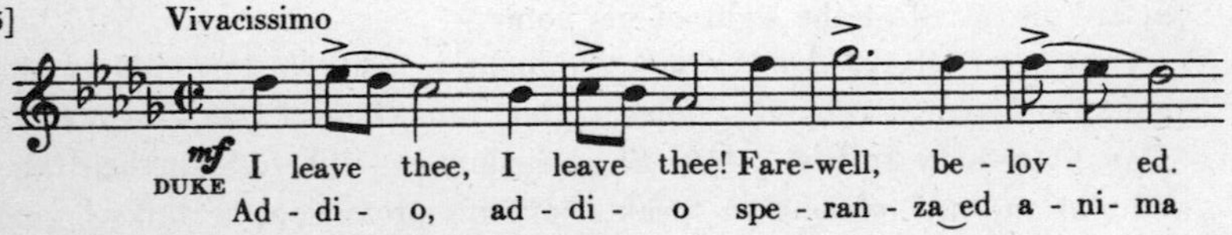
Vivacissimo
DUKE
I leave thee, I leave thee! Fare-well, be - lov - ed.
Ad - di - o, ad - di - o spe - ran - za ed a - ni - ma

[16] ARIA *CARO NOME* (Gilda)

Allegro moderato *dolcissimo*
Carv'd up - on my in - most heart Is that
Ca - ro no - me che il mio cor fe - sti
name for ev - er - more;
pri - mo pal - pi - tar,

love, his soaring melody is soon joined by Gilda in a tender counterpoint (Duet *È il sol dell' anima:* "Sun of the soul") [14]. They are interrupted by Giovanna, who fearfully informs them that she has heard voices in the street. After a fervent farewell [15] the Duke leaves, and Gilda, going up to her room, lovingly repeats his name. He had called himself Gualtier Maldé (Recitative *Gualtier Maldé*), and this name will be on her lips till her last breath (Aria *Caro nome:* "Carved upon my inmost heart") [16]. (Here the coloratura passages, far from being mere ornaments, eloquently suggest the flutterings of a young and pure heart in love for the first time).

The night is black now. By the light of the candle she carries, the courtiers, who have entered the street, admire her beauty. They have come, masked, to abduct the girl, for it is she whom Marullo has assumed to be the jester's sweetheart.

Rigoletto, still tortured by the curse [8], returns, but is told by the quick-witted Marullo that the courtiers have come to steal Ceprano's wife. Under the pretext of giving him a mask, he covers Rigoletto's eyes and ears; and it is the father who holds the ladder for the courtiers as they go about abducting the daughter [17]. Soon they bring out the struggling Gilda and triumphantly disappear with their victim. Rigoletto, finally weary of holding the ladder, tears off the mask to find the house open and Gilda gone. In horror he remembers the curse and falls fainting to the ground.

Act II: In great agitation, the Duke enters the antechamber of his suite at the palace. His beloved, Gilda, has been stolen from him. On his return to her house he had found it unlocked, and Gilda was gone. Where could she be, she who could bring him more happiness than all the angels in

[17] Allegro *sotto voce*

[18] ARIA *PARMI VEDER LE LAGRIME* (Duke)

Adagio

[19] Allegro assai moderato

[20] Allegro assai moderato

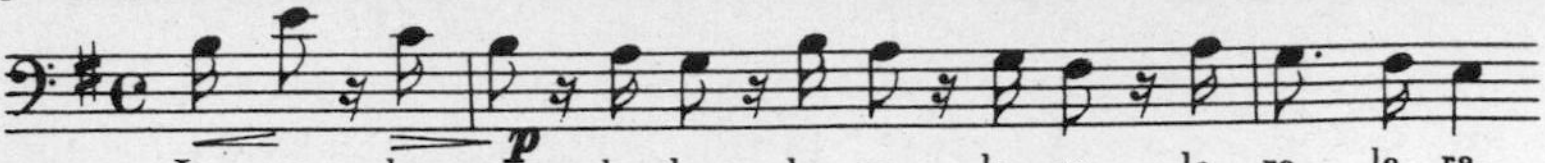

RIG. La ra, la ra, la la, la ra, la ra, la ra, la ra,
La rà, la rà, la la, la rà, la rà, la rà, la rà,

[21] ARIA *CORTIGIANI* (Rigoletto)
Andante mosso agitato

f Race of court - iers, vile rab - ble de - test - ed!
Cor - ti - gia - ni, vil raz - za dan - na - ta!

[22] Andante cantabile

p Oh my lords, will ye have__ no com - pas - sion
Miei si - gno - ri per - do - no, pie - ta - te

[23] ARIA *TUTTE LE FESTE* (Gilda)
Andantino

p On ev - 'ry fes - tal morn - ing, near to the ho - ly al - tar,
Tut - te le fe - ste al tem - pio men - tre pre - ga - va Id - di - o,

[24] DUET *PIANGI FANCIULLA* (Rigoletto, Gilda)
Cantabile

RIG. *mf* Daugh - ter, come let me com - fort thee in thy sor - row
Pian - gi, pian - gi, fan - ciul - la, fan - ciul - la, pian - gi.

[25] Allegro vivo

RIG. *f* Yes, my___ ven - geance__ fierce hath___ doom'd__ thee,
Sì, ven - det - ta,__ tre - men - da__ ven - det - ta

[26] CANZONE *LA DONNA E MOBILE* (Duke)
Allegretto con brio

mp Plume in the sum - mer wind, way - ward - ly play - ing,
La don - na è mo - bi - le qual piu - ma al ven - to,

[27] Allegro

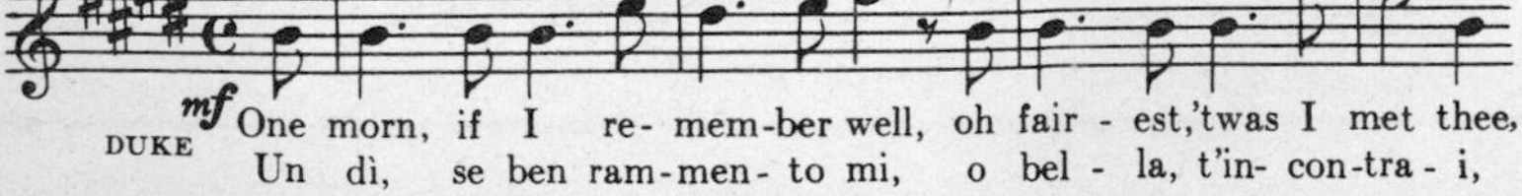

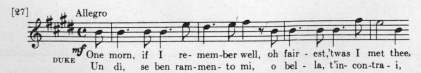

DUKE *mf* One morn, if I re - mem - ber well, oh fair - est,'twas I met thee,
Un dì, se ben ram - men - to mi, o bel - la, t'in - con - tra - i,

heaven (Aria *Parmi veder le lagrime:* "Art thou weeping in loneliness") [18]? When the courtiers come to inform him of their vengeance [19] and when they tell him that they have brought Gilda to the palace, his mood quickly changes. Filled with joyful anticipation (Aria—generally omitted—*Possente amor:* "Now hope renewed is glowing"), he enters his apartments, leaving the courtiers mystified by his strange behavior.

Rigoletto appears and, though mocked by the amused courtiers, makes a heroic effort to appear unconcerned and gay [20] while he is anxiously looking for signs of his daughter's presence. A messenger from the Duchess enters, and when the courtiers refuse to admit him to the Duke's apartments, Rigoletto realizes that Gilda must be with him. Desperately he tries to force his way into the Duke's rooms, but is frustrated by the courtiers. Furiously he reviles them (Aria *Cortigiani:* "Race of courtiers") [21], and then pleads with them [22], but in vain. Suddenly the door opens and Gilda, disheveled, rushes into her father's arms. Imperiously Rigoletto commands the courtiers to leave him alone with his daughter, then sorrowfully listens as Gilda relates the events leading up to her present disgrace (Aria *Tutte le feste:* "On every festal morning") [23]. Seeing all his hopes destroyed, Rigoletto nevertheless tries to console his daughter (Duet *Piangi fanciulla:* "Daughter, come") [24]. Monterone, under guard, is led past, despairing of the Duke's downfall, and Rigoletto, in a violent cabaletta to the duet, promises him revenge (*Si, vendetta:* "Yes, my vengeance") [25], despite Gilda's pleading for forgiveness [25].

Act III: Rigoletto and Gilda, through a crack in the wall, look into the house of Sparafucile, which is located on the banks of the Mincio River. The Duke enters, asking Sparafucile for wine and a room, and lightheartedly expresses his thoughts on women in one of the most durable hit tunes ever written (Canzone *La donna è mobile:* "Plume in the summer wind") [26]. Maddalena, Sparafucile's sister, joins the Duke, whose lovemaking [27] at first only amuses her. Outside the house, Gilda, heartbroken at the Duke's unfaithfulness, and Rigoletto, thinking of vengeance, join their voices to those within (Quartet *Bella figlia dell' amore:* "Fairest daughter of the Graces") [28, 29].

[28] QUARTET *BELLA FIGLIA DELL' AMORE* (Duke, Maddalena, Gilda, Rigoletto)

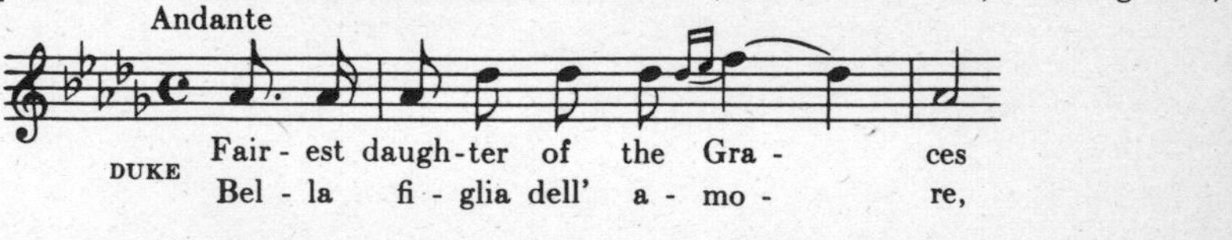

[29]

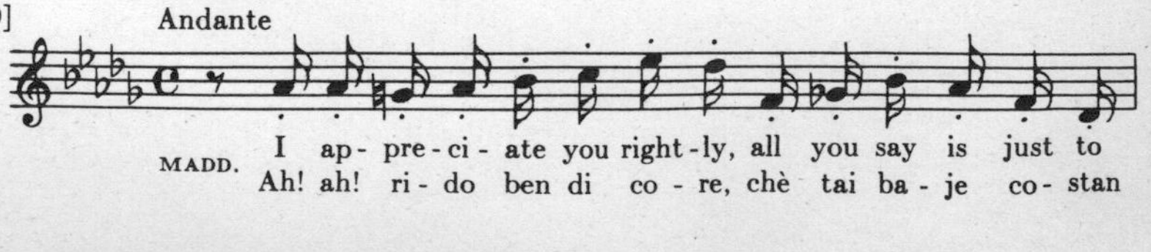

[29] *continued*

GILDA
flat - ter. Ah! ___ to ___ speak ___ of love ___ thus light - ly!
po - co. Ah! ___ co - si ___ par - lar ___ d'a - mo - re!

[30] Allegro

(Humming)

[31] TRIO *SE PRIA CH'ABBIA IL MEZZO* (Sparafucile, Maddalena, Gilda)

Allegro

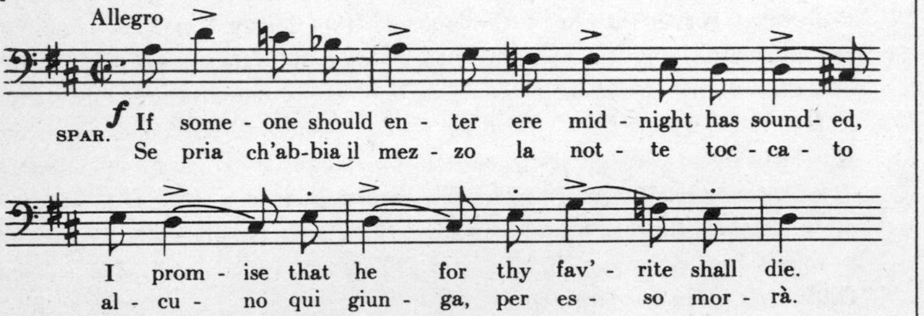
f
SPAR.
If some - one should en - ter ere mid - night has sound - ed,
Se pria ch'ab-bia il mez - zo la not - te toc - ca - to
I prom - ise that he for thy fav' - rite shall die.
al - cu - no qui giun - ga, per es - so mor - rà.

[32] Allegro

f
GILDA
God in ___ heav - en, oh ___ for - give! ___
Oh ___ cie - lo pie - - tà! ___

[33] Andante

pp
GILDA
From yon - der sky ___ with the blest an - gels fly - ing,
Las - sù, in cie - lo, vi - ci - na al - la ma - dre,

Rigoletto orders Gilda to precede him to Verona, dressed in men's clothes that he has prepared for her at home. While a few measures of music depict the proverbial calm before the storm, Sparafucile comes outside and receives from Rigoletto the customary advance of half the fee for the assassination of the man in the house. The jester will return at midnight to pay the other half and to receive the body, for he wants to commit it to the river himself.

The tempest is approaching, at first only with occasional lightning and thunder and an eerie moaning of the wind (suggested by the humming of male voices [30]). The Duke is shown to a bedroom and lies down, singing his favorite ditty [26]. As soon as he has fallen asleep, Maddalena is sent to secure his sword, but, moved by a strong affection for the handsome young man, she implores her brother not to harm him. Meanwhile, Gilda has returned, dressed in a man's riding habit, and hears Maddalena and Sparafucile bargaining for the Duke's life. Finally, while the storm gains in intensity, Sparafucile agrees that the man he was paid to kill may live if before midnight someone else comes in, whose body can be substituted (Trio *Se pria ch'abbia il mezzo:* "If someone should enter") [31]. Gilda's voice soars above those of the others as, asking God's pardon [32], she determines to offer her life for that of the Duke. Praying for the happiness of her unfaithful lover, she bravely enters the house. As Sparafucile stabs her, the tempest reaches its climax. The lamp inside the house is extinguished, and the darkness is interrupted only by lightning.

When the storm has gradually subsided, Rigoletto returns to complete his vengeance, and at the stroke of midnight he receives from Sparafucile a sack containing a body. Savagely he savors the triumph of the buffoon over the monarch. He is preparing to throw the sack into the waves when suddenly the voice of the Duke is heard in the distance [26]. Frantic, Rigoletto opens the sack, and by a flash of lightning he recognizes with a shudder his own daughter. Dying, she confesses her sacrifice and haltingly asks his forgiveness. With her last breath she tenderly promises to pray for him in heaven [33]. His daughter lifeless in his arms, Rigoletto cries out, "The Curse!" as he collapses over Gilda's body.

THEMES

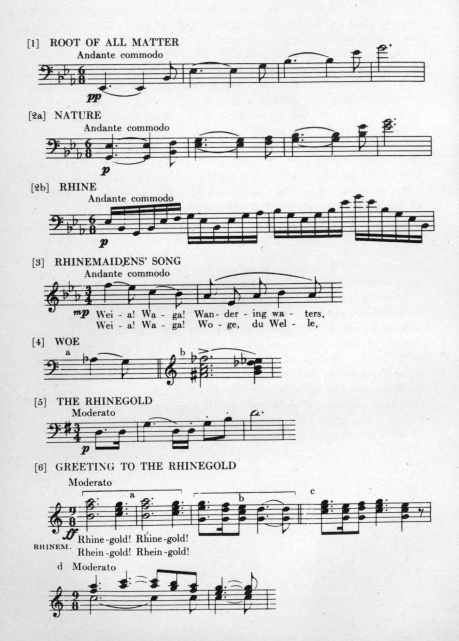

[1] ROOT OF ALL MATTER

Andante commodo

pp

[2a] NATURE

Andante commodo

p

[2b] RHINE

Andante commodo

p

[3] RHINEMAIDENS' SONG

Andante commodo

mp
Wei - a! Wa - ga! Wan- der - ing wa - ters,
Wei - a! Wa - ga! Wo - ge, du Wel - le,

[4] WOE

a
b

[5] THE RHINEGOLD

Moderato

p

[6] GREETING TO THE RHINEGOLD

Moderato

a
b
c
ff
RHINEM.
Rhine-gold! Rhine-gold!
Rhein-gold! Rhein-gold!

d Moderato

Der Ring des Nibelungen

THE RING OF THE NIBELUNG

Festival play for four nights by Richard Wagner. Libretto by the composer. First performance in its entirety: Bayreuth, August 13, 14, 16, 17, 1876.

Das Rheingold

THE RHINEGOLD

Opera in one act: first night (prologue) of *The Ring of the Nibelung.* First performance: Munich, September 22, 1869.

Characters: WOTAN, ruler of heaven and earth (bass-baritone); FRICKA, his wife, goddess of marital bliss (mezzo-soprano); FREIA, goddess of youth, Fricka's sister (soprano); DONNER (THUNDER), god of thunder (bass-baritone) and FROH (tenor), her brothers; ERDA, goddess of fate (mezzo-soprano or contralto); LOGE (FIRE), demigod (tenor); FASOLT, a giant (bass-baritone); FAFNER, his brother (bass); ALBERICH, a Nibelung (bass-baritone); MIME, his brother (tenor); WOGLINDE, a Rhinemaiden (soprano); WELLGUNDE (soprano) and FLOSSHILDE (mezzo-soprano), her sisters.
In the realms of Father Rhine, the gods, and the Nibelungs, in Germany of legendary times.

Scene 1: Ever peacefully flow the waters of the Rhine [1, 2ab]. In its rocky depths the three Rhinemaidens are merrily swimming and singing [3]. Actually, as they are well aware, they should be guarding the Rhinegold, which rests, at present wrapped in darkness, on top of one of the rocks.

The Nibelung Alberich emerges from a chasm and eyes the maidens lustfully. Woglinde invites him to approach, and he laboriously stumbles toward her over the slippery rocks; but whenever he is about to grasp her she smoothly floats out of reach. Now the other two, Wellgunde and Flosshilde, in turn, tease him in the same manner. As they all laugh at Alberich's helpless rage [4ab] and enjoy [3] his mounting excitement, the gold [5] begins to glow brilliantly in the rays of the sun. The Rhinemaidens greet its awakening [6cab]. Carelessly they reveal the story of the gold's secret: whoever can forge a ring [7] from the gold will rule the world, but only he who renounces love [8] can shape the ring. Suddenly Alberich climbs the crag, curses love, tears the gold from the rock, and disappears with it into the depths, leaving the distressed Rhinemaidens in deep darkness.

[7] THE RING

[8] RENUNCIATION OF LOVE

[9] VALHALLA

[10] TREATY

[11] WOMAN'S FASCINATION

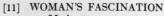

[12] FREIA

Scenic Transformation: As the scene changes into a mountain plain overlooking the Rhine valley, the music indicates that Alberich, having renounced love [8], now proceeds to forge the gold into the shape of the all-powerful ring [7].

Scene 2: Wotan and Fricka lie asleep on the ground. Fricka, awakening, discovers that on the mountain across the river the new castle of the gods [9abc] has been completed. In great anxiety she rouses Wotan, her husband, who in his sleep is muttering about ruling the world [7]. Awakened, he happily greets the mighty fortress [9abcd], but Fricka is worried about her sister Freia, who has been promised [10] by Wotan to the giants Fasolt and Fafner as payment for building the castle. She reproaches her husband for planning their new abode with little thought for creating a real home [11], instead being intent only on erecting a strong fortress.

Presently Freia [12a] appears, fleeing [13] from the giants Fasolt and Fafner [14]. Asked by Wotan to choose compensation other than Freia, the giants insist on the fulfillment of their contract [10]. Fasolt longs for the beautiful goddess of youth [12a] and warns Wotan to keep his bargain [15]. Fafner, less interested in Freia, is intent on destroying the gods by removing from their midst the keeper of the youth-preserving golden apples [16] that keep the gods eternally young. As the giants move toward Freia, her brothers, Donner and Froh, rush in to protect her, but Wotan bars [10] the use of force.

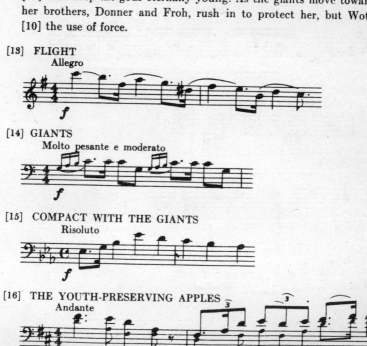

[13] FLIGHT
Allegro

f

[14] GIANTS
Molto pesante e moderato

f

[15] COMPACT WITH THE GIANTS
Risoluto

f

[16] THE YOUTH-PRESERVING APPLES
Andante

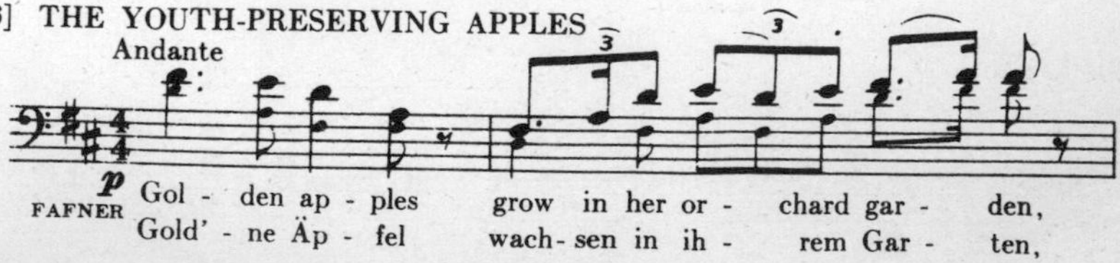
p
FAFNER
Gol - den ap - ples grow in her or - chard gar - den,
Gold' - ne Äp - fel wach- sen in ih - rem Gar - ten,

[17] LOGE (FIRE)

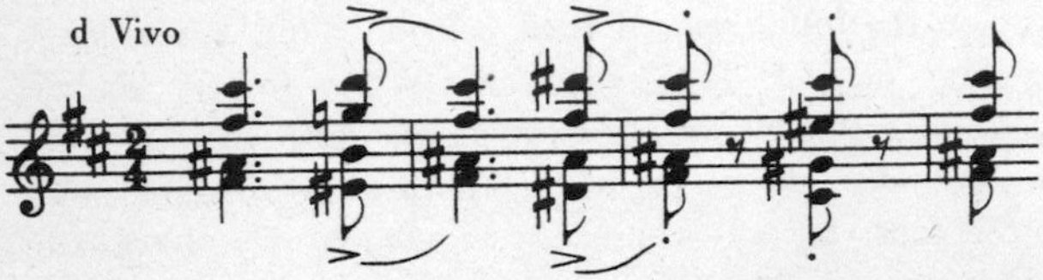

[18] BROODING

[19] RESIGNATION

[20] NIBELUNGS (SMITHS)

[21] TARNCAP

Last to arrive is Loge, the fickle god of fire, gifted with mysterious magic, sly [17abcde]. He had promised Wotan to search for a way to get around the bad bargain, but after checking the new fortress [9abcd] he had found it without fault. Although the other gods call Loge a traitor, Wotan flatteringly expresses his confidence in the wisdom [18] of the fire god. Thereupon Loge tells about his search for a recompense acceptable to the giants in place of Freia, and about his findings (Loge's Narrative *Immer ist Undank Loge's Lohn!:* "Thankless was ever Loge's toil!"): there is nothing in the whole world for which one would renounce [19] love [12b]. Only Alberich, he continues, preferred gold [5] to love—so the Rhinemaidens have told him [6ab, 3]. Alberich has stolen the Rhinegold [5] and forged a ring from it [7]. To do this, Alberich has had to renounce love [8], but in return the ring will give him power to rule the world [22ac].

Fricka learns from Loge that she could bind Wotan's love to her forever [11] by wearing jewelry forged by the Nibelungs [20] under the spell of the ring [12b, 5]. Wotan, too, would like to wield the power of the ring [7]. Gaily Loge replies that the ring, being already forged, can now be gained quite easily without renunciation by simply stealing it from Alberich. Sarcastically he adds that Wotan could then grant the Rhinemaidens' urgent entreaty [6ad] that the gold be returned to them [5, 3]. However, the giants decide that if Wotan can deliver the Rhinegold, they will accept it in exchange for Freia [12b, 16, 14]. As Wotan hesitates, they seize the goddess. Promising [10] to keep her as a hostage for the ring [7] till nightfall, they carry her off.

Loge looks after them curiously and then, turning to the gods, who have grown perceptibly pale because they have not partaken of Freia's [12a] golden apples [16] this morning, he mocks them. Quickly Wotan decides that he will descend with Loge to Nibelheim, the land of the Nibelungs inside the earth.

Scenic Transformation: Clouds of sulphur envelop the scene. The music indicates that Loge [17bce] is leading Wotan on his expedition [19, 13] to gain the Rhinegold [5, 7] and to free the goddess of youth and love [37].

Scene 3: The busy sound of hammers on anvils is heard in Alberich's realm [20, 4a] as its master forces his reluctant brother, Mime, to relinquish a piece of gold net which Alberich has had him forge. Putting this net [The Tarncap 21] over his head and murmuring an incantation, Alberich makes himself invisible. His laughter reverberates through the caves as his whip descends without mercy on the helplessly howling Mime, and presently he is off, invisible and invincible [7], to keep the Nibelungs slaving under his whip.

Mime is still sobbing with pain [4a] when Wotan and Loge arrive. In despair [18] he tells them about the ring [7], and how the formerly gay Nibelung smiths [20] must now slave [4ab] for Alberich [7]. Finally he relates his own most recent misadventure with the Tarncap [21]. He

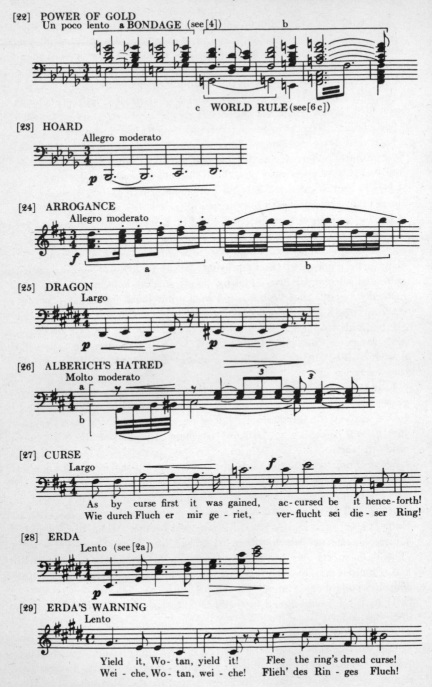

[22] POWER OF GOLD

Un poco lento
a BONDAGE (see [4])
b
c WORLD RULE (see [6 c])

[23] HOARD

Allegro moderato
p

[24] ARROGANCE

Allegro moderato
f
a
b

[25] DRAGON

Largo
p
p

[26] ALBERICH'S HATRED

Molto moderato
a
b
3
3

[27] CURSE

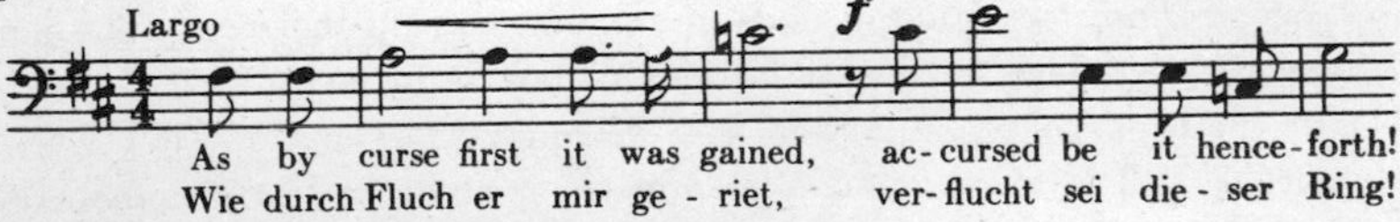
Largo
f
As by curse first it was gained, ac- cursed be it hence-forth!
Wie durch Fluch er mir ge - riet, ver- flucht sei die - ser Ring!

[28] ERDA

Lento (see [2a])
p

[29] ERDA'S WARNING

Lento
Yield it, Wo- tan, yield it! Flee the ring's dread curse!
Wei - che, Wo - tan, wei - che! Flieh' des Rin - ges Fluch!

flees when a group of Nibelungs appear [20 with 4a] carrying heavy loads of treasure, driven by the whiplash of their master [22]. When Alberich notices the strangers, he sends the Nibelungs back to work, forcing their obedience through the power of the ring [7, 22]. Loge [17ad] attempts to convince the suspicious Alberich of his friendly intentions, but the Nibelung has no need for Loge's friendship, preferring to rely on his treasure hoard [23]. With it he will defeat love and beauty [12b] and will force all to renounce love [8, 19]. With it he will conquer the gods [9bc], and the goddesses as well, when the Rhinegold [23, 5] is brought up from the bowels of the earth.

Loge keeps flattering Alberich's conceit [24] but at the same time feigns disbelief in the powers of the Tarncap [21]. Alberich offers a demonstration and transforms himself [21] first into a dragon [25] and then, at Loge's request, into a toad [21b]. Now the intruders seize their opportunity. They catch the toad, and as Loge snatches the Tarncap from the toad's head, Alberich reappears in his natural shape. He is bound and carried off by Wotan and Loge as they begin their ascent to the lånd of the gods.

Scenic Transformation: Behind clouds of sulphur the scene changes as before, but in reverse [24, 7, 19; 20 with 4a; 37, 14, 17, 16 minor, 6a, 4b].

Scene 4: Back where they had started, Loge and Wotan put down Alberich [4ab], and as Loge makes sport of the would-be master of the world, Wotan asks Alberich for the treasure in exchange for his freedom. Hoping to keep the ring [7], Alberich agrees and, kissing the golden band, he orders [22]the Nibelungs to bring the gold. They come [20 with 4a, 23], deposit the hoard, then rush off again at the sight of the ring on Alberich's outstretched fist [22]. Loge throws the Tarncap [21b] on the pile, and Wotan asks for the ring that Alberich has stolen from the Rhinemaidens [6a]. Despite Alberich's pleading and taunting [7], Wotan pulls the ring forcibly from the Nibelung's finger [10]. Alberich is crushed [19] but still seething with hatred [26]. He puts a curse on the ring [27]: it shall bring no gain, but only fear, grief, and death to its wearer. Quickly he descends through a cleft in the mountain and disappears [4b, 6a].

As the giants [14] approach with Freia [16], Fricka, Froh, and Donner come to ask about the success of Wotan's journey and are shown the hoard [26]. Fasolt, true to his word [15], will reluctantly give up the goddess [12a] if enough treasure is stacked in front of her so that she is hidden from his view [19]. When this is done [15, 20, 23], the Tarncap [21b] must go on top to hide Freia's hair [16] and, to fill a crack through which the eye of the goddess is still visible [12a, 37], the giants demand the ring. Loge mockingly pleads that the ring be returned to the Rhinemaidens [6a], but Wotan insists that he will keep it for himself [5, 22c]. Erda [28] appears from a cleft in a bluish light and soberly counsels Wotan to desist [29]. She, who knows past, present, and future, warns him of the end of the gods [26, 4b, 30] and advises him to give up the ring. She disappears again,

[30] TWILIGHT OF THE GODS

Adagio

[31] DONNER (THUNDER)

Allegro

He - da! He - da! He-do!

[32] RAINBOW

Andante

[33] WOTAN'S GREETING TO VALHALLA

Moderato

See how at eve the eye of sun - light,
A - bend-lich strahlt der Son - ne Au - ge;

THEMES

[34] STORM

Furioso

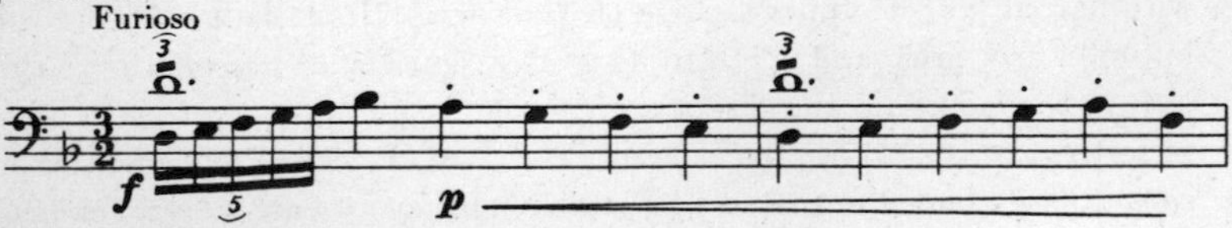

[35] SIEGMUND

Allegro

[36] SIEGLINDE'S PITY

Moderato

and Wotan, after a tense moment of consideration [28], announces [10] that he is buying back the goddess of youth [19] and throws the ring on the pile.

While the gods embrace the liberated Freia [12a], Fafner and Fasolt start gathering the treasure into sacks [14 with 20]. They begin to quarrel [4a, 26] over their shares, and as Fasolt snatches the ring [7] from his brother, Fafner kills him with his club and walks off with the hoard [27].

Gently rousing Wotan from his brooding [7, 28], Fricka invites him [11] to enter their new abode [9b]. As a dense fog has risen from the Rhine, Donner with his hammer summons lightning and thunder [31] to clear the atmosphere, and Froh causes the rainbow [32] to form a bridge across the Rhine. Wotan happily admires the castle [9ab], now seen brilliantly lighted in the evening sun. (Wotan's Greeting to Valhalla *Abendlich strahlt der Sonne Auge:* "See how at eve the eye of sunlight") [33 with 9bacd]. As he looks at the dearly bought [7] fortress, a great thought [43a] forms in his mind. He names the fortress Valhalla (Hall of the Heroes) [9] and leads the gods toward their new home.

Loge [17a] toys with the thought of returning to his original form of flaming fire [17cb] and consuming the gods, whose end is destined, but at last he turns reluctantly to follow them toward Valhalla.

As the Rhinemaidens' plaint over the loss of the gold [6adc, 5] rises from the river, the gods solemnly approach Valhalla [9b with 43a] over the rainbow bridge [32].

Die Walküre

THE VALKYRIE

Opera in three acts: second night of *The Ring of the Nibelung.* First performance: Munich, June 26, 1870.

Characters: Mortals: SIEGMUND, son of Wotan (tenor); SIEGLINDE, his twin sister (soprano); HUNDING, Sieglinde's husband (bass);

Gods: WOTAN, ruler of heaven and earth (bass-baritone); FRICKA, his wife (mezzo-soprano);

Valkyries, daughters of Wotan and Erda: BRÜNNHILDE (soprano); HELMWIGE (soprano); ORTLINDE (soprano); GERHILDE (soprano); WALTRAUTE (mezzo-soprano); SIEGRUNE (mezzo-soprano); ROSSWEISSE (mezzo-soprano); GRIMGERDE (mezzo-soprano); SCHWERTLEITE (contralto).

Germany, in legendary times.

Prelude to Act I: The music describes the raging of a thunderstorm [34, 31], through which occasional horn calls are heard. The storm is about to subside when the curtain rises.

[37] LOVE

Molto moderato

[38] Molto moderato

[39] THE VOLSUNGS' SUFFERING

Adagio

[40] HUNDING

Moderato

a

b Moderato

[41] "WOEFUL"

Adagio

[42] VOLSUNGS

Molto moderato

[43] SWORD

a Allegro moderato

Act I: Into Hunding's house, built around a tall ash tree, Siegmund staggers [35] and drops exhausted on the rug by the hearth, where he remains motionless. From an inner room Sieglinde enters, surprised to see a stranger. Her greeting remains unanswered, but as she tenderly bends over him [36] he asks for water, which she quickly fetches. As he drinks [35], he gazes fixedly at her [37, 38]. Refreshed, he asks who she is, and she tells him that she is Hunding's wife. The effects of the battle from which Siegmund has fled weaponless but unharmed, are quickly forgotten in the presence of his hostess [36], and when he drinks the mead offered him, he becomes conscious of the woman's attraction for him [38, 37]. Suddenly he proposes to leave, for he knows himself to be a carrier of misfortune; but Sieglinde stops him, exclaiming that hers is already an unhappy life [39]. As their eyes meet in silence [38], Hunding [40a] returns home and extends to the stranger the traditional rights of the guest. They sit down to the evening meal [36, 37], and Hunding notices how much his guest resembles his wife. Curious, he starts a conversation, and after introducing himself [40a] he asks his guest's name. Pensively [39] the guest tells of his father, whom, concealing his real name, he calls "Wolfe." With him he used to roam the woods after his mother had been killed and his twin sister abducted [40a]. However, one day after a battle his father [9a], too, had disappeared. Since then misfortune has followed him, and this explains why he must call himself "Wehwalt" (Woeful). Urged by Sieglinde, he tells about his latest fight [40b] and how that, too, ended in tragedy for the maiden he intended to help. As he sadly finishes his story [39, 41, 42], Hunding reveals [40b] that the battle had involved his kinsmen, and that on the morrow he intends to avenge them [40a].

Hunding sends his wife [36] to prepare his night cup. With her gaze fixed on Siegmund [41, 37] she complies, her eyes persistently indicating the ash tree [43a]. When she has gone, Hunding follows her, taking along his weapons [40a].

Siegmund is left to his somber thoughts [40b]. He needs a weapon [43a]. His father has promised him one in his direst need (Siegmund's Monologue *Ein Schwert verhiess mir der Vater:* "A sword my father foretold me") [44]. As he cries out to "Wälse"—the name by which he knows his father—he suddenly perceives a ray of light coming from a spot on the ash tree (43a trumpet]. But soon the fire in the hearth dies down, and Siegmund remains in darkness.

Sieglinde enters [41, 36]. She has drugged her husband, and now she has come to show Siegmund a sword driven up to the hilt into the trunk of the ash tree. At the time when, against her will, she was married to Hunding (Sieglinde's Narrative *Der Männer Sippe sass hier im Saal:* "The kinsmen gathered here for the feast"), an old man [9ab] had walked in. His single eye had glared fiercely at the men, but smiled comfortingly and soothingly at her [45] as he drove a sword [43a] into the tree, bequeathing it to the

b Vivace

[44] SIEGMUND'S MONOLOGUE

Molto moderato

f A sword my fa - ther fore - told me,
Ein Schwert ver - hiess mir der Va - ter,

[45] MAGIC SPELL

Moderato

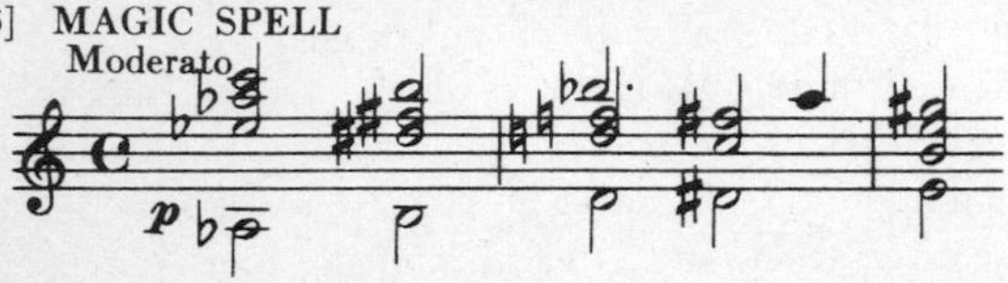

[46] VOLSUNGS' BATTLE-CRY

Molto vivace

SIEGL. To find him to - day
O fänd' ich ihn heut'

[47] HYMN TO SPRING

Andante

SIEGM. Win - ter storms have waned in the moon of May,
Win - ter - stür - me wi - chen dem Won - ne - mond,

[48] RAPTURE

Molto andante

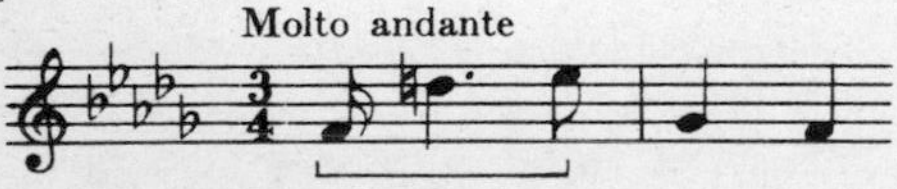
a

[49] RIDE OF THE VALKYRIES

Impetuoso

[50] VALKYRIES' GREETING

Impetuoso

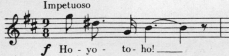

f Ho - yo - to - ho!

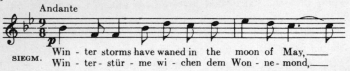

one who could remove it. When no one could do it, Sieglinde understood who the old man was [9a], and who would win the sword. Oh, she exclaims in a transport [46], if only the stranger before her were the one to unsheathe the sword and to avenge her sorrow and shame. Siegmund [42] embraces her jubilantly [46]. Suddenly the front door bursts open. Soft moonlight streams in on the pair. Siegmund exclaims (Aria *Winterstürme wichen dem Wonnemond:* "Winter storms have waned in the moon of May") [47] that Spring has entered the house to join his sister, Love [38, 37]. However, for Sieglinde it is the stranger who represents Spring [37] (Aria *Du bist der Lenz:* "You are the Spring") and the light and love [38] she has been waiting for. In ever increasing rapture they give expression to their love [48, 12b] until suddenly Sieglinde discovers how familiar the stranger looks [9ab]. He looks just like her own mirror image, his voice sounds like the echo of her own, and his eye looks like her father's, like the old man's who brought the sword [42, 43a, 9a]. Is "Woeful" the stranger's real name, she demands to know, and was his father truly called "Wolfe?" The stranger declares that he is Woeful no longer and that his father's [9a] real name was Wälse. Then, shouts the ecstatic Sieglinde, I will call you Siegmund! To prove that he really is Siegmund [42], the stranger grasps the sword [43a] and, aflame with love's desperation [8], names it Nothung (Need Sword) [motive 78a] as with a mighty heave he pulls it from the tree [43a]. Siegmund the Wälsung (Volsung) [42] now has a sword he can offer as a bridal gift; and triumphantly [46] he wants to take his bride away into the beckoning Spring night [47, 38]. But first Sieglinde reveals her own name and joyously tells him that she is his twin sister. Rapturously Siegmund takes her into his arms [38, 43a, 37].

Prelude to Act II: Motives [43a], [13], [37], [48a] gradually give way to [49].

Act II: Standing on a rocky mountain pass, Wotan, in full armor, orders Brünnhilde to assure Siegmund's victory in his imminent battle with Hunding. With the gay greeting of the Valkyries (*Hoyotoho!*) [50 with 49] Brünnhilde takes her leave, but before disappearing over the pass she announces to Wotan the approach of his angry wife.

Fricka arrives, furious [51]. Hunding [40a] has asked her, the guardian of marriage, for protection, and she has promised punishment for the Volsungs. Wotan proposes that true love [38] should have its way; though the Volsungs be brother and sister, their love [47, 38] is doubtless more deserving of the goddess' blessing than Sieglinde's loveless tie to Hunding. Thereupon Fricka violently [51] denounces Wotan (Fricka's Denunciation *So ist es denn aus:* "Is all, then, at end with the glory of godhood"): have all laws of the gods become invalid since Wotan begot the wild Volsungs? The Valkyries, those daughters of a wild love had been disgrace enough, but now he has fathered a pair of common mortals, to whose whims he subordinates his wife. Calmly Wotan explains that he needs a hero [43a] independent of the gods and their laws [10] to accomplish the

[51] **RAGE**

Molto vivace

ff

[52] **RESENTMENT**

Vivo

a
p
sf dim.
b REGRET

[53] **RESTLESSNESS**

Vivo

f

[54] **FATE**

Maestoso e sostenuto

p

[55] **PROPHECY**

Maestoso e sostenuto

pp
pp

[56] **RIDE**

Impetuoso

f

[57] **REDEMPTION**

Allegro

SIEGL.
O mar - - vel - ous bless - ing!
O hehr - - - stes Wun - der!

[58] **BRUENNHILDE'S PLEA** (see [59])

Larghetto

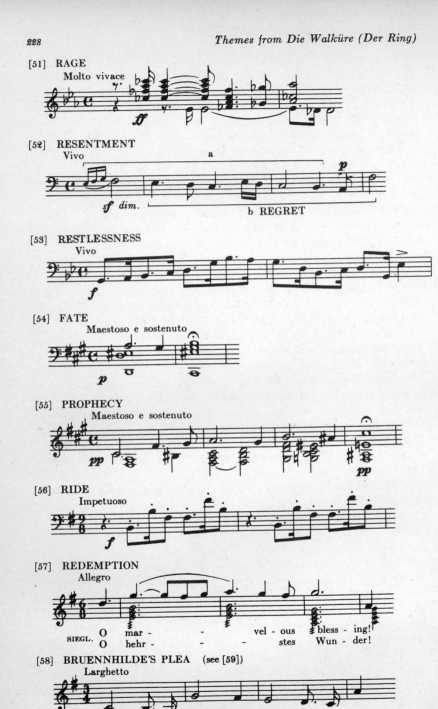

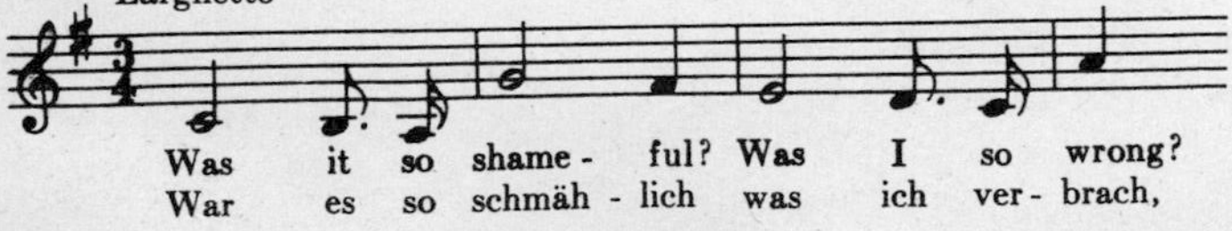
Was it so shame - ful? Was I so wrong?
War es so schmäh - lich was ich ver - brach,

deed [7] that Wotan is treaty-bound [15] not to undertake. However, Fricka points out that Siegmund is not at all independent of the gods, for Wotan has provided him with a sword [43a]. While Wotan's helpless anger [52a] and rage [51] increase, she demands that he give up the protection of Siegmund, that he turn Brünnhilde from him, and that he deprive the sword [43a] of its power.

As the Valkyrie's call [49, 50] announces her return, Wotan, in terrible dejection [52a], finds himself forced to comply with Fricka's demand that Siegmund die to preserve her honor. When Fricka leaves, Brünnhilde tenderly approaches the utterly defeated Wotan [27, 52ab] and asks the reason for his sadness. Miserable, he cries out [27, 51] at his impotence to create a free hero. Upon his favorite daughter's gentle inquiry [37, 38], he confides to her his story (Wotan's Recitative *Als junger Liebe Lust mir verblich:* "When youthful love's desire from me fled"). From the beginning he had lusted after power and love. Alberich, on the other hand, had renounced love and forged the all-powerful ring [7]. Wotan had stolen it and with it paid the builders of Valhalla [9bd]. Erda [28] had warned him against keeping the ring and had prophesied the end of the gods. Curious, Wotan had followed her to the womb of the earth and with a love spell had forced the all-knowing Erda to impart her knowledge to him. She had born him the nine Valkyries, whom he has employed to gather fallen heroes on the battlefield [49] in order to create a defense force for Valhalla [9bc]. Yet the doom, Erda had said [28], lies in the possibility of Alberich's regaining the ring [7]. Bound by treaty, Wotan cannot himself take back the ring [15]. Thus, he explains with growing anxiety [53, 52a], he needs an independent hero who—against the god's will, as it were, and without his help—would gain the ring for the helpless god [4b]. Alas [53, 52a, 51], Wotan can create only slaves: too easily Fricka had exposed Siegmund's [35] dependence. Wotan has touched the cursed ring [7], and Siegmund, whom he loves [37], he must now abandon [19, 27, 43a]. In a wild outburst he wishes only for the end, and he remembers Erda's [28] prophecy: when Alberich, filled with hate [26], produces a son, the destruction of the gods [108] will then be at hand. Forced by the power of gold, Wotan relates, a woman is now bearing the child of the loveless [19] Alberich. Let then, he exclaims in wild despair, the Nibelung's son rule over the empty splendor that is Valhalla [108].

Wotan now commands Brünnhilde to ensure Siegmund's [43a] defeat. As she attempts to oppose his order, he becomes more and more infuriated. He shouts that the Valkyrie is charged with the death of Siegmund [10], and rushes off in a rage [53, 4b].

Sadly the Valkyrie remains [19, 52a], her armor weighing heavily upon her [49, 45]. In deep sorrow [39, 73, 53, 52a] she moves into a cave in the background as Siegmund and Sieglinde approach [13].

Siegmund is trying to halt Sieglinde's hysterical flight. Tenderly [38] he attempts to calm her, but Sieglinde accuses herself of having dishonored

[59] BRUENNHILDE'S LOVE FOR THE VOLSUNGS

Larghetto

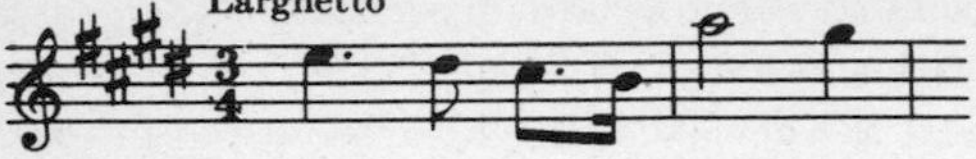

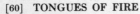

[60] TONGUES OF FIRE

Moderato

[61] WOTAN'S FAREWELL

Molto vivace

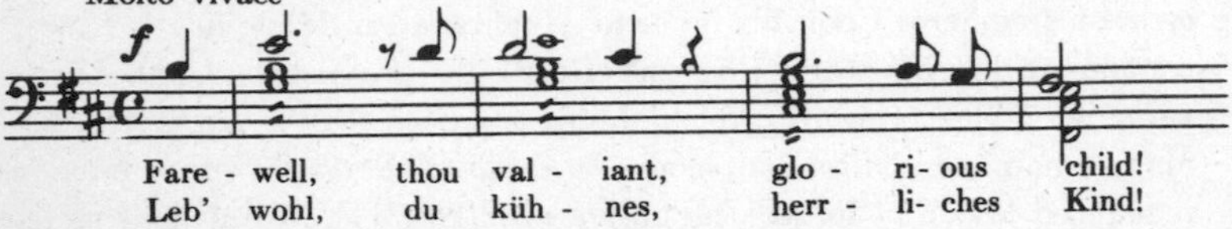
Fare - well, thou val - iant, glo - ri- ous child!
Leb' wohl, du küh - nes, herr - li- ches Kind!

[62] Adagio

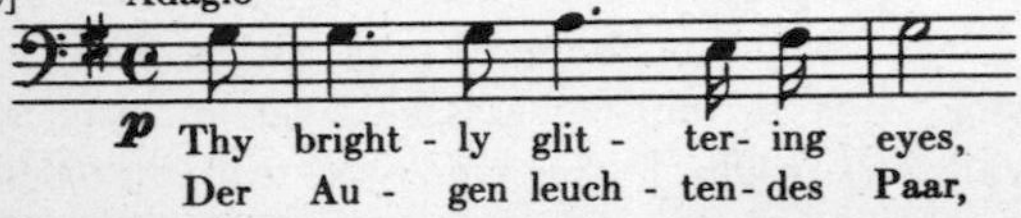
Thy bright - ly glit - ter- ing eyes,
Der Au - gen leuch - ten- des Paar,

Siegmund by giving herself to him after she had shamefully yielded to an unloved husband. Siegmund promises [42] to wipe out her shame by felling [43a] Hunding, whose horn can already be heard in the distance [40b]. Sieglinde's frenzied imagination already sees Siegmund being torn apart by Hunding's dogs, and she faints in his arms. As he sits on the ground, her head in his lap [37, 38], Brünnhilde appears [54, 55, 9bc] leading her horse from the cave, and announces to Siegmund his impending death. To his questioning, she answers that she will bring him to Valhalla [9ba], where he will find gods and heroes, his father, and Wotan's daughters [12b, 49], but not Sieglinde, who must remain on earth. Tenderly Siegmund kisses his bride [38] and declares that he will not leave her to follow Brünnhilde [54]. The Valkyrie informs Siegmund that Hunding will kill him and, when he shows only scorn, replies that his sword [43a] has been deprived of its power. With a vehement denunciation of the maker of the sword, Siegmund raises Nothung to kill Sieglinde, but Brünnhilde stops him. Moved by compassion, she now promises that she will change the course of battle [55 major]. Quickly she disappears among the rocks.

Thunderclouds envelop the scene in darkness. Siegmund turns to Sieglinde [38], who seems lost in a pleasant dream [47], and after a loving glance at her [37] he confidently draws his sword [43a] and goes to meet Hunding [40b]. As the storm draws ever closer, Sieglinde starts to mumble uneasily in her sleep [40b] and awakens frightened and shouting for Siegmund. She hears Hunding calling him to battle [4a]. As Siegmund brandishes his sword [43a] and confronts Hunding, Sieglinde rushes toward the men, but is stopped by a sudden light above the fighters in which Brünnhilde appears [49], protecting Siegmund with her shield. Just as Siegmund is about to deliver the death blow [43a], Wotan appears in a red glow above Hunding, and against the god's spear [10] Siegmund's sword breaks. The Valkyrie retreats in fright, and Hunding transfixes Siegmund with his spear [4, 42, 54]. Brünnhilde quickly lifts Sieglinde onto her horse and rides away [49]. Wotan has fulfilled his vow to Fricka [10]. At a contemptuous wave of the god's hand, Hunding falls dead. Then Wotan, remembering Brünnhilde [52], storms away in a terrible rage to overtake her [53].

Act III: The Valkyries, returning from battle, are riding (Ride of the Valkyries) [56, 49] to meet at the Brünnhildenstein (Brünnhilde's Rock). Some have already reached the rock. Gaily they exchange greetings with the new arrivals [50]. Finally Brünnhilde approaches [53 with 56]. In astonishment her sisters notice her desperate haste, and that, instead of a hero, she has a woman in her saddle [13]. Brünnhilde arrives and explains what has happened, but none of her sisters will lend her a horse to take the woman to safety. Sieglinde wants to die, but Brünnhilde tells her that she must live to bear Siegmund's child. When they see Wotan approaching in the distance, they decide to let Sieglinde flee alone into the woods where the Nibelung's treasure [7] is guarded by Fafner [25]. Brünnhilde will remain to delay Wotan. She prophesies to Sieglinde that she will bear the world's most glorious hero [69] and, giving her the pieces of Siegmund's sword [43a], which she had collected on the battlefield, she asks her to name the child Siegfried. Sieglinde greets the Valkyrie's miraculous revelation [57] with exultation, and, blessing Brünnhilde, she flees.

As Wotan reaches the rock, Brünnhilde hides behind her sisters. In a rage [51] Wotan demands to see her. The Valkyries' efforts to stave him off evoke a wild tirade against his favorite daughter, who, to his grief [52], has broken their happy alliance by turning against her father. As he calls her a coward, she humbly faces him to hear her punishment. Since she has turned all the god-given powers against the god, Wotan declares, she can no longer remain a Valkyrie, but will be stripped of her powers: no longer Wotan's helper [55], she will be banished [10] from his sight and lie in defenseless sleep on this rock until the first man passing by awakens her to be his mate. The horrified protest of the sisters cannot change Wotan's decision [10], and he orders them to leave Brünnhilde on peril of sharing her fate. Terrified, they flee [56 with 49].

Brünnhilde and Wotan remain alone [52b, motive 58; 54]. Timidly she asks whether her crime is really so grave as to merit such harsh punishment (Brünnhilde's Plea *War es so schmählich:* "Was it so shameful?") [58]. Has she not carried out his wish, if not his orders? To Wotan's remonstrances [52b] she replies that she knew how much he loved the Volsung [58], and when she talked to Siegmund [54, 55] his selfless grief touched her heart.

[63] WOTAN'S FAREWELL *continued*

Adagio

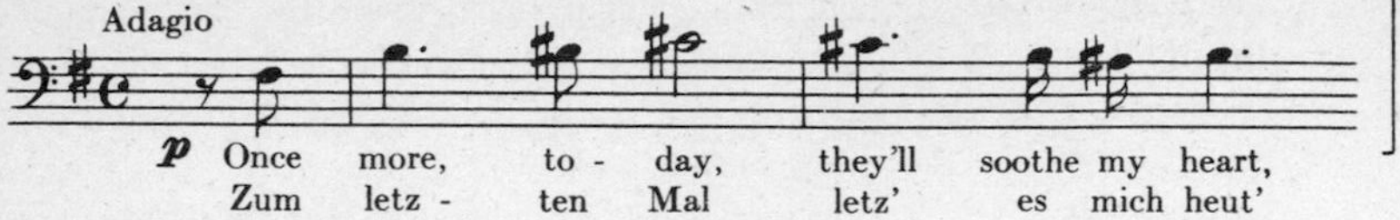
p
Once more, to - day, they'll soothe my heart,
Zum letz - ten Mal letz' es mich heut'

[64] MAGIC FIRE MUSIC (see [17d])

Allegro moderato

f

THEMES

[65] MIME'S LAMENT

Allegro moderato

ff
La- bor un- end- ing, toil with-out fruit!
Zwang-vol- le Pla - ge, Müh' oh - ne Zweck!

The love [59] she had learned from her father moved her to rebel against his command. Wotan comments with deep bitterness that, while he has had to overthrow his entire world and bury his dreams [19, 27], Brünnhilde has followed the call of love, and this is what she must do [10] henceforth [38]. Now Brünnhilde asks that the man who wins her should be not merely any bragging coward but of the noblest race [42], the glorious hero [69] yet to be born, whose mother she has saved together with the sword [43a]. Although Wotan still rages against the Volsungs, his sorrow is apparent when he reaffirms that she must lie sleep-bound [45] to become the wife of a mortal. Fervently Brünnhilde begs him to surround her with defenses [60] that only a hero, undaunted by god or man [69] will be able to pierce. Hungry tongues of fire [17d with 49; 45] shall encircle her to repel cowards.

Looking lovingly at his daughter [49, 60], Wotan bids her a proud farewell (Wotan's Farewell *Leb' wohl, du kühnes, herrliches Kind:* "Farewell, thou valiant, glorious child") [61]. If he must miss her henceforth in battle and at the banquet, a fire without equal shall surround her rock [45, 17d] to keep away all but the one who is freer than the god himself [69]. Embracing his daughter [59], he looks at her radiant eyes [60, 62] for the last time [63]. From now on they will shine for a mortal only, for a mortal luckier than the hapless god who must abandon her [8, 19] and with a last kiss deprive her of her godhood.

As he gently kisses her, a magic sleep [45] descends on Brünnhilde. Wotan lays her on the ground, covers her with her big shield [60 with 62 and 63], and slowly turns away from her [54]. Extending his spear commandingly [10], he calls on Loge [17cb] to return to the state of fire [64] and to surround the rock with flames [17a]. Flames leap from the stone [17c,b] and gradually envelop the entire rock [64, 60]. No one, vows Wotan, who stands in awe of his spear [69] shall ever pass the flames.

Sadly he looks at Brünnhilde [63] and turns to go; but once more he glances back at her [54] before he disappears through the flames.

Siegfried

Opera in three acts: third night of *The Ring of the Nibelung*. First performance: Bayreuth, August 16, 1876.

Characters: WANDERER (WOTAN) (bass-baritone); SIEGFRIED, the Volsung, a mortal (tenor); MIME, a Nibelung (tenor); ALBERICH, his brother (bass-baritone); FAFNER, a dragon, last of the giants (bass); ERDA,

[66] **FAFNER, THE DRAGON** (see [25])

Allegro moderato

[67] **SIEGFRIED'S HORN CALL**

Vivace

[68] **WORK**

Allegro vivace

[69] **SIEGFRIED**

Molto vivace

a

[70] **MIME, THE UGLY DWARF**

Vivacissimo

[71] **MIME, THE SMITH** (see [20])

Moderato

[72] **MIME'S NURSING SONG**

Molto moderato

The whim - per - ing babe kind - ly I reared,
Als zul - len - des Kind zog ich dich auf,

[73] **LONGING FOR LOVE**

Andante

goddess of fate (contralto); BRÜNNHILDE, Wotan's and Erda's daughter (soprano); THE VOICE OF THE FOREST BIRD (soprano).
Germany, in legendary times.

Prelude to Act I: The music describes the thoughts of Mime [18, 23, 20, 4a, 7, and 43a] as he will utter them when the curtain rises.

Act I: In his forest cave Mime sits at his forge, hammering [20] a sword and complaining about his useless toil (Mime's Lament *Zwangvolle Plage:* "Labor unending") [65]: he can make swords strong enough for giants, but Siegfried smashes them to bits as if they were toys. If only he could knit together the two pieces of Nothung [fragments of 43a], he muses [18], then Siegfried could slay Fafner [25, 66], and the ring [7] would belong to Mime [24]. As he returns, grumbling, to his work [65], Siegfried [67] gaily enters with a bear on a leash, but he sends the beast back to the woods after the frightened Mime assures him that he has forged [68] a sword for him. Siegfried [69a] looks contemptuously at the weapon. As he strikes the anvil with it, the sword breaks into pieces. In no uncertain words, Siegfried expresses his disgust with the incompetent dwarf [70], but Mime [71] calls him ungrateful. Has Mime not reared him, sparing no effort (Mime's Nursing Song *Als zullendes Kind:* "The whimpering babe") [72]? And in return the boy only hates him. Siegfried replies that he has learned much from Mime, but not how to like him. As a matter of fact, anything Mime does [71] upsets him so much that he would like nothing better than to finish off the ugly dwarf [70]. Mime tries to convince Siegfried that deep in his heart the boy does love him [73], that he, in fact, *must* love him as the nestling loves the parent bird. Siegfried, who has seen animals bring up their young in the forest, now asks Mime where he keeps the woman whom Siegfried could call mother [73]. Mime's claim to be both his father and his mother Siegfried calls a lie, for he has seen his reflection in the water [69, 42] and, luckily, he does not look at all like Mime. Yet all the animals he has seen resemble their parents. Taking the dwarf by the throat [70], Siegfried demands to know who his parents were.

Now Mime tells how one day in the woods he found Sieglinde [39, 36] about to give birth [38, 37], and how she died as Siegfried was born [69a]. Between Mime's determined efforts to sing his Nursing Song [72] all over again, Siegfried finds out that he received his name [69] from his dying mother, that her name was Sieglinde, and that his father [39] was killed in battle. He asks for proof and, after a moment's hesitation [18], Mime shows him the pieces of the sword [43a with 20]. Siegfried impetuously demands that Mime repair the sword at once [43b, 70]. Armed with a trusty weapon [43a], Siegfried will then go into the world, free and happy [74], never to see Mime again. He runs off [75], leaving Mime in despair [7, 20, 18, 25] and faced with a task he cannot accomplish [4a, 19].

Wotan enters, calling himself "Wanderer" [76]. He offers the suspicious

[74] WANDERLUST

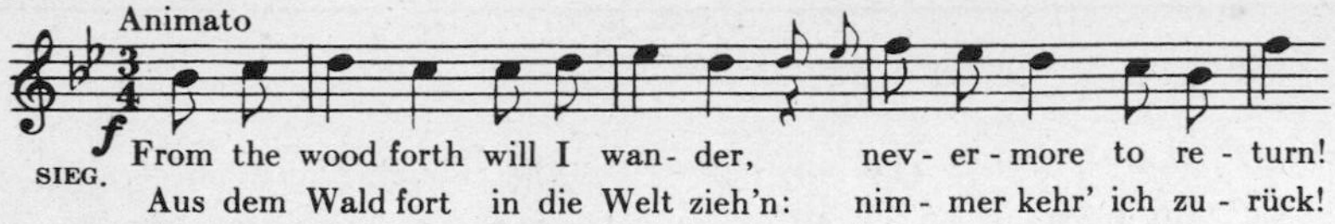
Animato
f
SIEG.
From the wood forth will I wan- der, nev- er - more to re - turn!
Aus dem Wald fort in die Welt zieh'n: nim- mer kehr' ich zu - rück!

[75] FREEDOM

Animato
f

[76] THE "WANDERER"

Moderato ed un poco maestoso
p dolce

[77] TRIUMPH (see[17])

Vivace

Mime his wisdom in exchange for a place at the hearth, and his head if he cannot answer Mime's questions [10]. Mime, after some thought [20, 18], accepts the challenge [10]. In an effort to frustrate the unbidden and uncanny visitor, he asks what race lives in the depths of the earth. It is the Nibelungs [20], answers the Wanderer. Forced by a magic ring [7], they produced a rich treasure [6a] for Alberich, who intended to win the world with it [24a]. To the second question, Wotan replies that the race dwelling on the surface of the earth is the giants [14]. Their rulers acquired the Nibelung's treasures [7]. Fafner, who killed his brother Fasolt, has since assumed a dragon's shape [25] to guard the hoard. To the final question, the guest answers that the race inhabiting the lofty heights is the gods [9ab], ruled from Valhalla by Wotan. He owns a spear on which are carved the treaties [10, 76] that subjugate [4b] the Nibelungs and the giants forever.

Now the Wanderer mockingly rebukes Mime for asking useless questions. He announces that, according to the rules of betting [10], it is now the dwarf's turn to wager his head against three answers. He asks the scared Nibelung [20] the name of the family against whom Wotan has raged [42] although he loves them [63]. After a satisfactory answer including the name of Siegfried [69], the visitor asks what sword Siegfried must wield to kill Fafner [25]. Nothung [motive 78a], answers Mime, quite forgetting his peril as he gaily relates the history of the sword [43a] through which a wise smith [20] intends to gain Alberich's treasure. Laughingly paying tribute to Mime's wit, the Wanderer now puts to the wise smith [20] his third question: who will piece Nothung together [69a]? As Mime becomes distraught [70] at being unable to answer [19], Wotan [76] tells him that he leaves the forfeited life of the would-be dragon-killer [20, 25] to him who will forge Nothung [43a]—that is, to him who knows no fear [69a]. As the Wanderer calmly leaves, little tongues of flame line his path [17c].

Mime, looking after him, has hallucinations of the fire [17cab, 45] approaching his cave and Fafner coming to swallow him, and he collapses with a wild outcry. Siegfried [43a] storms in [74, 75] and asks Mime [70] about the sword. Mime, still quite distracted, keeps mumbling about his latest troubles [25, 43a, 17c, 76]; finally, in an effort to save his head, he tells Siegfried that, complying with his mother's wish [39], he must teach him to know fear before he can let him go out into the world. He asks the puzzled Siegfried whether he has never, when alone in the dark woods, heard certain strange noises and seen uncertain flickers of light that made him tremble and his heart pound against his ribs [17cbd, 60]. When Siegfried regretfully declares that he has never mastered this art, Mime promises to guide him to Fafner [25, 60], who will teach him. But first Siegfried wants the sword. Mime [70, 71] has to admit that he cannot repair it. Thereupon Siegfried takes the pieces [43ba] and proceeds to file them into shavings [68]. As Siegfried works [67] and stirs the coal into triumphant flames [77], Mime watches with unbelieving eyes, realizing to whom his forfeited head belongs. However, he reasons that Siegfried must remain fearless to slay the dragon [25]. Therefore Mime must find a way to outwit him afterward in order to gain the ring [7]. Siegfried has meanwhile gathered the filings into a crucible, which he has put on the fire [43a]. Having learned from Mime the name of the sword [motive 78], he sings a song to Nothung (Siegfried's Smelting Song) [78, 68], describing, as he continues to work, what he is doing [79] and exhorting the bellows to blow their best.

Mime is now convinced that Siegfried will win the treasure [7]. He plans to offer him a drugged drink after the battle [23]; when he is in a stupor [45] Mime will kill him with his own sword [43b]. Now Siegfried pours the metal into the mold [78, 79], which he sinks in the hissing trough [43a]. He puts the blade [43a] on the coals and again works the bellows. Meanwhile, Mime has filled a kettle with herbs and put it on the fire. To Siegfried's inquiry, he answers [76] that he has given up forging to become cook for the boy, but Siegfried, who has had no use for Mime's weapons, wants none of his cooking either. He starts to hammer the blade

[78] **SONG TO NOTHUNG**

Risoluto, allegro ma non troppo

SIEG. No - thung! No- thung! Sword with-out peer!
No - thung! No- thung! Neid - li-ches Schwert!

[79] **SMELTING TUNE**

Animato

[80] **FORGING**

Pesante e risoluto, non troppo allegro

[81] **FAFNER, THE GIANT** (see [14])

Sostenuto

[82] **FOREST MURMURS**

Moderato

[83] **BIRD SONG**

Moderato

c Moderato

d Moderato

on the anvil [80], then dips it again in the water bucket. While Siegfried is attaching the hilt, Mime [20] revels in his future glory as ruler of the world. The boy now has finished Nothung [78]. Promising woe to all evil-doers, he flashes the shining blade before Mime [68] and with a mighty stroke he triumphantly splits the anvil neatly in two [43b].

Prelude to Act II: Motives [81], [66], [7], [27] indicate the locality where the act will take place. Then, just before the curtain is raised, the motive of the Nibelung's hatred [26] is introduced.

Act II: Alberich is keeping watch in front of Fafner's cave. He notices a weird light [56, 53], but it is not yet the light of day. After a moment the apparition vanishes [27, 81] and in a ray of moonlight the Wanderer [9a] appears. Alberich recognizes him and furiously demands that he stay away from this place. Wotan calmly assures him [76] that he has come merely to look, not to meddle, for he knows only too well what Alberich carefully points out to him: that he cannot seize the treasure in violation of the compact he made with Fafner [10, 15]. Unruffled by the Nibelung's threats [26, 27, 7, 4b, 24], Wotan declares that he is looking forward to seeing who will gain the ring, and in no way will he interfere with the hero [43a] who will slay the dragon. Perhaps Alberich could warn Fafner [25, 66, 81] and induce him to hand over the ring to him. The Wanderer himself wakes the dragon and proposes that, in exchange for a warning [43a], he give the ring [7] to Alberich. However, the only result of Wotan's and Alberich's combined efforts is a tired yawn as the dragon goes back to sleep. Gently reminding the Nibelung that fate will take its unalterable course [2a, 28], Wotan leaves [43a; 56 with 63 and 76], while the worried Alberich swears revenge [27, 26] and then hides among the rocks.

As the first light of morning falls on Fafner's cave [81], Siegfried [79] and Mime [70, 20] arrive, and Mime announces that they have reached the spot where Siegfried is to learn fear [60]. As the Nibelung describes the dragon [81], Siegfried plans how to combat [42] and kill him [78a], and he rails at Mime [70], for he feels sure he cannot learn fear from Fafner. Mime assures him that he will sense fear [60] as soon as he actually sees the dragon [81]. Then, yielding to Siegfried's demand to be left alone [71], he retires, hoping that Siegfried and Fafner will kill each other.

Siegfried, happy to be rid of Mime, stretches out under a linden tree [82]. He wonders what his father may have looked like. Certainly nothing like Mime [20]. And his mother [39]? Would that he could see her [73], a woman [12b]! Gradually he becomes conscious of the sounds of the peaceful forest (Forest Murmurs) [82]. A bird is singing in the branches above him [83abcd]. Hoping that he may learn to understand its song by imitating it, he tries to blow the same tune on a reed, then, disgusted with the poor result, he starts blowing his horn [67, 69]. This time the result is unexpected and, to Siegfried, amusing: a talking dragon [25, 81] appears from the cave. After a short exchange of taunts a battle ensues [43b, 25, 67] and Siegfried buries his sword in Fafner's heart [43b, 81]. Now Fafner

[84] LOVE'S ARDOR

Animato

[85] WANDERER'S EVOCATION

Allegro ma pesante

Wa - ken, Wa- la! Wa - la! a - wake!
Wa - che, Wa- la! Wa - la! er - wach'!

[86] LOVE (SIEGFRIED)

Un poco lento

[87] ADVENTURE

Vivace

warns the young hero against the one who has brought him here [26, 27], and he tells him whom he has killed [14, 7, 25]. As Siegfried tells the dragon his name [69], Fafner dies. Retrieving his sword [43b] from the dead body, Siegfried burns his fingers in the dragon's hot blood, and as he puts them to his lips to soothe the pain he finds that he suddenly understands the song of the bird in the tree [83dab]. The bird tells him [83cd] that there is a treasure in the cave and advises him to get the Tarncap and also the ring, which will make him ruler of the world. When Siegfried has gone into the cave, Alberich and Mime meet in front of it and quarrel wildly as to who shall have ring and Tarncap. Astonished to see the returning Siegfried holding both in his hands [7], they hide again. Siegfried decides that he will keep the treasures [6adc, 5, 6b] as souvenirs of this day. The bird now warns Siegfried not to trust Mime [83cd]. The dragon's blood will help him hear Mime's thoughts rather than his words.

Mime returns, hoping to outwit Siegfried [39]. After congratulating him, he talks to him in endearing tones, but Siegfried hears only his innermost thoughts [83c]. Thus he learns that Mime hates him, has cared for him only in order to obtain the gold through him, and now wants him to drink his brew so he can cut off Siegfried's head while the boy is drugged (meanwhile the gentle music indicates the tender feelings Mime intends to convey) [72]. In a sudden fit of disgust Siegfried kills [43b] him as Alberich's laughter [20] is heard from nearby. Siegfried lifts Mime's corpse [18, 20, 27], throws it into the cave [67], and he throws the dragon's carcass across the cave's mouth [81, 25]. Now both may guard the treasure [7].

Tired from his exertions [68], Siegfried stretches out again under the linden tree. He is lonely [73]. The only companion he has ever had was an ugly dwarf [20]. Perhaps the little bird in the tree can advise him how to find better company [84, 73]. The bird sings. It knows [83cba] of the most wonderful of women, who sleeps on a rock surrounded by fire. Her name is Brünnhilde. It also tells Siegfried that the strange feeling welling up in his breast [84] is love, and when Siegfried asks whether he will be able to break through the fire [69, 60], it answers that only one who knows no fear can do so [83abd]. Guided by his bird, Siegfried happily sets out for Brünnhilde's Rock [83abd, 84].

Prelude to Act III: The music describes Wotan's restless roving [56, 53, 52a], bound as he is by the contracts he made [10], and subject to his fate [2a, 30], as "Wanderer" [76].

Act III, Scene 1: It is night. Thunder and lightning fill the sky as Wotan approaches a cave at the foot of Brünnhilde's Rock [45, 54] and commands [10] Erda to rise from the depths of the earth (The Wanderer's Evocation *Wache, Wala:* "Waken, Wala") [85; 28, 2a, 30]. With his last imperious "Awake" [10], Erda, in a blue light, slowly ascends from the depths [54, 45], gradually awakening from her sleep. Wotan has come, he explains, to seek her counsel [28, 30, 2a], for in all his wanderings [76] he has not gained knowledge to equal hers. Why does he disturb her sleep of wisdom [45] instead of consulting her daughters, the Norns, Erda inquires. The Norns, replies Wotan, only weave fate according to Erda's wisdom. They merely obey fate and cannot control it [7, 19]. When Erda advises him to seek advice from Brünnhilde, the Valkyrie she bore him [9ab, 60, 54], Wotan delivers a tirade against the Valkyrie [59, 49]. On learning that Brünnhilde is asleep, to be awakened only as a mortal woman by a man [19, 63, 45, 54], Erda is outraged. When Wotan inquires about the end of the gods [30], she announces that he is a god no longer [7]. Thereupon Wotan wills [85a] the end of Erda's knowledge [28, 30]. He will leave his world to Siegfried [86, 69a, 85a, 9a], who has won the Nibelung's ring [43a, 7]. Safe from Alberich's curse, for he knows no fear [69], Siegfried will wake Brünnhilde [37, 38, 86], who, with her knowledge, will save the world. Now Wotan bids Erda [85a] sleep forever [45], and slowly she sinks back into the ground.

As dawn is breaking, Siegfried approaches, guided by his bird [83bda], which flies off on seeing the Wanderer. As Siegfried prepares to continue on alone [43a], he is stopped by the Wanderer, who elicits from him his story

[88] LOVE'S CONFUSION (see[39])

Animato

[89] AWAKENING

Molto lento

[90] DEVOTION

Molto lento

[91] RAPTURE

Ben tenuto

[92] ECSTASY

Animato

[93] PURITY

Molto tranquillo e moderato

[94] LOVE'S FULFILMENT

Tranquillo

[95] LOVE BOND

Allegro risoluto

molto forte e ben tenuto, ma non legato

[83c, 81, 43b, 68, 20]. Siegfried impatiently asks the old, one-eyed, funny-looking man [39, 70, 76, 9ad] to direct him to Brünnhilde or quickly get out of his way. Wotan loses his joviality [52ab] and forbids [10] Siegfried the path. As he waves his spear toward the mountaintop [49], a faint glow becomes visible [17, 64, 45] which increases in brightness and gradually draws nearer. When Siegfried [69a] shows that he is unafraid [87] of the fire, Wotan once more matches his spear against Nothung [10, 52a, 39], but this time it is the spear that is broken in two [10]. Wotan gathers up the pieces. His rule is over [28, 30, 19], and he leaves the field to Siegfried [39], who eagerly [69, 87] continues on his road [83bd] and, blowing his horn [67], plunges into the flames.

Scenic Transformation: The flames envelop the entire scene [17d, 60, 69, 87, 17a, 45]. Gradually they subside as Siegfried [60, 69, 87] reaches the top of the rock, where Brünnhilde and her horse, Grane, lie motionless under the spell of a magic sleep [54, 60, 12b].

Act III, Scene 2: Looking about in wonderment [11], Siegfried notices first the horse [49], then the armor [63]. He lifts the shield from Brünnhilde and exclaims, "A man in armor!" He takes off the helmet [11], cuts the breastplate open with his sword [43a], and recognizes in sudden fear and amazement that the sleeping warrior is not a man [11]. Troubled [84], he calls on his mother for help as he is seized with trembling [88]. He thinks that a sleeping woman may have taught him fear [60, 12b], and he must wake her [43a, 84]. Exhausted, he bends down to kiss her lips [54] even if it should mean his death [19]. Under his kiss [12b] Brünnhilde slowly awakens and ceremoniously greets the sun and the radiant day [89, 90]. On learning that it is Siegfried [69a] who has awakened her, she is overcome with a tender joy [90], and both exuberantly [91] hail their fate [90]. Brünnhilde jubilantly tells about her long love for him [92, 69a, 91, 86, 90, 59]. While Siegfried, his eyes fixed upon her, remains confused by his new feelings [88, 92], Brünnhilde notices Grane [49] and looks wistfully at her weapons, which no longer protect her. The fire he has traversed now burns in Siegfried's breast [17c], and he attempts to embrace Brünnhilde, but violently she frees herself: no god ever dared to approach the holy maiden [9c]. As he reminds her of her own confession of love [86], she becomes confused [27]. With a shock [51, 13] she realizes that, loving Siegfried, she must lose her former wisdom. Although she always was, is, and will be Siegfried's [93, 94], she begs him frantically not to desecrate her [60]; but soon she can no longer resist his pleading [84, 86, 92] and her own feelings [91]. Is she now his [54]? Vehemently [25] and wildly [49] she embraces Siegfried, who has quite forgotten again what fear is [69, 83bda]. Laughing in love [49, 50], the Valkyrie gladly sacrifices Valhalla and the gods [95], and the lovers jubilantly pledge themselves [95] to each other for life and death [91, 92].

THEMES

[96] **SIEGFRIED THE HERO** (see [67])

Molto moderato

[97] **BRUENNHILDE, THE WOMAN**

Molto moderato

[98] **LOVE (BRUENNHILDE)**

Moderato

[99] **WORLD RULE** (see [22c])

Un poco lento

[100] **HAGEN**

a Pesante b Pesante

[101] **GIBICHUNGS**

Commodo

[102] **LURE**

Molto moderato

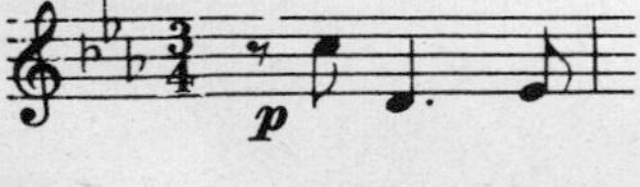

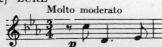

Die Götterdämmerung

THE TWILIGHT OF THE GODS

Opera in three acts and a prologue: fourth night of *The Ring of the Nibelung*. First performance: Bayreuth, August 17, 1876.

Characters: Mortals: SIEGFRIED the Volsung (tenor); GUNTHER the Gibichung (baritone); GUTRUNE, his sister (soprano); HAGEN, his half-brother, son of Alberich (bass); BRÜNNHILDE, daughter of Wotan (soprano); ALBERICH, a Nibelung (bass-baritone); WALTRAUTE, a Valkyrie (mezzo-soprano); WOGLINDE, a Rhinemaiden (soprano); WELLGUNDE (mezzo-soprano) and FLOSSHILDE (contralto), her sisters; THREE NORNS, daughters of Erda, goddess of fate (contralto, mezzo-soprano, soprano).
Germany, in legendary times.

Prologue: It is night on Brünnhilde's Rock, where the three Norns, the weavers of fate, sit motionless near the entrance to a cave [89 with 2; 54]. As it is still dark, they decide to resume their weaving and singing. The first Norn, singing of days long past, relates how a brave god [9dac] once came to the holy ash tree and paid with one of his eyes to drink from the nearby well of wisdom, and how he cut a branch from the tree and fashioned from it a spear [10]. Thereupon the tree died [30]. She throws the rope to the second Norn and asks her to continue the story [55]. The sister tells that the spear [109], inscribed with compacts [10], was shattered by a young hero, and that Wotan [76, 9a] ordered the holy ash tree cut into logs [30]. The third sister receives the rope [55] and adds that the logs are now piled around Valhalla. When they catch fire and burn Valhalla [109], that will mean the end of the gods [30]. Do the sisters know more [54]? The distant flickering of Loge [77] makes the weaving difficult. The Norns sing of Loge [17ab], turned into fire again by Wotan and ordered [10] to guard Brünnhilde's Rock. One day Wotan will have him light the splinters of his spear and he will throw them into the logs heaped around Valhalla [109, 9a minor, 45]. What then [54]? The strands of the rope become entangled. What has happened to the Rhinegold [7, 19, 5, 6a]? What has happened to the ring [22, 43a, 67]? Suddenly the rope breaks [27, 30]. The Norns realize that their hour has struck. They must return forever to Erda [45, 54].

At break of day, Siegfried [96] and Brünnhilde [97], leading Grane [49], come from the cave. Brünnhilde has given her husband [98] all her knowledge, and has joyously [91] sacrificed the strength she possessed as a Valkyrie. Now she sends Siegfried happily off to new adventures [96, 67, 69]. With all the knowledge offered him, Siegfried confesses, he has learned but one thing: to think lovingly of Brünnhilde. They embrace [86], and Siegfried gives her his ring [7], the symbol of his achievements [69, 25].

[103] FORGETTING

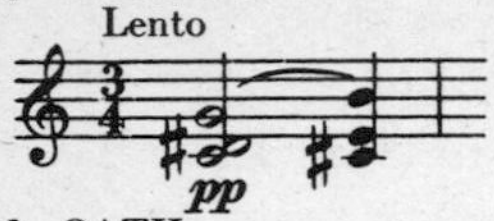
Lento
pp

[104] OATH

Misurato
b
c Vivace
f
a
ff

[105] GUTRUNE

Moderato
a
b

[106] BLOOD BROTHERHOOD

Misurato
f

[107] VIOLATION OF OATH

Allegro vivace
f

When in exchange [5] he receives Grane [49, 56], it appears to him that all his future deeds and thoughts will be as much Brünnhilde's as his own [98, 96, 75]. Together they extol the love that has made them thus inseparable, and after a fervent farewell Siegfried leaves, guiding Grane down the hill. Brünnhilde looks after the disappearing hero (Siegfried's Rhine Journey) [96, 75, 97, 91, 67, 37, 95].

Scenic Transformation: The curtain is lowered as the journey continues [67 with 77; 2b, 30, 6adcb, 7, 19, 5]. With [22ab] the curtain rises again.

Act I, Scene 1: In the Gibichung throne hall, open toward the banks of the Rhine, Hagen [100a] is asked by Gunther [101] to appraise his fame. Hagen replies that he has learned from their mother to respect his true-blooded, first-born half-brother. Yet Gunther's fame could bear increase, for Hagen knows of possessions [12b] that the Gibichung does not yet own; Gunther should marry the most glorious woman, Brünnhilde [49, 17d, 83abd]. However, only Siegfried the Volsung [42, 41, 43b, 67] is fated to win her. He has vanquished the dragon [25, 81] and won [43b] the Nibelung's treasure [7, 5] with its magic power [22ac]. Siegfried, counsels Hagen, might be persuaded to win Brünnhilde for Gunther in order to obtain Gutrune for a wife. Gutrune, Gunther's sister, is pleased [102] by this thought, but doubtful regarding her chances to win Siegfried. Hagen reminds her [102] of the drug that destroys one's memory [21a, 103] of all women [12b]. This idea [100a, 99] is greatly appreciated by Gunther [101] and Gutrune [102], but how may Siegfried be found [27]? Already his horn can be heard [67], and Hagen [100b, 4b, 102], who has gone down to the riverbank, sees him approaching on the Rhine [6adc, with 67; 43a, 7]. Welcomed by Hagen [27], he lands under the admiring glances of Gutrune [102]. He steps from the boat [69] and asks Gunther [101] to fight or be friends. Gunther invites him in and, while Hagen tethers Grane [56, 97, 49], swears friendship [104a], offering land, people, and himself into the pact. Siegfried, equally, brings all he owns—his body [42] and the sword he has made himself [79, 43b]—as he swears the oath [104b]. Hagen, rejoining them, alludes to the treasure, but Siegfried places little value on it [20 with 23; 25, 6ab]. However, he mentions the Tarncap, which he is carrying, and Hagen explains its power of changing shapes and places [21]. Siegfried also tells about the ring [7], which he has given to a noble woman [98].

Gutrune [105ab], who has gone into the house, returns with a drink of welcome [102]. Raising it to his lips with a toast to Brünnhilde [91, 86, 90], Siegfried drinks the drugged mead [103]. When he returns the cup to Gutrune [105ab], her glance arouses his desire [102] and he offers her marriage. Meeting Hagen's eye [100b], Gutrune [105ab] bashfully leaves, and Siegfried looks after her, spellbound [27]. Gunther now tells about the woman he would like to marry [49, 17d, 83ad], and it becomes clear from Siegfried's reaction that he has completely forgotten [103] Brünnhilde. He offers to break through the fire [77] for Gunther and, using the Tarncap to assume Gunther's shape, to bring him the maid in exchange for Gutrune [105a]. They prepare to swear blood brotherhood [106]. First Hagen fills a drinking-horn with wine [27, 10], and then Siegfried and Gunther draw blood from their arms with their swords and let it run into the horn [43a, 101]. Putting their hands on the horn held by Hagen [100b, 10], they swear [104b] brotherhood [106], threatening revenge [107] on whoever breaks the oath. They drink [27] and Hagen smashes the horn [100b, 10, 104a]. To the mistrusting Siegfried [102] Hagen explains his non-participation in the oath [107], saying that his impure blood [20 against 16; 7] would not mix with theirs.

Siegfried and Gunther leave for Brünnhilde's Rock [49, 102, 77], where Gunther is to wait one night in the boat until Siegfried [21] brings Brünnhilde. Gutrune appears and looks lovingly [105] after Siegfried [67] before she re-enters the house.

Hagen remains alone [100b with 26a] to guard Gunther's house (Hagen's Monologue *Hier sitz' ich zur Wacht:* "Here I sit on guard"). Gunther, he

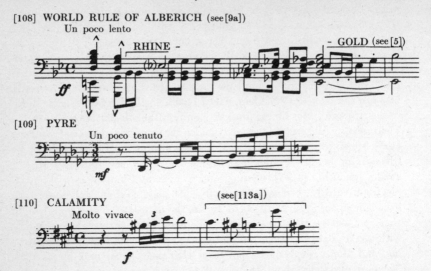

[108] WORLD RULE OF ALBERICH (see[9a])

Un poco lento
RHINE -
- GOLD (see[5])
ff

[109] PYRE

Un poco tenuto
mf

[110] CALAMITY

(see[113a])
Molto vivace
3
f

muses [4b, 99], will, with Siegfried's help [69], bring home a bride—Siegfried's own bride [49]. To Hagen they will bring the ring [100b, 19, 5], and soon they all will have to serve him, the son of Alberich [108, 4b, 99].

Scenic Transformation: As the curtain is closed, the music seems to continue Hagen's thoughts [7, 26a, 67, 100b, 69, 10]. Then the music joins Siegfried and Gunther on their journey [69] as gradually motives [97] and [90] gain in importance; when the curtain is raised, the scene is the same as in the prologue—Brünnhilde's Rock.

Act I, Scene 2: Brünnhilde sits in front of the cave, lost in contemplation of Siegfried's ring [94]. She hears Waltraute [56, 49, 50] approaching [13] through the air. Leaving her horse in the grove, Waltraute enters. Brünnhilde asks whether her sister has come, braving Wotan's anger, or whether the god has forgiven her—for has he not permitted Brünnhilde to be found by Siegfried [59], thus making her the happiest of women [90, 69, 91]? Or has Waltraute come to share her fate? No, answers Waltraute [52ab]. It is terrible fear that has brought her here (Waltraute's Narrative *Seit er von dir geschieden:* "Since he has parted from you"). Since Wotan renounced Brünnhilde, he no longer sends the Valkyries to battle. He has wandered about alone [53]. One day he returned to Valhalla, his spear [10] in pieces [108]. He ordered the holy ash tree cut, and the logs ranged [109] around the big hall, where he now sits with all the gods and heroes [9ac], not moving, not speaking [54], paying no attention to the Valkyries' silent entreaties [52ab]. Only once, when thinking of Brünnhilde [63], he had murmured: "If to the Rhinemaidens [6a] she'd return the ring [7, 19], she would lift the curse [27] from god and world" [9c]. Hearing this, Waltraute had stolen away [110] and had hastened to her sister [56] to ask her to save the gods [19]. Brünnhilde does not understand [110]. She will not part with the ring [7]. In spite of Waltraute's frenzied warning of impending doom for Valhalla [4b, 99], she will not part with the symbol of Siegfried's love [90, 86], the token of her marital bliss [97, 91]. Though Valhalla tumble into ruins [110], never will she give up [8, 19] her ring. She bids her sister leave [27], and Waltraute in despair [4b, 51] rides away [49, 50].

Darkness has set in. The fire from the bottom of the rock [17d, 45] suddenly leaps upward [17cb, 64]. The sound of Siegfried's horn is heard [67, 69a], but the man who jumps through the flames, his head partly covered by the Tarncap [21, 103], has Gunther's form [101]. When he claims Brünnhilde as a wife, she vehemently denounces Wotan [4ab] for making her punishment so harsh [110]. The disguised Siegfried [100b, 26ab] commands her to precede him into the cave. She tries to threaten him with the ring [7, 99], but Siegfried pursues her [27] and, after overcoming her strong resistance [49], pulls the ring from her finger [27]. As Brünnhilde [94, 97], trembling, obeys and precedes him into the cave [100a, 26ab, 110], Siegfried draws his sword [105c; 43a with 10]. He will keep faith with Gunther [104a] and Gutrune [105a], and will place Nothung between himself and Gunther's bride, Brünnhilde [21b, 103, 97].

Act II, Scene 1: Before the Gibichungs' hall, Hagen, on his night watch, seems to be asleep [26, 4b]. Alberich crouches at his feet [7]. He reminds his son, joyless as he, of the power they will wield [99, 19]. He tells him about Wotan's defeat by Siegfried [7]. Hagen must destroy [111] Siegfried, who has shattered [43a] Wotan's rule [10] and who holds the ring [81, 7] in happiness [67], for his innocence protects him from the curse. Hagen must act quickly, for if Brünnhilde [59] should return the ring to the Rhinemaidens [3], it would be lost forever. Will Hagen, though too weak to gain the ring from Fafner [81], swear to win it from Siegfried [43b, 111, 108]? Hagen vows he will [27], and Alberich fades away into the darkness.

Day begins to dawn. There is a sudden movement in a bush [21b] and Siegfried [67] stands before Hagen. The Tarncap on his head has brought him here in an instant from Brünnhilde's Rock. He calls for Gutrune [105a, 112] and tells how in Gunther's shape [101, 21a] he won the bride [103] but remained faithful to Gutrune [105a, 104c, 43a], and how he returned [21, 67]. Gutrune bids Hagen gather the men [112] for the wedding while she will gather the women [105b], and she goes with Siegfried into the house. Hagen sounds his cow-horn and calls for the vassals [113] to come [112] well armed to meet an emergency [101 minor, 30]. As the men arrive, he tells them, to their vast amusement, that Gunther needs his army to celebrate his wedding [112] and to join him in feasting and drinking.

When the bridal pair arrives on the Rhine [112 minor, 100a], they are ceremoniously welcomed by the men [101], and Gunther proudly introduces his bride. As Brünnhilde [49, 110] sees Gutrune [43a] happily clinging to the arm of Siegfried [54, 21b, 103], she nearly faints [97]. Suddenly

[111] MURDER

Molto vivace
tr
f

[112] WEDDING CALL

Allegro
f

[113] HAGEN'S CALL

Allegro
(see [4a])
a
ff
Hoi- ho!
Hoi- ho,
ho-ho!

she notices her ring on Siegfried's hand [7, 27, 19] thereby discovering the deception [26, 5, 99, 103, 7], but Siegfried clearly recalls that he won the ring from a dragon [25; 81 with 6ac]. Encouraged by Hagen [100b, 103], Brünnhilde shouts "Betrayal" [4b] and, crying out to the gods [9a] for letting her suffer so [110], she asks for Siegfried's destruction [26, 45]. Raging, she declares that it is Siegfried with whom she has shared the joys of love, but he claims to have been faithful to his oath [106, 104c] and that Nothung [43a with 10] separated him from the woman. When Brünnhilde denies this [98], he swears on Hagen's spear [100b, 107] (The Spear Oath *Helle Wehr, heilige Waffe:* "Shining steel, hallowed weapon") [114, 110] and dedicates it to his own destruction [111] if he has broken his oath. Thereupon Brünnhilde in a fury [50 with 49] also takes the oath [114, 110] and dedicates the weapon to Siegfried's death [111] for perjury. Siegfried gives up the argument, feeling that it is useless to argue with a woman [98, 38]. Expressing his regret to Gunther that the deception [17a, 21] did not succeed, he bids all proceed with the feast [112].

Brünnhilde remains alone with Hagen and Gunther [27, 19, 26a, 98, 21b, 107, 26, 111], unable to explain what demon must be at work [110, 54]. Alas [4a], she has given all her wisdom to Siegfried [86]. Where can she find help [111, 113]? Hagen offers revenge [114] and learns that Siegfried [67] is invulnerable in battle, but that Brünnhilde, knowing he would never flee [69, 43a], used no magic spell [45] on his back. There, Hagen says, his spear will find its mark [113]. He tells the unhappy Gunther that only Siegfried's death can help him [110, 107], and Brünnhilde's [97] determination, together with Hagen's reminder that this is the only way to obtain the ring [7, 99], eventually overcome Gunther's reluctance. Gutrune [105ab] will be told [102] that Siegfried was killed [67 minor] by a boar at the hunting party which they will arrange for the morrow. "Thus shall it be," they swear, as Hagen promises the ring to Alberich, and Gunther and Brünnhilde call on Wotan to listen to their vows [107, 114]. As they turn to the hall, they are met by the wedding procession [112] led by Siegfried and Gutrune, who are carried high by the vassals. Gunther and his bride join the procession [113] and all move up the hill for the ceremony.

Prelude to Act III: The music describes the hunting party. Horns, among them Siegfried's [67], resound from various directions [4a, 112]. Nearby flows the Rhine [1, 6adc, 5, 115a].

Act III, Scene 1: In the Rhine, where it passes through wild, rocky woodland, the Rhinemaidens are swimming about as, bemoaning the loss of the Rhinegold [115ba, 5], they wait for Siegfried. When he approaches [67], they first try to tease him into giving them the ring [7], then they threaten him [4, 27, 19, 113]. The dragon [81] had warned him of a curse, Siegfried remembers, but he did not teach him fear. The Rhinemaidens make fun of his stinginess and decide to ask the woman [97] who will inherit the ring from Siegfried this very day to give it to them. They swim away [115ab]. Hagen [27, 4a], Gunther, and the rest of the hunting party join Siegfried [112, 67] for food and drink. Hagen asks whether it is true that Siegfried can understand the birds' singing [83ab]. Siegfried has a drink with Gunther [101] and, to cheer the gloomy man [107, 113], begins [83] to tell of his youth [72], of Mime the dwarf [20, 18], how he restored Nothung [43b, 78a], and how he killed Fafner [25]. When his tongue touched the dragon's blood, he recalls, he could understand a bird that sang to him from a linden tree [82]. It told him [83cd] about the Tarncap and the ring, and later about Mime's treachery. When the vassals ask to hear more, Hagen gives Siegfried another drink into which he has squeezed some herbs [102] to refresh the memory, he says [21b]. Siegfried slowly drinks [103, 98, 39, 97]. The bird, he now relates, told him where to find Brünnhilde. He went to the rock, traversed the fire [17d], and found a beautiful woman [12b] lying in profound sleep [60]. He awakened her to burning love's delight [86, 90]. As Gunther jumps up in terror, Hagen buries his spear in Siegfried's back [27, 4a]. Siegfried tries to throw his shield at Hagen [69], but sinks to the ground, fatally wounded [116]. All reproach Hagen [54], but he calmly leaves, stating that he has avenged perjury [107].

Siegfried raises his head in a last greeting to Brünnhilde (Siegfried's Farewell to Brünnhilde *Brünnhilde, heilige Braut:* "Brünnhilde, holy bride") [89, 90], recalling how he wakened her with a kiss [69] to all the joys of love [91, 92]. He dies [54]. His body is raised on his shield [39] and carried off in solemn procession (Funeral March) [116, 42, 41; 36, 37, 38; 43a, 69, 96, 97].

[114] SPEAR OATH

Molto vivace

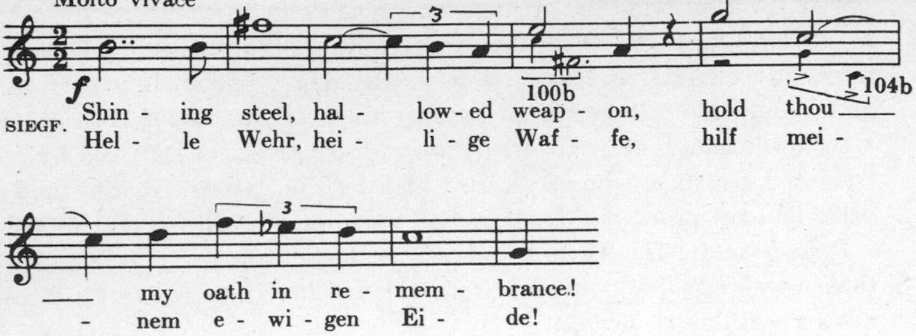

[115] FROLIC OF THE RHINEMAIDENS

a Andante commodo

b Andante commodo

[116] FUNERAL MARCH

Maestoso

Scenic Transformation: During the Funeral March a dense fog has gradually enveloped the scene. With motive [4b] the fog clears and the Gibichungs' hall becomes visible in the uncertain light of the moon [27 with 99].

Act III, Scene 2: Gutrune [105a], wakened by frightening dreams [96 minor, 67], steps into the hall. Was the woman she just saw walking toward the banks of the Rhine [6] Brünnhilde [49, 97, 54]? As she listens anxiously [112, 110], she hears Hagen calling for lights [113] and for Gutrune to come [112] and greet her husband [67 minor], who is dead [107], the victim of a wild boar [4b]. When Siegfried's body is borne in, Gutrune falls on it with a heart-rending cry and calls Gunther, who tries to console her, a murderer. Gunther now violently denounces Hagen [111], who proudly admits that his spear avenged perjury [114, 107] and claims the ring as his just spoils [113a, 7]. When Gunther opposes him, the son of the Nibelung draws his sword [27] and after a short fight kills him [4b]. However, when he reaches for the ring [99], the dead Siegfried raises his hand in a threatening gesture [43a]. In this moment of horror Brünnhilde approaches solemnly from the Rhine to fulfill her revenge [30, 2a] on all who have betrayed her, and to prepare a fitting ceremony for the dead hero [54, 55]. When Gutrune accuses her of causing all this disaster, Brünnhilde answers that long before Siegfried had ever known Gutrune [105a] she, Brünnhilde, had been his wife [86], and Gutrune recognizes Hagen's trickery [103, 105b].

After looking solemnly at Siegfried [54], Brünnhilde orders the men (Immolation Scene *Starke Scheite schichtet mir dort:* "Pile up mighty logs over there") to erect a mighty pyre [109, 17d] for Siegfried [69, 30] and to bring his steed [49], which, together with Brünnhilde, will share Siegfried's last rites. While the pyre is erected, Brünnhilde extols Siegfried's purity in friendship and love [91, 43a, 37]. Yet, she adds, he broke his every oath and vow [104c]. How did this come to pass [55]? She calls on the gods [9a] to listen to her plaint [59] and to look at the calamity their perfidy has brought about. But now, since she has regained all her knowledge [54], Wotan's ravens may return with a message [27] that will bring the god peace [6a, 9c, 53, 9d]. As she silently orders the men to place Siegfried's body on the pyre [109, 30, 2a], she takes the ring [7] and puts it on her finger. May the Rhinemaidens take it from her ashes [115b with 6b; 4bdc] and forever keep their gold [5] shining and pure in the waters [115a], cleansed from the curse [7, 27] by the fire.

She takes a firebrand and orders [10] Loge [17bd, 77, 17a] from Brünnhilde's Rock to Valhalla [30]. As she throws the brand onto the pyre, so shall fire fall [2a, 4b] into the hall of the gods [9a]. Quickly the pyre bursts into flame [17cb]. Brünnhilde unbridles Grane [50, 49]. There in the fire [57], she says, lies their master [69], whom they both desire to join. She mounts the steed and rides him into the pyre [50 with 49]. Immediately the flames blaze up high [17d, 45], but they quickly subside when the Rhine [2b] overflows its banks and the Rhinemaidens appear [6ad] at the place of immolation. Hagen, who has watched the scene motionless but with increasing anxiety, now throws down his weapons and plunges, as if possessed, into the waters to take the ring. Two of the Rhinemaidens pull him with them into the depths [27 ending without completion] while the third jubilantly swims away [3] holding the ring.

In the sky, Valhalla becomes visible [9a] with gods and heroes sitting motionless in the great hall. While the Rhinemaidens are gaily and gracefully swimming about in the now calm waters of the Rhine [3], Valhalla is gradually engulfed by the cleansing flames [simultaneously 9a, 3, 57, 2b; 9ad, 69, 30, 57].

THEMES

[1a] OCTAVIAN–THE ROSE-BEARER

Con moto agitato

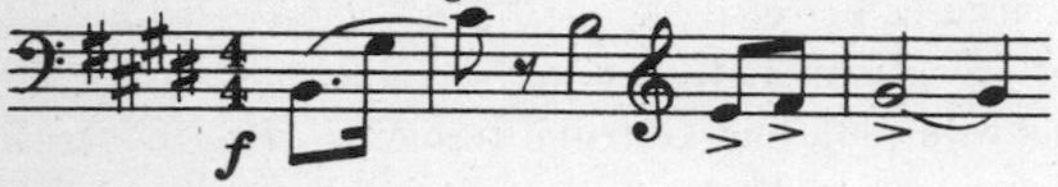

[1b] MARIANDEL WALTZ

Vivo

[2] THE MARSCHALLIN'S LOVE

Agitato

[3] OCTAVIAN'S LOVE

Agitato

[4] PASSION

a Con moto agitato

b Vivo

[5] RENUNCIATION

Andante mosso

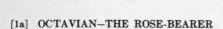

Der Rosenkavalier

THE ROSE-BEARER

Opera-comedy in three acts by Richard Strauss. Libretto by Hugo von Hofmannsthal. First performance: Dresden, January 26, 1911.

Characters: THE MARSCHALLIN,* Princess of Werdenberg (soprano); OCTAVIAN (called QUINQUIN), a young gentleman of the highest nobility, her lover (mezzo-soprano); BARON OCHS VON LERCHENAU, a country nobleman (bass); VON FANINAL, rich merchant, newly ennobled (bass); SOPHIE, his daughter (soprano); MARIANNE LEITMETZERIN, duenna (soprano); VALZACCHI, an Italian gentleman for hire (tenor); ANNINA, his accomplice (contralto); A SINGER (tenor); A POLICE OFFICER (bass); THE INNKEEPER (tenor). *Vienna, about the middle of the eighteenth century.*

Prelude to Act I: The themes of Octavian [1a] and of the Marschallin [2] are followed by those of Octavian's love [3] and of passion [4a]. The themes build up to a climax, then quickly ebb away as a motive of languid renunciation [5] appears, followed by a strain of great tenderness [6]. Without interruption in the music, the curtain opens.

Act I: The birds are already heard singing outside, when Octavian, kneeling by the bed of the Marschallin, exuberantly congratulates himself on his luck [7, 2, 6, 4a] and describes the turmoil the words "You and I" arouse in him [7, 4a, 6, 3]. Tenderly the Marschallin calls him her young darling, and they embrace [6]. Suddenly, Octavian becomes conscious of the singing of the birds, and he angrily closes the window and draws the curtains tight. Just then a noise [8] is heard outside, which turns out to be the servant arriving with the morning chocolate. Although Octavian has just loudly proclaimed himself master of the premises [1], he quickly hides behind a screen as the little Negro page enters [9ab]. The boy puts the chocolate on a little table in front of the sofa and, bowing, retires again.

The Marschallin, stepping from the bed in a negligee, scolds Octavian because she had to remind him to take his sword with him into hiding. When he sulks [1], she gently asks him to sit beside her on the sofa [2, 5] for breakfast. They eat [Breakfast Waltz 10] and exchange endearments [4b, 2]. Octavian rejoices in his good fortune—thanks to the Field-Marshal's predilection for hunting in far-off Croatia—but the Marschallin stops him. To Octavian's violent distress, she tells him that this very night she dreamed of her husband, and that he had returned quite unexpectedly. As

* Wife of field-marshal.

[5] *continued*

[6] **TENDERNESS**

Un poco andante

[7] **OCTAVIAN'S ARDOR**

A tempo mosso

[8] **DISTURBANCE**

[9] **THE LITTLE BLACK PAGE**

a Alla marcia con grazia

b Alla marcia con grazia

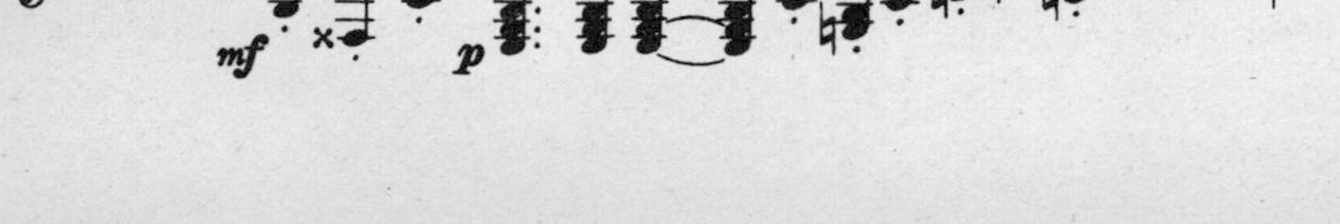

a matter of fact, she is still upset [fragments of 2], for she keeps hearing a noise [8a] in the courtyard just as she did once when the Marshal arrived suddenly and she . . . But that is none of Octavian's [1a] business; he had better calm down [2] and hide quickly, for there is definitely someone approaching through the dressing room, and it can only be the Field-Marshal. When Octavian, after some bravado [1a] and some anxiety [5], has hidden behind the bed curtains, the Marschallin recognizes to her great relief that the vulgar voice, now clearly distinguishable in an argument with the Princess' lackeys, is only that of Baron Ochs. Good Lord, she had received a letter from this country cousin of hers a week ago but, thanks to Octavian [1a], she had found no time to look at it.

Octavian reappears from behind the bed, dressed as a maid-servant (later called Mariandel by the Marschallin) [Mariandel Waltz 1b; 4b]. As "she" tries to slip out through the dressing room, she bumps into the Baron, who enters just at this moment, forcing his way past the objecting servants, with no doubt in his mind that the Marschallin will be delighted to see him even at this early hour [11]. When the lackeys finally succeed in diverting his attention from the maid to the Marschallin, he makes his obeisance [11]. Then, very much at his ease [12], he complains about the lackeys, and the Marschallin explains that they had acted on orders, for she was suffering from migraine [7, 6]. However, this does not discourage the Baron at all. He sits down comfortably without letting the "maid" out of his sight, while she tries to busy herself in the background. Between remarks about her attractiveness, he tells the Marschallin what she—as he indignantly points out—should have known from his letter: he is going to marry a pretty, fifteen-year-old girl, the daughter of the recently ennobled Faninal. Well, he, Ochs, has enough nobility [11] in him for the whole family, and Faninal has the money and is reputedly in rather poor health. Oh, the maid should not remove the breakfast; Ochs is rather hungry. In whispers he tries to make a rendezvous with the maid [1b] while, in a loud voice, directed toward the Marschallin, he asks her to propose a rose-bearer [26a] whom he might entrust with the honor of bringing the customary silver rose to his future bride. Besides that, Ochs would just like to ask the Marschallin's attorney a few questions, but one should not send a darling [13] like Mariandel to go looking for him among the vile lackeys.

Just then the major-domo, come to make his morning report, confirms the presence of the attorney in the antechamber. Covered by the broad figure of the major-domo, Ochs again proposes a tête-à-tête to the bashful maid [Invitation Waltz 14]. When the major-domo leaves, the tender scene is suddenly exposed to the Marschallin's view [1a], and she laughingly expresses her surprise at such behavior in a bridegroom. Thereupon Ochs (Aria *Macht das einen lahmen Esel aus mir?*: "And why should that make me a three-legged ass?") [15] explains that for him love is a real profession to be pursued in its infinite variety at any hour of the day and at any

[10] BREAKFAST WALTZ

Tempo di Waltz

[11] POMPOUSNESS

Pesante

[12] NONCHALANCE

Commodo

[13] Con moto

[14] INVITATION WALTZ

Tempo di Waltz

[15] ARIA *MACHT DAS EINEN LAHMEN ESEL AUS MIR* (Ochs)

Presto

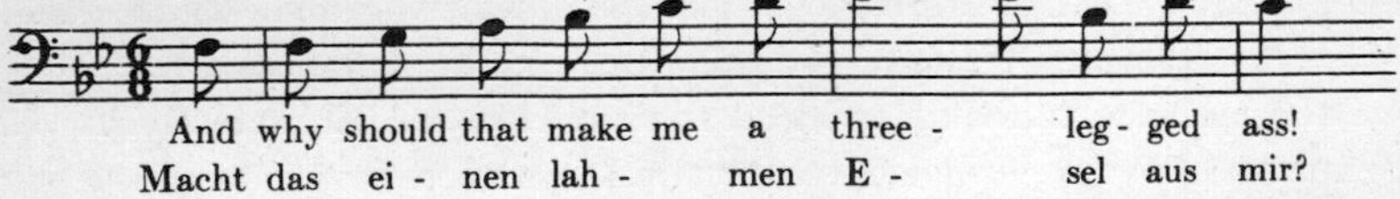
And why should that make me a three - leg - ged ass!
Macht das ei - nen lah - men E - sel aus mir?

[16a] VALZACCHI

Presto

time of the year. Warming up to his subject, he spares no effort in enlightening the Princess on all the aspects of his favorite metier. The bashful Mariandel acts somewhat embarrassed (Trio), and the Marschallin, after some philosophical reflections, asks Ochs to leave her servant in peace. Ochs, however, suggests that the Marschallin give him Mariandel as a maid for his future bride, for the girl surely has some noble blood in her. As a matter of fact he, too, has a lackey with blue blood, Lerchenau blood, and he keeps him as his personal servant. Suddenly the Marschallin has an idea. Overruling Octavian's objections, she has him bring her medallion and asks Ochs whether he might like the gentleman depicted there [13], the young Count Rofrano, for a rose-bearer. When Ochs looks at the picture [1a], he is astounded by its resemblance to the maid, and the Marschallin fondly confesses that, the relation being so obvious, she keeps the "maid" as a very special servant always near her [4b]. But now she orders Mariandel to go and admit the people in the antechamber for the levee. Mariandel complies, managing to escape the pursuing Baron.

A host of people enter, including a noble widow with three children who, in blaring chorus, begin to ask for assistance but are interrupted by a milliner and an animal vendor who, at the top of their voices, praise the wares they have brought along. Valzacchi [16a], a specialist in shady dealings, unsuccessfully offers the Marschallin a scandal sheet. Now the hairdresser enters to arrange the Princess' coiffure, while a flutist has started to play a solo. A tenor follows with an Italian aria [17], but an argument between the Baron and the attorney regarding the former's impending nuptials [18] results in an outburst by the Baron which brings the singer's aria to an abrupt conclusion. Valzacchi and his companion, Annina [16ab], offer their services to the Baron, but he turns to the Marschallin and ceremoniously [11] puts the case containing the silver rose [26a] on her desk. The audience meanwhile has come to an end, and the Marschallin, after promising again to obtain the services of Count Rofrano [6] as bearer of the rose [26a], dismisses Ochs. With formal bows [11], he leaves, followed by his shabby and awkward retinue of peasants and by Valzacchi and Annina.

In a thoughtful mood, the Marschallin looks after the pretentious oaf [11] who will marry a young, pretty, and rich girl [5], firmly believing he deserves her, even feeling that he is condescending in marrying her. Alas [19], says the Marschallin, looking into her mirror, she can remember another young and pretty girl who, straight from the convent, was ordered into holy matrimony (Mirror Aria *Kann mich auch an ein Mädel erinnern:* "There was once a young girl, I remember"). Gone is the girl, and soon it will be the old Marschallin instead. But such is the lot of every woman [5], and wise are those who accept it with grace.

Octavian enters in riding habit, but his exuberance is met by the Marschallin with great restraint [7, 5, 8a, 3, 4a, 1a, 6]. She feels the force of the inexorable flow of time [20] which soon will cause Octavian to leave her

[16b VALZACCHI *continued*

b Vivace possibile

[17] THE TENOR'S ARIA

Un poco sostenuto

Di ri - go - ri ar - ma - to il se - no

[18] WEDDING FORMALITIES

Allegro non troppo

[19] THE YOUNG MARSCHALLIN

Grazioso

[20] Moderato

MARSCH.
There's some - thing ver - y strange a - bout time.
Die Zeit, die ist ein son - der - bar Ding.

[21] WEDDING PREPARATIONS

Molto allegro

[22] OCHS, THE BRIDEGROOM

Moderato

for a girl younger, and, yes, more beautiful than she is. Although Octavian remonstrates violently [7, 6], she repeats her warning. They should both be prepared for the shock which must come one day.

Right now, the Marschallin tells Octavian, she must go to church [5]; but in the afternoon she will take a drive, and he will be welcome to ride beside her carriage. With a stiff greeting, Octavian leaves. The servants sent immediately after him—he has left without so much as a kiss—cannot catch up with him, so the Marschallin calls for her little page [9a] and orders him to take the silver rose to Count Octavian [6]. As the little Negro boy trips out, she remains motionless, rapt in thought [1a, violins *pianissimo*].

Act II: There is great excitement [21] in the town house of Von Faninal as preparations for the wedding [18, 22] and for the reception of the rose-bearer [23] are in full swing. Faninal sounds a solemn note before leaving his daughter [24] to bring in the groom. The duenna, standing by the window, excitedly reports everything taking place in the square in front of the house, where a huge crowd of spectators has gathered—while Sophie earnestly but without much success tries to face her future with humbleness [25]; for vanity and pride, she knows, are grievous sins.

Now the call "Rofrano! Rofrano!" [23] is heard from the street, and the duenna at the window describes Octavian's arrival in detail [1a and the entire Mariandel Waltz *maestoso*]. He enters, splendidly dressed [23]. The two young people are so deeply impressed with each other's appearance that they can barely speak as they go through the ceremony of the presentation of the silver rose [26ab]. Both feel that they have never been so happy [27]. When they are finally seated for a more informal conversation [28], they quickly develop an affectionate intimacy, but after a while they are interrupted by the entrance of Faninal and Ochs [22]. The groom critically surveys Sophie, then goes to meet Octavian and immediately prattles about his illegitimate sister and about his own personal servant. Eventually he turns to the already outraged Sophie and revolts her further with his suggestive remarks—to the violent disgust of Octavian [1a]. Finally she turns on Ochs. "Who do you think you are?" she cries. Calmly he replies, quoting his favorite waltz [29], that he will soon be her only thought and desire. In his company, he adds with a leer, she will never be at a loss as to how to pass the time [30]. However, the notary has just arrived, and Ochs had better attend to business [22]. Meanwhile, he says, Octavian can stay with the girl and give her some "education." He leaves [22, 29] with Faninal and the notary.

Immediately, in whispers so that the duenna should not hear, Sophie asks Octavian for help. She will not marry that ruffian. Their conversation is interrupted by the Baron's retainers, who are drunkenly chasing after Faninal's maid-servants. With considerable difficulty they are restrained by the major-domo and the lackeys. In the confusion, the duenna, too, has

[23] ROFRANO

[24] SOPHIE'S HUMILITY

Allegro non troppo

[25] ARIA *IN DIESER FEIERLICHEN STUNDE* (Sophie)

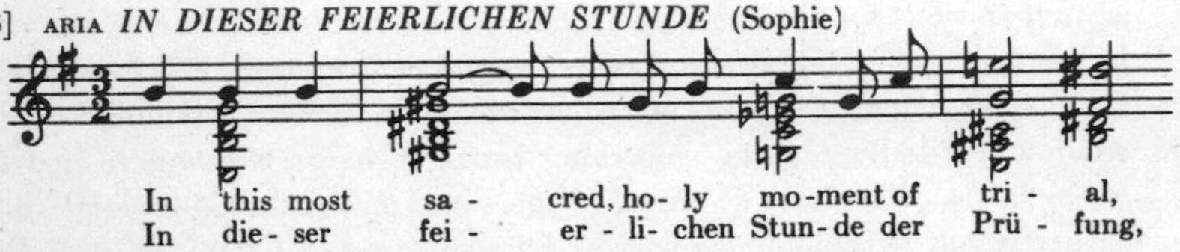
In this most sa- cred, ho- ly mo-ment of tri - al,
In die- ser fei - er - li- chen Stun- de der Prü - fung,

[26] THE PRESENTATION OF THE ROSE

Piuttosto lento

a
b
b

[27] Moderato

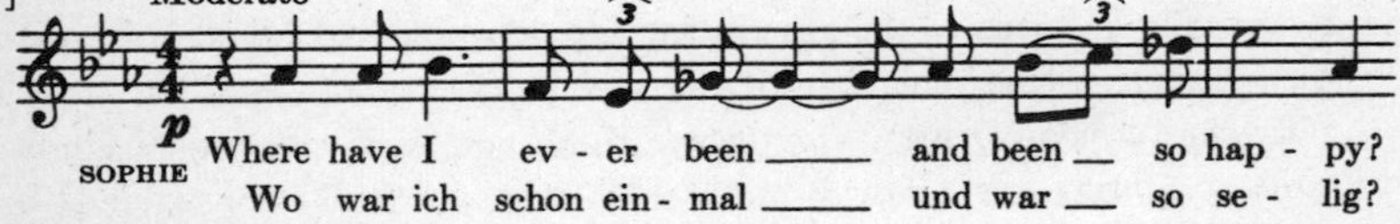
SOPHIE
Where have I ev - er been ___ and been __ so hap - py?
Wo war ich schon ein- mal ___ und war __ so se - lig?

[28] Animato grazioso

SOPHIE
I know you ver - y well, ___ mon cou - sin!
Ich kenn' Ihn schon recht wohl, ___ mon cou - sin!

[29] OCHS' FAVORITE WALTZ

Tempo di Waltz tranquillo

left, and Sophie is alone with Octavian. She expresses her confidence in him [31], and he declares that he will stand by her if first she will get rid of the Baron as a suitor, for Octavian's sake [1] as well as her own. They kiss [32] and give expression to their tender feelings (Duet *Mit ihren Augen voll Tränen:* "Your eyes are dim with crying") [33, 32].

While they are still gazing into each other's eyes [1, 32], Valzacchi and Annina enter stealthily. Suddenly they spring forward [16b], take hold of Sophie and Octavian, and call for Baron Ochs von Lerchenau. When Ochs arrives, he calmly asks Sophie to explain the situation. Octavian [1, 3] speaks up for her and informs the Baron that she has changed her mind. However, this by no means fazes Ochs. He grabs Sophie by the hand [22] and tries to pull her into the adjoining room, but Octavian bars his way and challenges him to cross sabers [22 minor]. Ochs replies that he is busy now, and when Octavian calls him a contemptible cheat and a dowry hunter, he whistles for his servants. Emboldened by their arrival, the Baron bids Octavian move out of his way [22]. However, Octavian draws his sword [3], Ochs's men retreat, and the Baron, finally forced to defend himself, draws and is immediately nicked in the arm by Octavian [1]. Ochs howls "Murder!" and shouts for a physician and for the police, while Octavian holds the Lerchenau servants at bay with his sword. The entire household gathers, and Annina recounts the fight to them [26a, 22, 1], while Ochs keeps bawling for help [34]. Eventually Faninal arrives. When he sees Ochs and hears from the officious Annina [16b] what has happened, he is beside himself, hurriedly sends for a doctor, and berates his lackeys for their negligence. Then he turns violently on the rose-bearer [23, 26a, 1], who politely refers him to Sophie. Sophie humbly [24] but firmly declares that she will not marry such an uncouth individual as Ochs [22]. Faninal laments the upset of his marriage plans [18], asks Octavian to leave [21], and tells Sophie she must marry the Baron [18]. Sophie's [24] furious objections earn her the threat of being sent to a convent. Octavian finally leaves with a last word of comfort to Sophie, and the duenna leads her away.

Faninal now turns to Ochs and promises to put everything to rights, but the Baron, whose wound has meanwhile been bandaged by a doctor, is at the moment more interested in a drink [11 *alla marcia*]. Faninal leaves to order it for him. Soon Ochs receives his wine and stretches out comfortably on the sofa (Monologue *Da lieg' ich:* "Here I am"). The things that can happen to a cavalier in Vienna [22, 11]! An outburst against Octavian is echoed by the Lerchenau servants, but after another sip of wine, Ochs comes to find the young buck's antics rather amusing; also, he would not have missed the girl's rage for anything. He sends the physician on to make him a comfortable bed and, refilling his glass, he softly sings his favorite ditty [29].

Annina enters with a personal letter for Ochs [34], and as she reads it to

[30] RIBALDRY

Con spirito

[31] Andante mosso

SOPHIE
I feel that I could trust you, mon cou-sin,
Zu Ihm hätt' ich ein Zu - traun, mon cou-sin,

[32] Andante

see [1]
see [45]

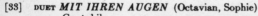

[33] DUET *MIT IHREN AUGEN* (Octavian, Sophie)

Cantabile

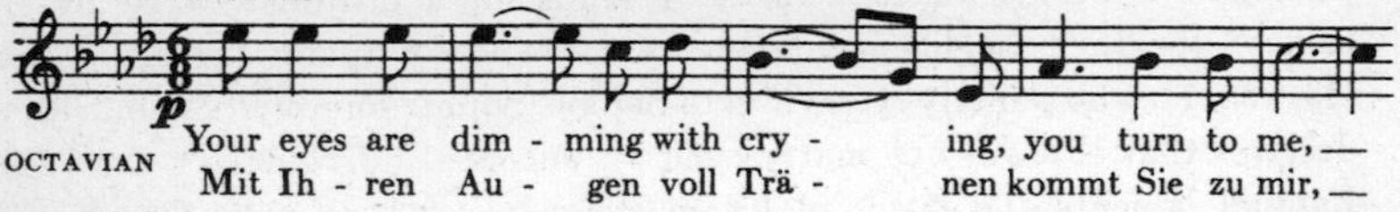
OCTAVIAN
Your eyes are dim - ming with cry - ing, you turn to me,
Mit Ih - ren Au - gen voll Trä - nen kommt Sie zu mir,

[34] THE LUCK OF THE LERCHENAUS

Waltz mosso

[35] THE SUSPICIOUS CHARACTERS

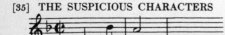

him [1b, Mariandel Waltz], he learns to his joy [34] that "Mariandel" will be free the following evening, that she adores him, and that she awaits his answer. Repeatedly ignoring Annina's outstretched hand, Ochs asks her to return later to write his reply; then, continuing his interrupted melody [29, 30], he saunters merrily off to bed.

Introduction to Act III: The music, *pianissimo*, interspersed with sudden *fortes*, is somewhat spooky, setting the mood for the odd developments which Valzacchi and Annina [16b], with the help of some strange characters [35], are preparing. These two are now in the employ of Octavian [1] as well as of Ochs, and the joke will be on the prospective bridegroom [22]. Without interruption in the music, the curtain opens.

Act III: In the private room of an inn of somewhat dubious reputation, Valzacchi is putting the last touches on Annina to make her look like a middle-aged widow in mourning [16b]. Mariandel [1b] enters, hardly recognizable as Octavian [1a], and throws them a purse. Five suspicious-looking individuals come in [35], and Valzacchi, after having sped away Octavian [1a, Mariandel Waltz] to his rendezvous with Ochs, places them behind trap doors and in secret compartments throughout the room. Then he claps his hands [16b] and their heads appear suddenly out of walls, chests, etc., and, at his command, disappear without a sound [35]. Now Valzacchi opens the door [14] and begins to light the candles (runs and trills in the flutes). Through the open door the sounds of a little orchestra are drifting in [36]. Mariandel enters on the arm of Ochs [Waltz 36 with 3]. The noisily obsequious waiters [37 with 36; 38] are quickly thrown out by the Baron with the help of Valzacchi, and Ochs remains alone with Octavian.

He has extinguished most of the candles and now sits down to dinner with "Mariandel." His tender advances are interrupted when the girl, after taking one sip from the goblet, decides that she wants no wine [39] and adds, with a fine show of anguish, that she does not want a tête-à-tête, either. She jumps up, opens a curtain, and with unbelieving eyes sees a bed. Ochs calms her and takes her back to the table. As he renews his caresses, she sighs and reminds him that he is a bridegroom. However, he has forgotten all that; he is just a cavalier dining with his lady-love [40a, b]. Octavian plays the languid maiden [41], but the moment Ochs attempts to kiss "her" he is stopped by Mariandel's resemblance to Octavian [1a], and when suddenly, by mistake, one of the men sticks his head out of a trap door [35], Ochs fears he has hallucinations. The playing of his favorite song [29] by the inn's orchestra helps him to recover his balance. Mariandel, with languishing glances at Ochs, sings a melancholy tune about the futility of everything [42]. Ochs can resist her charms [41] no longer, but when he approaches her [1], strange heads begin to pop out here, there, and everywhere [35]. In panic, Ochs swings the table bell. The disguised Annina appears and claims to be his abandoned wife. Valzacchi, the innkeeper, and

[36] DINNER MUSIC I

Tempo di Waltz *con anima*

[37] WAITERS' WALTZ

Tempo di Waltz *con spirito*

[38] DINNER MUSIC II

Molto animato

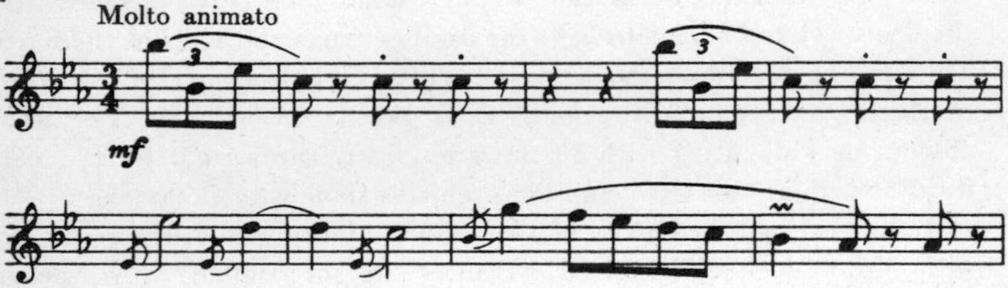

[39] ABSTINENCE WALTZ

Un poco languido

[40] CAVALIER WALTZ

a Tempo di Waltz

b Tempo di Waltz *con grazia*

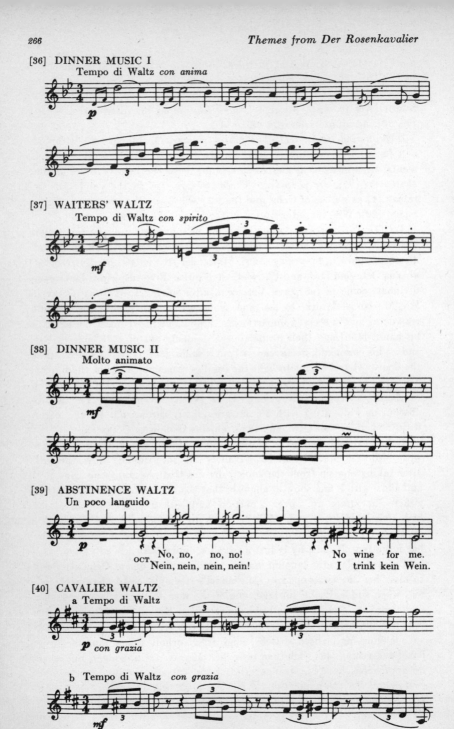

waiters enter. Four children rush in calling him "Papa." Valzacchi meanwhile whispers to Octavian that he has already sent for Faninal. The Baron, desperate, and threatened by those present, calls for the police. Immediately, an officer comes in with two men, whereupon Ochs regains his composure and asks him to clear the room of the riffraff. However, the officer ignores him and starts his inquiry. Mariandel draws his attention, and Ochs, pressed to identify her, claims that she is his bride, the daughter of Von Faninal. To the bewilderment of Ochs, Faninal appears just at this moment. After futile attempts at diversion [22], Ochs is forced to recognize Faninal as his prospective father-in-law [21]. However, Faninal, asked to recognize Mariandel as his daughter, vehemently denies any such allegation [21]. Ochs tries to send him home [22], but Faninal insists that his daughter be brought up from the carriage downstairs. She arrives [24], to the scandalized delight of those present, and Faninal explains the situation to her [22]. Sophie is happy about the developments, but Faninal collapses. With the help of some servants, Sophie takes him into the adjoining room [24, 21].

Ochs now attempts to leave with Mariandel [22, 26a], and although he almost succeeds in placating the officer [42, 34], he cannot persuade Mariandel to go with him, not even with a promise of marriage [44c, 42]. She runs to the officer, whispers something to him, and disappears behind the curtains. When Ochs sees the officer looking in amusement between the curtains while Mariandel's clothes are being thrown out piece by piece [42], he gets more and more excited [22]; but as he is about to break away from the two policemen who have been restraining him, the innkeeper rushes in, announcing the Marschallin.

Followed by the Baron's personal servant, who had apparently gone to her for help, she enters, completely ignoring the delighted Baron, who now talks loftily to the police officer [22]. The latter, also ignoring Ochs, humbly introduces himself to the Marschallin. Octavian, in men's clothes, steps from behind the curtains—unnoticed by Ochs—and expresses his surprise at the presence of the Marschallin, who regards him silently and somewhat haughtily [5]. Sophie comes from the adjoining room [24, 26], and despite Ochs's efforts to silence her, she warns him of the consequences should he ever dare be seen again in the vicinity of the Faninal mansion [21]. She goes back to her father, and Ochs wants to follow her; but the Marschallin advises him that he had better say no more and beat a quick retreat. Then she dismisses the officer by telling him that the entire affair [26a] was merely a farce. Ochs is astonished but by no means willing to give up [11]; and when Octavian comes forward [3] to add force to the Marschallin's order, the Baron takes a good look at the young Count [1a] and slowly begins to understand the whole masquerade [1b, Mariandel Waltz, 6]. He tries to trade his silence against another chance with

[40b] *continued*

[41] SURRENDER WALTZ

Waltz un poco commodo

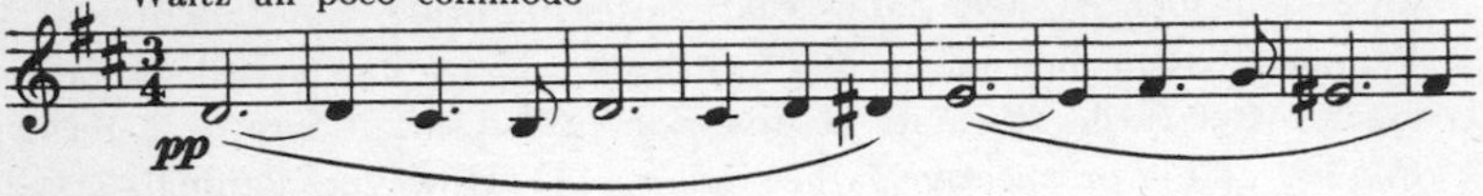

[42] MELANCHOLY WALTZ

Moderato assai

OCTAVIAN When it's all said and done,
Es is ja eh alls eins,

[43] Moderato

OCTAVIAN Eh bien,___ do you not say a word to me?
Eh bien,___ hat Sie kein freund- lich Wort für mich?

[44] TRIO *HAB' MIR'S GELOBT* (Marschallin, Sophie, Octavian)

Moderato e molto cantabile

MARSCH: I___ gave my word that I ___________ would love him
Hab'___ mir's ge - lobt, ihn lieb ___________ zu ha - ben

c Moderato e molto cantabile

[45] DUET *IST EIN TRAUM* (Sophie, Octavian)

Andante tranquillo

SOPHIE. It's a dream and it can - not be, ___ I'm with you ___ and you
Ist ein Traum, kann nicht wirk-lich sein, ___ dass wir zwei ___ bei - ein-

OCT. You are all that I feel and see, _____ I'm with you ___ and you
Spür' nur dich, spür' nur dich, al - lein _____ und dass wir ___ bei - ein-

are with me! ___
an - der sein, ___

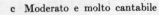

are with me!
an - der sein!

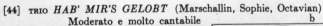

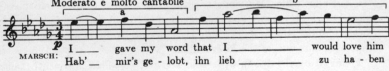

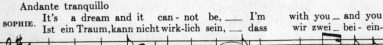

Faninal [22, 12], but the Marschallin declares with finality that this whole affair in all its ramifications has herewith come to an end [22, 18]. "To an end," repeats Sophie, who has just reentered; "to an end," murmurs Ochs, not at all reconciled. "To an end," repeats the Marschallin sadly to herself [5].

Now the suspicious characters [35] come from their hiding places; Annina takes off her disguise [14]; the innkeeper enters with a long bill, and behind him waiters, musicians, coachmen, doormen, all seeking out Ochs. This is too much for him; he is ready to leave, but Annina insolently bars his way [34], and all crowd around him demanding money [14, 29, 30, 38, 37] while the four children keep shouting "Papa." Finally Ochs manages to reach the door [40b] and is followed out by the entire crowd.

Sophie remains with the Marschallin and Octavian, and sadly contemplates the end of the affair [41]. The Marschallin angrily bids the embarrassed Octavian to join Sophie, who is standing awkwardly alone [42, 2]. Sophie, however, is not in the mood for Octavian's efforts at conversation [43]. He asserts his love, but she refuses to believe him. The Marschallin, alone on the other side of the room, repeats to herself her vow that she will face the new situation with tranquility [6]. Sophie wants to rejoin her father [24], but Octavian won't let her [3, 26a]. As he stands in embarrassment between the two women, the Marschallin walks over to Sophie and, after looking at her intently but kindly [5], she declares that she will try to cheer Faninal by driving him home in her carriage, together with the Count Rofrano and Sophie. As for Sophie, perhaps Rofrano will be better able to cheer her up. Octavian can only stammer the Marschallin's name: Maria Theresa [5, 27]. There is an awkward pause before the three, each to himself, confess their innermost thoughts and emotions in this moment of decision (Trio *Hab' mir's gelobt:* "I gave my word") [44ab]: the Marschallin repeats her vow to love Octavian in the only way proper for her; Sophie expresses her awe before the Marschallin, feeling, yet not wanting to know, that she receives Octavian as a gift from her; and Octavian, despite a feeling of helplessness and guilt before the Marschallin [5], can think only of Sophie. Finally he joins her in the expression of their mutual love [44ac], and the Marschallin, quite forgotten by the pair, resignedly [5] goes to join Faninal.

Sophie and Octavian remain alone [26a, 27]. In a tender embrace, they feel they are dreaming (Duet *Ist ein Traum:* "It's a dream") [45], and Octavian joyfully recalls their first meeting [26a, 27]. The Marschallin and Faninal pass with an indulgent glance [5] at the youngsters, who embrace once more [26a, 45, 26b, 27] and then quickly follow their elders [26ba].

The little black page boy comes in [9a], finds a handkerchief dropped by Sophie, and gaily trips off with it [9b].

THEMES

[1] SALOME

a Andante mosso

p
b

[2] Andante mosso

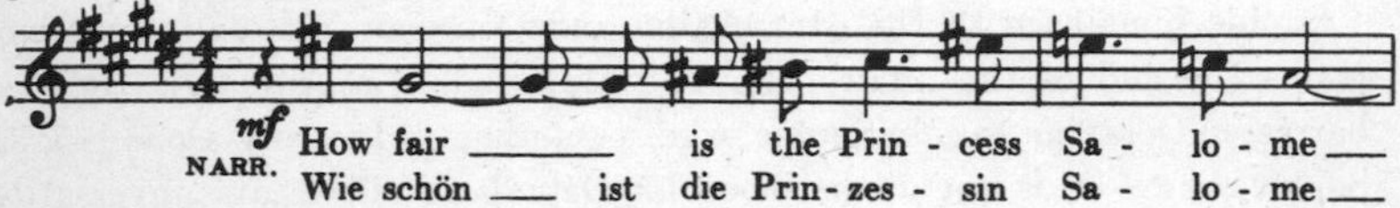
mf
NARR.
How fair ___ is the Prin - cess Sa - lo - me ___
Wie schön ___ ist die Prin - zes - sin Sa - lo - me ___

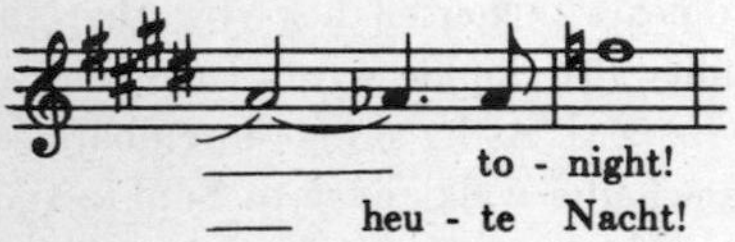
___ to - night!
___ heu - te Nacht!

[3] NARRABOTH'S LOVE

Andante mosso

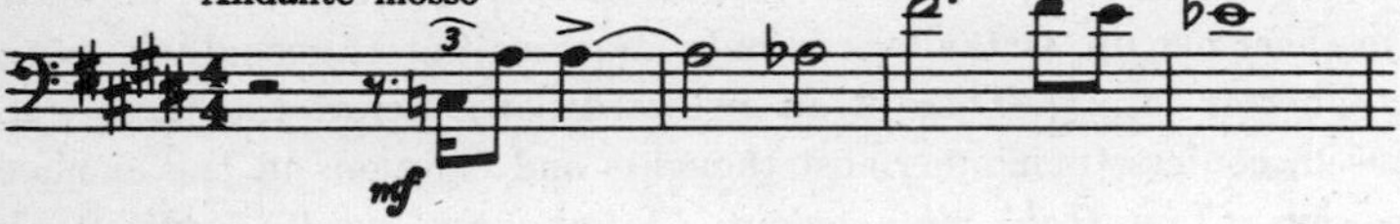
mf

[4] THE JEWS

Mosso

a
b
f
ff

[5a] Andante mosso

THE PAGE
You al - ways look at her. You look at her too much.
Du siehst sie im - mer an. Du siehst sie zu viel an.

Salome

Opera in one act by Richard Strauss. Libretto translated from Oscar Wilde's play by Hedwig Lachmann. First performance: Dresden, December 9, 1905.

Characters: HEROD ANTIPAS, Tetrarch of Judea (tenor); HERODIAS, his wife (mezzo-soprano); SALOME, daughter of Herodias (soprano); JOKANAAN (JOHN THE BAPTIST) (baritone); NARRABOTH, captain of the guard (tenor); THE PAGE of Herodias (contralto); FIVE JEWS (4 tenors, bass); TWO NAZARENES (tenor, bass); TWO SOLDIERS (bass); A CAPPADOCIAN (bass).
A great terrace in the palace of Herod, about 30 A.D.

(The music starts after the curtain for the single scene has been raised.)

On a terrace at the palace of Herod, Narraboth, the young Syrian captain of the guard, gazes through the door of the banqueting hall at Salome [1a, in its most tender version], admiring her beauty [2 with 3]. The young page looks up at the moon. To Narraboth the moon resembles a little dancing princess [3, 1a], while the page compares it to a woman rising from the grave.

A sudden commotion [4] is heard from inside the hall. It is a quarrel among the Jews about their religion, as one soldier explains to another. As Narraboth continues admiring Salome, the page, greatly concerned, warns him of the possible dangerous consequences of his admiration [5ab], but without success [1a].

From the depth of a cistern, a voice proclaims the coming of Him who will bring light and joy to the world. It is the voice of a prophet [6] named Jokanaan, an inquiring Cappadocian is told; the Tetrarch has forbidden that anyone see him.

Narraboth observes Salome [1a, 3] rising and coming toward the terrace. She appears in great excitement [7, 1a], exasperated [8] by the way Herod, her stepfather, keeps looking at her [9]. She relishes breathing the sweet night air [10, 7, 1a], but is still shuddering [8] at the thought of the quarreling Jews [4a], the cagey Egyptians, and the brutal Romans at the banquet tables.

As the page again warns Narraboth [5b], Salome delights in looking at the moon [10, 7, 1a], whose beauty she likens to that of a virgin, chaste and pure. But now Jokanaan speaks again, and Salome, filled with curiosity [7 minor, 1b], inquires about the prophet of whom, she knows, the Tetrarch is afraid and who says such terrible things [8; 8 with 1b] about her mother. Despite an order from Herod that she return to the banquet [8, 10], and ig-

[5b] Andante mosso

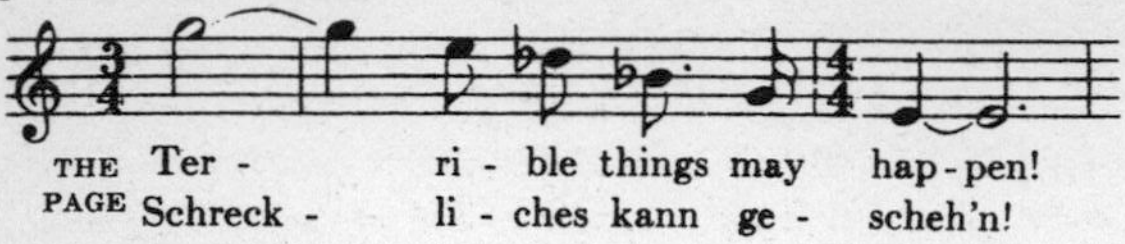
THE PAGE
Ter - ri - ble things may hap - pen!
Schreck - li - ches kann ge - scheh'n!

[6] **THE PROPHET**
Maestoso

[7] **EXCITEMENT**
Presto

f
3

[8] **CAPRICE**
Presto

3

[9] **HEROD'S COAXING**
Presto

[10] Tempo di Waltz

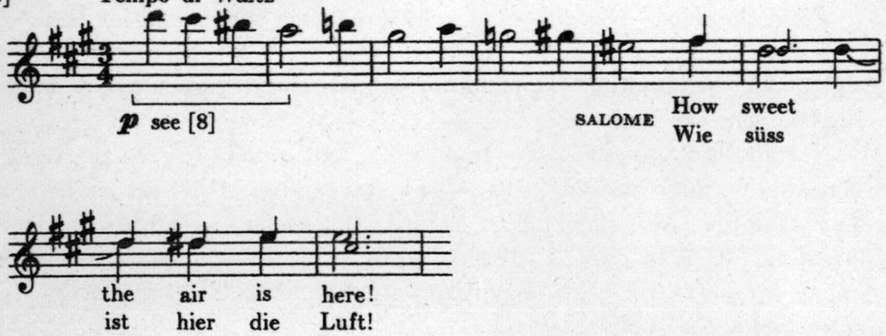
p see [8]
SALOME
How sweet the air is here!
Wie süss ist hier die Luft!

[11] Con moto

JOK.
f
Pa - les-tine, why art thou re - joic - ing?
Jauch- ze nicht, du Land Pa - lä - sti - na

noring Narraboth's entreaties [1a], she stays and learns from the soldiers that the prophet is still a young man. Presently the voice from the cistern prophesies doom for Palestine [11]. Salome insists [7, 1ab] on speaking with Jokanaan, but the soldiers dare not comply with her wish. With horror she looks down into the blackness of the cistern. When the soldiers continue to refuse her demand, Salome suddenly takes notice of Narraboth. The page senses disaster in the offing [5a] as Salome uses all her wiles on the captain [7, 12, 1b, 3] until he complies with her demand and orders the cistern opened. While the grate is being lifted by the soldiers, Salome alternately looks down and nervously paces to and fro [7, 12, 6, 1b, 13a], in curious anticipation [motive 17 with 7; 6]. The prophet issues from the dark opening [13a] and summons "him whose measure of sin is overflowing" [6, 13a]. Salome listens aghast [7, 14]. Harshly, the prophet accuses [15] her "whose lust has driven her to the summit of abomination," and he summons her to come before his presence [6] and to repent.

Salome realizes that he is talking about Herod and about her mother, and in shuddering fascination [14] she can only whisper: "He is terrible, truly terrible!" His eyes are especially frightening [14, 1a]. And he is so emaciated [13a]! He must be chaste as the moon and cool to the touch as a statue of ivory [7, 12]. In vain has Narraboth [3] been trying to distract Salome; she *must* take a closer look at the prophet [14, 1b]. Jokanaan, however, does not want her near him [13a]; he does not even want to know who she is [15], but she proudly and defiantly introduces herself [16 with 7 and with 1b; 1a]. In horror the prophet bids her stand back [15], to pour ashes on her head, and to seek the Son of Man [6], but Salome is fascinated by the whiteness of Jokanaan's body [14]. Nothing, she declares, ignoring Narra-

[12] SALOME'S SEDUCTIVE CHARMS

Presto

[13] JOKANAAN

a Maestoso

b Vivace

[14] LUST

Dolce cantabile

a
b
p

[15] REBUKE

Andante

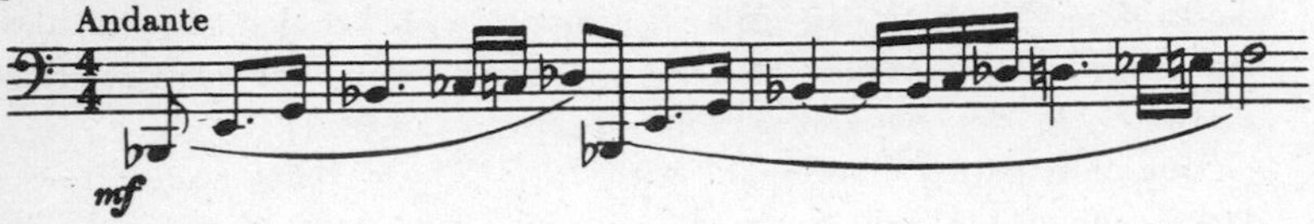
mf

[16] Vivace

f
SALOME
I am Sa - lo - me, the daugh- ter of He - ro - di- as,
Ich bin Sa - lo - me, die Toch - ter der He - ro - di- as,
the Prin - cess of Ju - dae - a.
Prin-zes - sin von Ju - dae - a.

[17] Agitato

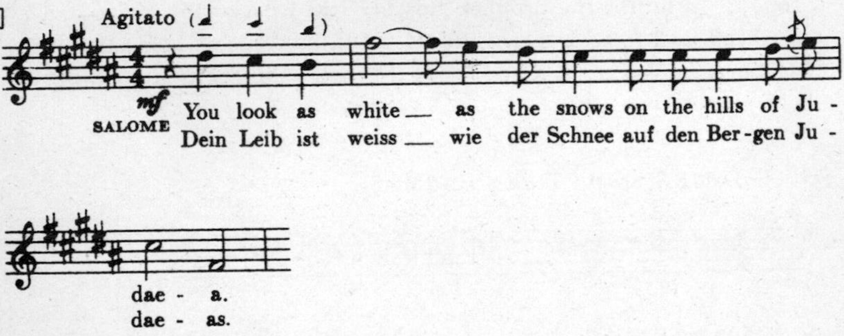
mf
SALOME
You look as white — as the snows on the hills of Ju -
Dein Leib ist weiss — wie der Schnee auf den Ber-gen Ju -
dae - a.
dae - as.

[18] Molto allegro

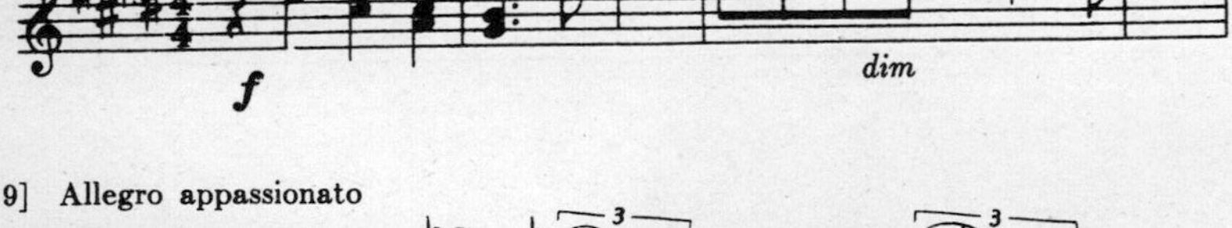
f
dim

[19] Allegro appassionato

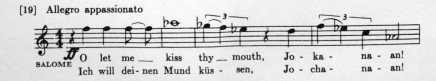

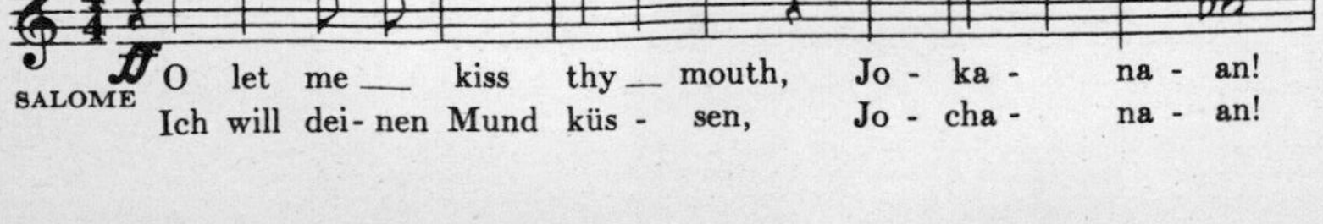
3
3
ff
SALOME
O let me — kiss thy — mouth, Jo - ka - na - an!
Ich will dei- nen Mund küs - sen, Jo - cha - na - an!

both's frantic efforts to lead her away [3], nothing in the whole world can compare with this whiteness [1a, 14, 17]. Jokanaan, however excited [6], will not listen to the voice of woman, creator of evil [7, 1a], but only to that of the Lord, his God [6]. Thereupon Salome suddenly finds his body horrible [13b, 14ab, 13a]. Rather [15] is it the prophet's hair, ravishing [7, 10] in its unique blackness [13a], which she desires to touch [14a with 15; 1a]. As Jokanaan again tells her to stand back [13b, 1a, 6], it is now his hair that has become horrid to the princess [15, 13a]. It is the mouth of the prophet [15 with 6], his scarlet lips which make her tingle [18, 14b, 14a] and which, undaunted by the prophet's stern rebuff, she longs to kiss [19]. She does not hear Narraboth's supplications [3] to cease addressing the prophet and she barely notices when, dead by his own sword [3], he falls between her and Jokanaan [7, 1a, 15]. Passionately she keeps repeating her longing to kiss Jokanaan's lips [19]. Once again the prophet [6] points the way to salvation: Salome shall go forth [13a with 19] to find Him [20] and ask for His forgiveness [6 against 19]. But not even the strong personality of Jokanaan [13a] can stay Salome's desperate desire [19]. Thereupon Jokanaan curses Salome [13a, 14] and returns to his dungeon [13, 12, 14; 17 minor with 15; 13a, 19, 6]. The grate is replaced, but Salome [1a, 21] continues staring down after Jokanaan [13b, motive 35b].

There is a commotion in the banquet hall [4] and Herod [22] comes out on the terrace, followed by Herodias and their dinner guests. He is looking for Salome and is as content as Herodias is annoyed when his eyes [23] find her. But now the moon attracts his attention [23, 22]. It seems to him a drunken harlot—but to Heriodias the moon looks only like the moon and nothing else. She wants to return to the hall, but Herod orders that the feast be continued outside. Suddenly his foot slips on something and, frightened [24a], he discovers that it is the blood of Narraboth. Clearly he remembers [1a] the handsome captain's longing glances toward Salome [3, 1a, 7]. "Away with him," he shouts. An icy wind [24] which touches no one else makes Herod shiver: it sounds to him like the rustling of mighty wings [13a], but his attention wanders back to Salome [23, 7]. He has wine poured and invites Salome to share it with him [25 with 7; 1b, 7]. "I am not thirsty, Tetrarch," [1b] she answers, to the satisfaction of her mother. So Herod has fruit brought in and asks Salome to take just one bite [26]. "I am not hungry, Tetrarch" is her answer. As Herodias insultingly calls her husband a vulgar upstart, he asks Salome to come and sit on her mother's throne [7]. Salome's refusal [1a] and Herodias' triumph [21] drive him to utter confusion [7].

The voice of Jokanaan is heard again. Herodias wants to see him delivered to the Jews, but Herod [22] holds that Jokanaan is a holy man who has seen God. Thereupon a lively theological discussion is stirred up among the five Jews [4a, 4b]. Eventually Herodias stops them. The prophet's ringing voice announces the coming of the Savior [6], and two Nazarenes

[20] Cantabile

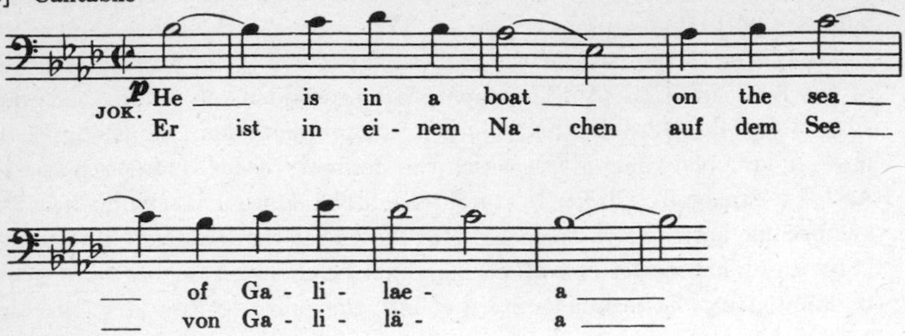
p
JOK.
He is in a boat on the sea
Er ist in ei - nem Na - chen auf dem See
of Ga - li - lae - a
von Ga - li - lä - a

[21] REVENGE

f

[22] HEROD
Allegro

f

[23] HEROD'S GAZE
Allegro

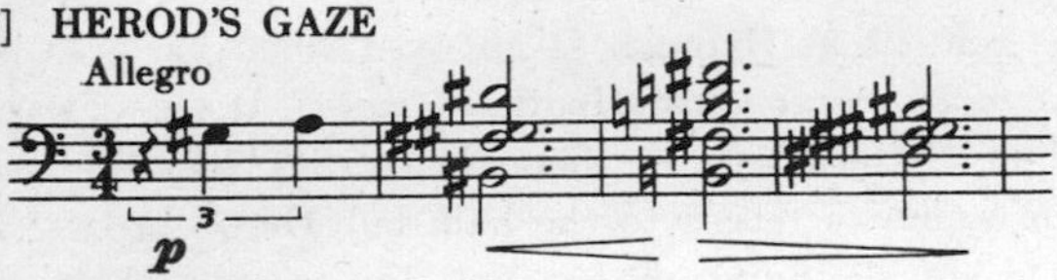
3
p

[24] THE ANGEL OF DEATH
Allegro molto

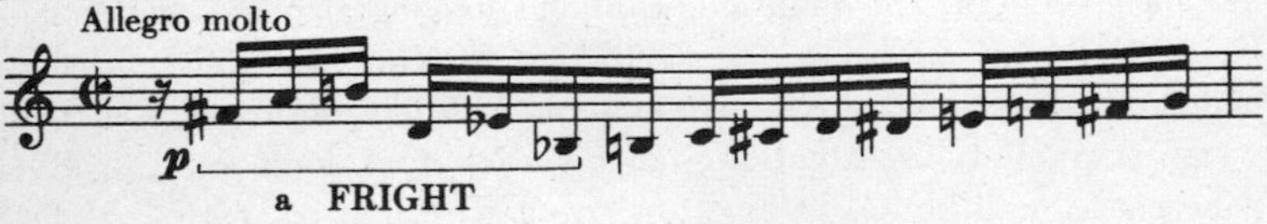
p
a FRIGHT

[25] Molto allegro

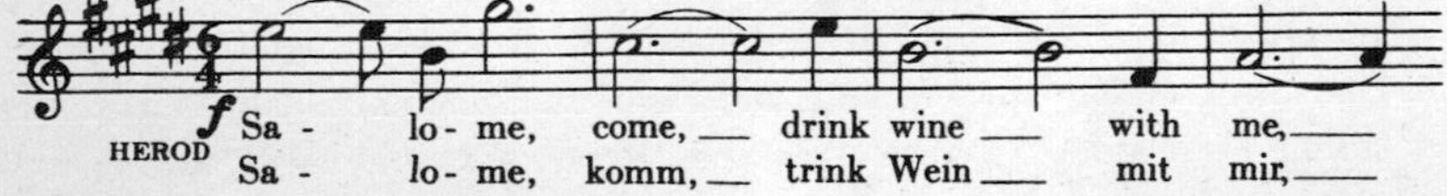
f
HEROD
Sa - lo - me, come, drink wine with me,
Sa - lo - me, komm, trink Wein mit mir,

[26] Molto vivace

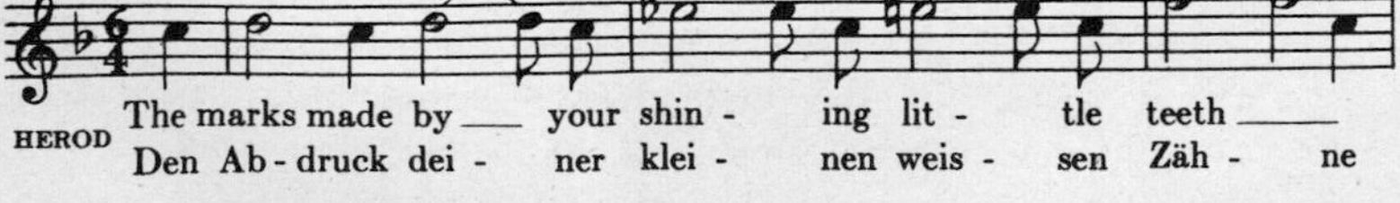
HEROD
The marks made by your shin - ing lit - tle teeth
Den Ab - druck dei - ner klei - nen weis - sen Zäh - ne

tell about the wonders He has wrought [20], including the reviving of the dead—a report which greatly frightens Herod [6].

While Jokanaan [6, 15, 13a] renews his prophecies of violent ends for the harlot (meaning Herodias) and for the king, Herodias shrilly demands that he be silenced. However, the Tetrarch's mind is again occupied with Salome. When he asks her to dance for him [7], she declines [8], but Herod insists [22, 7]. He will give her anything she desires if she dances for him. A weird interest (the trill of a lonely flute in the orchestra grows in eeriness with every repetition) seems to awaken in Salome as she rises [1b] and draws from the Tetrarch the solemn oath that he will give her anything she will ask, be it half his kingdom [27]. Exuberant [28] with expectation of the dance, Herod suddenly hears again the sound of the giant wings [1a, 24, 13a] which he cannot see [23, 14b] gliding over the terrace. He is freezing and then again suffocating from heat [13a, 7, 1a, 24]. Finally he tears the garland from his head [7] and feels relieved [22]. Once more he asks Salome whether she will dance for him. In spite of her mother's objections, she consents [1a]. Immediately slaves start to dress Salome while Jokanaan continues to prophesy the arrival of the Lord [6]. Herodias urges that they go inside, but Herod wishes to watch Salome dance [7].

She emerges from among the group of her attendants, dressed in the seven veils, ready to dance for Herod [motive 35b with 23]. The musicians who have meanwhile appeared now start a wild tune [29a, 30], but on a sign from the princess [motive 35b] they change to a slower rhythm. Salome dances the dance of the seven veils [mainly 31 with 29; 1a. Reminiscences of 17, 13, 19, 3. 33, 14, 32, 34, 10. Then 29a with 7. 33 with 30 and

[27] Molto vivo

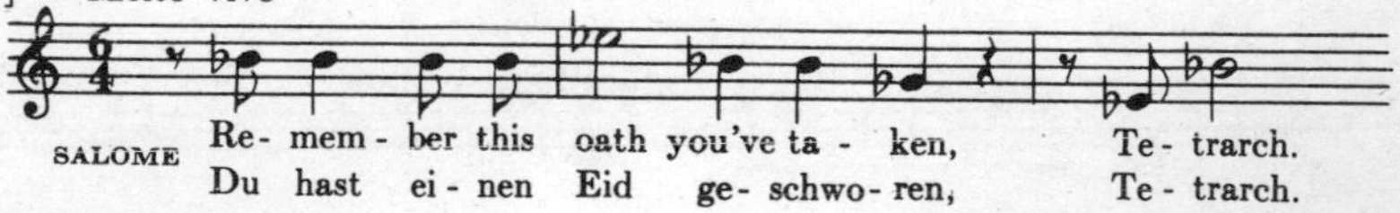
SALOME
Re- mem - ber this oath you've ta - ken, Te - trarch.
Du hast ei - nen Eid ge- schwo- ren, Te - trarch.

[28] Allegro molto

HER.
Thou'lt be fair as Queen Sa - lo - me, like a God- dess fair!
Du wirst schön sein als Kö - ni - gin, un - er - mess- lich schön.

[29] SALOME'S DANCE
Moderato

a

[30] Molto presto e furioso

f

[31] Moderato (see [35b])

p
a
b

[32] Agitato (see [17])

8va
f
3

[33] Moderato

p
3

[34] Moderato

accel.
mf
3

[35a] Lento

rit.
a tempo
p
pp
SALOME
The head of Jo - ka - na - an
Den Kopf des Jo - cha - na - an

[35b] Lento e feroce

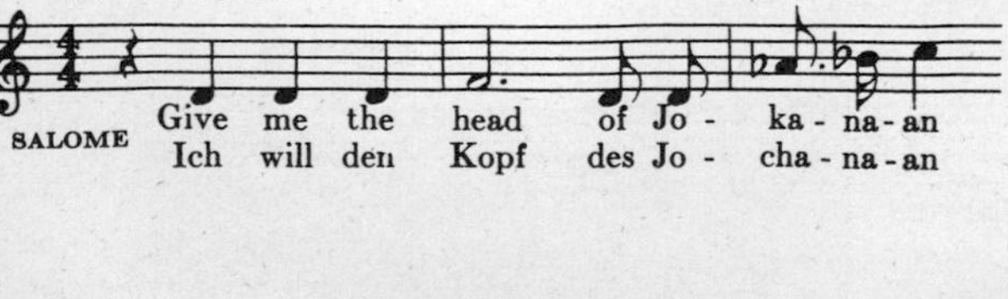
SALOME
Give me the head of Jo - ka - na - an
Ich will den Kopf des Jo - cha - na - an

21; 32 with motive 35b]. For an instant she remains immobile at the cistern [the flute trill with 14a], then, removing the last veil [14b], she throws herself at Herod's feet.

Herod, who has been watching with fascination, expresses his delight [23] and asks what Salome desires as her reward. "I should like to have, on a silver platter . . ." Salome says sweetly [the trill with 14a], and when the gushing Herod [23] finally permits her to finish the sentence, she smilingly adds: ". . . the head of Jokanaan" [35a]. Herodias is most happy with her daughter's choice, but the Tetrarch, nearly beside himself, begs Salome to reconsider [22, 1a]. However, Salome insists on the head of Jokanaan [35b, 21]. She and her mother repeatedly remind Herod that he has sworn an oath [27], but he desperately asks the Princess to choose something else [7 minor]. Herodias continues to encourage her daughter to insist on the head [35b]. Herod tries to persuade [9] Salome to take instead the world's most beautiful emerald, which he possesses; then he offers her [36]—he finds it difficult to concentrate [22, 23]—his hundred white peacocks in exchange for the life of a man who may have been sent by God [6]. Still Salome insists that she wants nothing but the head of Jokanaan [35b]. Herod, forcing himself to suppress his rage [21], offers her all his jewels and wonder-working stones [36], even the curtain of the holy of holies [4b], but Salome's determination is inflexible [35b]. Exhausted, Herod subsides into his chair [22] and finally accedes to Salome's demand [35b]. The queen draws from his hand the signet ring which is the symbol of authority over life and death [14a]. The ring is immediately given to the executioner, who thereupon descends into the cistern carrying his immense sword high for all to see. Herod recovers and, missing his ring, trembles with fear of impending disaster [22, 6].

Salome, who in the meantime has gone to the cistern, anxiously peers down into the dark cavern and listens hysterically for every sound. Why doesn't anything happen? she wants to know. Why can't she hear anything? Why doesn't the executioner strike [31ab, 21, 1a]? And what has she just heard falling—was it his sword [12]? Is he afraid [6]? Why, she shouts [8], doesn't the Tetrarch see to it that she receive the head of Jokanaan [31, 21]?

The huge arm of the executioner rises from the cistern holding, on a silver charger, the head of the prophet. Triumphantly [37], Salome takes the platter [1a, 21]. Jokanaan willing or not, she now will kiss his lips [14a, 13b, 1a], with rapture [26, 19, 15]. The once terrifying eyes [13b, 14a] and the poisonous tongue [26, 1b, 13b] are now dead, but Salome, Princess of Judea, is alive to take her revenge [31, 6, 37, 1a; 7 minor; 21]. Alas, Jokanaan had been fair [14]. There was nothing in the world more beautiful [17] and awe-inspiring [15], or more mysterious [13a]. But he saw only his God [6] and never did he see Salome [7, 1a, 18], else he would have loved her as much as she craved him [19, 14, 35b; 13a with 1a].

[36] PERSUASION

Agitato

[37] TRIUMPH

Andante

The moon has disappeared. Herod is horrified [14a minor, 23, 1b] and frightened [24a]. He orders all the lights extinguished. Terrible things will happen, he feels [23]. From the darkness now reigning, Salome whispers that she has kissed Jokanaan's lips [trill with 14a]. Was the bitter taste blood? Or love? No matter; she has kissed his lips, the lips of Jokanaan [19; 17 with 19 and with 1a; 15, 17].

As a sudden ray of moonlight illuminates the grisly scene, Herod, filled with revulsion, shouts an order, and the soldiers crush Salome to death under their shields [1b, 31a].

THEMES

[1] SALVATION (RETURNING PILGRIMS)

Andante maestoso

[2] REPENTANCE

Andante maestoso

[3] VENUSBERG MUSIC

Allegro

[4] Allegro

[5] Allegro

[6] Allegro

[7] Allegro

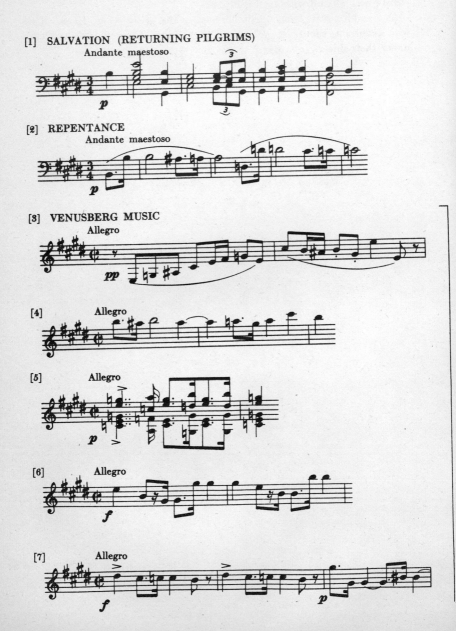

Tannhäuser

Opera in three acts by Richard Wagner. Libretto by the composer. First performance: Dresden, October 19, 1845; Paris, March 13, 1861.

Characters: Minnesingers: HEINRICH VON OFTERDINGEN, called TANNHÄUSER (tenor); WOLFRAM VON ESCHENBACH (baritone); BITEROLF (bass); WALTHER VON DER VOGELWEIDE (tenor); HEINRICH DER SCHREIBER (tenor); REINMAR VON ZWETER (bass);

HERMANN, Landgraf of Thuringia (bass); ELISABETH, his niece (soprano); VENUS (soprano or mezzo-soprano); A YOUNG SHEPHERD (soprano).

The subterranean realm of Venus (Venusberg); a valley near the Wartburg; the Wartburg. The beginning of the thirteenth century.

Prelude: * The "Pilgrims' Chorus" with its themes of salvation [1] and repentance [2] gives way to strains of Venusberg music [3–7], including the "Hymn to Venus" [8] and the "Lure of the Grotto" [motive 11]. In the Dresden version the Pilgrims' Chorus [1, 2] now returns to bring the "Overture" to a triumphant conclusion. In the Paris version, the "Prelude" leads directly into the "Bacchanal."

Act I, Scene 1: In the realm of Venus in the Hörsel Mountain, Tannhäuser lies asleep, his head reclining against the couch of the goddess, who is attended by the Three Graces. The amorous games of nymphs and youths [3] are spurred into an orgy by the arrival of bacchantes [5, 4] and of satyrs and fauns [9], till cupids (to the blast of trumpets) send a hail of arrows among them. Overpowered with longing, the couples withdraw, and the Graces take their leave while the sirens call from the distance [10, 6].

Tannhäuser awakens with the desire to return to earth, and with a longing for change, strife, and, if need be, death. All his praises of Venus [8] end with a plea for freedom. Fruitless are the goddess' efforts to tempt him with the love grotto [11]. In vain she warns him that, rejected by mortal men, he will come begging for her love [12]. When she asks him to promise that he will return if denied salvation elsewhere, Tannhäuser answers: "My salvation is with Mary." With the name of the Blessed Virgin still on his lips, Tannhäuser suddenly finds himself before a Madonna at a crossroads in a valley near the Wartburg.

* "Prelude": so called in the Paris version; in the original, Dresden, version there is an "Overture."

[7] VENUSBERG MUSIC *continued*

[8] HYMN TO VENUS

Allegro

f

[9] Allegro

ff

[10] CALL OF THE SIRENS

Molto moderato

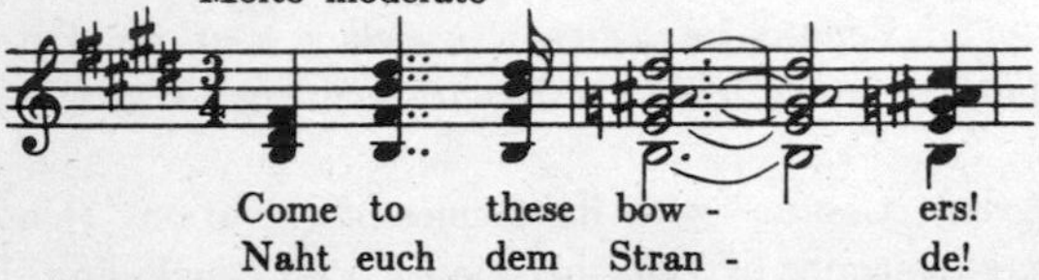
Come to these bow - ers!
Naht euch dem Stran - de!

[11] LURE OF THE LOVE GROTTO

Moderato

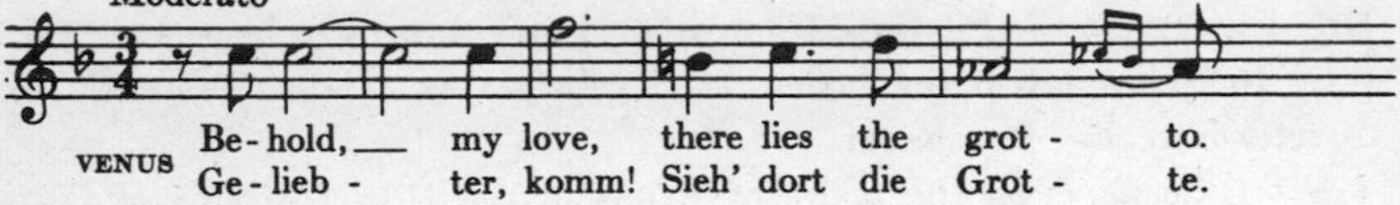
VENUS
Be-hold, my love, there lies the grot - to.
Ge-lieb - ter, komm! Sieh' dort die Grot - te.

[12] Allegro

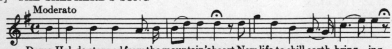

VENUS
Fly to the frig - id breed of man,
Hin zu den kal - ten Men - schen - flieh',

[13] THE SHEPHERD'S SONG

Moderato

Dame Hol-da stepped from the mountain's heart New life to chill earth bring - ing.
Frau Hol- da kam aus dem Berg her-vor zu zieh'n durch Flur und Au - en.

[14] DEPARTING PILGRIMS' CHORUS

Moderato

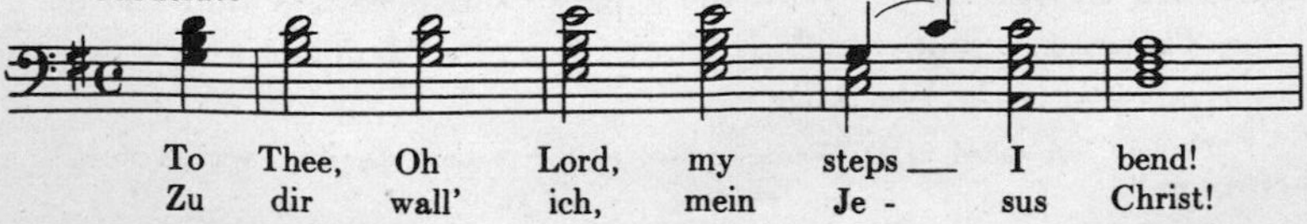
To Thee, Oh Lord, my steps I bend!
Zu dir wall' ich, mein Je - sus Christ!

Act I, Scene 2: A shepherd is playing his shawm and singing a welcome to spring [13] as pilgrims set out on their journey to Rome [14, 2, 15]. With a heart-rending cry Tannhäuser falls on his knees to praise God and to repent [2].

The Landgraf and his hunting party, gathering to the sound of their hunting horns, find Tannhäuser and invite him to rejoin their fellowship. When he violently refuses, Wolfram mentions Elisabeth and, with the Landgraf's permission, tells about the spell Tannhäuser has apparently cast upon her [16]. Since he has left, Elisabeth has not attended the singing contests. All join Wolfram when again he asks Tannhäuser to stay with them [16], and Tannhäuser, jubilantly reawakening to the beauty of the earth [17], begs to be taken to Elisabeth.

Act II: The air is filled with joyous excitement [18] and jubilation [17] as Elisabeth once again enters the great hall at the Wartburg (Aria *Dich teure Halle:* "O Hall of Song") [19]. With Tannhäuser absent, she has been sad and the hall joyless, but now all is radiant again [18] and she rejoices at being in the hall once more [17].

Tannhäuser enters, and she asks him to explain the overpowering effect of his song on her, and her sadness when he was away [20]. Together they

[15] DEPARTING PILGRIMS' CHORUS *continued*

[16]

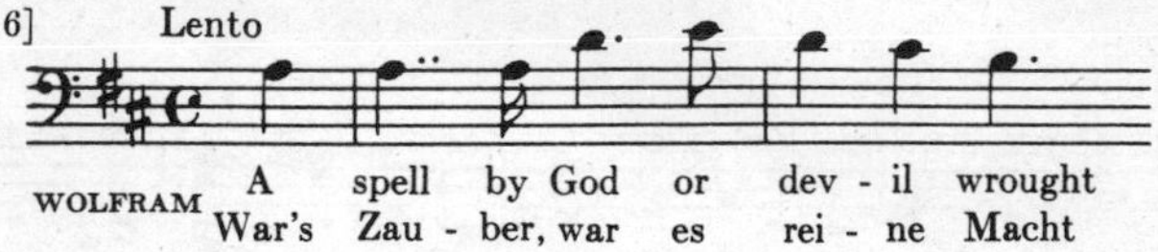

[17]

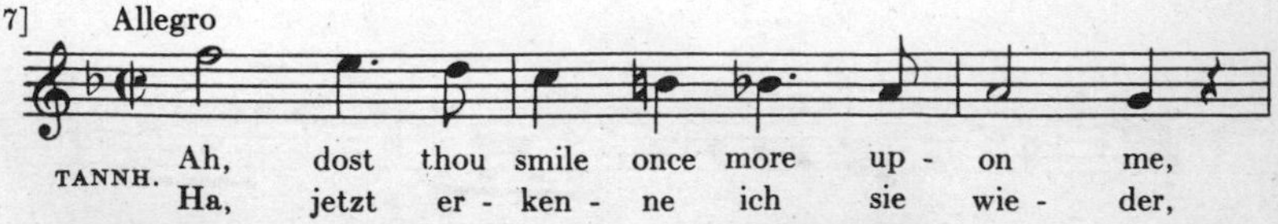

[18] Allegro

[19] ARIA *DICH, THEURE HALLE* (Elisabeth)

Allegro

O Hall of Song, I give thee greet - ing!
Dich, theu - re Hal - - le, grüss' ich wie - der!

[20] ARIA *DER SAENGER KLUGEN WEISEN* (Elisabeth)

Allegretto

In min - - strels' lays de - light - - ing,
Der Sän - - ger klu - gen Wei - - sen

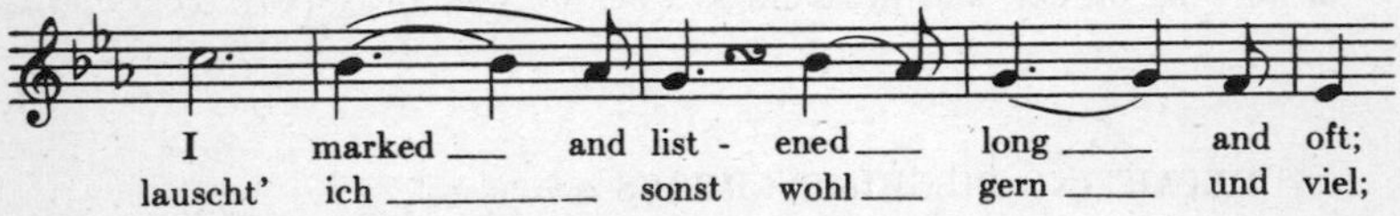
I marked and list - ened long and oft;
lauscht' ich sonst wohl gern und viel;

[21] Allegro

ELIS. Let's praise this won - drous hour,
& TANNH. Ge - prie - sen sei die Stun - de,

[22] FESTAL MARCH

Allegro

[23] Allegro

p

[24] Allegro

p

exalt the power of love which has brought him back [21]. Elated, Tannhäuser takes his leave.

The Landgraf comes to welcome the guests to the singing contest. Happy to find Elisabeth in the hall and divining the reason, he decides that "Love" shall be the theme of the impending competition.

Trumpets [22] herald the arrival of the nobles [23, 24, 25], who take their places and hail their host. After the singers have entered [26], the Landgraf announces the subject for the contest and offers as prize to the winner whatever he may desire. Lots are drawn [26], and it is Wolfram who opens the contest. He greets the assembly (Wolfram's Address *Blick' ich umher in diesem edlen Kreise:* "Proud to address this great and noble gath'ring") [27] and praises the beauty of chaste love. Tannhäuser rises to sing [3], but his ideal is a love of a more sensuous nature. (In the Dresden version Walther reproaches Tannhäuser, only to draw a more outspoken reply.) Biterolf sternly rises in the defense of virtue and, to the loud approval of the assembly, grimly expresses his scorn for Tannhäuser's youthful lack of restraint. When Tannhäuser tauntingly accuses Biterolf of lacking experience in matters of love, swordplay is barely avoided. Wolfram sings again, extolling love that (like his own love for Elisabeth) follows the beloved at a distance [28]. In answer, Tannhäuser ecstatically intones the Hymn to Venus [8] and scoffs at the ideals of those who have never been to the Venusberg.

Chaos ensues, and all the attendant ladies flee, scandalized. Only Elisabeth remains and, by shielding Tannhäuser's body with her own, prevents the knights from "bathing their swords in his blood." She pleads [29] that he be saved from dying in mortal sin and be given a chance to repent and to receive pardon. Gradually Tannhäuser awakens from his rapture. As the knights comment on the sinner being saved by a veritable angel [30], he cries out in anguish for God's mercy [31]. The Landgraf banishes Tannhäuser, but reminds him that he still can find salvation by going to Rome [14]. The knights bid him [32] join the young pilgrims of the land, who are at this very moment preparing to follow their elders; they threaten death if he should return without having obtained absolution. Meanwhile, Elisabeth is offering her life to God for Tannhäuser's redemption [32]. The

[25]

[26]

[27] WOLFRAM'S ADDRESS

Moderato

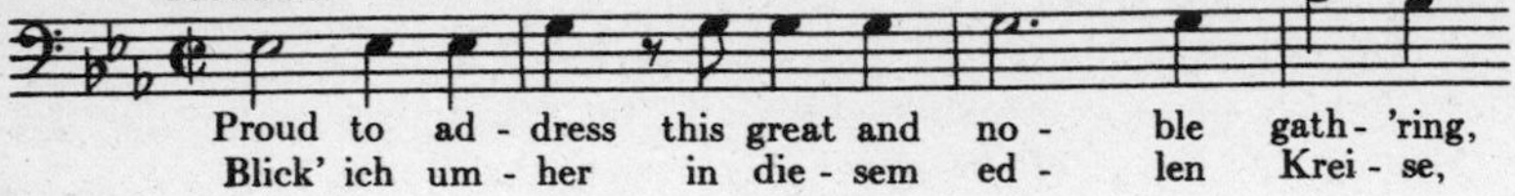
Proud to ad - dress this great and no - ble gath - 'ring,
Blick' ich um - her in die - sem ed - len Krei - se,

[28] Cantabile

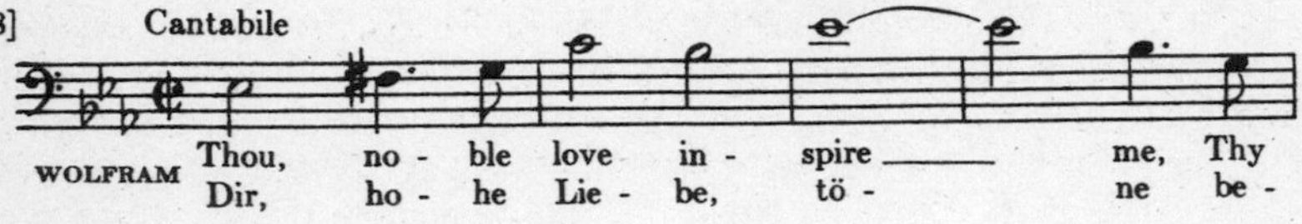
WOLFRAM
Thou, no - ble love in - spire me, Thy
Dir, ho - he Lie - be, tö - ne be -

glo - ry let me sing,
gei - stert mein Ge - sang,

[29] Adagio

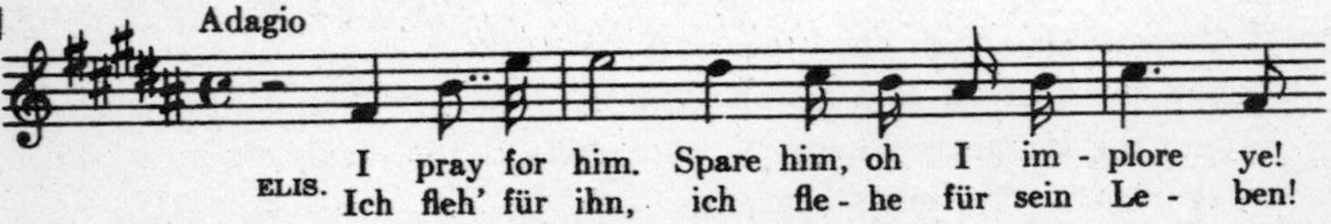
ELIS.
I pray for him. Spare him, oh I im - plore ye!
Ich fleh' für ihn, ich fle - he für sein Le - ben!

[30] Molto moderato

CHORUS
An an - gel pure, from heav'n de - scend - ed,
Ein En - gel stieg aus lich - tem Ae - ther

[31] Molto moderato

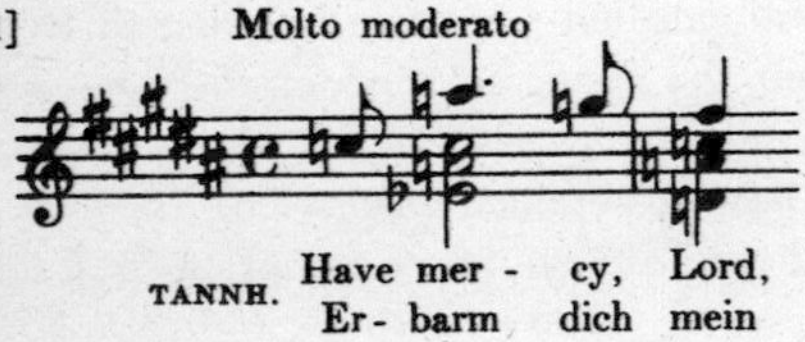
TANNH.
Have mer - cy, Lord,
Er - barm dich mein

[32] Con moto

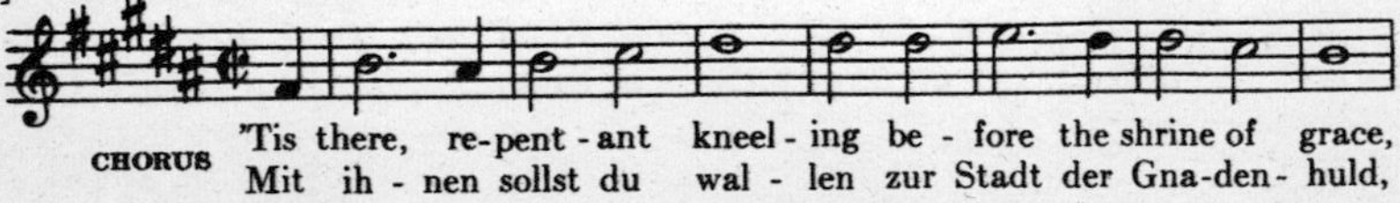
CHORUS
'Tis there, re - pent - ant kneel - ing be - fore the shrine of grace,
Mit ih - nen sollst du wal - len zur Stadt der Gna - den - huld,

[33] TANNHAEUSER'S PILGRIMAGE

Andante assai lento

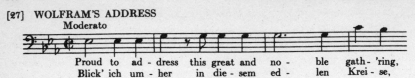

song of the departing pilgrims is heard from below [15], and Tannhäuser, filled with new hope, kisses the hem of Elisabeth's gown and with the cry "To Rome!" rushes away [32].

Introduction to Act III (*Tannhäuser's Pilgrimage*)*:* The music describes Tannhäuser on his way to Rome [14]. The thought of Elisabeth's intercession [29] sustains him while, in deep contrition, he chooses the roughest road [33, 2, 15]. Finally he arrives before the Pope, who grants absolution [34] to all the pilgrims: but for Tannhäuser there is only the papal curse [35]. Meanwhile, Elisabeth has never stopped praying for him [29].

Act III: Wolfram descends to the crossroads where Elisabeth, who has been wasting away in constant prayer, lies prostrate before the Madonna. As the pilgrims return from Rome [1, 2], she rises to look anxiously for Tannhäuser among them, but in vain. Crushed, she kneels again, asking the Virgin's forgiveness for her own sins, so that, admitted to heaven, she may dedicate all her prayers to the redemption of Tannhäuser (Elisabeth's Prayer *Allmächt'ge Jungfrau, hör' mein Flehen:* "All-holy Virgin, hear and cherish") [36]. Solemn and wordless, but with gratitude [20], she declines Wolfram's offer to accompany her back to the Wartburg. Wolfram remains alone in the twilight [28]. Sensing the shadow of death over the land [37], he asks the evening star to give the greetings of a truly loving heart to Elisabeth when her soul passes on its way toward the angels (Aria *O du mein holder Abendstern:* "O star of eve") [38].

[34] ABSOLUTION

Andante assai lento

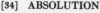

[35] THE POPE'S CURSE

Lento

[36] ELISABETH'S PRAYER

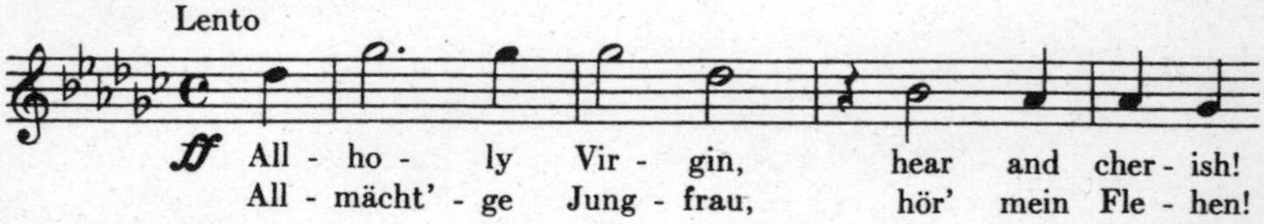
Lento
ff
All - ho - ly Vir - gin, hear and cher - ish!
All - mächt' - ge Jung - frau, hör' mein Fle - hen!

[37]

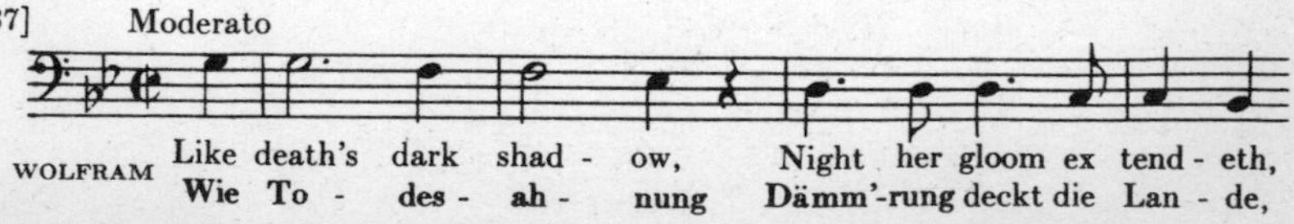
Moderato
WOLFRAM
Like death's dark shad - ow, Night her gloom ex tend - eth,
Wie To - des - ah - nung Dämm'-rung deckt die Lan - de,

[38] ARIA *O DU MEIN HOLDER ABENDSTERN* (Wolfram)

Moderato

p
pp
O star of eve, thy ten - der beam
O, du mein hol - der A - bend - stern,

[39] TANNHAEUSER'S NARRATIVE

Andante

Con - trite in spir- it as no pil - grim yet on
In - brunst im Her- zen, wie kein Büs - ser noch sie
earth has been, I bent my steps toward Rome.
je ge- fühlt, sucht'ich den Weg nach Rom.

[40] Allegro vivo

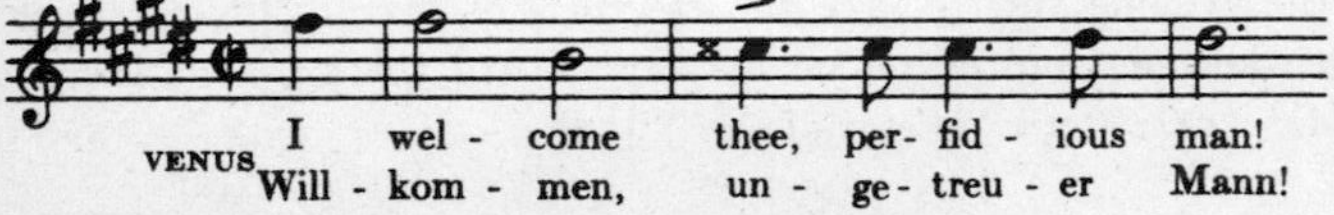
I wel - come thee, per- fid - ious man!
VENUS Will - kom - men, un - ge - treu - er Mann!

One more pilgrim appears [35]. It is Tannhäuser, searching for the Venusberg [3, 4]. However, to Wolfram, whose sincere sympathy [29] has touched him, he relates the story of his pilgrimage [33] (Tannhäuser's Narrative *Inbrunst im Herzen:* "Contrite in spirit") [39 with 33]—how he thought only of penance as he tortured himself on the road to Rome, how the glorious day of forgiveness dawned [34], and how he prostrated himself [33] before the benign Pope. But the Pope damned him eternally [35], adding that there would be no forgiveness for Tannhäuser as surely as there would be no bloom on the crozier in his hand. When Tannhäuser eventually awoke from a dead faint [34], his only feeling was a wild loathing for the Church, and his only desire was, as still it is, a speedy return to Venus [3, 4, 11].

Presently his wish is granted [4] as the valley seems to be absorbed by the magic of the Venusberg [3, 6, 5, 7] and the goddess herself appears [10] to welcome back her unfaithful lover [40]. Wolfram, in shock and fear, tries desperately to hold back the raving Tannhäuser. Finally he stops him from joining Venus by mentioning Elisabeth's name. As Tannhäuser repeats "Elisabeth" the Venusberg disappears. A funeral procession with the body of Elisabeth approaches. Tannhäuser kneels at her bier and, with his dying breath, whispers: "Blessed Elisabeth, pray for me."

The younger pilgrims return bearing the Pope's miraculously blooming crozier [34]. All praise God's mercy [1].

THEMES

[1] SCARPIA

Andante molto sostenuto

[2] TERROR

Vivacissimo con violenza

[3] ANGELOTTI'S SISTER

Vivacissimo con violenza

[4] THE SACRISTAN

Allegretto grazioso

[5] Allegretto grazioso

[6] THE UNKNOWN WORSHIPER

Andante moderato

[7] TOSCA

Andante moderato

Quotations used by permission of G. Ricordi & Co.

Tosca

Opera in three acts by Giacomo Puccini. Libretto by G. Giacosa and L. Illica after the play by Victorien Sardou. First performance: Rome, January 14, 1900.

Characters: FLORIA TOSCA, celebrated singer (soprano); MARIO CAVARADOSSI, painter (tenor); BARON SCARPIA, Chief of Police (baritone); CESARE ANGELOTTI, Consul of the former Republic of Rome (bass); A SACRISTAN (baritone); SPOLETTA, police agent (tenor); SCIARRONE, guard (bass); A JAILER (bass); A SHEPHERD (contralto).
Rome, June 1800.

Introduction: Only three measures, the theme of Scarpia, the ruthless police chief of Rome [1], precede the raising of the curtain.

Act I: Angelotti, Consul of the former Republic of Rome, fleeing [2] from the Castle of Sant' Angelo, where he has been imprisoned by Scarpia, enters the church of Sant' Andrea della Valle. After a short search he finds the key to the chapel of the Attavanti, left for him by his sister [3], and quickly enters it.

The Sacristan [4, 5] brings in painting materials for Cavaradossi, whose scaffold is erected near the Attavanti chapel. His grumbling comes to a sudden halt when he discovers that the painter is not there. The bells are chiming, and he kneels to pray.

Cavaradossi comes and uncovers a painting of a blue-eyed, blonde Madonna [6, 7a], which the Sacristan, to his disgust, recognizes as that of a woman who has recently been a frequent worshipper here. The artist begins to paint, then stops to compare his work with a medallion of Tosca, his dark-eyed, black-haired beloved (Aria *Recondita armonia:* "Strange harmony of contrasts") [8], satisfied that in the Madonna the likenesses of both, Tosca [9] and the unknown blonde woman [10], have been successfully amalgamated. However, it is always and only Tosca whom he loves [9]. On leaving, the grumbling Sacristan indicates a basket containing food, but Cavaradossi declares he is not hungry, and continues to paint.

Suddenly there is a movement in the chapel [2] and Angelotti [11] appears. The painter recognizes him, and, on learning that Angelotti has just escaped from Sant' Angelo [12], offers his help. However, just then Tosca calls from beyond the now locked door. Quickly Cavaradossi gives Angelotti the basket of food and sends him back into the chapel [11] before opening the door for Tosca.

She enters [13], her suspicions aroused by the delay [11], but she is re-

[8] ARIA *RECONDITA ARMONIA* (Cavaradossi)

Lento
pp
Strange har - mo - ny of con - trasts
Re - con - di - ta ar - mo - ni - a

[9]

Lento
sostenendo
My Flo - ria's dusk - y glow
E bru - na, Flo - ri - a,

[10]

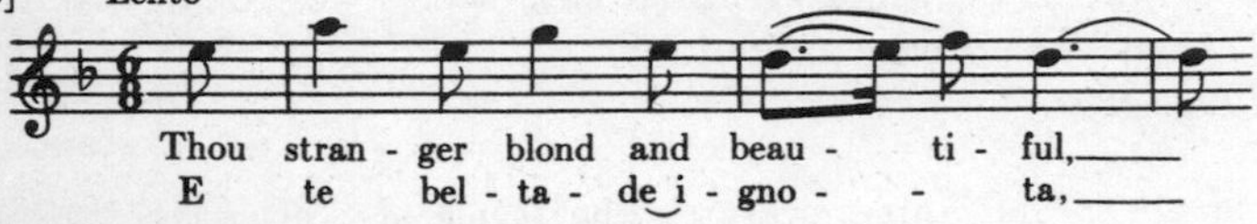
Lento
Thou stran - ger blond and beau - ti - ful,
E te bel - ta - de i - gno - ta,

[11] ANGELOTTI

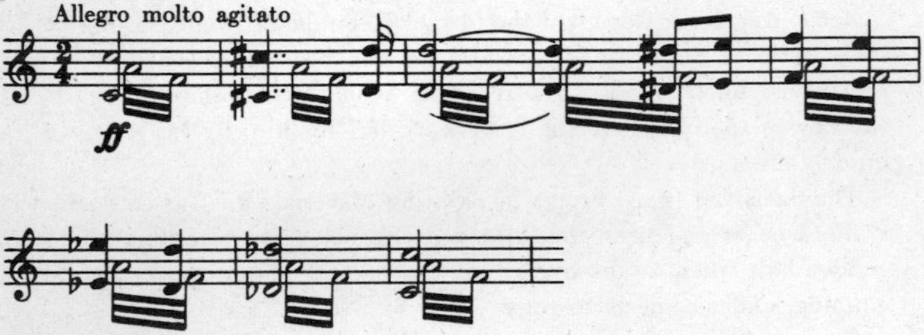
Allegro molto agitato
ff

[12]

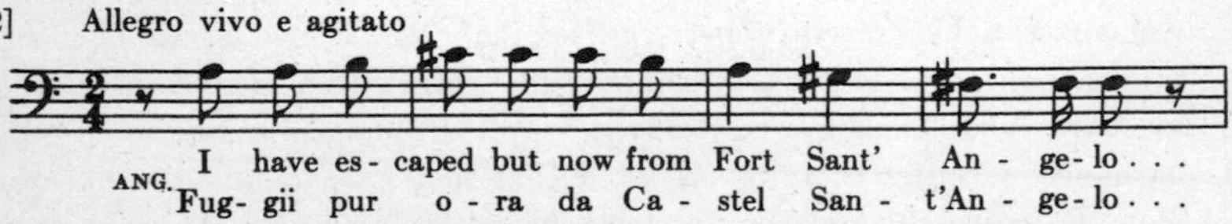
Allegro vivo e agitato
I have es - caped but now from Fort Sant' An - ge - lo . . .
ANG. Fug - gii pur o - ra da Ca - stel San - t'An - ge - lo . . .

[13] PIETY

Andantino sostenuto
pp

[14]

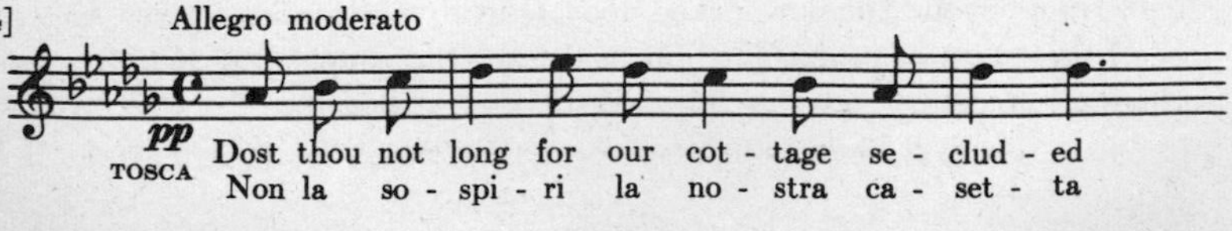
Allegro moderato
pp
TOSCA Dost thou not long for our cot - tage se - clud - ed
Non la so - spi - ri la no - stra ca - set - ta

assured by Cavaradossi. She offers flowers to a statue of the Madonna [13], and then tells him that he may expect her tonight at his villa. Although for a moment Cavaradossi fails to show enthusiasm [2], he is soon overwhelmed by the sensuous picture she paints for him [14]. However, he asks her to leave, as he is busy [2]. As she turns to go, she happens to look at the painting and recognizes it as a portrait of the Countess Attavanti, but her jealousy [11] is quickly allayed by Cavaradossi's tender assurance [15] that her beauty has no equal. After a fervent exchange of vows of love [7] she leaves.

Angelotti [2] comes from the chapel carrying women's clothes that his sister, the Countess Attavanti, has left there for him [3, 6] to help him escape from the villainous hypocrite Scarpia [1]. Cavaradossi gives him the key to his villa and suggests that he hide in a cave in the side of the well if danger should threaten [1]. When the cannon of the fort is heard thundering the alarm [2], Cavaradossi decides to accompany Angelotti, and both quickly leave.

The Sacristan enters [4, 5], again surprised at finding nobody there. He tells the noisily gathering church staff [16] that news has just arrived of the defeat of Napoleon, and he informs them about the festivities to take place in the evening [17]. The choirboys' frolicking [16, 17] at the prospect of extra pay is interrupted by the appearance of Scarpia [1] with Spoletta and other assistants. Scarpia orders all to go about their business. Then, telling the Sacristan that a political prisoner from the castle [12] has fled toward the church, he asks to be shown the chapel of the Attavanti. They find the chapel open, and in it Scarpia discovers a fan [12, 2] decorated with the coat of arms of the Countess Attavanti. Then he sees her picture [10] and learns that it was painted by Cavaradossi [6], whom he knows to be a revolutionary and the lover of Tosca. The Sacristan [4] shows Scarpia the empty food basket, and the police chief quickly deduces the facts [2].

Tosca returns [7] to call off her rendezvous, as she must sing for the victory celebration. When she doesn't find Cavaradossi, she again suspects

[15] Andante sostenuto

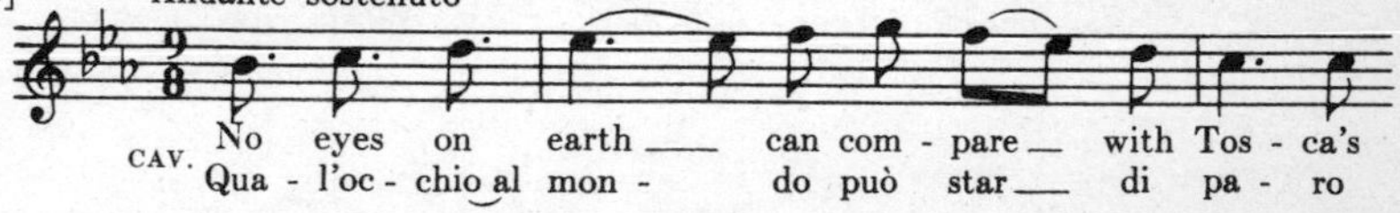
CAV.
No eyes on earth can com - pare with Tos - ca's
Qua - l'oc - chio al mon - do può star di pa - ro

[16] THE CHOIR BOYS

Allegro con spirito

f

[17] Allegro con spirito *tratt.* *tornando a tempo*

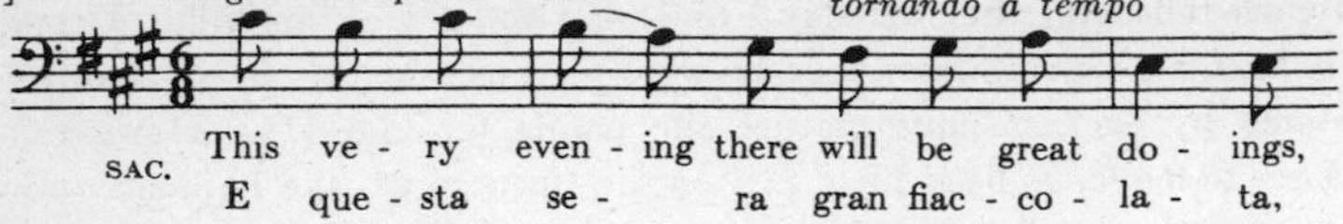
SAC.
This ve - ry even - ing there will be great do - ings,
E que - sta se - ra gran fiac - co - la - ta,

[18] Andante mosso

BELLS

[19] Largo religioso sostenuto molto

[20] DINNER
Andante

[21] GAVOTTE
Tempo di Gavotta molto moderato

[22] ARIA *HA PIU FORTE SAPORE* (Scarpia)
Andante un po' agitato

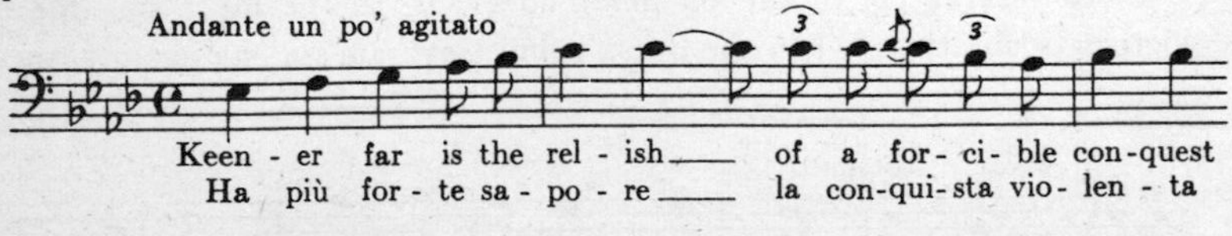
Keen - er far is the rel - ish of a for - ci - ble con - quest
Ha più for - te sa - po - re la con - qui - sta vio - len - ta

[23] QUESTIONING
Andante mosso

[24] SUFFERING
Lento

unfaithfulness. Scarpia addresses her smoothly [18] and finds occasion to mention the fan [12], which he claims to have found on the scaffolding [10]. Tosca bursts into tears, convinced that she has been betrayed. Scarpia insinuatingly assures her of his readiness to console her [18], but she is thinking only of the betrayal [12] and, in a fit of violent jealousy [2], she vows that she will surprise Cavaradossi at his villa. Weeping, she leaves [7].

Scarpia, satisfied with the success of his trickery, sends Spoletta to follow Tosca. While the church is gradually filling for the thanksgiving service [19], and the Cardinal advances with his retinue toward the main altar, Baron Scarpia joyously envisions Angelotti and Cavaradossi on the gallows and Tosca in his arms [19]. The mere thought excites him to such a degree that he quite forgets the *Te Deum,* but, roused from his dream at last, he fervently joins the chant of the worshippers and sinks on his knees [1].

Act II: Scarpia is sitting at dinner [20] at his office in the Palazzo Farnese. The window is open, and the strains of a gavotte [21] are heard from the ballroom below, where the victory celebration is in progress. Scarpia writes a note to Tosca and gives it to the guard for delivery to her as soon as she arrives at the palace. As surely as she loves Mario, he exclaims, the note will force her into submission [1]. It is violent conquest that excites Scarpia (Aria *Ha più forte sapore:* "Keener far is the relish") [22] as he pursues, wins, and then discards what beauty the gods create.

Spoletta is announced and reports how he entered Cavaradossi's villa after Tosca had left. Since he could not find Angelotti, he arrested Cavaradossi. As Scarpia orders the painter brought in [23], the sounds of the victory cantata are heard through the window. Cavaradossi meets Scarpia's suave insinuations, bland accusations, and brutal menaces with irony and scorn while Tosca's voice is heard soaring over those of the choristers until Scarpia violently shuts the window. Finally he threatens torture [1, 24], but to no avail. Just then Tosca enters [15]. Cavaradossi can only quickly whisper to her not to betray him, before he is taken into an adjoining room [23]. Scarpia gives instructions to the executioner [24], whom he had summoned at the news of Cavaradossi's arrest; then he turns to Tosca and with the greatest nonchalance asks her what she had found at the villa. She refuses to talk until he tells her that a tightening steel band is making Cavaradossi's head run with blood [25]. Thereupon she offers to speak, but when the torture is stopped, she calls to Cavaradossi and, encouraged by Mario's response, she refuses to reveal Angelotti's hiding-place. At this,

[25] TORTURE

Andante sostenuto

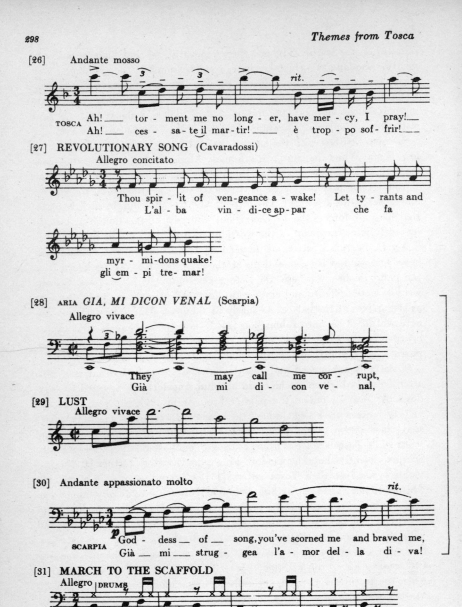

[26] Andante mosso

rit.
TOSCA
Ah! tor - ment me no long - er, have mer - cy, I pray!
Ah! ces - sa - te il mar - tir! è trop - po sof - frir!

[27] REVOLUTIONARY SONG (Cavaradossi)

Allegro concitato

Thou spir - it of ven - geance a - wake! Let ty - rants and
L'al - ba vin - di - ce ap - par che fa

myr - mi - dons quake!
gli em - pi tre - mar!

[28] ARIA *GIA, MI DICON VENAL* (Scarpia)

Allegro vivace

They may call me cor - rupt,
Già mi di - con ve - nal,

[29] LUST

Allegro vivace

[30] Andante appassionato molto

rit.
p
SCARPIA
God - dess of song, you've scorned me and braved me,
Già mi strug - gea l'a - mor del - la di - va!

[31] MARCH TO THE SCAFFOLD

Allegro

DRUMS
p
col 8va

[32] ARIA *VISSI D'ARTE* (Tosca)

Andante lento appassionato *dolcissimo con grande sentimento*

p
Love and mu - sic, these I have lived for,
Vis - si d'ar - te, vis - si d'a - mo - re,

Scarpia has the torture resumed and, with the door to the torture chamber open, he repeatedly orders the screws tightened [25]. Tosca's anguish [26] grows unbearable, and when Cavaradossi utters an agonizing cry of pain, she can resist no longer and tells Scarpia [1] where Angelotti can be found.

The torture is ended and Cavaradossi, more dead than alive, is brought in [23, 24], painfully supporting himself on the shoulders of two men [24]. Tosca kisses him tenderly [15], but when Scarpia orders Spoletta to get Angelotti from the well [1] Cavaradossi violently repulses and curses her. At this moment Sciarrone comes in to tell Scarpia that the supposed victory over Napoleon was, in reality, a crushing defeat. This news is greeted by Cavaradossi with the defiant singing of a revolutionary song (*L'alba vindice appar:* "Thou spirit of vengeance awake!") [27] while the frantic Tosca vainly tries to stop him and Scarpia promises him an early execution. Cavaradossi is taken away.

Scarpia remains alone with Tosca, who has been brutally stopped in her desperate efforts [26] to follow Cavaradossi. Calmly Scarpia returns to his interrupted meal [20] and suavely suggests that there may still be a possibility of saving her friend. Tosca's offer of money only makes Scarpia smile. It is true, he admits, that people call him corrupt (Aria *Già, mi dicon venal:* "They may call me corrupt") [28], but no woman could ever bribe him with money [29]. He is filled with a wild desire for Tosca [30], and he must possess her [29]. If she hates him, so much the better. As Tosca, vainly shouting for help [26], tries to flee from him, the sound of drums is heard in the distance. This is the sound, Scarpia explains, that escorts the condemned to the execution [31], and while Tosca hesitates, Cavaradossi has barely one hour to live. In helpless despair, Tosca asks (Aria *Vissi d'arte:* "Love and music") [32] why the Lord whom she has served so devoutly [13] has called this misery down upon her [26]. On her knees she begs mercy from Scarpia, but he is inflexible [28, 29].

Spoletta enters and reports that Angelotti has committed suicide at his approach [2]. When Scarpia asks about Cavaradossi, Spoletta answers that "all is ready." At this, Tosca silently nods assent to Scarpia's whispered question about her decision, and she hears him order a "simulated" death by the firing squad for Cavaradossi in "just the way it had been handled once before." Scarpia dismisses Spoletta [1] and declares that his duties in the bargain are completed, but Tosca now demands a safe-conduct to flee the country with Cavaradossi. While Scarpia writes it, Tosca, lost in an abyss of misery [33], suddenly spies a knife on the table, and when Scarpia, bearing the safe-conduct, comes to embrace her [29], she stabs him. Triumphantly she sees him die [1 *pianissimo*]. Then she cleans the blood from her fingers [33], frantically searches for the safe-conduct, and finally finds it in Scarpia's clenched fist. She extricates it and turns to leave, but stops [29] to light two candles, which she places at either side of Scarpia's head [1*ppp*]. Then she removes a crucifix from the wall and places it reverently on his breast. Cautiously she leaves the room.

[33] DISTRESS

Andante sostenuto
pp

[34] STARLIT NIGHT

Andante sostenuto
pp

[35] THE SHEPHERD'S SONG

Andante molto sostenuto
Fly, sighs of sad- ness, ______ to her who does not
Io de' so- spi- ri, ______ Te ne ri - man - no
love me! ______
tan- ti, ______

[36] NOSTALGIA

Andante lento appassionato molto
p
rit. rubando rit. a tempo

[37]

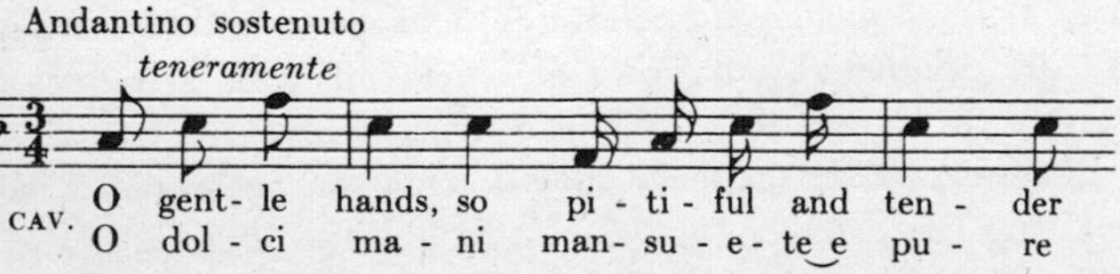
Andantino sostenuto
teneramente
CAV.
O gent- le hands, so pi - ti - ful and ten - der
O dol - ci ma - ni man- su - e- te e pu - re

[38] THE MOCK EXECUTION

Andantino moderatamente mosso

Introduction to Act III: Motive [39], then [34] and [1].

Act III: A clear night sky [34] arches over the Castle of Sant' Angelo, Rome's prison and place of execution [1]. In the distance a shepherd is heard singing his age-old tune [35 with 34]. At the first uncertain light of dawn, Rome's church bells ring the matins. Cavaradossi is brought to the casemate atop the fort to spend his last hour [36]. The jailer, bribed with a ring, permits him to write a letter to his beloved [7]. Nostalgically remembering the times spent with her [36] (Aria *E lucevan le stelle:* "When the stars were brightly shining"), he gives voice to his despair at dying so young. Spoletta appears with Tosca [7] and, after a few words with the jailer, leaves again, while Tosca rushes toward Cavaradossi and shows him the safe-conduct signed by Scarpia [1]. She tells him about the loathsome bargain: Scarpia asked for her love in exchange for Cavaradossi's life. In vain she prayed to all the Saints [13]. Pointing through the window toward the gallows ready to receive her lover [31], he smilingly [29] forced her to agree. In her deep distress [33] she found a knife while he was writing the safe-conduct and killed him as he approached her. Mario looks in wonderment at the delicate hands [37] that could commit murder [33]. She now tells him about the simulated execution [38] he must submit to before they can flee together. Ecstatically they plan the future of their love. She reminds him that he must pretend to be shot, and fall at the discharge of the rifle blanks [38]. In radiant hope, they sing to the future [39] as the firing squad is arriving. Tosca whispers to Cavaradossi to continue lying on the ground until she calls him [38]. Then he is taken away [40]. Tosca remains to watch the execution from a distance and admires the artistry with which Cavaradossi falls. Anxiously she waits until all have left [40]; then she calls to him. As she approaches and finally lifts the blanket with which he has been covered, she discovers with a scream that he has in fact been executed. From below, Sciarrone is heard reporting to Spoletta that Scarpia has been killed. Spoletta rushes in with soldiers to arrest Tosca. When he is about to lay hands on her, she violently pushes him back, jumps onto the parapet, and hurls herself into space [36].

[39] Andante sostenuto

TOSCA & Hope is nigh, fil-ling my heart with heav-en-ly ar- dor,
CAV. Tri - on - fal di no- va spe - me l'a - ni-ma fre- me

[40] THE EXECUTION

Largo con gravità

THEMES

[1] Adagio

[2] Allegro brillantissimo e molto vivace

[3] THE BRINDISI *LIBIAMO* (Alfredo, Violetta)

Allegretto *con grazia leggerissimo*

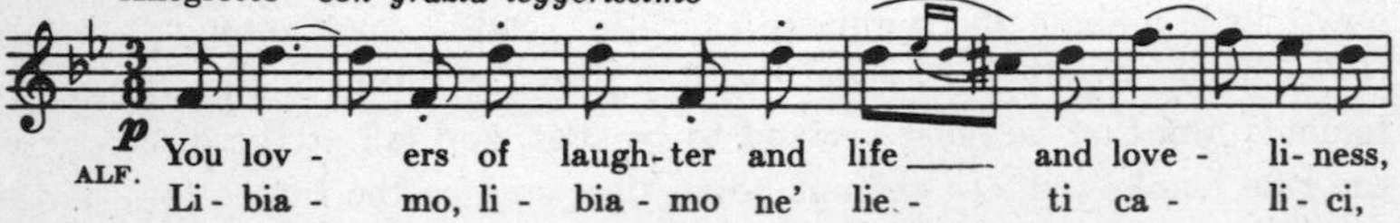
ALF.
You lov - ers of laugh-ter and life ___ and love - li-ness,
Li - bia - mo, li - bia - mo ne' lie - ti ca - li - ci,

[4] Allegro brillante

[5] DUET *UN DI FELICE* (Alfredo, Violetta)

Andantino

ALF.
The day I met you, O bless - ed day, When first you
Un dì fe - li - ce, e - te - re - a mi ba - le -
came be - fore ___ me,
na - ste in - nan - te,

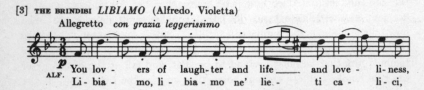

La Traviata

Opera in three acts by Giuseppe Verdi. Libretto by Francesco Maria Piave after Alexander Dumas' *La Dame aux Camelias* ("Camille"). First performance: Venice, March 6, 1853.

Characters: VIOLETTA VALERY (soprano); ALFREDO GERMONT (tenor); GIORGIO GERMONT, his father (baritone); FLORA BERVOIX (mezzo-soprano); GASTONE (tenor); BARON DOUPHOL (baritone); DR. GRENVIL (bass); ANNINA, Violetta's maid (soprano).
In and near Paris, in the late 1840's.

Prelude to Act I: A theme of most tender sadness opens the prelude—the same theme that introduces the last act, in which Violetta is slowly dying [1]. There follows the motive of Violetta's desperate plea for Alfredo's love [16]; but here—although contrasted by violin passages characteristic of Violetta's lighter nature—it is dressed in the most sensitive hues. Gradually the music dies away.

Act I: At Violetta's house a glittering party is in progress [2]. Gastone approaches the hostess and introduces to her Alfredo, who, he explains, has long admired her from afar. Violetta asks her guests to take their seats for supper, and Alfredo is called upon to propose a toast, in which he is joined by the hostess and the guests (The Brindisi *Libiamo:* "You lovers") [3].

Music is heard from the inner rooms [4], and Violetta invites her friends to go in and dance. A sudden attack of weakness—her chronic ailment, she explains—forces her to remain behind for the moment. Regarding her pale face in the mirror, she suddenly notices that Alfredo has not left with the others. He tells her that he has loved her since the first time he saw her (Duet *Un dì felice:* "The day I met you") [5], and that this love is still burning in his heart [6], but Violetta suggests that he forget her, for her own emotions follow a lighter pattern [7] and she is not given to serious affection. Alfredo obediently takes his leave, but, to his great joy, he is invited to return the next day [4].

The guests re-enter, and, thanking their hostess for the splendid entertainment [8], they depart. Violetta remains in deep thought (Recitative *È strano:* "How strange!"). For the first time she is experiencing true love. Alfredo has awakened a new feeling in her heart (Aria *Ah, fors' è lui:* "Ah, can it be") [9]—love, the power that moves heaven and earth [6]. But no, all this must be folly (Recitative *Follie!:* "What follies!"); for her there

[6] DUET *UN DI FELICE* (Alfredo, Violetta) *continued*

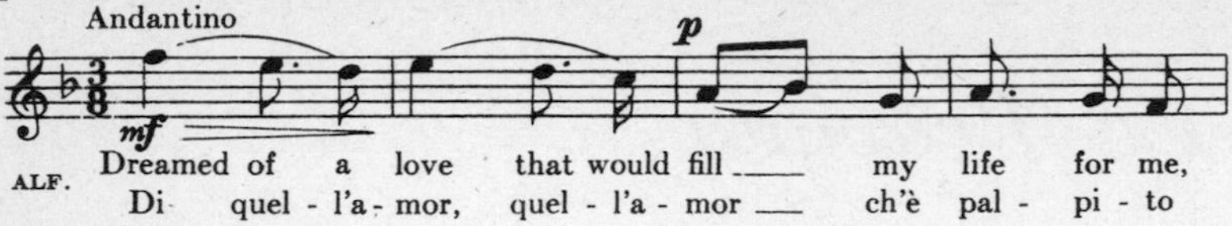
Andantino
p
mf
ALF.
Dreamed of a love that would fill ___ my life for me,
Di quel - l'a - mor, quel - l'a - mor ___ ch'è pal - pi - to

[7]

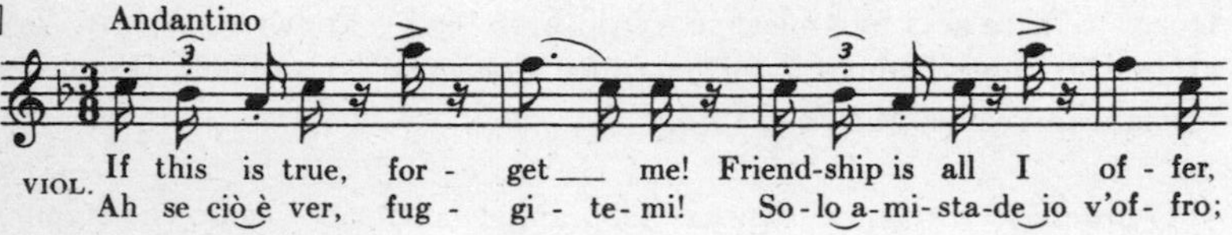
Andantino
VIOL.
If this is true, for - get ___ me! Friend-ship is all I of - fer,
Ah se ciò è ver, fug - gi - te- mi! So-lo a-mi-sta-de io v'of- fro;

[8]

Allegro vivo
pp
CHORUS
See, the morn - ing sun is ___ gleam - ing, Let us
Si ri - de - sta in ciel l'au - ro - ra, e n'è
now de - part from hence. ___
for - za di par - ti - re

[9] ARIA *AH FORS'È LUI* (Violetta)

Andantino
p
Ah, can it be that this is he
Ah, for - s'è lui che l'a - ni - ma
Of whom my heart fore - told me,
so - lin - ga ne' tu - mul - ti,

[10]

Allegro brillante
tr
Ev - er free to take ___ my chanc - es in the
Sem - pre li - be - ra ___ deg - g'i - o fol - leg -
game of fol - ly and pleas - ure!
gia - re di gio- ja in gio - ja!

is only the unshackled life of never ending pleasure (Cabaletta *Sempre libera:* "Ever free") [10]—and Alfredo's pleading from the garden [6] remains unheeded.

Act II, Scene 1: At a country house near Paris, Alfredo is happily reflecting on the past three months, which Violetta has been spending with him here (Aria *De' miei bollenti spiriti:* "Fevered and wild my dream of youth") [11] (the Cabaletta is generally omitted). Quickly his happiness gives way to preoccupation when Violetta's maid, Annina, informs him that her mistress is selling all her possessions in town to pay for this house. He rushes off to prevent the sale.

Violetta enters and is given a letter in which Flora invites her to a ball that evening, but such invitations no longer interest her.

Unexpectedly Alfredo's father arrives (Duet *Madamigella Valery?:* "Is it Violetta Valery?") to accuse her of ruining his son. He is forced to change his opinion of Violetta when he is shown the sales contract through which she is disposing of her Paris apartments. Giorgio Germont demands nevertheless that she leave Alfredo forever in order that the engagement of Alfredo's sister may be brought to a happy conclusion [12]. Although Violetta swears that she has renounced her former life and that her only happiness lies in Alfredo's love, without which she would prefer to die [13], Germont convinces her that God and the world will not grant to women like herself the blessing of a permanent love. Sorrowfully acceding to Germont's demand, she asks in return only that Alfredo's sister be told about this sacrifice [14] that surely will cause Violetta's death. Germont's consoling voice joins Violetta's heart-rending farewell to love. Grateful and with a blessing, Germont leaves.

With a superhuman effort Violetta gathers her strength to compose a letter promising a rendezvous to Baron Douphol—the only means of convincing Alfredo that she no longer loves him—and sends Annina to deliver it. Now for a farewell note to Alfredo: how to find words to cover up her grief [15]? Just as she is signing the missive, Alfredo returns. Quickly she hides the note and, in a state of utter confusion, she hysterically assures him of her love and begs him to love her always [16].

[11] ARIA *DE' MIEI BOLLENTI SPIRITI* (Alfredo)

[12] FROM DUET *MADAMIGELLA VALERY* (Germont, Violetta)

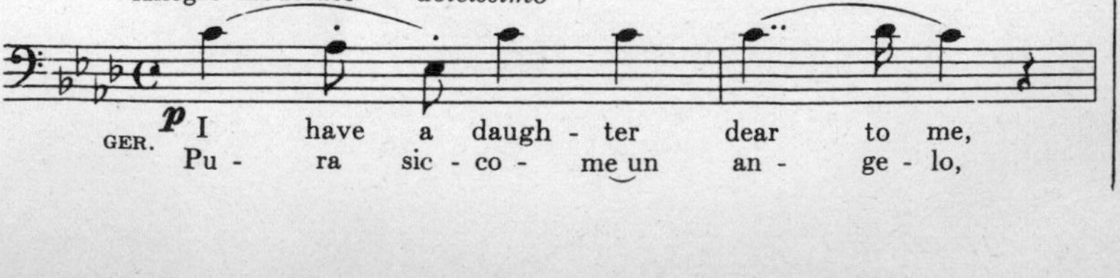

[13] Vivacissimo

VIOL.
Ah, you know— not how I love— him, how I
Non sa - pe - te qua-le af - fet - to vi- vo, im-
treas - ure___ naught a - bove— him,
men - so ___ m'ar- de in pet - to?

[14] Andantino cantabile

VIOL.
Speak to your bless - ed child, Say, when you see___ her,
Di - te al - la gio - vi - ne sì bel - la e pu - ra,

[15] Adagio

[16] Allegro assai mosso

VIOL.
Love me, Al - fre - do
A - ma - mi, Al - fre - do

[17] ARIA *DI PROVENZA* (Germont)

Andante piuttosto mosso

In Pro-vence, the south-ern sea soft - ly cools the sun- lit shore,
Di Pro- ven-za il mar, il suol, chi dal cor ti can- cel- lò?

[18] Allegro brillante

8va

[19] Allegro moderato

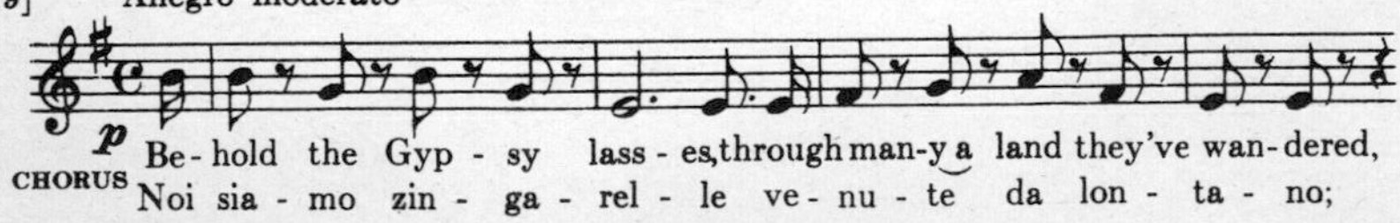
CHORUS
Be- hold the Gyp - sy lass - es, through man-y a land they've wan- dered,
Noi sia - mo zin - ga - rel - le ve - nu - te da lon - ta - no;

[20] Allegro assai vivo

CHORUS
Young ___ Pi - quil - lo in ___ Bis - cay - a
E ___ Pi - quil- lo un bel ___ ga - gliar - do

Alfredo is left alone, and presently a messenger brings the farewell note from Violetta, who is already on her way to Paris. Trembling, Alfredo opens it and reads. As he turns in desperation, he is met by Germont, who has entered from the garden to console his son and to ask him to return to the family home in Provence (Aria *Di Provenza:* "In Provence") [17]. (The Cabaletta always omitted.) But Alfredo finds Flora's invitation, and rushes off to look for Violetta at the ball.

Act II, Scene 2: At Flora's house the festivities are about to begin [18]. Masqueraders enter dressed as gypsy girls [19] and bullfighters [20]. Alfredo's entrance without Violetta causes general surprise, but soon all the guests sit down to gamble [21]. Violetta appears on the arm of Baron Douphol and is greatly perturbed when she discovers Alfredo's presence [22]. Provoked by Alfredo, the Baron challenges him but, thanks to Violetta's intervention, only to a game of cards in which the rich Baron hopes to ruin Alfredo. However, Alfredo wins consistently until the game is interrupted by the announcement of supper. As soon as all have left the room, Violetta returns in agitation and Alfredo, whom she has summoned to meet her, also comes back. In great perturbation and anxiety, she asks him to leave. Under his ruthless questioning, Violetta, who has sworn to Germont not to reveal the truth, is forced to pretend that she loves Douphol. Thereupon in a rage, Alfredo calls back all the guests and, in repayment

[21]

[22]

[23]

[24] Largo

CHORUS
Sad heart, have cour- age, we share thy woe.
O quan - to pe - ni! ma pur fa cor.

[25] Largo

VIOL.
O Al - fred, Al - fred, a - las, thou know'st not How true and
Al- fre-do, Al-fre - do, di que - sto co - re non puoi com-

ten- der- ly this heart has lov'd thee!
pren- de- re tut- to l'a - mo - re!

[26] ARIA *ADDIO DEL PASSATO* (Violetta)

Andante mosso

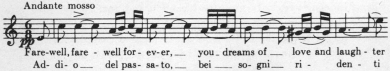

Fare-well, fare - well for - ev- er, you dreams of love and laugh - ter
Ad- di- o del pas- sa- to, bei so- gni ri - den - ti

[27] Allegro vivacissimo

CHORUS
Crown him with gar- lands, sur- round him with danc- es,
Lar - go al qua- dru - pe - de sir del - la fe - sta,

[28] DUET *PARIGI O CARA* (Alfredo, Violetta)

Andante mosso

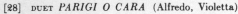

ALF.
Pa - ris, be - lov - ed, we'll leave for - ev - er,
Pa - ri - gi, o ca - ra, noi la - sce - re - mo,

[29] Allegro

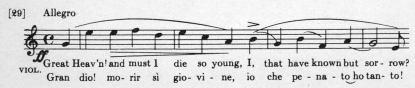

VIOL.
Great Heav'n! and must I die so young, I, that have known but sor - row?
Gran dio! mo- rir sì gio- vi - ne, io che pe - na - to ho tan- to!

[30] Andante

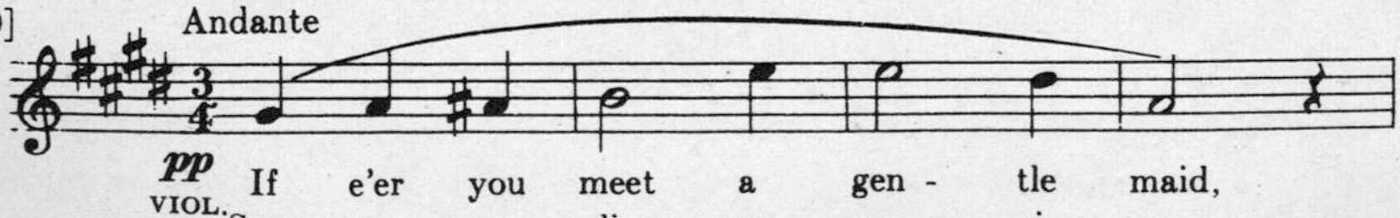
VIOL.
If e'er you meet a gen - tle maid,
Se u - na pu - di - ca ver - gi - ne,

for her expenses, throws his winnings at Violetta's feet. The guests are shocked [23], and Giorgio Germont, who has just entered, sternly rebukes his son for his behavior. Alfredo is now overcome with remorse; and as the guests try to console Violetta [24], she declares, her voice soaring over theirs, that her love for Alfredo is greater than he can ever comprehend [25]. As Alfredo is led away by his father, Douphol challenges him by throwing a glove at his feet.

Introduction (*Prelude*) *to Act III:* The strains that open the overture [1] are heard, infinitely sad and resigned, as is the mood of Violetta, who, lonely and forgotten by her friends, awaits her approaching death.

Act III: In her poor quarters, Violetta, with the faithful Annina by her side, is asleep. She awakens and, in a voice that betrays her condition, asks Annina for some water. Dr. Grenvil comes in on his daily visit. Although he talks encouragingly to Violetta, he tells Annina that her mistress has but a few hours to live.

Violetta demands to know how much money she has left. Informed by Annina that the amount is pitifully small, she nevertheless orders that half of it be distributed to the poor immediately. At the same time, she asks Annina to see whether there is any mail for her. Left alone, she draws a letter of Germont's from her bosom [6] to reread it once again: Baron Douphol is recovering from wounds sustained in the duel. Alfredo has gone abroad, but, informed by Germont himself of Violetta's sacrifice, he is returning to ask for her pardon. Germont will also come.

"Too late," exclaims Violetta in despair. Gone are the rosy dreams of the past; all is over for Violetta (Aria *Addio del passato:* "Farewell, farewell forever") [26]. As she breaks down in tears, the gay sounds of the Paris carnival penetrate from the street [27].

Annina enters excitedly, followed by Alfredo. After a passionate embrace, Alfredo and Violetta ask each other's forgiveness and promise to remain together for the rest of their lives. They will go far away from Paris (Duet *Parigi, o cara:* "Paris, beloved") [28], and Violetta's health will soon be restored. But, attempting to dress, Violetta collapses and realizes in desperation that her end is at hand just at the threshold of her love's fulfillment [29].

Annina, who has gone for the doctor, now returns with him and with the elder Germont, come to accept Violetta as a daughter. With a shock he realizes that she is dying as a result of his interference. Violetta turns to Alfredo and, in a halting voice, gives him a medallion bearing her likeness, to remind him of the days when she still looked beautiful. "Someday," she says, as the helpless bystanders fight to repress their tears, "you will marry a pure maiden. Give her this portrait and tell her that I will be praying in heaven for you and her." [30] Suddenly she feels all pain disappearing [6] and new life surging through her body, and, with an expression of supreme happiness on her face, she falls dead in Alfredo's arms.

THEMES

[1] LONGING [2] MYSTERY

Lento e languido

[3] TRISTAN

Lento e languido

[4] THE GAZE

Lento e languido

[5] LOVE POTION

Lento e languido

[6] DEATH POTION

Tristan und Isolde

Opera in three acts by Richard Wagner. Libretto by the composer. First performance: Munich, June 10, 1865.

Characters: KING MARKE (bass); TRISTAN, his nephew (tenor); KURWENAL, Tristan's warrior-companion (baritone); ISOLDE, heiress to the Irish throne (soprano); BRANGÄNE, her companion (soprano or mezzo-soprano); MELOT (tenor or baritone); A SHEPHERD (tenor); A HELMSMAN (baritone); THE VOICE OF A YOUNG SAILOR (tenor).
Cornwall and Brittany, in the Middle Ages.

Prelude to Act I: The music starts with the motives characterizing the transcendental love of Tristan and Isolde. This is a love capable of fulfillment only in death—a love, therefore, which in this world of the living must be marred by suffering and longing [1]. Its mystery [2], springing from Isolde's magic potions, is manifest also in Tristan [3], in whose gaze [4] are revealed all the emotions stirred by the love potion [5 ending with the motive of the death potion 6]—all the emotions that comprise the love of Tristan and Isolde [7]. A motive of frenzied yearning [8; 8 with 2] leads to a climax on [1] and [2]; then the fabric of motives [1] to [7] gradually thins out, and the curtain opens.

Act I: Brangäne holds open the tapestry that separates Isolde's tent from the rest of the deck of Tristan's ship. The voice of a young sailor is heard singing to the wind to continue its blowing [9], and mixing into his song ironical phrases about a wild and lovely Irish maiden.

Isolde, who has been lying on her couch hiding her head in the pillows, jumps up, looking wildly about her [4],* outraged at the mockery. To her distraught question as to their whereabouts, her companion answers that under prevailing conditions [9] they should reach Cornwall by evening. Never, shouts Isolde, and, trying to reawaken within herself her mother's long-unused powers over the winds [9, 2], she violently calls for a raging hurricane to swallow up the ship and everyone on it. Brangäne implores her to reveal the cause of her strange behavior—why she left home without a tear [2] and with scarcely a farewell [4], and why she has remained silent and without food during the entire voyage. Isolde, gasping for air, bids Brangäne open the tent. As the maid obeys, the deck toward starboard

* Themes [2–6] often appear with changed meter and at times in a fast tempo, thereby radically changing character and meaning.

[7] TRISTAN AND ISOLDE

Lento e languido

[8] LOVE'S YEARNING

Lento e languido

[9] FROM THE SONG OF THE YOUNG SAILOR

Moderato

The west wind wild blows home - ward now,
Frisch weht der Wind der Hei - mat zu:

[10] CONSECRATION TO DEATH

Moderato

f
p
p
pp
a
b

[11] KURWENAL'S MOROLD-SONG

Vivace

To lay a tax on Cor - nish_ backs, Sir
Herr Mo - rold zog zu Mee - re__ her, in

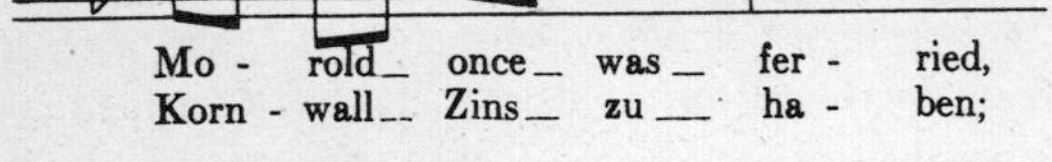
Mo - rold_ once_ was_ fer - ried,
Korn - wall_ Zins_ zu__ ha - ben;

[12] Molto vivace

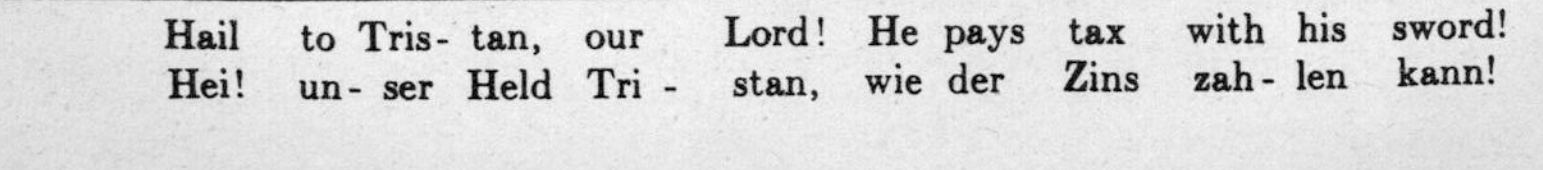
Hail to Tris- tan, our Lord! He pays tax with his sword!
Hei! un- ser Held Tri - stan, wie der Zins zah- len kann!

becomes visible, disclosing sailors and soldiers and, at the helm, Tristan, with Kurwenal, his faithful companion, beside him. The young sailor is singing again [9], but Isolde's attention is centered on Tristan [2 with 1], whose death she has vowed to bring about [10]. Scornfully commenting to her companion on the hero [3] who does not dare look at her [4], afraid that he may bring his King a corpse for a bride [2], she asks Brangäne to go and bid Tristan come and pay obeisance to his mistress. Brangäne, approaching Tristan, startles him from his dreaming. Although he courteously addresses his mistress' messenger [3], he replies evasively to her polite invitation. When finally she is forced to quote Isolde's command, Kurwenal rudely answers that Tristan need not bow to anyone. Over the objections of Tristan, his booming voice intones a lampoon on Morold—Isolde's late fiancé—who had come to Cornwall to exact tribute and whose head Tristan had sent to Ireland as payment [11, 12]. Brangäne has fled in confusion, and as the men repeat the refrain of Kurwenal's song [12] she quickly lowers the tapestry, once more closing off the tent. Isolde, with a desperate effort to maintain composure, makes her repeat everything Tristan has said, and then tells Brangäne how it happens that, to her bitter shame, she is now sailing to Cornwall as a tribute paid by Ireland [10a, 12]: One day an ailing man [13] calling himself "Tantris" landed in a small, battered boat on Ireland's coast to seek healing from Isolde's skill, but she recognized him as "Tristan" [12] when she noticed in his sword a dent corresponding to the scrap of steel she had extracted from Morold's head. She was standing before his couch, the sword raised high, ready to strike, when Tristan [3] gazed into her eyes [4]. Unable to strike the blow, she healed him quickly to be rid of this haunting look. It is this poor, sick man's praise they have just heard sung [12], she tells the surprised Brangäne. Although he swore eternal gratitude, she continues, he returned quickly to demand the heiress of the Irish throne as a bride for old King Marke, who had paid tribute as long as Morold was alive. All this because she had once weakened [4] when he was in her power [13]. Though she had saved him in silence, he had braggingly offered to fetch the beautiful Irish maiden for Marke [12], as he was familiar with the country [13] and looked forward to the adventure [12]. May he be accursed! May death be his fate, and hers!

Affectionately Brangäne tries to calm her, pointing out that Tristan resigned succession to Marke's throne by making Isolde Marke's queen and the wife of a ruler of unequaled power, of a man both gentle and noble-minded. However, Isolde can see only an unbearable future living near Tristan and not being loved by him [7, 3]. Brangäne enthusiastically claims that no man ever saw Isolde without loving her, and if there were such, the magic resources [2] of Isolde's mother, the queen, would come to her aid. Isolde comments that these resources will help her in her revenge [10], and orders her companion to bring the casket containing the magic potions. Brangäne places it before her mistress [7, 8] and points out among

[13] TRISTAN'S AILING

Mosso

[14] SAILORS' CRIES

Allegro

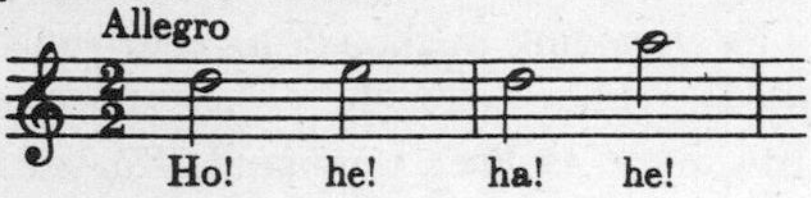
Ho! he! ha! he!

[15] TRISTAN, THE HERO

Lento

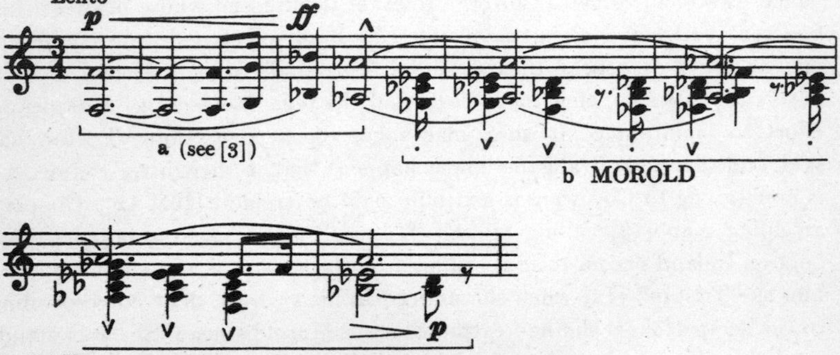
p
ff
a (see [3])
b MOROLD
p

[16] DAY

Molto vivace

ff

[17] IMPATIENCE

Molto vivace

p

[18] ARDOR

Molto vivace

p
3
a

[19] ECSTASY

a Molto vivace

c

the flasks [2] what she considers the most important one [3, 5], but Isolde is interested only in the death potion [6, 2].

The sailors' calls [14] are heard as they begin to take in the sails, and Kurwenal enters [14, 9] to order the women to prepare for the landing, and to tell Isolde that Tristan is looking forward to escorting her to the King. However, Isolde sends a message informing Tristan that she will not go until he has come to atone for his guilt and to receive her pardon [10]. When Kurwenal has gone, Isolde bids her companion a fervent farewell, but when Brangäne anxiously asks where she is going, she quickly regains her composure: she will stay here [6] and wait for Tristan [15a], who will expiate his guilt by drinking the potion she now indicates to the horrified Brangäne. Mockingly she thanks her companion for reminding her of the magic resources of the queen [2], who as a remedy for deepest sorrow has provided the death potion [6, 10].

Kurwenal announces his master and retires when Tristan enters [15ab, 6]. Tristan asks his lady's wish, and Isolde, after complaining at length about his negligent behavior toward her, declares that Morold's blood [15b] still cries for revenge [10a]. If the nations have made peace, Isolde has a private score to settle [13] because it was for her that Morold [15b] went to battle and was killed [15a]. Isolde then spared the ailing Tristan [13], she claims, so that a man could defeat him and thereby gain Isolde's hand. But now the men have all made peace with Tristan and the task of vengeance has fallen on her shoulders. Somberly [4] Tristan takes his sword and holds it out to her [15b], but Isolde refuses it. King Marke would take it amiss; furthermore, she has tried that once [13] in vain [4]. Instead, she suggests, as she nods commandingly to Brangäne, they will drink expiation [6]. At the call of the sailors [14], Tristan, startled from his brooding, asks: "Where are we?" and is ironically answered by Isolde: "Close to our destination!" [10] Soon, she goes on, Tristan will be able to tell King Marke what a mild and forgiving spouse he is bringing in, for all he had to do to atone for killing her fiancé and for bringing her country into dishonor was to sip a peace potion [6]. Impetuously Tristan takes the cup that Brangäne has filled. He knows the Queen's arts well, he declares, and the potion will be a welcome balm. With his honor unblemished [15a] he will find relief from his eternal sorrow in the potion of oblivion [10]. He drinks, but before he can finish the draught, Isolde snatches the cup from him [4] and drinks [1, 2] her half of it. Motionless, they stare at each other [10b], but the expressions on their faces gradually change. With quivering voices they call each other's names and a moment later they are rapturously embracing [1, 2, 3, 4, 7]. Shouts of "Hail King Marke" penetrate the tent and drive home to Brangäne what disaster she has caused by her misguided loyalty. Tristan and Isolde are aware only of their feelings for each other [2, 7, 4, 8; 8 with 2; 5 with 1; 4]. When the tapestry is lifted [14], Brangäne rushes between the lovers and puts the royal robe around Isolde. Kurwenal approaches [14, 9] to inform Tristan

b Molto vivace

[20] HUNTING CALL

Molto vivace

[21] LOVE

Andante con moto

p

[22] YEARNING FOR DEATH

Un poco tenuto

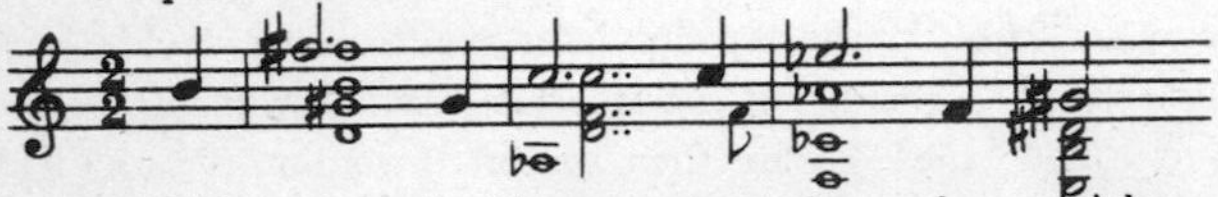
TRISTAN
Bid yearn - ing hence to ho - ly night,
Das Seh - nen hin zur heil' - gen Nacht,

[23] NIGHT OF LOVE

Molto moderato

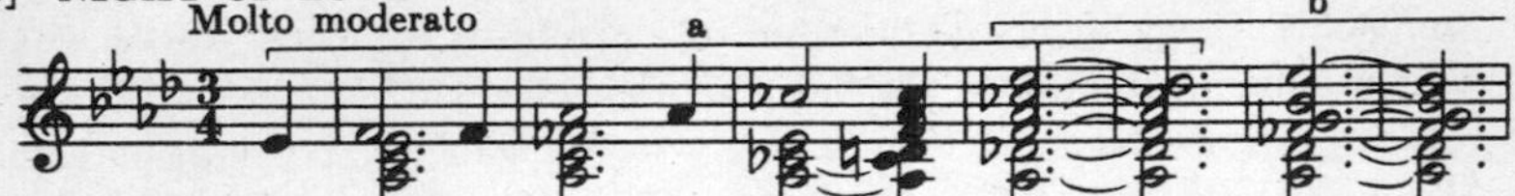
a
b
TRISTAN
O night of love, de - scend up - on us
O sink' her - nie - der, Nacht der Lie - be

[24] BLISS OF NIGHT

Molto moderato *tranquillo*

p
ISOLDE
Could our hearts — the sun but im - pris - on,
Barg im Bu - sen uns sich die Son - ne,

[25] LOVE OF TRISTAN AND ISOLDE

Tranquillo

pp

of Marke's arrival in a boat. When the desperate Brangäne confesses to her mistress that she has poured the love potion [5], instead of the death potion, Isolde faints. Tristan stands torn between bliss and bitter despair [10] as all hail the approaching Marke.

Prelude to Act II: The music sets the mood for the following scene, contrasting the motive of the glaring light of day [16] with Isolde's impatient longing [17] for night and its wonders [18 with 17; 2, 19a].

Act II: Isolde, standing in her garden on the steps leading to her rooms, anxiously listens to the varied sounds of the summer night [20, 18, 2, 19a]. No longer can she hear the horns of the royal party leaving for a night hunt [20], but Brangäne warns her that only the force of her desire [19a] makes her deaf to the sound of the horns. Isolde, in her turn, accuses her companion of wanting to keep Tristan from her [18, 19a]. She discounts Brangäne's warning that Melot has planned this sudden hunt [20], not out of friendship for Tristan, but with treachery in mind. She orders her companion to extinguish the torch, thereby giving Tristan the sign to approach [18, 18a]. Brangäne, in desperate fear for her mistress, bemoans the hour when she exchanged potions [2] and, instead of quick death [6, 10], prepared shame and eternal grief for her. However, Isolde considers it the mysterious work of the Goddess of Love [2], who came to claim for herself those whom Isolde had destined for death [10, 6]. Whatever Love commands, Isolde will obey [21], she declares, and the torch must be extinguished so that Love may shine [19a]. She sends Brangäne to the watch tower and in furious ecstasy [18] throws the torch to the ground [10]. Anxiously she listens [17], waves her veil, sees Tristan approaching, and, when he arrives, rushes jubilantly into his arms [19ac].

Their incoherent ejaculations [21, 18] eventually turn into a condemnation of light in general and, more specifically, of the hated torch [16], but Isolde gently reminds Tristan that he himself has once been a creature of the day [12]. Yet Isolde has always been his [21]: only the trickery of day [16] could have made it seem otherwise. Tristan tells [16] how his love for Isolde was so distorted by the day that, under pressure of the quest for honors and glory, he decided, spiting himself, to bring her to Cornwall as the King's bride. Isolde relates [16] how she, in consequence, had to hate the man she loved, for he was blinded by the day, and how she attempted to flee day and to take Tristan with her [10] into the land of eternal night [2]. Tristan recalls how, the fateful cup in his hand, he felt the peace of night pervading his entire being [motive 23a]. But the potion deceived him [2], interrupts Isolde, in his hope for death [10a]. Blessed be the potion [2]! exclaims Tristan. Although it restored him to the day [16], it afforded him a clearer vision of the mysteries of night [21]. Now, consecrated to night, they can no longer be deceived by day's splendor [2 with 16]. Having understood the mystery of death [10], they will, even though surrounded by the vain glitter of day [16], see

[26] **LOVE IN THE BEYOND**

Tranquillo
p
TRISTAN
So might we die as ne'er —— to part,
So stür - ben wir, um un - ge - trennt,

[27]

Allegro molto

[28] **MARKE'S GRIEF**

Molto moderato
p espressivo
f
3
dim
p

[29]

Molto moderato

[30] **THE LAND OF OBLIVION**

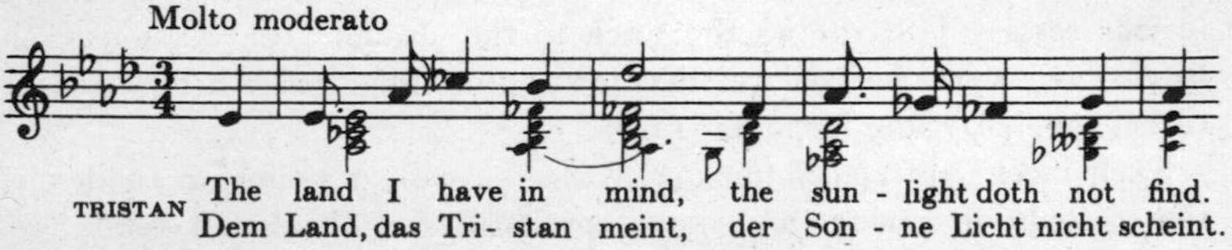
Molto moderato
TRISTAN
The land I have in mind, the sun - light doth not find.
Dem Land, das Tri- stan meint, der Son - ne Licht nicht scheint.

[31] **DESPAIR** (see [16])

Molto moderato
f

[32] **SOLITUDE**

Molto moderato

[33] **LANGUID SUFFERING**

Molto moderato
p dolcissimo

through its falseness [2 with 16] and retain the longing [18] for night [22], where alone true love's bliss can be found.

As Isolde sits on a hillock, Tristan kneels at her side [19; 16 gradually fading out], and together they invoke the night of love to envelop them (Love Duet *O sink hernieder, Nacht der Liebe:* "O night of love, descend upon us") [23]. They feel that all light is disappearing [16] except the light of bliss within their hearts [24] which unites them [25] and, in contrast to the false world of day [16], creates for them a world of love all their own [2, 24, 22], from which they hope never again to awake.

From the tower Brangäne sounds her warning call [23b, 24, 25], but Tristan and Isolde [25] would rather die [22], than awaken. Death cannot destroy their love [22], but only that which impedes it. Death, then, would mean eternal bliss (continuation of Love Duet *So stürben wir, um ungetrennt:* "So might we die as ne'er to part") [26]. Again Brangäne warns that the night is passing, and again they decide to escape day by dying [25, 22] and to flee the light forever [16, 19a]. Ecstatically they dedicate themselves once more to night and love [22, 23b, 26, 27, 19bc]. At the height of their exultation Brangäne suddenly utters a horrified cry and Kurwenal enters with bared sword, shouting to Tristan to save himself. Immediately behind him the hunting party [20] follows [17] and its members stop aghast before the lovers. Isolde turns her head away, and Tristan, half unconsciously, attempts to protect her from their view [26, 27]. Finally he murmurs: "The bleak day for the last time" [16].

Melot proudly asks the King whether he has not proved his accusation [16], but Marke is filled only with deep sadness [28]. Why, he wishes to know, would Tristan, the noblest champion of virtue and honor, deal thus with him? Why, he asks in deepest sorrow [29], would Tristan crown his innumerable services with such a deed? Why did he insist on bringing him this noble bride whom Marke dared admire only from afar—this wonderful woman who was his pride and who filled his heart with new tenderness—if now he must strike him where he has become most vulnerable? Why has he inflicted on him a wound from which there is no recovery [6] and destroyed his honor beyond repair and redemption?

Sadly Tristan professes himself incapable of an explanation [1, 2]. He turns to Isolde [25] and gently asks whether she will follow him to his destination [22], to the land of darkness [30], the mysterious realm of the night [23, 30] to which he now invites her [25, 22].

Once, Isolde recalls, a hostile Tristan bade her follow him to a foreign land, and she could not but obey. How happy will she be now to leave with him for the land that is his true realm [30], his home [25], if he will but show the way [22]! Tenderly Tristan kisses her on the forehead [3, 27].

When Melot, scandalized, draws his sword, Tristan sarcastically recalls their former friendship, and then sadly explains to Isolde that Melot, blinded by her beauty [2] and moved by jealousy, turned traitor to his friend who himself had turned traitor to the King! Suddenly he calls out

[34] THE SHEPHERD'S SAD TUNE

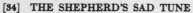

Molto moderato
a
p
f
b
3
p
cresc.
f
dim.
p
c Molto moderato
p
sf
p

[35] CAREOL

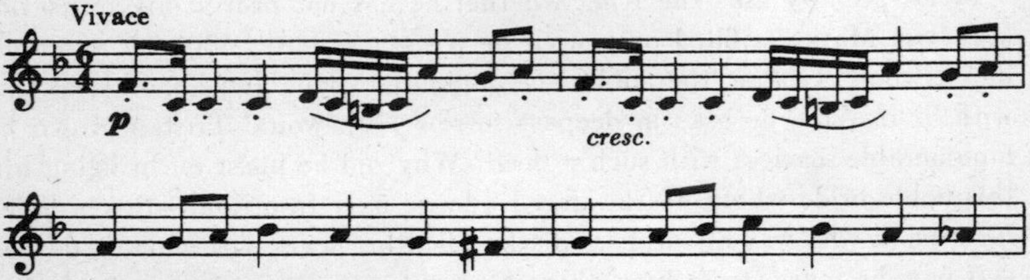
Vivace
p
cresc.

[36] TRISTAN'S PROTECTOR

Molto vivace

[37] LOVE'S CURSE

Un poco strascinando
ff

to Melot to defend himself and draws his sword, but purposefully drops it when Melot reacts with a thrust. Mortally wounded, Tristan sinks into Kurwenal's arms.

Prelude to Act III: Motive [31] seems to describe Tristan's unspeakable weariness of the day as, in spite of his fatal wound, the gates of death will not open for him. Equally bleak, motive [32] pictures the empty expanse of the vast and motionless sea. Interspersed between repetitions of these motives, a strain of languid suffering [33] is heard.

Act III: On a rough couch under a tree, on the grounds of his family castle, Tristan lies motionless, as if dead. Kurwenal sits beside him, anxiously watching him. From beyond the ramparts, toward the sea, the sad tune of a shepherd is heard as he blows his shawm [34abc]. Now the shepherd looks in over the wall and compassionately asks Kurwenal whether Tristan has regained consciousness. Kurwenal, however, is afraid that Tristan might die if he were to awaken before the one who can cure him arrives [31, 33]. Is there no ship in sight? There is not [32, 34b], the shepherd says, but as soon as he sees one he will signal its arrival with a gay tune. His question about Tristan's ailment remaining unanswered [31], he leaves again to resume his watch [32, 34cab].

Awakened [31] by the shawm, Tristan weakly asks where he is. The overjoyed Kurwenal tells him that he is at Careol [35], and when Tristan does not seem to understand, he adds that he is at the castle of his fathers [35], which he had left to gain glory and honor in Cornwall [11, 12]. Now Kurwenal has brought him back home [35], there to recover from his wound. Tristan knows otherwise [31], but he cannot explain; nor can he explain where he has been.

It was the land of his origin and his destiny [30], the land of night and of oblivion [16]. Only the longing [2, 22] for Isolde has brought him back —for Isolde, who is still alive [16]. The longing to see her [1 with 4] brought him back from the very gates of death [10], back to the day [16] to find her [25], back to the bleak [31], the hated day [16]. When, he asks, will Isolde extinguish the torch, that he may find happiness and peace [18, 2, 19a]? Kurwenal now reveals that he expects Isolde here this very day, for when he saw Tristan so ill [13], he thought he knew who could heal his wound [21] and sent for Isolde [19a].

Tristan, beside himself, exuberantly praises Kurwenal [36] for sharing his affections and hatreds, his joys and his sufferings [36, 33], although Kurwenal cannot fathom the tremendous pain of his longing [22]. Could he do so, he would hurry to the tower to look for Isolde [33] as her boat approaches [23b]. Can't he see it? The sad tune of the shawm [34] is heard from below, and Kurwenal informs Tristan that there is no ship in sight. Sadly Tristan listens to the tune, recalling all the moments of grief in his life for which it has been the background. Even now it spells his fate: longing and death. But no [16 with 34a], he exclaims in despair, it means a yearning [2] that prevents him from dying. Dying [13], he had sailed

[38] ISOLDE, ANGEL OF DEATH

[39] THE SHEPHERD'S JOYOUS TUNE

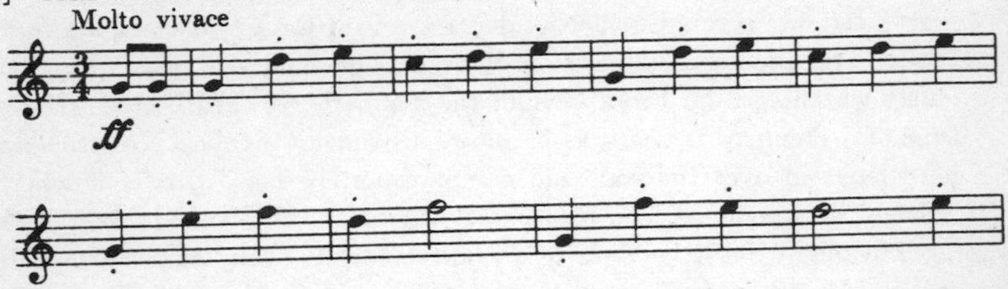

[40] DEATH

to Ireland, and Isolde had healed him. Then she gave him the poisoned potion [6] and he had hoped to find peace, but instead it caused him unending suffering [34a with 2; 34a with 16; 31; 2 with 34c; 2 with 34a and 34c]. Violently he curses the poisoned potion [1, 37; 37 with 2; 16] and faints.

Kurwenal hovers anxiously over him [37, 1] until he finally notices a faint breathing [2]. Softly Tristan again inquires about the ship [2], and in his mind's eye he already sees Isolde [37] standing on the ship and drinking to reconciliation with him [5], approaching in bliss [25] and beauty [38] to bring him rest. He bids Kurwenal ascend the tower, certain that he, too, will be able to see her [24, 38]. At this moment the shepherd is heard playing a gay tune [39], and Kurwenal hurries to the look-out, from where he reports the progress of the ship past the cliffs and into port [24, 38, 39].

Tristan sends Kurwenal to bring Isolde, and in great excitement [24] he gives expression to his frenzied joy as he tears at his bandages [21, 22, 8; 8 with 24; 25, 38]. When Isolde approaches [18], he staggers to meet her [18a and 24 with 10] and sinks slowly into her arms [1, 2, 3]. With a last look into her eyes [4], and with her name on his lips, he dies. Isolde cries that she has come to die with him [40], but he remains mute [15a]. She has suffered through many hours and days [33] just to spend one more waking hour with him, she laments, and now he deprives her of her last joy in this world [22, 40, 15a]. Will he not let her heal the wound so that they can share the bliss of night [26, 27] and then die together [5, 6]? Tristan is dead [40, 15a] and does not respond to her love [27], but suddenly it seems to her that he has come to life again, and she swoons over his body [26].

The noise of weapons is heard from the beach, and the shepherd comes [34c] to inform Kurwenal, who had been a speechless witness to the meeting of the lovers, that another ship has arrived. Kurwenal, looking over the wall, recognizes Marke and Melot, and, furious, he prepares to defend the castle [36]. The helmsman of Isolde's ship rushes in [34c], reporting that his men are in flight, but Kurwenal stands firm and ignores a call from the approaching Brangäne that he should not fight. When Melot enters, demanding surrender, Kurwenal with a jubilant outcry [36] transfixes him and shouts to the King that he, too, can expect only death if he comes nearer [37]. While the battle still rages [36, 34c], Marke and Brangäne enter, horrified at the sight of Tristan and Isolde [40]. The fight ceases when Kurwenal falls, his last steps carrying him to Tristan's body, where, holding his master's hand, he dies [36 *pianissimo*; 35, 2].

Marke is grief-stricken [29] at having caused death [40], for, informed by Brangäne about the potion, he has come only to unite the lovers. Meanwhile, Brangäne has brought her mistress back to life [26, 1, 2], but Isolde does not hear either her or King Marke's explanations. Gazing transfigured at Tristan, she seems to see him smiling at her (Isolde's Love Death *Mild und leise wie er lächelt:* "Fair and gently he is smiling") [26] as his loving presence envelops her whole being [26, 27, 15a, 2, 19bc] and she dies the love death (motive [2] finally finding a conclusion).

THEMES

[1] ARIA *ABIETTA ZINGARA* (Ferrando)

Allegretto con mistero
p
Swar - thy and threat - en - ing, a ___ Gyp - sy wom - an
Ab - biet - ta zin - ga - ra, fo - sca ve - gliar - da!

[2]

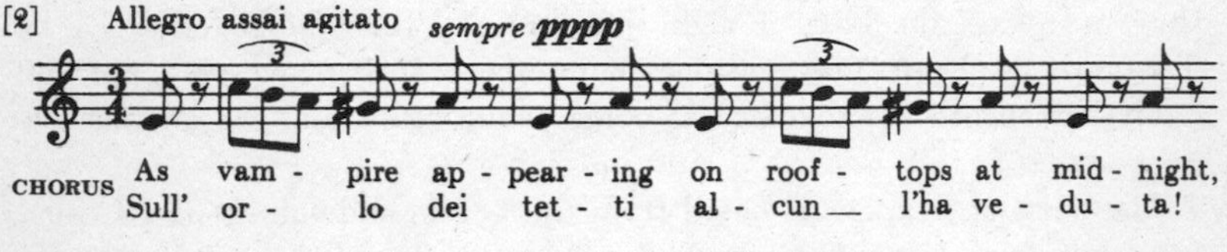
Allegro assai agitato
sempre pppp
CHORUS
As vam - pire ap - pear - ing on roof - tops at mid - night,
Sull' or - lo dei tet - ti al - cun ___ l'ha ve - du - ta!

[3] ARIA *TACEA LA NOTTE PLACIDA* (Leonora)

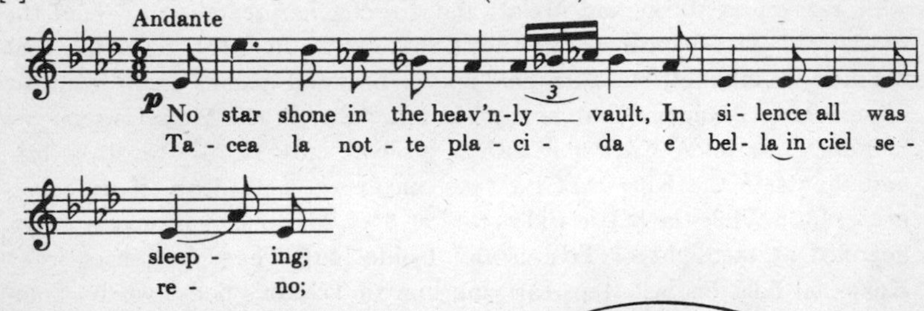
Andante
p
No star shone in the heav'n-ly ___ vault, In si - lence all was
Ta - cea la not - te pla - ci - da e bel - la in ciel se -
3
sleep - ing;
re - no;

[4]

Allegro giusto
tr
The love my heart o'er - flow - - ing,
Di ta - le a - mor, che dir - - si

[5] MANRICO'S SERENADE

Andante
3
Naught ___ on earth ___ is left ___ me,
De - ser - to sul - la ter - ra,

[6]

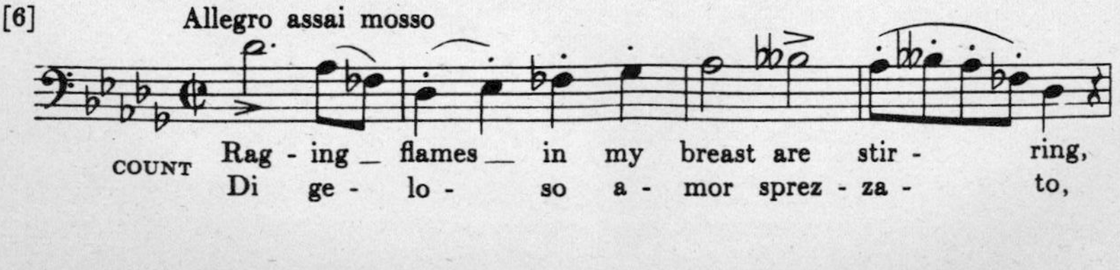
Allegro assai mosso
COUNT
Rag - ing _ flames _ in my breast are stir - ring,
Di ge - lo - so a - mor sprez - za - to,

Il Trovatore

THE TROUBADOUR

Opera in four acts by Giuseppe Verdi. Libretto by Salvatore Cammarano after the play by Antonio García Gutiérrez. First performance: Rome, January 19, 1853.

Characters: LEONORA (soprano); INEZ, her attendant (soprano); AZUCENA, a gypsy (mezzo-soprano); MANRICO, her son (tenor); RUIZ, his lieutenant (tenor); COUNT DI LUNA (baritone); FERRANDO, captain of the guard (bass). *Spain, in the fifteenth century.*

After a short introduction the curtain rises.

Act I ("The Duel"), Scene 1: Ferrando, captain of Count di Luna's guard, on duty in front of his master's apartments, admonishes his soldiers to stay alert: they must be awake at the return of the Count, who tonight, as every night, is keeping watch in front of the royal palace for the "Troubadour," his unknown rival for the love of Lady Leonora.

To make the time pass faster, Ferrando tells the guards and the servants who gather around him the story of the kidnapping of Garcia, the Count's younger brother (Recitative *Di due figli vivea padre felice:* "There lived once a happy father of two boys"). One day, he relates, a fierce-looking gypsy woman was found near the boy's cradle (Aria *Abietta zingara:* "Swarthy and threatening") [1], and when the child fell ill, the gypsy was burned at the stake. However, her daughter remained alive, and it must have been she who stole the child and burned it, for the half-charred body of a baby was found at the place where they had burned the witch. The ghost of the burned gypsy, Ferrando continues, is said to be still haunting the mansion at midnight, and the soldiers and servants agree in hushed voices [2]. Just then the clock strikes twelve and all disperse in fright.

Act I, Scene 2: In the garden near her apartments, vaguely lit by a clouded moon, Leonora tells her companion, Inez (Recitative), about the youthful stranger whom she once crowned champion of the tournament and who disappeared at the outbreak of the civil war. Then, one night a troubadour sang to her in the garden (Aria *Tacea la notte placida:* "No star shone in the heavenly vault") [3], and it was he. Inez has dire forebodings, but to Leonora the unknown youth embodies all she longs for, and for him alone will she live and, if need be, die (Cabaletta *Di tale amor:* "The love my heart overflowing") [4].

Hardly have they returned to the house when the Count appears, but he stops abruptly near the entrance when he hears the voice of the Troubadour, whose serenade (*Deserto sulla terra:* "Naught on earth is left me") [5] floats softly through the night. Leonora comes from the house and

[7] Allegro assai mosso

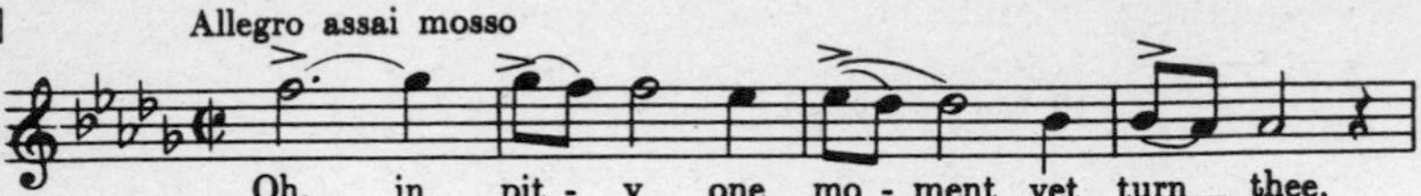

LEON. Oh, in pit - y one mo - ment yet turn — thee,
Un i - stan - te al - men — di - a lo - co,
MAN. Vain his threat - 'ning, and vain — his an - ger,
Del su - per - bo è va - na l'i - ra;

[8] **ANVIL CHORUS**

Allegro

See how the dark- ness of night dis - solves a - way when the
Ve - di! le fo - sche not-tur - ne — spo - glie — de' cie - li

sun - light from Heav'n de - scend - eth;
sve - ste l'im - men - sa — vol - ta;

[9] Allegro

Who cheers the days — of the rov - ing — Gyp - sy?
Chi del gi - ta - no i gior - ni ab - bel - la?

[10] ARIA *STRIDE LA VAMPA* (Azucena)

Allegretto

Fierce flames are soar - ing, draw - ing fren - zied
Stri - de la vam - pa! la — fol - la in-

mul - ti - tudes
do - mi - ta

[11] ARIA *CONDOTTA ELL' ERA* (Azucena)

Andante mosso

In chains to her — doom they dragg'd her,
Con - dot - ta el - l'e - ra in cep - pi

[12] ARIA *MAL REGGENDO* (Manrico)

Allegro

I as - sault - ed, he feeb - ly de - fend - ed,
Mal reg - gen - do al - l'a - spro as - sal - to,

rushes into the Count's arms. The Troubadour, his visor closed, steps forward from the shadows, calling Leonora unfaithful, and she realizes her mistake. The Count dares his rival to show his face, and recognizing him as Manrico, a follower of Urgel (the rival leader in the civil war), he challenges him to a duel. He rages with jealousy [6] while (Trio) Leonora tries to direct his wrath against herself [7] and Manrico looks forward joyously to overcoming his enemy [7]. Leonora faints as the men rush off with drawn swords.

Act II (*"The Gypsy"*), *Scene 1:* Many weeks later, in the mountains of Biscay, the gypsies, at break of day (The Anvil Chorus *Vedi! le fosche notturne spoglie:* "See how the darkness of night dissolves") [8] are commencing their work and singing in praise of their women (*Chi del gitano:* "Who cheers the days") [9]. However, they leave their anvils to listen to Azucena, who, seated near Manrico by the fire, relives the scene of her mother's death at the stake (Aria *Stride la vampa:* "Fierce flames are soaring") [10] and implores Manrico to avenge her: *"Mi vendica!"* Soon the gypsies are on their way again, but Azucena and Manrico remain. When Manrico asks his mother to continue her tale, she relates how, her baby in her arms, she helplessly watched as her mother, from the stake, shouted a last *"Mi vendica!"* before being consumed by the flames (Aria *Condotta ell'era in ceppi:* "In chains to her doom they dragged her") [11]. She tells how she succeeded in kidnapping the Count's baby and how she prepared to throw him into the flames. Although his tears moved her heart, the vision of her mother's execution [10] and of her last cry for vengeance compelled her to cast the victim into the flames. But when the dread vision left her, she discovered to her horror that she had sacrificed her own son. But no, she continues, her mind always becomes confused by these terrifying recollections (Recitative). Manrico is her son, of course! Has she not always been a most tender mother to him? Was it not she who nursed him back to life when Luna left him for dead on the battlefield—Luna, whom Manrico once saw helpless and at his mercy, but whom he spared in a feeling of unexplained sympathy? And Manrico tells (Aria *Mal reggendo:*

[13] Allegro sostenuto

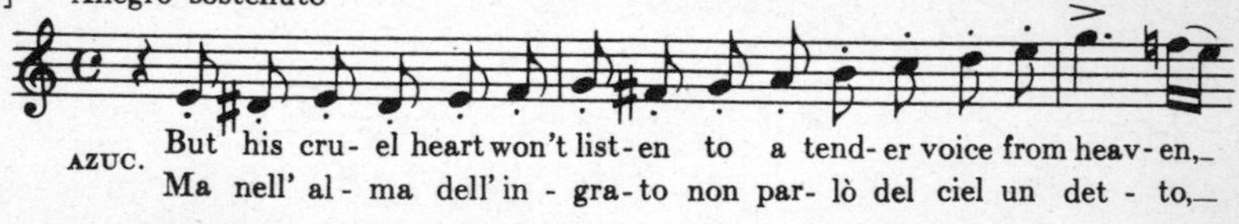
AZUC.
But his cru- el heart won't list-en to a tend- er voice from heav- en,_
Ma nell' al - ma dell' in - gra- to non par- lò del ciel un det - to,_

[14] Velocissimo *agitato assai*

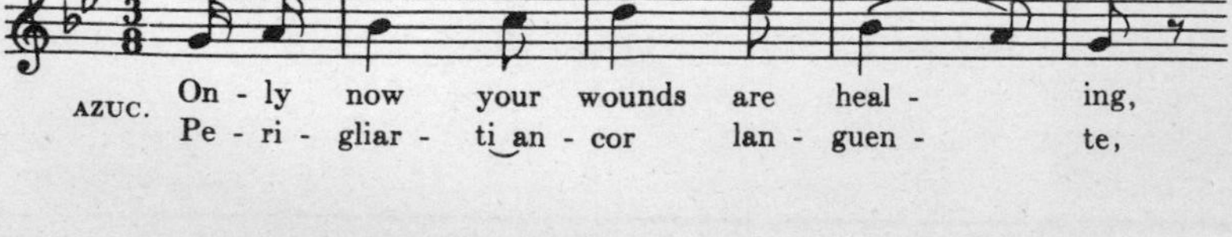
AZUC.
On - ly now your wounds are heal - ing,
Pe - ri - gliar - ti an - cor lan - guen - te,

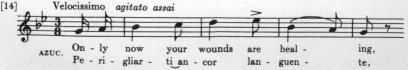

[15] Velocissimo

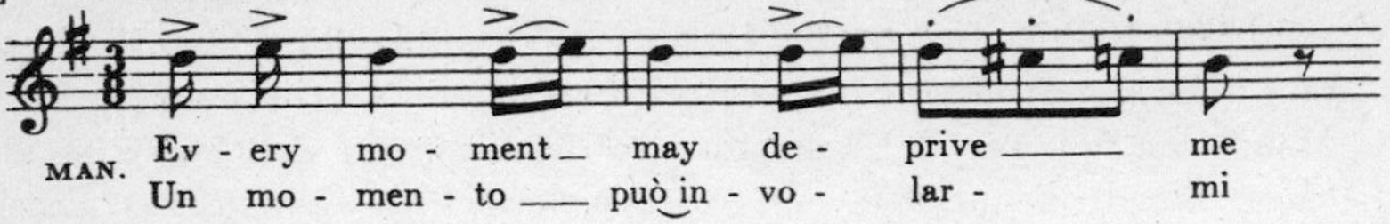
MAN.
Ev - ery mo - ment may de - prive me
Un mo - men - to può in - vo - lar - mi

[16] ARIA *IL BALEN* (Count)

Largo *cantabile*

In the light of her sweet glan - ces,
Il ba - len del suo sor - ri - so

[17] Allegro assai mosso *sotto voce*

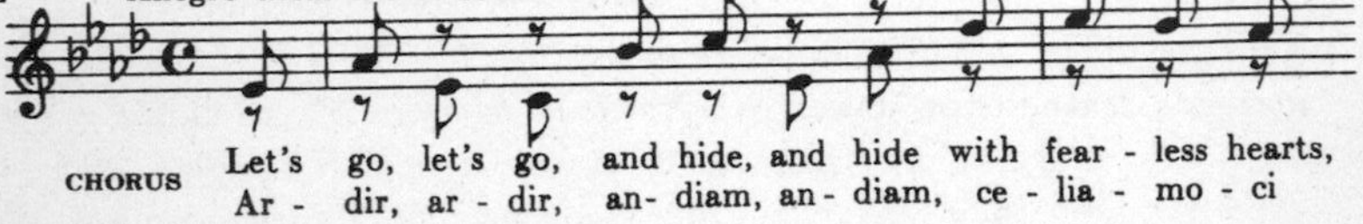
CHORUS
Let's go, let's go, and hide, and hide with fear - less hearts,
Ar - dir, ar - dir, an- diam, an- diam, ce - lia - mo - ci

[18] Allegro mosso

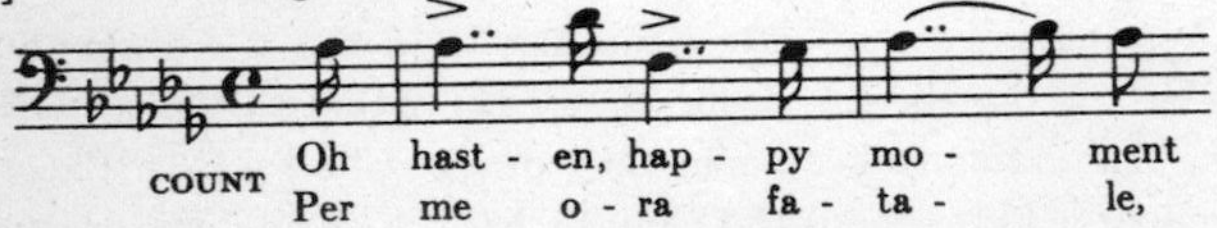
COUNT
Oh hast - en, hap - py mo - ment
Per me o - ra fa - ta - le,

[19] Andante

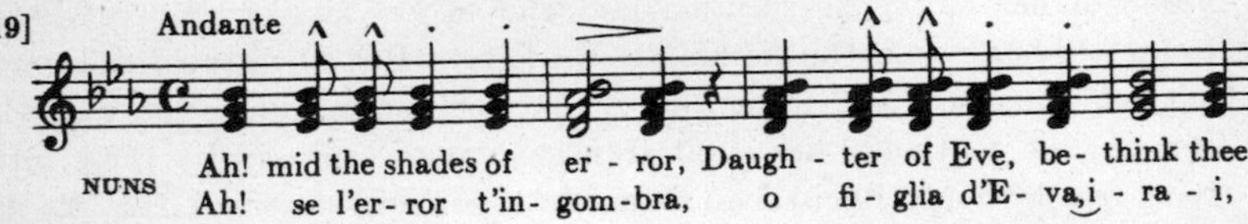
NUNS
Ah! mid the shades of er - ror, Daugh - ter of Eve, be- think thee!
Ah! se l'er- ror t'in- gom- bra, o fi - glia d'E - va, i - ra - i,

[20] Andante mosso *con tutta forza di sentimento*

LEON.
Can I be- lieve the vis - ion blest?
E deg - gio e pos - so cre - der- lo?

[21] SOLDIERS' CHORUS

Allegro

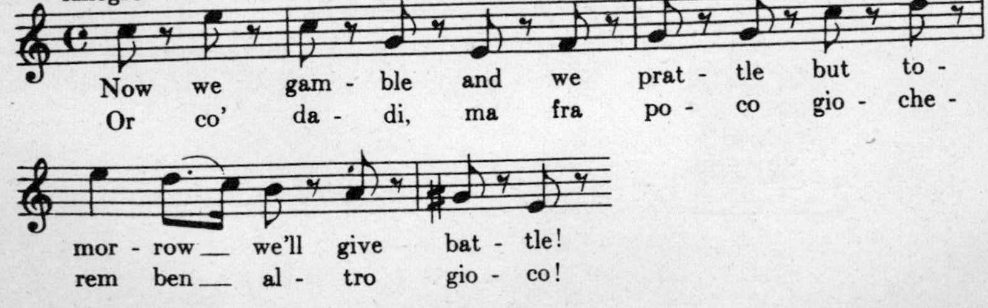
Now we gam - ble and we prat - tle but to -
Or co' da - di, ma fra po - co gio - che -
mor - row we'll give bat - tle!
rem ben al - tro gio - co!

"I assaulted") [12] how in the duel he had his sword raised over the fallen Luna when a voice from heaven restrained his arm from dealing the fatal blow. Azucena finds no such sympathy apparent in Luna [13]. Spurred by his mother, Manrico swears that at the next chance he will not spare his enemy [13].

A messenger arrives with orders for Manrico to head the defenses of Castellor. He also brings the news that Leonora, believing Manrico dead, will take the veil this very evening at a nearby convent. In vain are Azucena's efforts to stop her son from leaving [14]. He must be off on the instant [15].

Act II, Scene 2: The Count, with a number of men, wrapped in cloaks, cautiously enters the cloisters of the convent to abduct Leonora before she can make her vows. For she alone can give content and purpose to his life (Aria *Il balen del suo sorriso:* "In the light of her sweet glances") [16]. The sound of a bell is heard, and all hide [17]. The Count is anxiously looking forward to the joyous moment when he will take Leonora away from the arms of the church [18].

From inside the convent a procession of nuns appears [19], and with them Leonora, Inez, and companions. Leonora stops for a few parting words to her friends. As she turns to enter the church, the Count steps forward and declares that she must follow him, but suddenly Manrico appears and stands between them. Leonora, delirious with joy [20], rushes into Manrico's arms. Luna, confronted by his enemy and rival, whom all believed slain in the last battle, remains for an instant perplexed (Ensemble), and now a superior force of Manrico's followers enters with the shout *Urgel viva!* ("Long live Urgel!"). The Count is consumed by impotent fury as Manrico carries off Leonora.

Act III ("The Gypsy's Son"), Scene 1: Ferrando tells the gay soldiers [21] camped near Castellor that the coming dawn will see them victorious and in possession of the castle. They are eager for battle and bravely look forward to gaining booty and honor [22]. As they slowly disperse, the Count comes from his tent, bitterly reflecting on his recent misfortune. Suddenly

[22] SOLDIERS' CHORUS *continued*

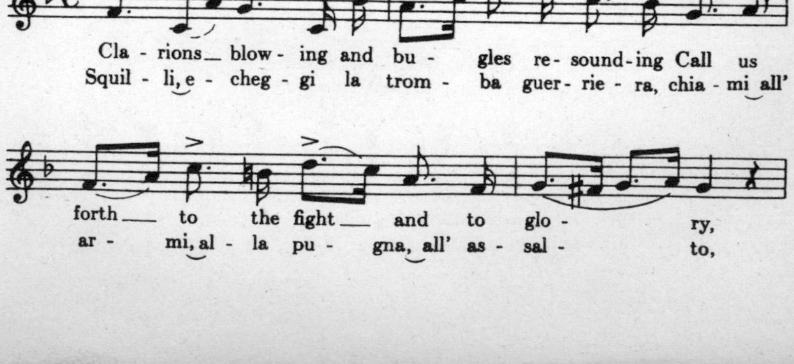
Allegro moderato maestoso *grandioso*
Cla - rions blow - ing and bu - gles re - sound - ing Call us
Squil - li, e - cheg - gi la trom - ba guer - rie - ra, chia - mi all'
forth to the fight and to glo - ry,
ar - mi, al - la pu - gna, all' as - sal - to,

[23] Andante mosso

AZUC. There my days ob - scure - ly glid - ed,
Gior - ni po - ve - ri vi - ve - a,

[24] Allegro

AZUC. O ty-rants, loose these cru - el bonds that griev - ous - ly con - fine me,
Deh! ral - len - ta - te, o bar - ba - ri, le a - cer - be mie ri - tor - te

[25] Allegro

COUNT *p* Of him, the vile se - duc - er, wick-ed Gyp-sy, you're the moth-er?
Tua pro - le, o tur - pe zin - ga - ra, co - lui, quel tra - di - to - re?

[26] ARIA *AH SI, BEN MIO* (Manrico)
Adagio *cantabile con espressione*

Oh, come let links e - ter - nal bind the vows we fond-ly plight-ed;
Ah, si, ben mio; coll' es - se - re io tuo, tu mia con - sor - te,

[27] ARIA *DI QUELLA PIRA* (Manrico)
Allegro

Trem - ble, ye ty - rants. I will chas - tise ___ ye!
Di quel - la pi - ra l'or - ren - do fo - co

[28] ARIA *D'AMOR SULL' ALI* (Leonora)
Adagio *con espressione*

Love, fly on ro - sy pin - ions,
D'a - mor sull' a - li ro - se - e

[29] THE "*MISERERE*" (Leonora, Manrico and Chorus)
Andante assai sostenuto *a mezza voce*

p
CHORUS Mi - se - re - re a - gain the wail of sor - row,
Mi - se - re - re d'un' al - ma già vi - ci - na

there is a commotion, and Azucena is dragged in by guards. On being questioned, she reveals that she has come from Biscay in search of her son [23]. Ferrando recognizes her as the gypsy who stole Luna's brother, and the Count is doubly happy when he finds out that she is the mother of his rival, Manrico. He orders her chains tightened. Azucena warns him of God's wrath [24], while the Count gives vent to his feeling of triumph [25], and the soldiers are happy in the expectation of seeing the gypsy burned at the stake.

Act III, Scene 2: At Castellor, Manrico and Leonora are about to be married. In spite of the expected assault on the fortress, Manrico, transported by love [26], is hopeful of victory.

Now the sound of the organ is heard from the chapel, but as they turn to enter, Ruiz hurries in to inform Manrico that Azucena has been taken by the Count and is to be burned alive. The glow of the fire is already visible through the trees. Manrico feels the flames enveloping his heart and spurring him to fierce destruction (Aria *Di quella pira:* "Tremble, ye tyrants") [27], and he rushes away with his men to save his mother or to die with her.

Act IV ("The Execution"), Scene 1: Ruiz brings Leonora to the tower in which Manrico is imprisoned. Left alone, Leonora bids her sighs rise and bring hope to the dejected prisoner (Aria *D'amor sull' ali rosee:* "Love, fly on rosy pinions") [28]. The sound of a *Miserere* chorus [29] from inside the tower shakes her to the depths of her being [30], and Manrico's farewell to her [31] makes her nearly faint, as with hysterical outbursts [32] she joins his last declaration of love. She decides (Aria *Tu vedrai che amore in terra:* "Thee I love with love eternal"—usually omitted) that she will die for him or with him.

The Count comes from the tower (without noticing the woman hidden in the shadows) and gives orders for the execution of Manrico and Azucena. As he wonders about the whereabouts of Leonora, she comes forward

[30] THE *"MISERERE" continued*

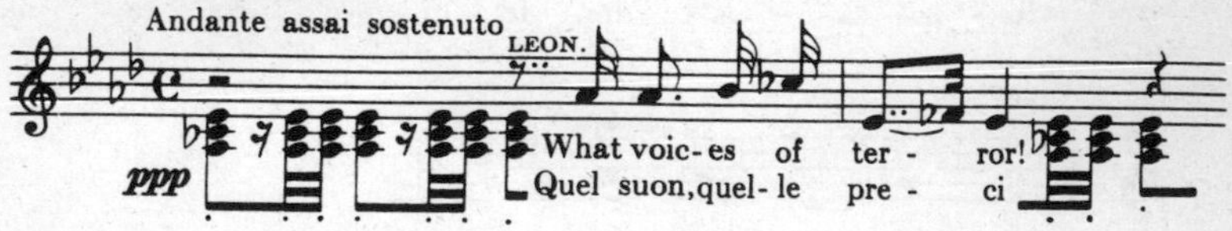

[31]

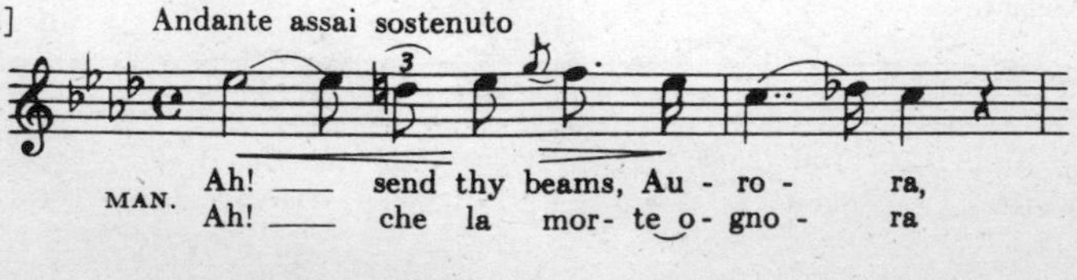

[32] THE "*MISERERE*" *continued*

Andante assai sostenuto

6
6
3
LEON.
For - get? Oh nev - er, nev - er!
Di te, di te scor - dar - mi!

[33] Andante con moto

LEON.
Kneel - ing, oh let me move your heart, oh let my tears im-plore you!
Mi - ra, di a-cer- be la - gri- me spar-go al tuo pie-de un ri- o!

[34] Andante con moto

COUNT
Oh, would that with a thou-sand deaths I could pro-long his an-guish,
Ah! dell' in-de-gno ren-de-re vor- rei peg- gior la sor- te,

[35] Allegro brillante *molto vivace*

LEON.
Oh joy, he's saved, my beat-ing heart with thanks to heav'n o'er-flow-eth,
Vi- vrà! Con-ten - de il giu - bi- lo i det- ti a - me, Si- gno- re,

[36] Andantino *a mezza voce*

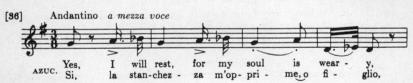

AZUC.
Yes, I will rest, for my soul is wear - y,
Si, la stan-chez - za m'op- pri - me, o fi - glio,

[37] Andantino *a mezza voce*

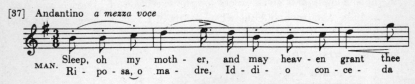

MAN.
Sleep, oh my moth - er, and may heav - en grant thee
Ri - po - sa, o ma - dre, Id - di - o con - ce - da

[38] Andantino

AZUC.
Home to our moun - tains
Ai no - stri mon - ti

[39] Andante

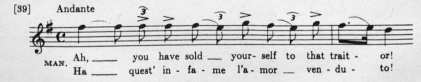

3
3
3
MAN.
Ah, you have sold your- self to that trait - or!
Ha quest' in - fa - me l'a - mor ven - du - to!

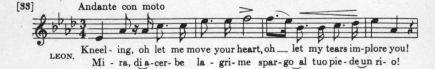

and asks mercy for Manrico. But he will not hear of it. At his feet, she begs that he take her life for Manrico's [33], but he becomes only more incensed [34]. Finally she offers herself to the Count on condition that he free Manrico and that she herself be allowed to bring him the news. As he calls the guards to give the necessary orders, she swallows poison from a ring on her hand, murmuring: "I will be yours, but cold and lifeless." The Count announces that Manrico is now free. Both rejoice, Leonora at having saved Manrico [35] and the Count in the expectation of possessing Leonora [35].

Act IV, Scene 2: Azucena, imprisoned with Manrico, cannot sleep. The air in the dungeon, she complains, is choking her. But it will not be for long. She will escape prison and the tyrants—for the hand of death is already upon her. Suddenly a vision of the flaming stake appears before her eyes. Is it hers, is it her mother's [10]? Gradually calmed by Manrico, she lies down to rest [36] and, as Manrico tries to soothe her tortured mind [37], she gradually falls asleep, dreaming of a return to the peace of her Biscayan mountains [38].

Suddenly the door opens and Leonora enters. Manrico's exuberant joy gradually gives way to suspicion as she tells him to hurry to freedom although she must stay. As he accuses her of infidelity [39], Leonora tries in vain to placate him and frantically begs him to flee while there still is time [40]. Azucena meanwhile continues to dream of her mountains [38]. Manrico harshly orders Leonora to leave, but the poison is already taking possession of her. Rather than live for another, she confesses as she sinks at his feet, she has chosen to die for him [41]. Manrico, stunned, blames himself for distrusting Leonora. As she dies, the Count who has come in unnoticed, finds that he has been cheated and brutally orders Manrico to be taken to the block. Azucena, wakened by the shouting, tries in vain to get the Count's attention. As he triumphantly observes the execution through the window, Azucena shouts: "He was your brother! Mother, you are avenged!"

[40]

Andante
Ah you are blind - ed by rage, by jea - lou-sy blind-ed!
LEON.
O co-me l'i - ra ti ren - de, ti ren - de cie- co!

[41]

Andante
Rath- er a thou-sand deaths I'd die, than with-out you to live!
LEON.
Pri- ma che d'al - tri vi - ve- re i - o vol- li tua mo- rir!

THEMES

[1] OVERTURE

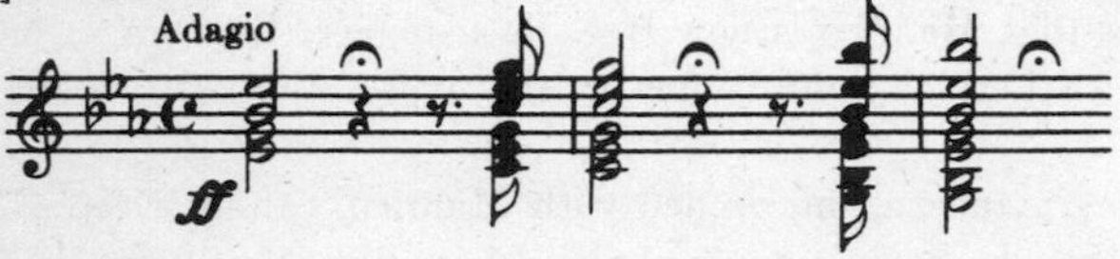

[2]

[3]

[4]

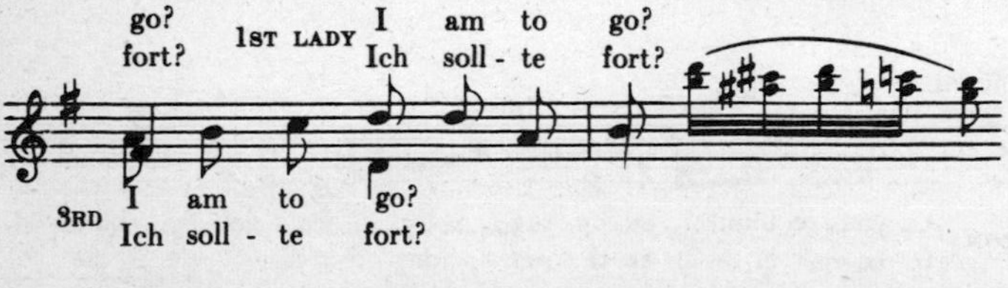

[5]

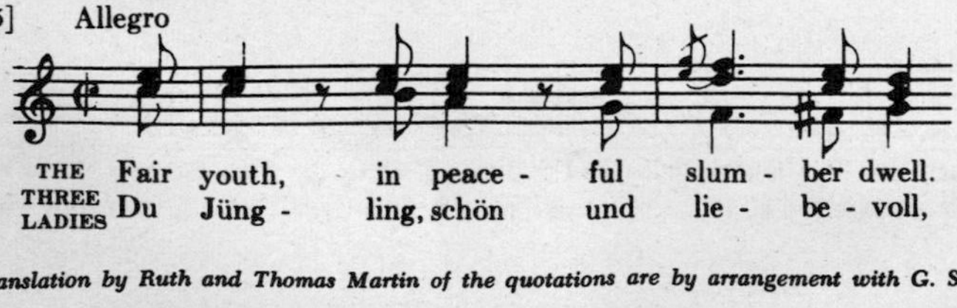

Translation by Ruth and Thomas Martin of the quotations are by arrangement with G. Schirmer, Inc.

Die Zauberflöte

THE MAGIC FLUTE

Opera in two acts by Wolfgang Amadeus Mozart. Libretto by Emanuel Schikaneder. First performance: Vienna, September 30, 1791.

Characters: TAMINO, a foreign prince (tenor); THE QUEEN OF THE NIGHT (soprano); THREE LADIES, in her service (sopranos and mezzo-soprano); PAMINA, her daughter (soprano); SARASTRO, High Priest of Isis and Osiris (bass); MONOSTATOS, a Moor, his overseer (tenor); TWO MEN IN ARMOR (tenor, bass); THREE PRIESTS (tenor, basses); THREE SPIRITS (sopranos and mezzo-soprano); PAPAGENO, bird-catcher (baritone); PAPAGENA, at first disguised as OLD WOMAN (soprano).
*Egypt, in the days of antiquity.**

Important parts of this opera are cast in the form of spoken dialogue, indicated in the text by (Dialogue).

Overture: An adagio introduction begins with three solemn chords [1] (supposed to have Masonic connotations). The allegro section that follows is built mainly on theme [2], interrupted once by [1].

Act I, Scene 1: In a forest Tamino, his last arrow spent, flees from a giant serpent [3]. As he falls fainting to the ground, the Three Ladies appear and kill the serpent with their spears. They extol their own prowess (Trio) and look with delight at the handsome youth. Each tries to send the others back to their mistress, the Queen of the Night, for each desires to remain alone with Tamino, but none of them will give way [4]. Eventually they bid a tender farewell to the still unconscious charmer [5] and leave together.

When Tamino regains consciousness, he has just time to hide as Papageno, clothed all in feathers and playing his pan's pipes [6], descends toward the clearing and introduces himself as the happy bird-catcher (Song *Der Vogelfänger bin ich ja:* "I am a man of widespread fame") [7].

Tamino comes forward (Dialogue) to introduce himself as a prince, and Papageno tells him that he is catching birds for the Queen of the Night. When Tamino asks whether it was he who killed the serpent, Papageno, quickly overcoming his initial shock on discovering the monster, boasts that he strangled it with his bare hands. The returning Ladies punish him for this lie by padlocking his mouth. They give Tamino a medallion bearing a likeness of Pamina, the daughter of their mistress, and leave again, followed by the unhappy Papageno. Tamino immediately falls in love with the portrait (Aria *Dies Bildnis ist bezaubernd schön:* "O image angel-like

* The ideals and rituals governing life at Sarastro's Temple of Wisdom are obviously analogous to those of Freemasonry. The main characters of the opera have been interpreted as personages and factions involved in the battle around Freemasonry in the Austria of Mozart's time.

[6]

8

[7] SONG *DER VOGELFAENGER BIN ICH JA* (Papageno)

Andante

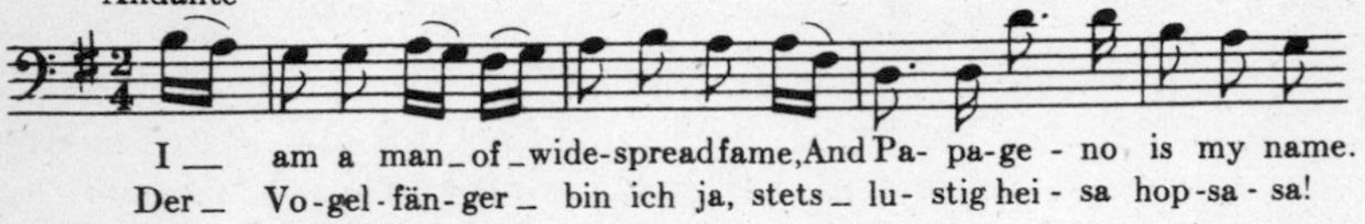
I _ am a man _ of _ wide-spread fame, And Pa- pa-ge - no is my name.
Der _ Vo-gel-fän-ger _ bin ich ja, stets _ lu- stig hei - sa hop-sa - sa!

[8] ARIA *DIES BILDNIS* (Tamino)

Larghetto

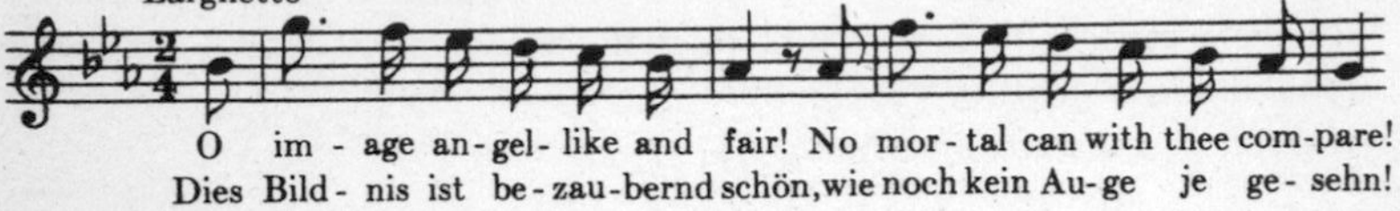
O im - age an-gel- like and fair! No mor - tal can with thee com-pare!
Dies Bild - nis ist be-zau-bernd schön, wie noch kein Au-ge je ge- sehn!

[9] ARIA *ZUM LEIDEN* (Queen of the Night)

Larghetto

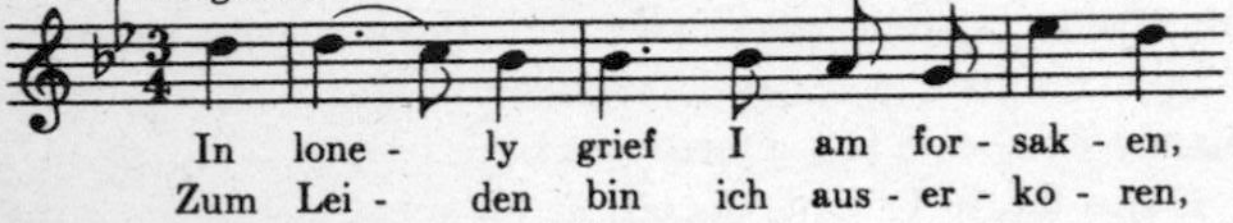
In lone - ly grief I am for-sak - en,
Zum Lei - den bin ich aus - er - ko - ren,

[10] Allegro moderato

You, you, you shall _ free _ her from bonds of slav - 'ry,
Du, du, du wirst _ sie _ zu be - frei - en ge - hen,

[11] QUINTET *HM, HM* (Papageno, Tamino, the Three Ladies)

Allegro

PAPAGENO Hm! hm! hm! hm! hm! hm! hm! hm! hm! hm! hm! hm! hm! hm! hm! hm!

[12] Andante *sotto voce*

THE THREE LADIES
Three spir - its young and wise will guide you, And
Drei Knäb - chen, jung, schön, hold und wei - se, um -
on your jour - ney stay be - side you.
schwe - ben euch auf eu - rer Rei - se.

and fair!") [8], whereupon the Three Ladies return, announce the approach of the Queen, and withdraw respectfully. Suddenly darkness falls and the Queen of the Night becomes visible on her throne against the background of a sky brilliant with stars. She greets the youth (Recitative *O zittre nicht:* "Oh tremble not") and tells him that an evil man has carried off her daughter (Aria *Zum Leiden bin ich auserkoren:* "In lonely grief I am forsaken") [9]. If Tamino can save her, Pamina shall be his [10]. As she disappears, daylight returns, and Papageno comes back, vainly appealing to Tamino for help [Beginning of Quintet 11]. However, the Three Ladies, rejoining them, relieve the bird-catcher of the lock and advise him never to lie again. They bring a magic flute for the Prince and a charmed set of bells for Papageno, whom they order to accompany Tamino on his journey to free Pamina from the villain, Sarastro. After promising that three Spirits will serve the men as guides [12], the Ladies bid them farewell.

Act I, Scene 2: In a room of Sarastro's palace three servants rejoice (Dialogue) over the news of Pamina's escape, but, to their dismay, they soon see Sarastro's vile overseer, Monostatos, approaching with the recaptured girl. He drags her in [13], has her fettered, and sends the slaves away. As Pamina faints, Papageno enters. He and Monostatos are so scared at the sight of each other that both take flight, but Papageno returns just as Pamina regains consciousness. He tells her (Dialogue) about Tamino, and both extol the joys of love (Duet *Bei Männern welche Liebe fühlen:* "The man who feels sweet love's emotion") [14].

Act I, Scene 3: The Three Spirits lead Tamino toward the temple [15] and leave. Tamino tries to enter, but he is stopped at two doors by voices from within. As he approaches the third door, a priest appears and confirms that this is Sarastro's realm, but intimates that Tamino has been misinformed about the High Priest, for there is no evildoer within the sacred halls of friendship. The priest returns to the temple. Sadly Tamino starts playing his flute [16], whereupon wild animals approach and listen happily to its sweet sounds. Now Tamino hears the pan's pipes of Papageno in the distance [6]. He quickly goes off to find him and—he hopes—Pamina with him.

Papageno and Pamina just miss the Prince as, following the sound of his flute, they enter the temple square. However, their hopes of flight [17] are short-lived, for Monostatos catches them and orders his slaves to put them in chains. At this moment Papageno starts playing his bells [18], and their sound forces the slaves and Monostatos to dance against their will.

[13]

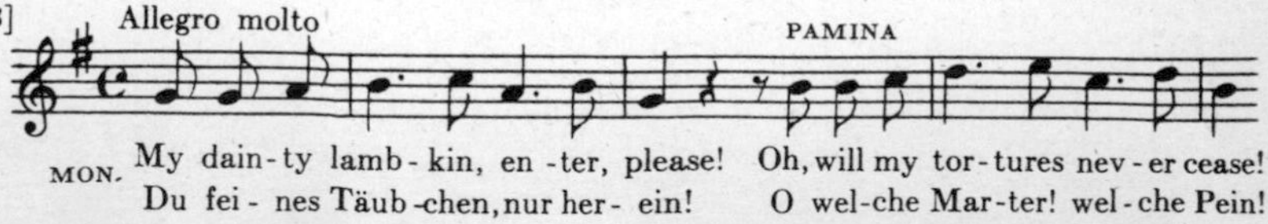
Allegro molto
PAMINA
MON.
My dain-ty lamb-kin, en-ter, please! Oh, will my tor-tures nev-er cease!
Du fei-nes Täub-chen, nur her-ein! O wel-che Mar-ter! wel-che Pein!

[14] DUET *BEI MAENNERN* (Pamina, Papageno)

Andantino
PAMINA
The man_ who feels_ sweet love's_ e - mo- tion Will al - ways
Bei Män - nern, wel - che Lie - be füh - len, fehlt auch_ ein

have_ a kind - ly heart!
gu - tes Her - ze nicht.

[15]

Larghetto
THE THREE SPIRITS
Your jour-ney's end you soon will reach; Yet win you must by man-ly dar - ing.
Zum Zie - le führt dich die - se Bahn, doch musst du, Jüng-ling, männ-lich sie-gen.

[16]

Andante

[17]

Andante
PAM. & PAP.
Noth- ing ven-tured, noth-ing won; To es-cape them_let_ us_ run!
Schnel- le Füs- se, ra - scher Mut schützt vor Fein-des_List_ und_ Wut!

[18]

Allegro
8va

[19]

Andante
sotto voce

Dancing and singing, they withdraw. Again the joy of the fleeing pair is of short duration, for now they hear the trumpets and drums that announce Sarastro. He appears with his suite, and Pamina on her knees confesses that she wanted to flee, but only to escape the Moor's caresses. Sarastro will not force her love, but neither will he let her return to her mother, for woman, to be happy, must ever be guided by man.

Monostatos brings in Tamino, and as soon as Pamina sees him she is in his arms. Monostatos asks his master to punish the impertinent intruders and, at the same time, points out his diligence in preventing their attempt to abduct Pamina. But Sarastro—to the great acclaim of his followers—rewards Monostatos by ordering him lashed. Now Sarastro directs that the two strangers be veiled and subjected to the order's initiation trials, and while Tamino and Papageno are led away, he himself conducts Pamina to the temple.

Act II, Scene 1: In solemn procession [19] the priests arrive in a palm grove. Sarastro (Dialogue) asks and gets their approval (three blasts on their horns) [1] of his plan to allow the Prince to become one of their number and to unite him with Pamina, whom Sarastro has taken from her mother for this purpose, in accordance with the will of heaven. The High Priest prays that the gods may guide the newcomers through the trials and, should they perish, to accept them in their midst (Aria *O Isis und Osiris:* "O Isis and Osiris") [20].

Act II, Scene 2: At night Tamino and a badly shaken Papageno are led by two priests into a small temple court and their veils are removed. Though informed of the dangers awaiting them (Dialogue), Tamino is anxious to undergo the trials. Papageno accedes only when promised that he can see his predestined mate, Papagena. Silence is imposed on the two men, and they are warned to beware of woman's trickery [21]. Hardly have they been left to themselves when the Three Ladies appear (Quintet) and warn them not to trust the deceitful and crafty priests [22], but Tamino places no credence in their gossip. With effort he restrains Papageno from talking to them. As the Ladies admit defeat and turn to leave,

[20] ARIA *O ISIS UND OSIRIS* (Sarastro)

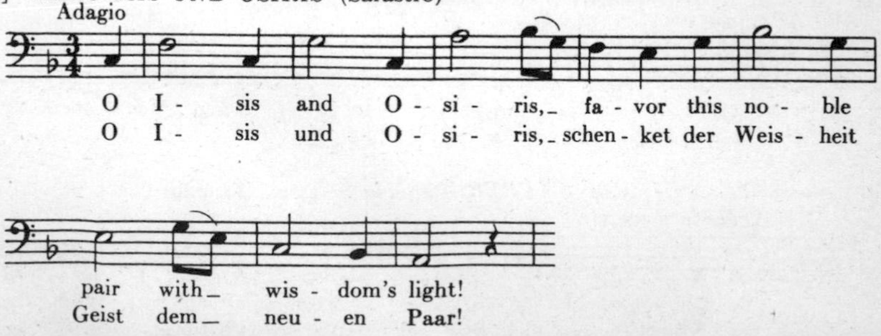

[21] Andante

TWO PRIESTS
Be- ware of wo - man's craft - y — schem - ing,
Be - wah - ret euch vor Wei - ber - tük - ken,

[22] QUINTET *WIE? WIE? WIE?* (Three Ladies, Papageno, Tamino)

Allegro

THE THREE LADIES
Ye? ye? ye? in this place of night and gloom?
Wie? wie? wie? ihr an die -sem Schrek -kens- ort?

[23] ARIA *ALLES FUEHLT DER LIEBE FREUDEN* (Monostatos)

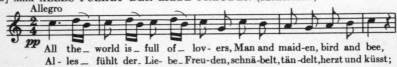

Allegro

All the — world is — full of — lov- ers, Man and maid-en, bird and bee,
Al - les — fühlt der — Lie- be — Freu-den, schnä-belt, tän-delt, herzt und küsst;

[24] ARIA *DER HOELLE RACHE* (Queen of the Night)

Allegro assai

The wrath of hell with- in my breast I cher - ish;
Der Höl - le Ra - che kocht in mei - nem Her - zen!

[25] Allegro assai

ah ——————————

[26] ARIA *IN DIESEN HEIL'GEN HALLEN* (Sarastro)

Larghetto

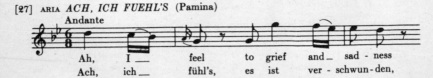

With- in these ho - ly — por - tals Re-venge re-mains un- known, —
In die - sen heil'- gen — Hal - len kennt man die Ra - che nicht, —

[27] ARIA *ACH, ICH FUEHL'S* (Pamina)

Andante

Ah, I — feel to grief and — sad - ness
Ach, ich — fühl's, es ist ver - schwun- den,

[28] TRIO *SOLL ICH DICH, TEURER* (Pamina, Sarastro, Tamino)

Andante moderato

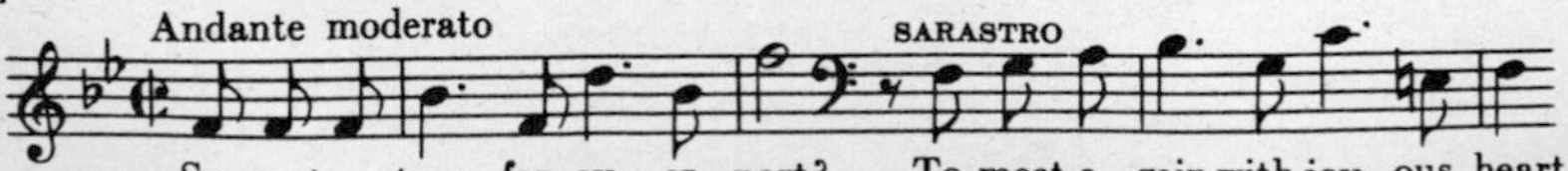

PAMINA
So must we two for- ev - er part? To meet a- gain with joy - ous heart.
Soll ich dich, Teu- rer, nicht mehr seh'n? Ihr wer -det froh euch wie- der sehn!

an unseen chorus consigns them to hell, and, with a stroke of thunder and lightning, they disappear. The Speaker comes (Dialogue) to guide Tamino to further trials. The bird-catcher has been prostrate on the ground since the clap of thunder, and when a priest enters and encourages him to proceed, he insists at first that he is lying in a faint, but eventually he complies.

Act II, Scene 3: Monostatos discovers Pamina (Dialogue), who has fallen asleep on a garden bench, and feels he cannot refrain from giving her just one little kiss. After all, he, too, has a heart (Aria *Alles fühlt der Liebe Freuden:* "All the world is full of lovers") [23], but the Queen of the Night suddenly appears (Dialogue), and he quickly retreats. The Queen gives Pamina a dagger destined for Sarastro. Pamina must accomplish the Queen's revenge (Revenge Aria *Der Hölle Rache kocht in meinem Herzen:* "The wrath of hell within my breast I cherish") [24] or else, the Queen swears in a fury [25], Pamina shall be her daughter no longer. Hardly has she gone when Monostatos returns (Dialogue). He has overheard the conversation, but he promises to forget it if Pamina will love him. As she refuses, he draws a dagger, but just then Sarastro enters. When Pamina begs him not to take revenge on her mother, Sarastro declares (Aria *In diesen heil'gen Hallen:* "Within these holy portals") [26] that the word *revenge* is unknown within the walls of the temple of wisdom.

Act II, Scene 4: Papageno and Tamino are conducted into a bare room and warned again (Dialogue) that the breaking of silence will be punished by thunder and lightning. Left alone, the bird-catcher immediately starts complaining that they are badly treated—they don't even get water. Immediately an Old Woman appears with the drink he has demanded. She claims (Dialogue) that she is only eighteen years old and has a lover named Papageno, but when she is about to reveal her own name, a loud thunder clap is heard and she quickly limps away.

The Three Spirits enter (Trio), sent by Sarastro to return the flute and the bells, which had been taken from the men at the beginning of the trials. They also invite them to partake of the food and drink on a table that magically rises out of the ground. They encourage Tamino, and warn Papageno to keep silent. When they have gone, Papageno immediately begins to eat while the Prince plays on his flute [8]. Guided by its sound, Pamina excitedly arrives (Dialogue), but when Tamino refuses to speak to her, her joy is soon transmuted into grief (Aria *Ach, ich fühl's:* "Ah, I feel") [27] and she sadly leaves. Three trombone blasts signify to the men that they should proceed, and eventually Tamino succeeds (Dialogue) in dragging the frightened bird-catcher off with him.

[29] ARIA *EIN MAEDCHEN ODER WEIBCHEN* (Papageno)

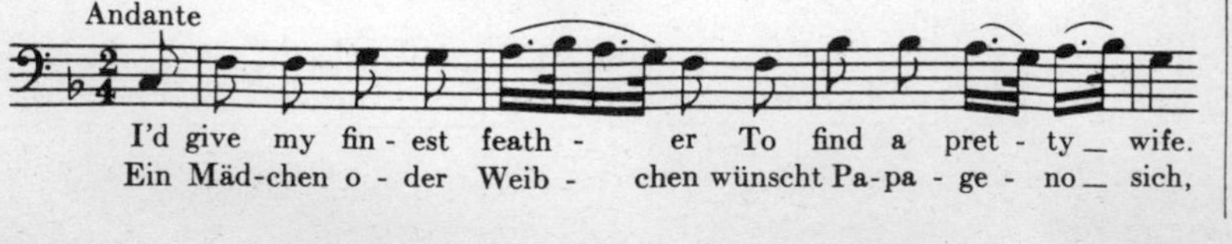
Andante
I'd give my fin - est feath - er To find a pret - ty wife.
Ein Mäd-chen o - der Weib - chen wünscht Pa-pa - ge - no sich,

[30] ARIA *EIN MAEDCHEN ODER WEIBCHEN* (Papageno) *continued*

Allegro

And hap - pi - ly then ev - er aft - er, We'd
Dann schmeck-te mir Trin - ken und Es - sen, dann
frol - ic in glad - ness and laugh - ter!
könnt' ich mit Für - sten mich mes - sen,

[31] Andante

THE THREE SPIRITS
Soon speeds the morn - ing light pro - claim - ing The
Bald prangt, den Mor - gen zu ver - kün - den, die
sun - shine's gol - den ___ way ___
Sonn' ___ auf gold' - ner ___ Bahn. ___

[32] Andante

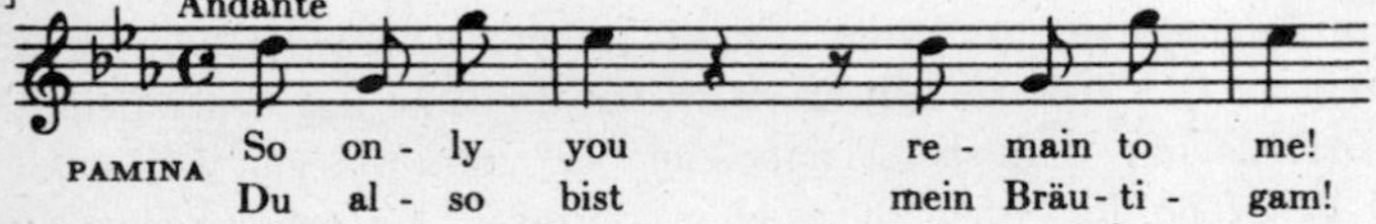
PAMINA
So on - ly you re - main to me!
Du al - so bist mein Bräu - ti - gam!

[33] Andante

PAMINA
Ta - mi - no ___ mine! Oh hap - py fate!
Ta - mi - no ___ mein! O welch ein Glück!

[34] Andante

PAMINA
We wan - der ___ by sweet mu - -
Wir wan - deln ___ durch des To - -
TAMINO
We wan - der ___ by ___ sweet ___
Wir wan - deln ___ durch ___ des ___
TWO MEN IN ARMOR
You wan - der ___ by ___ sweet ___
Ihr wan - delt ___ durch ___ des ___

Act II, Scene 5: Sarastro, at the head of his priests, enters a hall inside a pyramid (Chorus). Tamino is brought before him (Dialogue) and affirms that he is willing to undergo the two last and dangerous trials. Pamina is led in to bid him farewell. She fears for Tamino's life (Trio *Soll ich dich, Teurer, nicht mehr seh'n?:* "So must we two forever part?") [28], but both he and Sarastro bid her trust in the gods. Pamina is led away, and all leave, Sarastro guiding Tamino. Darkness sets in.

Papageno comes stumbling in, but as he attempts to move on, thunder and fire bar his progress in every direction. However, the Speaker enters and declares that the gods will not punish Papageno any further, although acceptance into the brotherhood will be denied him. Papageno cares little about the brotherhood; all he wants at this moment is a glass of wine. The Speaker leaves, and a great goblet filled with wine rises from the ground, but when Papageno has drunk from it, he experiences a new desire: he needs a wife (Aria *Ein Mädchen oder Weibchen:* "I'd give my finest feather") [29] if he is to be completely happy [30]. Immediately the Old Woman appears and (Dialogue) asks him to promise to marry her—else he will remain incarcerated in this very room with nothing but bread and water to sustain him. As he reluctantly—and not without mumbled reservations—swears fidelity, she changes into young Papagena, dressed all in feathers just like Papageno. However, at that moment the Speaker returns and leads her away.

Act II, Scene 6: The Three Spirits enter a palm grove [31] and prevent Pamina, who thinks that Tamino has ceased loving her, from committing suicide with her mother's dagger—her only friend, as she believes [32]. The Spirits tell her that she is mistaken and that the gods always protect those who are truly in love. They lead the joyous maiden away to find Tamino.

[35] SCENA *PAPAGENA!* (Papageno)

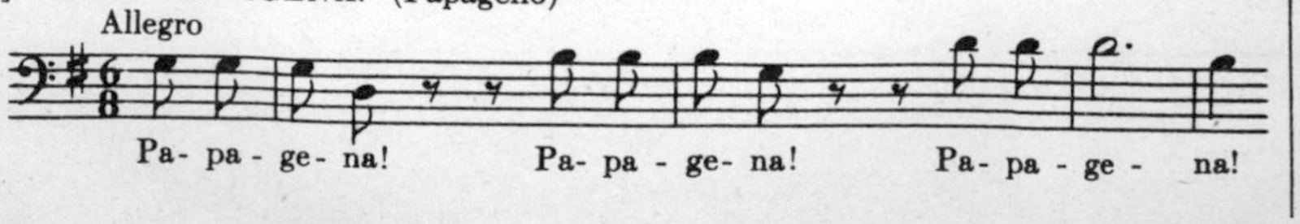

[36] SCENA *PAPAGENA!* (Papageno) *continued*

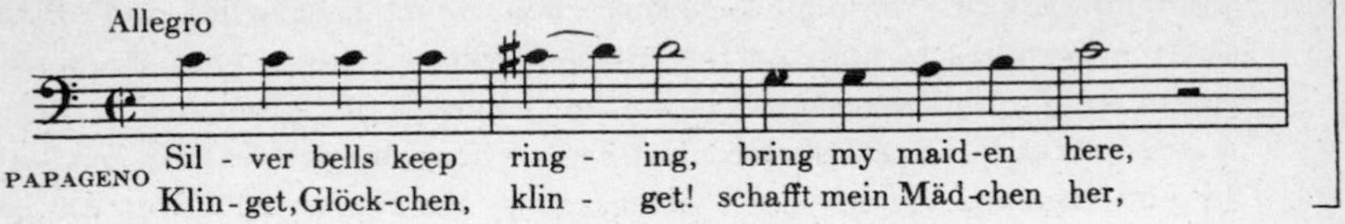
Allegro
PAPAGENO
Sil - ver bells keep ring - ing, bring my maid-en here,
Klin - get, Glöck-chen, klin - get! schafft mein Mäd-chen her,

[37] DUET *PA-PA-PA-* (Papageno, Papagena)

Allegro
PAPAGENA
PAPAGENO Pa - pa - pa, Pa - pa -
PAPAGENO
PAPAGENA
pa, Pa - pa - pa - pa, Pa - pa - pa - pa,

[38] QUINTET *NUR STILLE* (Monostatos, Queen of the Night, The Three Ladies)

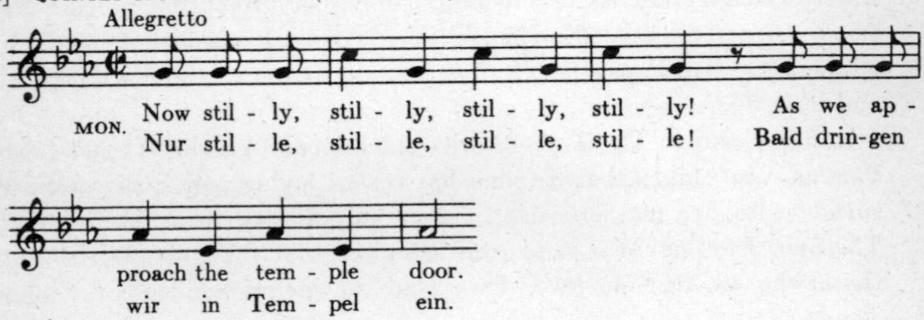
Allegretto
MON.
Now stil - ly, stil - ly, stil - ly, stil - ly! As we ap -
Nur stil - le, stil - le, stil - le, stil - le! Bald drin-gen
proach the tem - ple door.
wir in Tem - pel ein.

[39]

Allegro
p

Act II, Scene 7: Two Men in Armor enter a dark cave where embers are glowing on one side and a waterfall is visible on the other. They declare (Chorale) that those who have traversed these paths of hardship will, cleansed by the elements, be worthy to enter the mysteries of Isis. Tamino is brought in, and just as he is ready to embark on the road of trials, Pamina's voice is heard calling for him. She desires to join him on his dangerous road, and is permitted to do so. Jubilantly they embrace [33] and prepare to pass through fire and water, fortified by love and protected by the playing of the flute [Quartet 34]. Unharmed, they pass first through the fire, then through the water, whereupon unseen voices joyously invite the pair to enter the temple that appears suddenly before them in all its splendor.

Act II, Scene 8: Papageno wanders through a garden, vainly looking, calling, and whistling [6] for his Papagena (Scena *Papagena!*) [35]. When neither she nor any other girl answers his appeal, he sadly makes ready to end his misery by hanging himself. Just as he is about to tighten the noose, the Three Spirits hurry in and advise him to try his bells. He follows their counsel [36], and soon he is joined by Papagena. Immediately they start to plan for a future rich in little Papagenos and Papagenas (Duet *Pa-pa-pa*) [37].

Act II, Scene 9: Monostatos, promised Pamina as his reward, leads the Queen of the Night and the Three Ladies through the darkness toward the temple (Quintet *Nur stille:* "Now stilly") [38] to destroy "the unctuous pietists" as they call them. Suddenly they hear a strange distant roar that soon grows into thunder; a bolt of lightning cleaves the earth, and the evil band is plunged into eternal night.

Scenic Transformation: Without interruption in the music, the scene changes to the Temple of Wisdom.

Act II, Scene 10: Before the assembled brotherhood, Sarastro, with Tamino and Pamina near him, rejoices in the victory of light and truth over night and falsehood, and [39] all thank the gods and hail the newly ordained pair.

INDEX

Numbers in brackets refer to musical quotations as given in order of their appearance in the scores of each opera. Numbers without brackets refer to the page on which the entry is referred to in the story of the opera. For example, the very first entry tells the reader that Abendlich strahlt der Sonne Auge *is the 33rd musical quotation in* Das Rheingold, *and in the account of the plot it is referred to on page 223.*

A

B

Numbers in brackets refer to musical quotations as given in order of their appearance in the scores of each opera. Numbers without brackets refer to the page on which the entry is referred to in the story of the opera.

Numbers in brackets refer to musical quotations as given in order of their appearance in the scores of each opera. Numbers without brackets refer to the page on which the entry is referred to in the story of the opera.

I

J

K

L

Numbers in brackets refer to musical quotations as given in order of their appearance in the scores of each opera. Numbers without brackets refer to the page on which the entry is referred to in the story of the opera.

M

N

Numbers in brackets refer to musical quotations as given in order of their appearance in the scores of each opera. Numbers without brackets refer to the page on which the entry is referred to in the story of the opera.

O

P

Q

R

Numbers in brackets refer to musical quotations as given in order of their appearance in the scores of each opera. Numbers without brackets refer to the page on which the entry is referred to in the story of the opera.

Numbers in brackets refer to musical quotations as given in order of their appearance in the scores of each opera. Numbers without brackets refer to the page on which the entry is referred to in the story of the opera.

U

V

W

Z

Numbers in brackets refer to musical quotations as given in order of their appearance in the scores of each opera. Numbers without brackets refer to the page on which the entry is referred to in the story of the opera.

ABOUT THE AUTHOR

RUDOLPH FELLNER *has degrees in musicology from both Austrian and American universities. He teaches in the Opera Department of the Mannes College of Music in New York, and has served on the conductorial staffs of the San Francisco, Montreal, NBC, Cincinnati, and Chicago Opera companies.*